Humble Apologetics

HUMBLE APOLOGETICS
Defending the Faith Today

John G. Stackhouse, Jr.

OXFORD
UNIVERSITY PRESS

2002

OXFORD
UNIVERSITY PRESS

Oxford New York
Auckland Bangkok Buenos Aires Cape Town Chennai
Dar es Salaam Delhi Hong Kong Instanbul Karachi Kolkata
Kuala Lumpur Madrid Melbourne Mexico City Mumbai Nairobi
São Paulo Shanghai Singapore Taipei Tokyo Toronto

Copyright © 2002 by John G. Stackhouse, Jr.

Published by Oxford University Press, Inc.
198 Madison Avenue, New York, New York, 10016

www.oup.com

Oxford is a registered trademark of Oxford University Press

Library of Congress Cataloging-in-Publication Data
Stackhouse, John Gordon.
Humble apologetics : defending the faith today / John G. Stackhouse, Jr.
p. cm.
Includes bibliographical references and index.
ISBN 0-19-513807-4
1. Apologetics.
I. Title.
BT1103.S73 2002
230—dc21 2002008382

1 3 5 7 9 10 8 6 4 2
Printed in the United States of America
on acid-free paper

To
Trevor, Joshua, and Devon

Contents

Acknowledgments

I have been thinking about apologetics for almost 30 years. Over that time, I have accumulated intellectual debts far too numerous to record or even, alas, remember. I have acknowledged several of these debts in the text that follows. Several more, however, deserve mention here.

Among authors, I am chiefly indebted to C. S. Lewis, the twentieth century's most popular apologist. After discovering Lewis in my teens, I flattered myself briefly (I am ashamed to say) that I had "gotten beyond him" in graduate school. Returning to his work once I became a professor, I have found over the successive years endless riches in his thought and expression. Lewis isn't right about everything, of course. But he is right about so many things, and suggestive about so many more, that I have found him an inexhaustible resource.

Os Guinness inspired and informed me about how to engage in apologetics in a mode other than the typical evangelical style that was all I knew as a youth—namely, what I call "apologetics as martial arts." Ever since meeting him as an impressionable undergraduate, I have been grateful for the impress of Os's brilliant writing and speaking. I trust he will forgive me for failing to recall the source of each of the many ideas I first received from him somewhere along the way.

The so-called Reformed epistemologists, especially Alvin Plantinga and Nicholas Wolterstorff, have shaped my general views of thinking, and thus my particular views of apologetics, in fundamental ways. I am the more grateful to Nick for originally recommending this project to Oxford, and then generously agreeing to read and comment on the manuscript.

Several other readers also read previous versions of this book, and each offered astute suggestions that have improved it: Craig Barnes, Donna-Jean Brown, Alan Bulley, and Paul Griffiths. Students in apologetics courses I have offered at Regent and elsewhere refined these materials at earlier stages through their questions in class and reflections in assignments. Editor *extraordinaire* Cynthia Read shaped this book at several stages, and I am thankful for her gifts of insight, wit, and conscientiousness throughout this project. Elizabeth Powell assisted ably with the research and production, and she also compiled the index.

Regent College granted me a research leave in 2001 during which I wrote the first draft. The Social Sciences and Humanities Research Council of Canada provided necessary funds for early stages of the project, and the Louisville Institute provided a grant to support its completion. To these benefactors, I offer my thanks.

I am grateful to my parents, Yvonne and John Stackhouse, for a home in which asking questions about religious matters was welcomed, not resisted. I am grateful to my wife Kari for more than 20 years of love that began, indeed, with a first date during which we began asking each other apologetic questions. (How, indeed, could love fail to bloom in such soil?) And I am grateful to God for my three sons, the delight of my eyes, to whom this book is dedicated in hope that they, too, will be humble apologists for the gospel.

Some parts of Chapters 3 and 11 were revised from earlier versions appearing in the following: "From Architecture to Argument: Historic Resources for Christian Apologetics," in *Christian Apologetics in the Postmodern World*, ed. Timothy R. Phillips and Dennis L. Okholm (Downers Grove, IL: InterVarsity Press, 1995), 39–55; and "Why Our Friends Won't Stop, Look, and Listen," *Christianity Today* 41 (3 February 1997): 48–51. Some parts of Chapter 6 were revised from passages in *Can God Be Trusted? Faith and the Challenge of Evil* (New York: Oxford University Press, 1998). Rich Carl's poem, "Apologetics," originally appeared in *HIS* 38 (March 1978): back cover; used by permission of the author.

Introduction

In this time of rapidly increasing awareness of religious differences around the world, we need to consider carefully how members of one faith can properly offer what they take to be the blessings of that faith to others. How can believers both defend and commend their religion without needlessly offending their neighbors and exacerbating the tensions of the global village?

"Apologetics" is the study and practice of such "defending and commending," and this book presents guidelines for apologetics that should make such encounters truly profitable for everyone who engages in them. I should say at the outset that I am a Christian and this book centers on Christian apologetics. My research and teaching of world religions, however, encourages me to affirm that many of its observations and principles will be applicable to adherents of other faiths. So I hope that such believers also will find this book useful.

Apologetics in the past has often been destructive. In fact, this book is the result of two life-changing encounters that drove me to two conclusions: Apologetics can bless, and apologetics can curse. The first encounter was with my own high-school English teacher. The second was with a friend's account of a devastating experience he had had with a professional religious apologist. The first encounter sparked within me a lifelong passion for commending the faith to my neighbors. The second warned me about how harmful apologetics can be.

When I entered high school, I was a voracious reader of science fiction. By the time I hit the tenth grade, I had read a couple of hundred novels and an equal number of short-story collections. I knew something of the "old guys," such as Jules Verne, H. G. Wells, and C. S. Lewis; I knew the reigning kings, such as Ray Bradbury, Robert Heinlein, and Isaac Asimov; and I was discovering some of the edgier new writers of the time, such as Harlan Ellison, Philip K. Dick, or Larry Niven.

Then I met Mr. Eichenberg.

Mr. Eichenberg was in his early thirties, already balding, with longish hair down his neck and a Fu Manchu mustache—it was the early 1970s. He was my English teacher, and he was terrific. Sarcastic, enthusiastic, vivacious, lucid, he was everything a teacher should be—at least by my standards at the time.

He was also, however, a convinced ex-Roman Catholic. Encountering my shiny, confident, and largely untested Protestantism, Mr. Eichenberg (as he told me much later) thought it would be salutary for my education if he were to scuff up my religion a little.

So he did. In class after class, in discussion of poem after poem and story after story, Christianity (which is, after all, unavoidable in English literature) constantly came in for heavy weather, as did my own little bark of faith. I had never before experienced such challenges.

So I went home to my parents and told them what was going on. Being good Anglo-Canadians and respectful of public institutions, they didn't march down to the principal's office to complain. Instead, they directed me to books in my father's library that addressed the issues I was confronting in class: creation versus evolution; the impossibility of miracles; the unreliability of the Bible, both historically and religiously; the problem of evil; and more.

I read and read, and put science fiction aside. (I have, science fiction fans should note, picked it up again along the way.) After a while I began to hold my own with Mr. Eichenberg. He taught me the next year also, and I began to think that he was now pulling punches from time to time, perhaps a little wary of the Protestant kid who seemed to have learned a thing or two. He still got the best of most arguments, to be sure. And I knew throughout this exchange that he wasn't trying merely to annoy or embarrass me. He himself cared about these questions and posed them both for his own benefit and for mine. It was true teaching. And it launched me into the fascinating world of serious religious conversation among people who do not agree on much, but who do agree on the importance of the issues and therefore of the importance of good conversation about them. It launched me into apologetics.

Five years later, I was an undergraduate student. A young professor at the university served as an elder in the church I attended. Bob and I became friends, and he told me a story one afternoon about an experience he had had a decade before. If my own story with Mr. Eichenberg had turned me on to apologetics, Bob's story nearly turned me off forever.

Bob had grown up in the same sectarian, anti-intellectual tradition in which I also had been raised. Having completed an engineering degree at the state university, he was now going on in computer science—a relatively new discipline in the late 1960s. He had been worried about maintaining his Christian faith while an undergraduate, and now was worried further as he went to graduate school at a major research university.

He joined a campus Christian group and began to gain confidence in the presence of other bright, convinced Christians. A few months into the new academic year, however, he found that his group was going to host a well-known professional Christian apologist on campus early in the next term. (I have changed his name in the following account.) Bob began to fret: What if this guy couldn't make the grade? What if he couldn't cope with the high-powered challenges that surely would arise at this sort of university? Would the Christian group ironically sponsor the event that would humiliate them all?

The weeks went by, and finally the night of the public lecture arrived. Bob trudged from his dorm room toward the student union, where the Christian group had rented the main auditorium. He was worried that hundreds of students would come to witness a debacle. As he walked, he then began to worry instead that no one would come! But he turned the last corner and saw streams of students heading inside the union building.

He joined the throng and found his way into the auditorium. The room was a roar of animated conversation, students shouting and waving greetings to each other, the seats now nearly full and some students beginning to sit in the aisles and in front of the stage. Bob found one of the few remaining seats against one wall and began to pray that God would help the Christians not embarrass themselves.

Five minutes after the scheduled start time, a student in jeans and a university sweatshirt came to the lectern. He welcomed the audience and then introduced the speaker. The student went on fulsomely: The audience learned that the speaker had earned a half-dozen academic degrees (each of them identified in turn); had written a handful of "classic" books; had held numerous posts in schools across North America; and had accumulated various "amazing" honors along the way. At last the paean was over and Dr. Ward stood up to a round of applause.

"This is it," thought Bob with a dry mouth and pounding pulse. But he needn't have been afraid.

Dr. Ward was clearly in his element. He spoke for a solid hour, presenting a cascade of reasons to believe that Christianity was true, that Christianity was far superior to all other religions and philosophies, and that Christianity was the only sensible and adequate answer to human problems. He concluded with a dramatic conversion account and then expansively asked for questions from the audience.

Bob was impressed. This guy really knew his stuff.

Suddenly, however, he was gripped with fresh panic. Now that the floor was open, anything could happen. It's one thing for a speaker to pick his own topic, select his own turf, and sound pretty convincing. But what about the X–factor, the question from left field, the unanticipatable query that explodes the very foundations of the faith?

Bob began to pray again, just as fearfully as before.

The first questioner came to the microphone in the center aisle. Hundreds of heads swiveled to watch the neatly dressed undergraduate as he held up his clipboard and began to read his question.

Dr. Ward smiled encouragingly as the student finished, and it was obvious he had heard this question a hundred times before. He answered smoothly, as if from a prepared text, and the student took his seat. Bob was feeling a bit better.

Then the next student spoke. She had long, wild hair and wore hippie clothing. But her question, as powerful as she apparently thought it was, ruffled not a hair of Dr. Ward's well-combed head. He replied in the same confident tone, and the questioner retreated. Bob was beginning to brighten.

Indeed, Bob's mood improved dramatically as question after question was lobbed at Dr. Ward, and he knocked them all quite easily out of the park. It seemed that the Christian champion would defeat all comers and without any evident exertion.

The student master of ceremonies signaled for just one more question, and Dr. Ward smiled again to greet the last student at the floor microphone.

This guy, however, was a graduate student. Indeed, he might have been a professional graduate student. Well into his thirties, with a thick, black mop of hair matched by an unkempt black beard, his eyes flashed as he began his question. His question went on and on, and the student's voice rose higher and higher as he began to rail against the Bible, Christianity, and finally Dr. Ward himself. Bob stared at Dr. Ward to see if he could possibly endure such an onslaught, and indeed Dr. Ward's smile had become somewhat tight. At last, however, the student concluded his tirade, and Dr. Ward began to answer.

He replied by asking the student, who was still at the microphone with his arms folded across his chest, if he would first make clear whether he meant option A or option B of the two possibilities Dr. Ward suggested were implied by his question. The student, a bit nonplussed by this distinction that obviously hadn't occurred to him, hesitantly replied, "Option A."

"Well, then," Dr. Ward continued, "do you then mean either option A1 or option A2?"

The student was now evidently a bit distressed, and a murmur swept the hall. "Uh, I guess I mean option A2."

"Fine," replied Dr. Ward. "Then do you mean option A2-alpha or A2-beta?"

The student suddenly realized, as the entire audience realized simultaneously, that Dr. Ward had set up these three pairs of distinctions to box the student in. He now could select no option without contradicting his own case. He stood helplessly for another moment at the microphone while Dr. Ward's smile looked bigger than ever. Finally, the student said, "I don't know."

"Quite," said Dr. Ward, and turned magnificently to the student emcee, who was patently in awe of what he had witnessed.

The emcee then recovered himself, and cried, "Let's give a big hand to Dr. Ward for his wonderful presentation tonight!" and the room resounded with applause.

Bob was thrilled with relief. As the audience began to disperse, he got up from his seat and began to hum a little hymn to himself as he made his way to the aisle: "Onward, Christian soldiers! Marching as to war." The Lord's champion had triumphed! God had delivered the enemy into our hands! What a great night for the gospel!

And then he found himself walking behind two women as the crush pushed its way through the doors outside. As they passed through the last set of doors, and just before they moved away out of earshot, Bob heard one of them say to her friend, "I don't care if the son of a bitch *is* right. I still hate his guts."

Bob was stunned and literally stopped walking as the students moved off into the night.

And when he told me that story a decade later in a campus cafeteria, I was stunned, too. For I realized, with sickening clarity, that I was already well down the road to shaping myself into another Dr. Ward.

It was right then, at eighteen years old, that I decided apologetics *had* to be done differently. Encountering Mr. Eichenberg had taught me that apologetics could be interesting and important. Encountering Dr. Ward, however, now taught me that apologetics could be offensive and therefore self-defeating. I intend this book, therefore, to present a way of engaging in worthwhile apologetical conversation without perverting it into a destructive exercise in triumphalism.

Part One sketches salient features of the contemporary context in which most of us engage in such conversation. Apologetics makes connections between believers and their neighbors, and in this first part I describe what I judge to be the features of North American society most salient for the apologetic exchange.

Part Two then shifts from the historical and sociological to the theological and epistemological. Its main concern is to define apologetics: its proper role in Christian mission, its limitations, and its possibilities.

Part Three then is the payoff section in which I offer a series of guidelines for making apologetics as beneficial and effective as possible. In doing so, however, I maintain that apologetics is best understood as developing one's authentic self so as to present one's faith as helpfully as possible to one's neighbor. Apologetics is not primarily the acquisition and deployment of techniques. We are to become better versions of ourselves, not to resemble some ideal type of "apologist."

The book concludes with some reflections on how our apologetics must be reconceived as, in a word, *humble*. We ought to engage in apologetical conversation as we engage in anything else in the Christian walk: with full recognition of the smallness and weakness of our abilities and efforts, but also with gratitude to God for calling us to work with him in such a grand project. We do so, furthermore, with hope that God will generously make of those efforts something truly worthwhile: the increase of faith, or at least of mutual understanding, among neighbors in a world riven by fear and conflict.

PART ONE

CHALLENGES

I

Pluralism

THREE DEFINITIONS OF PLURALISM

If everyone already belonged to one religion, apologetics might still be necessary as a way to provide believers with the best possible grounds for faith. But clearly that is not the world we live in. Instead, we live in a deeply diverse world, a world characterized by pluralism.

Now, *pluralism* is a word we encounter all the time, but few speakers or writers pause to define what they mean by it. Pluralism has at least three definitions. Defining the term is crucial, since someone might well *recognize* pluralism in the first sense; *endorse* some kinds of pluralism in the second while rejecting others; and then perhaps *endorse* or *reject* this or that form of pluralism in the third. Thoroughly exploring what we mean by "pluralism" will help us clarify a lot of what we encounter in contemporary society. And getting that clear is necessary for any apologist who wants to understand and address her audience accurately.

Pluralism as Mere Plurality: At the most elementary level, pluralism means the state of being "more than one." The typical supermarket confronts a shopper with thirty kinds of breakfast cereal—just one instance of a bewildering pluralism of choices. The Yellow Pages merely begin to list the wide range of goods and services available in the modern city. Sociologists suggest that such proliferation of varieties of goods, services, and even ideologies is characteristic of modernizing societies—a process they call *pluralization*.[1] So pluralism in this first sense is a condition, a state of affairs, a

3

matter of value-free description. Is there more than one? Then there is pluralism.

When it comes to religions and other worldviews, Canada and the United States have always been characterized by diversity. Each group of native people practiced a distinct form of religion. When European traders and soldiers, and then colonists, arrived, they brought several forms of Christianity and Judaism to the Americas.[2]

But before the nineteenth century, most settlements—whether native or white—were homogeneous: one religion in one place. Since that time, pluralism has increased dramatically, and especially in our own day. Changes in immigration policy since the Second World War have allowed greater immigration to North America from Asia, Africa, and Latin America. This has meant the rise of Islam, Hinduism, Buddhism, and less-well-known religions in cities and towns across the continent. So-called New Religions, whether the indigenous faiths of the Mormons and Jehovah's Witnesses or imports such as Hare Krishna and *santerìa*, have been widely reported. (Indeed, because of the popular media's fascination with the new and unusual, New Religions have probably been over-reported, given their still-tiny proportions in North America.)

So when someone remarks on religious pluralism nowadays, he might mean simply the strict sense of "there is more than one." But he probably means, "Wow, are there ever a lot of choices—and such *different* choices!"

Pluralism as Preference: This second definition goes beyond mere recognition that "there is more than one" to affirm that "*it is good* that there is more than one." Here pluralism moves from sociological description to ideological prescription, from "what is" to "what ought to be."

This preference can apply to a wide range of things. I prefer ice-cream shops that offer more than one flavor of ice cream, for example, because sometimes I feel like having chocolate and sometimes I would rather eat butter pecan. The preference for pluralism can be expressed about more significant matters (although I myself am not indifferent to the matter of ice-cream flavors). When I moved to a small town in Iowa for a few years, I learned quickly that everyone patronized *both* grocery stores, *both* service stations, *both* pharmacies, and so on, in order to keep both in business. Economic pluralism meant preferring competition to monopoly.

Pluralism can be expressed even about ultimate questions of life and death. Someone might prefer there to be more than one philosophy, more than one ideology, more than one religion, in a society because the presence of competing alternatives prevents any individual or any group from asserting unchallenged claims to truth, justice, and power. Such pluralism, on this understanding, also can lead to mutual and complementary instruction from each particular point of view.

Each of us therefore is probably a "pluralist" in this or that respect. But preferring plurality in some instances does not, of course, commit one to preferring it in all instances. Someone who held to every one of the pluralist views in the previous illustration still might resist, shall we say, "matrimonial pluralism," as she strongly prefers monogamy to polygamy. Someone else might well prefer private property to communal ownership, or the rule of law to anarchy, and so on. We must resist, therefore, the aura of correctness that attends the word *pluralism* in some circles nowadays, as if it is always good to be pluralist. Most of us are pluralistic in only some matters and definitely not pluralistic in others.

The aura of correctness around the word extends to the third level of definition as well.

Pluralism as Relativism: Someone might recognize a situation as pluralism: "There is more than one." Someone might actually prefer a situation to be pluralistic: "It is good that there is more than one." But this third level of pluralism goes beyond both of these to declare that no single option among the available varieties in a pluralistic situation can be judged superior to the others. And on this level, there are several varieties.

Everything Is Beautiful: To hold the attitude that everything is beautiful is to see every option as good. Vanilla is good and so is chocolate, and so opting for one or the other is a matter of subjective preference, not objective judgment. (This illustration will be contested by those who believe that chocolate, in fact, is truly superior to vanilla, and I shall not stand in their way.) What is said of ice-cream flavors is true of other spheres as well. All have their merits, and all should be affirmed.

This attitude surfaces especially when one encounters the bewildering variety of religions. Hinduism, Buddhism, Christianity, Native religion, New Age varieties, Wicca—all are good and simply different from each other, not better or worse than each other. They all ought to be affirmed as valid spiritual paths.

I recall students in my religion courses who introduced themselves as having a particular religious outlook. Some were Jews, some were Sikhs, some were Buddhists or Hindus or Jains or Muslims or Christians of various sorts. Many of them were lifelong believers in their traditions, each convinced that his or her tradition was in fact the best of all. But a lot of them confessed that they felt that they *shouldn't* think that way. Somehow, they had received the notion that truly educated, sophisticated, and wise people saw the world's religions as equally good. I have heard the same testimony many times from journalists who belong to a particular religion but who feel obliged by their profession, so they say, to treat all religions as equally good. To be sure, this attitude is commercially advantageous: Avoid offending people with value judgments and you'll keep more readers, listeners, or viewers. But this attitude also seems to be part of an ethos of proper, not merely profitable, journalism in a pluralistic society.

Before analyzing the next form of pluralism, let's pause to note how this one can be easily challenged by referring to extremes. Do you really believe, one might ask such a pluralist-as-relativist, that Nazism is just as good as Judaism? Do you really not distinguish morally between the rites of infant baptism and infant sacrifice? Does offering widows social and economic support in their bereavement make the same sense to you as expecting them to be immolated on their husbands' funeral pyres? This naive relativism rarely stands up to a question of this sort.

All the Good Options Are Good—and We Say Which Ones: A more sophisticated version of pluralism-as-relativism says that all of the options in a particular sphere are partially good and partially bad: They all can be appreciated as more or less approximate versions of

6

ultimate reality. An elite, however, can see through these various alternatives to the truth that transcends them all. This is ultimate reality itself, and it is recognizable to those who have the panoramic and critical ability to see it.

Such an outlook, whether it shows up as a particular approach to literary criticism, or politics, or religion, should be recognized as being actually pseudorelativistic and not really pluralistic at root. For it maintains that there is indeed one "best" position among those available, and it is the position held by those who possess this ultimate insight.

In the spheres of religion and spirituality, this sort of thing abounds. Whether it be the New Age celebrity who blesses "all religions" in some sweeping way while maintaining that her particular take on things is the key to life, or a scholar of religion (such as John Hick) who articulates what he believes to be the core truths of Ultimate Reality that lie behind the world's faiths,[3] the claim to affirm all spiritual paths finally amounts to a limited and condescending approval of what are seen to be merely various approximations of the final and supreme truth that is recognized by those "in the know." This view, in short, pretends to pluralism while offering one version as in fact the best of the lot. Let's pass on, then, to other forms of pluralism that are truly pluralistic—that actually do not privilege one viewpoint as better than all others.

The more sophisticated, and rarer, forms of pluralism-as-relativism assert that whatever one's own revulsion toward this or that idea or practice, one possesses no universal, objective standard against which to assess it as good or evil, true or false, beautiful or ugly, helpful or harmful. Indeed, one cannot even affirm that "one option is as good as another" because there is no standard of *good* that is not itself the product of one or another option.

Allan Bloom, in *The Closing of the American Mind*, complains that most students nowadays believe that everything is relative.

There is one thing a professor can be absolutely certain of: almost every student entering the university believes, or says he believes, that truth is relative. . . . The students' backgrounds are as various as America can provide. Some are religious, some atheists; some are to the Left, some to the Right; some intend to be scientists, some humanists or professionals or businessmen; some are poor, some rich. They are unified only in their relativism and in their allegiance to equality. . . .

Relativism is necessary to openness; and this is the virtue, the only virtue, which all primary education for more than fifty years has dedicated itself to inculcating. Openness . . . is the great insight of our times. The true believer is the real danger. The study of history and of culture teaches that all the world was mad in the past; men always thought they were right, and that led to wars, persecutions, slavery, xenophobia, racism, and chauvinism. The point is not to correct the mistakes and really be right; rather it is not to think you are right at all.[4]

Pluralism here runs well beyond the recognition of different moral codes and even the preference for the presence of different ethics. Here pluralism becomes radical: There is no final judgment to be made among competing systems of ethics.

My own university students have displayed a deep ambivalence about ethics other than their own. In introductory religion courses, many frequently opine that the way this or that religion treats women appalls them. Yet in the very next paragraph of an essay, such students commonly switch back with what they intend to be a relativistic judgment, namely, that they would probably agree with that religion's understanding of gender if they had been raised in it. This latter admission seems to imply that the students' disgust toward what they judge to be sexism is nothing more than an effect of their particular upbringing. Morality, in sum, is nothing more than a social construction and not reflective of any objective moral order that lies beyond any person's or any civilization's preference. This reduction of values to mere historical happenstance ("I was raised in Canada by Christians and not in Iran by Muslims") pervades ethical conversation in our time.

Let's notice in passing, however, that such a remark can reflect nothing more than a banal belief about how ethical convictions are formed. *Of course* we learn our ethics primarily from our society, as we do most of the culture we learn! To remark on this fact as if it says something important about the *validity* of this or that ethical conviction is a version of what philosophers call the genetic fallacy. By discrediting the origin (or genesis) of an idea, we supposedly discredit the idea itself: Because cultures generate at least some convictions that aren't universally valid, we cannot accept any of their convictions as being universally valid. Or perhaps it is a version of another common, but fallacious, belief: Because various people hold various opinions on this matter, then none of those opinions can be taken as finally true—as if everyone has an equal claim to authority on disputed matters and thus the mere existence of disagreement means no judgment can be made. Just because students in a mathematics course disagree about the correct answer to a problem doesn't mean that one answer isn't in fact correct and the others wrong. Just because people disagree about the best way to build an automobile doesn't mean that some cars aren't in fact better than others.

Despite this widespread relativism, however, we should also note that few people in our culture seem prepared to endorse sheer relativism, particularly in ethical questions. Leaving aside the colossal social and political implications of such anarchy (implications that seem not to occur to people who easily mouth relativistic sentiments), many of our neighbors do place limits even on private morality. Usually these limits amount to either a sentimental altruism ("X is okay if and only if it is a loving thing to do") or a vulgar liberalism ("X is okay if it does not hurt anyone else"), but they are limits indeed. So, despite students' testimony that they are relativists, I must testify that I have encountered very few students who do, in fact, believe in sheer moral or ideological relativism.

It also is true that after the events of September 11, 2001, it is considerably easier to press the case with many of our neighbors that some forms of religion are indeed worse than others.

There remain, however, two intellectually serious versions of this pluralism-as-relativism that warrant attention.

There Is No Way to Tell Good from Evil: The view claiming that we can't distinguish good from evil is sometimes called simply *skepticism*. It suggests that regardless of whether or not there exists an objective, absolute standard by which to adjudicate things, we human beings probably can't know it. To be sure, we might stumble on this or that truth in some absolute form. Maybe in a given instance we are indeed in possession of absolute truth. But we still could not know for certain that what we think we know as true is in fact true. We cannot escape our limitations to see things from a universal perspective. Thus it is more accurate and more helpful to describe our so-called judgments as provisional. We should say that *A* or *B* is our conviction "as far as we know—and we could very well be wrong." We must not treat our views as if they were certainly right—even our most important views, including our religions.

It will surprise some readers to find that I think that there is much to say in favor of such skepticism, even from (and even particularly from) a Christian point of view. Let me just register this opinion for now, and defend it below once we discuss the various ways of thinking (that is, the cognitive styles) of our time. For the present, let's encounter the last form of pluralism-as-relativism.

There Is No "Good" or "Evil": Nihilism (from *nihil*, nothing) asserts that there simply is no universal standard: no God or gods; no *karma, dao, brahman,* or *logos*; no structuring principle of the universe in terms of right or wrong, better or worse. We can indeed make judgments about true or false: Nihilism itself is a firm belief that things are a certain way and not otherwise. But statements of moral and aesthetic judgment must be recognized for what they are: mere statements of individual or group preference— and, usually, individual or group *interest*. (We can look to Marx, Freud, Nietzsche, Sartre, and Foucault for variations on this theme.) The universe itself simply is devoid of such standards beyond what we invent for ourselves and are pleased to call (in our delusion, or in our desire to manipulate others) anything other than our own preferences.

In sum, the term *pluralism* can mean a wide range of things, some of which are matters of fact, some of which are inimical to Christian faith, and some of which are compatible with it. The Christian who wants to share her faith in a world suffused by all of these forms of pluralism will need to be clear as to which sorts she is encountering in any given situation.

If she is engaged in apologetical conversation, however, she will need to attend particularly to the intellectual pluralism of our time in the first sense of *plurality*, that is, the sheer complexity of the intellectual landscape we all traverse. This landscape in which we make our decisions about matters great and small thus deserves more extensive mapping.

DIMENSIONS OF INTELLECTUAL PLURALITY

We can look at intellectual plurality on a couple of levels. The first is relatively easy to remark; the second requires considerably more attention.

Ideological Options

The term *ideology* was given an ironic definition by Karl Marx who saw ideologies as mere intellectual rationalizations for what were at root economic and political states of affairs. So, for instance, Marx examined the typical nineteenth-century English conviction that God had assigned to each person a particular "station" in life. Marx concluded that this idea was in reality an ideology that served the capital-holding classes by adding the church's blessing to the social status quo. In what follows, though, ideology will mean the neutral, classical sense of the term as simply "a system of ideas or a set of convictions." Some of these ideologies may well be ideologies in Marx's sense, but we will not delay over this point.

Indeed, the point at hand is simply to note the sheer variety and volume of such options, which are unprecedented in world history. A useful illustration might be to engage in a sort of parlor game of naming as many ideological "isms" as one can. A brief list of options that flow in and out of each other would include capitalism, socialism, communism, liberalism, neoliberalism, conservatism, neoconservatism, libertarianism, liberationism, Marxism, Marxist-Leninism, Maoism, feminism, womanism, ecofeminism, environmentalism, survivalism, existentialism, structuralism, poststructuralism, modernism, postmodernism, idealism, realism, empiricism, positivism, pragmatism, utopianism, and so on. One could add to these, of course, the world's religions, great and small, old and new, from Hinduism to the latest version of Pentecostalism or the New Age. The list seems endless, with new versions emerging on the pages of *au courant* journals almost weekly.

Such a list reminds us of several realities when it comes to apologetical conversation. First, controversy over Christianity is almost never conducted in the terms in which it is usually discussed by professional apologists, namely, "theism versus atheism." The options are far wider than these anachronistic choices—choices that smack of Enlightenment-era European debates. To be sure, one might encounter nowadays a discussion between a theist and an atheist, but the theist could well be a Muslim, a Sikh, or a Hindu and the atheist a Thervadin Buddhist, philosophical Confucianist, or postmodern pragmatist. More commonly, however, the question is not, "Do you believe in God?" but "Which God or gods do you believe in?"

Second, no one can possibly list, let alone understand, much less master, the range of ideological options on offer to North Americans today. Thus the claim that "my ideology is superior to all others" proves immediately difficult, if not flatly impossible, to demonstrate. So one's enthusiasm for one's own ideology ought to be expressed in a way appropriate to this situation.

Finally, the apologetically sensitive person would profitably inquire as to just why there are so many options. Many religions have, of course, disappeared into the sands of history. But why have the centuries not reduced the possibilities to just a few great alternatives? And what is it about our contemporary culture that so many of these still flourish and new ones proliferate? Some understanding of these dynamics would help the Christian to communicate a missionary message more effectively, it would seem. The remainder of this chapter, and the other chapters that complete Part One, will offer some clues.

Cognitive Styles

Intellectual pluralism (in this case, pluralism as plurality) is not just a matter of ideology, not just a matter of intellectual *content*. Pluralism is also manifest in varieties of ways of thinking, of intellectual *forms*—what are sometimes called "cognitive styles." When we seek to engage our neighbor on a matter of faith, it is crucial to make sure that we are thinking together in the same mode, not just about the same subject matter. If we look together at the same question but in quite different cognitive styles, it is unlikely we will come to the same conclusion. (For example, if we're trying to decide whether that bridge over there is a good one, it will matter a great deal whether we're looking at it as engineers or as artists.) Indeed, we might wonder if the other is actually thinking correctly at all!

In what follows, there are several patterns to notice. First, these styles emerge consecutively, and so the following sketches draw primarily on standard intellectual histories of the modern West from the eighteenth century to the present. Second, later styles do not supplant earlier ones. Instead, they accumulate, layering on each other, so that by the time we reach the twentieth century in this survey, there are several major, and many minor, different cognitive styles in play in our culture. Third, in recent decades this multiplicity of cognitive styles has extended even into the minds of many individuals, so that someone may well think in a particular way about some things in her life while deploying a different cognitive style for other things. This multiplicity, fragmentation, and versatility is characteristic of advanced modern societies and their inhabitants—it is, in fact, what some call the postmodern or hypermodern condition. This last condition is sufficiently important, controversial, and complicated as to warrant a separate chapter.

To begin, then, we turn to the first modern cognitive style, that of the Enlightenment.[5]

The Enlightenment: This movement in Western thought arose out of the Scientific Revolution of the seventeenth century and came into its own in the eighteenth. It was called the "Age of Reason" or, as the French put it, *le siècle des lumières* (the century of lights). Like any major development in civilization, the Enlightenment is a complex phenomenon, whose nature and effects are perhaps infinitely debatable. But standard descriptions of it include the following emphases.

First, when it came to matters of epistemology—that is, the philosophy of knowledge—the Enlightenment put its confidence in reason and experience. Rationalists might follow René Descartes's lead and emphasize the former; empiricists might follow John Locke instead and emphasize the latter. But both sorts believed that the surest route to knowledge of the world lay in the appropriate use of what the senses said, what people felt within, and what disciplined reflection made of it all.

According to the most enthusiastic proponents of the Enlightenment, here was human emancipation from superstition and tradition. Now human beings were free to think for themselves, looking forward to new discovery rather than backward to the glories of the past. As Immanuel Kant would say, humanity had now "come of age." German idiom includes the idea of a young man's first sexual experience as his enlightenment (*Aufklärung*), implying his exit from dependent childhood into independent adulthood. With this new status and responsibility, Kant famously encouraged his civilization to "dare to know," *sapere aude!*[6]

Atheists happily went further and discarded divine revelation as well, and the prestige of Voltaire, Diderot, and others gave the Enlightenment an "anti-Christian" taint in some circles. But this is to oversimplify. Even Christian thinkers as orthodox as John Wesley and Jonathan Edwards took the basic Enlightenment themes for granted as they examined the world for signs of God's gracious providence.[7] They, too, saw science as a reliable means of understanding the natural world. They, too, saw reason and experience as unlocking secrets of human life as well, even probing the depths of the human soul and spiritual matters such as conversion and sanctification. They shared the confidence of most of the scientists of the preceding century—who inspired the Enlightenment—that science explored the divinely authored Book of Nature while theology explored the divinely authored Book of Scripture. Because they had a single Author, the Books would never ultimately disagree, and one profitably consulted both.

For a second Enlightenment theme—no matter what one's view of God and revelation—was that truth was discoverable and objective. Truth was not shrouded in mystery, dispensed only on occasion by individual proclamation, whether Delphic oracle or charismatic prophet. Instead, the so-called scientific method asserted that truth was apprehended as the community of scholars investigated data, hypothesized explanations, and then confirmed each other's conclusions by going over and over the same ground. Truth was not something revealed arbitrarily by some divinity, nor too complicated for humanity to understand. Truth was "out there" to be had.

The third Enlightenment theme spoke to *who* possessed the truth. Truth was not the province of magicians or priests or other privileged elites. It was open to all through society's scholars. To be sure, specialists then as now might well converse in terminology and concepts well above the heads of the general population. But there was, ideally, no deliberate mystification, no secrecy. Anyone with the intelligence and skill to engage in such conversation was welcome. Truth was universal, for the benefit of all. And when it was discovered, it was made public—literally, *published.*

Such convictions are still readily apparent three centuries later. Most day-to-day "bench science" proceeds this way, in physics, chemistry, biology, and geology. This model of data, hypothesis, and confirmation—all processed according to objective standards—also continues to inform much sociology, psychology, economics, and other social sciences. At times, some of the humanities—including history and even theology—proceed this way as well. Perhaps supremely, though, the Enlightenment persists in the applied sciences, notably engineering and medicine. Terms here are univocal: No one is supposed to mistake a 0.5 mm screw for anything else. Ambiguity and impulse are dangerous in both airplane construction and surgery. Reason and experience are the reliable routes to knowledge. No one designs an engine or treats a disease because of a vague hunch or because an ancient authority says so.

Romanticism: Toward the end of the eighteenth century, intellectuals in various European centers began to react against Enlightenment ideas. In everyday speech, the word *romantic* now conjures up images of moonlight, soft breezes, hillsides, rippling water, and love. These stereotypes are not far off the mark in directing us to important themes in the Romantic movement.

Where the Enlightenment had looked to reason and experience, Romanticism looked to intuition and feeling. Truth was reality to be felt and absorbed, not data to be retrieved and analyzed.[8] Over and over again, the images in Romantic writing are organic, as opposed to the mechanical metaphors of the Enlightenment. One senses the way things are, not in the Enlightenment sense of acquiring data through the senses and then rationally processing that information, but by literally feeling the world through one's intuitive union with it—as one simply knows whether one's fingers are cold or hot, or whether one is happy or sad. It is direct access to things by organic and mystical union. As even the scientist Humphry Davy felt it, "Every thing seemed alive, and myself part of the series of visible impressions; I should have felt pain in tearing a leaf from one of the trees."[9]

The paragon of Enlightenment virtue was Isaac Newton. As Alexander Pope so memorably wrote: "Nature and Nature's laws lay hid in night: / God said, Let Newton be! and all was light."[10] The characteristic Enlightenment thinker was a *philosophe*. The leading Romantic authors instead were poets and playwrights such as William Wordsworth and Wolfgang von Goethe. Try to think of a "Romantic scientist"—it's a contradiction in terms.

For, second, where the Enlightenment had been coolly objective in its acquisition of truth, Romanticism was hotly subjective. Both movements agreed that truth was discoverable, but Romanticism declared that truth was something to be experienced individually and personally. Enlightenment thinking, in the powerful phrase of William Wordsworth, murders to dissect.[11] As Romantics viewed

Enlightenment thought, the object of study is pinned down on a cold, hard surface amid gleaming metal apparatus. Illuminated by harsh artificial light, it is slowly disintegrated under the probing of scientific instruments. To the contrary, the Romantics argued, truth was a matter of being a part of things, not of taking them apart. Reality was the warm-blooded life of particularity, not the frozen death of abstraction; the movement of dancers, not the fixedness of mannequins and models; flow and freedom, not universal constants and scientific laws.

Alfred, Lord Tennyson, provides an example of the Romantic view of Christian faith:

> That which we dare invoke to bless;
> > Our dearest faith; our ghastliest doubt;
> > He, They, One, All; within, without;
> The Power in darkness whom we guess;
>
> I found him not in world or sun,
> > Or eagle's wing, or insect's eye;
> > Nor through the questions men may try,
> The petty cobwebs we have spun:
>
> If e'er when faith had fallen asleep,
> > I heard a voice "believe no more"
> > And heard an ever-breaking shore
> That tumbled in the Godless deep;
>
> A warmth within the breast would melt
> > The freezing reason's colder part,
> > And like a man in wrath the heart
> Stood up and answered "I have felt."[12]

Third, then, if one were to open oneself up to the world in this way, truth was "out there" to be apprehended "in here," in the personal center of one's life. This was not the same sort of public truth as championed by the Enlightenment, the truth of generalizations verified by a community of scholars. But it is yet a public sort of truth. Anyone who will cultivate the right cognitive attitudes and skills—not scientific ones, now, but intuitive, poetic ones—will see the way things are. The confidence of the Romantics was a reflection of the confidence of the Royal Society: If we look at the right things in the right way, we all will come to the same (correct) conclusions. Modern intellectual life seems to offer little space for Romanticism. Some theories of literary and other artistic interpretation do emphasize intuitive apprehension of the truth. Some university departments of women's studies, aboriginal studies, social work, education, and other departments that emphasize "empowerment" strike back at what they see as excessive objectification by emphasizing Romantic modes and themes. In such dialogues, intuition, freedom, harmony with nature, and so on are set against rationality, oppression, alienation from nature, and the like.

The presence and importance of this movement lingers in other zones of contemporary life. Perhaps this is most conspicuous with respect to music. Few of us even attempt to justify our preference for this artist or for that composition by objective criteria of aesthetic excellence. We lack the musical and aesthetic vocabulary to champion our favorite song as, say, "reminiscent of Josquin Des Prés in its polyphonic richness, built over the stable chord progressions of bluegrass, but foreshadowing the misty lyricism of Claude Debussy." To do so would appear (as perhaps it did just now) impossibly pretentious. Instead, we simply hand over the CD to a friend and say, "Listen to this!" with the confidence that, if our friend is properly oriented to art, he will surely agree that this song is not just pleasant to his ears, but is objectively good.

Romanticism also continues to exert powerful influence in the area of religion: People take on a religion because it simply feels right. Some forms of Wicca or native spirituality purport to offer the wisdom of the ancients despite powerful historical evidence to the contrary—evidence that the beliefs and rituals go no further back than a few decades or so. I remember encountering on an Internet discussion list the claim that nine million women were executed as witches during the European witch-hunts. When I suggested that this was a preposterously high figure, I was told that no matter what historical scholarship I presented, "We know in our bones that nine million of our sisters died." So how is such a belief held to be true? It is true in the Romantic sense: It feels right.

Christians inclined toward Enlightenment-style thinking must not, as some do, paint Romanticism only in unflattering colors. Our faith has a strong tradition of valuing such perceptions of the world. Mystical experiences that seem overwhelmingly true, if rationally unverifiable, show up across the Christian spectrum. "You ask me how I know he lives? / He lives within my heart," runs the popular gospel song. The worldwide explosion of Pentecostalism shows that Christian interest in Romanticism has hardly disappeared. From Augustine through Thomas Aquinas to John Calvin and even contemporary Christian philosophers such as William Alston and Alvin Plantinga, Christian intellectuals have sought to preserve a place for feeling and intuition in Christian apprehension of the world.[13] Christianity has room for Romantic themes—as one of the first great Romantics, S. T. Coleridge, tirelessly maintained.

Process: As the nineteenth century progressed, new currents developed that both carried forward previous elements and added new ones. An increasingly dominant mode of thought saw *process* to be the chief category in which to understand reality. As in the Enlightenment, reason and experience were again championed as the high roads to truth. Now, however, these were qualified by a third element, *history*. The Enlightenment had hoped to devise universal laws that governed all things past, present, and future. But in the nineteenth century a number of influential thinkers began to see that, while such universal laws might still be discoverable, what they described were processes that could be understood properly only over time—and sometimes very long periods of time indeed.

One needed to look beneath the surface of things and beyond the present moment to understand reality. Truth was still discoverable and objective, but one needed to know where and how to look for it. Thus all could partake of truth, but only as many as would take the long view, the view of Process.

So G. W. F. Hegel formulated a sweeping philosophy that sought to explain the entire cosmos in terms of a vast process of Spirit and Matter interacting over all of time toward a great, final realization of Spirit's self by Itself. In this context, Hegel interpreted human history as a process of continual interaction of new combinations that would produce better results each time—thus his so-called dialectic. Karl Marx famously turned Hegel on his head and taught that human history was fundamentally the story of the struggle between economic classes over material power, not the story of Spirit coming to self-realization. His call to revolution was based on the strong sense that he knew precisely where he was in the material dialectic of history and thus (particularly in Lenin's and Mao's versions) what needed to be done at a particular juncture in that story. Charles Darwin joined other scientists in overturning much of the static mentality of early nineteenth-century science. He provided a mechanism (natural selection) for the increasingly popular idea of the evolution, rather than the divine direct creation, of species. Finally, Sigmund Freud turned to the study of human psychology and suggested that adult feelings, behaviors, and values were largely the results of childhood experiences—the end results of lifelong processes.

Hegel, Marx, Darwin, and Freud were simply brighter luminaries in a whole constellation of thinkers that decisively introduced process as a fundamental category of thought. This was, so to speak, the Enlightenment in a new mode, the mode of "becoming," not simply "being."[14]

There aren't many Hegelians around any more, although some recent convergences between Eastern mysticism and science call to mind Hegel's conviction that the cosmos is fundamentally spiritual. In the twentieth and twenty-first centuries, a good deal of social science, history, and other forms of cultural study has been influenced by Marxism of one form or another. Darwin, of course, has provided the reigning paradigm in biology, but also has contributed to the popularity of evolutionary models in geology and cosmology. For at least the last generation, Freud has been under heavy attack for this or that aspect of his theory or his scientific practice (or the lack of the latter, according to some). But the clock cannot be turned back to before his basic recognition of the developmental nature of human psychology. More general "ideas of progress"—ideas that impelled so much of the dynamism of European culture in the nineteenth century and of American culture throughout the twentieth—continue to inform much economic theory as well as popular politics. And the recognition that many ideas are merely the results of particular historical circumstances rather than the discovery of timeless truths informs jurisprudence and legislation. They follow precedents into the past in order to guide, but not simply determine, the laws being made and interpreted today and tomorrow.

All three of these currents—Enlightenment, Romanticism, and Process—continue to flourish in the intellectual culture of our own time. But none of them dominate, and thus there is no set of "rules of engagement" by which all intellectual disputes can be resolved. In this pluralized situation, sometimes the only recourse is to alliances, agreements, compromises, and coercions—in short, to matters of power.

Recognition of this pluralized situation has taken intellectual and more broadly cultural forms, forms sometimes identified as postmodern. The next chapter looks at this term in several dimensions, and then concludes our discussion of pluralism with a set of common sense questions: What is really new about all this? Haven't we always had pluralism? Is there anything distinctive about the contemporary situation?

2

Postmodernity and Postmodernism(s)

First Speaker: "Here's The Answer. This is The Way It Is."
Second Speaker: "I doubt it."

Welcome to postmodernity.

Postmodernity is sometimes touted as the most important challenge for religious belief and proclamation today. Prophets of the postmodern sometimes sound as if the whole world—or, at least, the intelligentsia—"went postmodern" recently, and the rest of us better wake up to that fact and adapt to it. Others agree that the world is now postmodern, but we must resist postmodernism to the death. Still others tout postmodernity as a time of new cultural opportunities to be selectively exploited by the discerning believer.

So what is postmodern?

If, as the opening of this chapter suggests, the heart of postmodernity is *doubt* regarding any claims to having The Truth, then postmodernity is not a brand new phenomenon. In important respects, it is merely the latest version of skepticism. The lineage of skepticism in Western civilization goes back at least as far as the ancient Greeks (who produced the first Skeptics) and to the world-weary Ecclesiastes of the Hebrew Scriptures.

Medieval philosophers argued about how well our view of things correlates with the way things actually are, an argument perhaps most significantly carried on by the so-called realist-nominalist controversy of the later middle ages. Realists—such as Thomas Aquinas—believed that our names for things arise out of our recognition of actual essences in reality. So we call this thing a tree and that other thing a tree because they share a similar essence of "tree-ness." Nominalists—such as William of Ockham—believed that our names for things are simply matters of convention and could easily have been otherwise. We call these two different things trees because from our particular point of view they seem similar. But the similarity isn't essential. Thus the terms or names we devise (hence *nominalism*) are just the labels we happen to stick on things rather than recognitions of the way things are in themselves. Followers of postmodern debates about the relationship—or lack of one—between the "signifier" and the "signified" will see antecedents in this dispute.

In the seventeenth century, the great empiricist philosopher John Locke recognized that our minds do shape the way we perceive and think about things. He is well known for his suggestion that the human mind is a *tabula rasa*, a blank slate, on which experiences are simply imprinted. He is less well known, however, for his recognition of some properties of things as being essential to them (such as their extension in space—their shape) and some of their properties as being dependent on circumstances (such as their color, which depends on the light available and the optical apparatus of the beholder).[1]

It was not a new thing, then, for Immanuel Kant to come along a century later and declare an unbridgeable divide between a thing as it is "in itself" (*an Sich*) and that thing as it appears "to me" (*für mich*). Kant's extensive analysis and argument, however, have been immensely influential on all sorts of later thinkers up to our own day. It is his statement that has set the terms for most epistemology—philosophy of knowledge—in the modern era.

It is really only in the second half of the twentieth century, however, that implications of this philosophical question have been carried by a wave of large-scale social change. The result is a cultural situation enough different from what has gone before to warrant a new term, namely, *postmodernity*.[2]

THE SITUATION OF POSTMODERNITY

Words that begin with "postmodern" are notoriously hard to define to everyone's satisfaction. That problem is in itself something of a postmodern joke: an irony to be observed with the wry smiles and knowing winks of the postmodern cognoscenti.

I shall try to explain the joke by distinguishing between what I call the *condition* or *situation* of postmodernity and the characteristic *response* to this condition, for which I reserve the term postmodernism.

The postmodern situation is literally "after the modern." So far we have looked at three cognitive styles: Enlightenment, Romanticism, and Process (Enlightenment-via-History). Each of these is distinctly modern, and it is over against their common modernity that the postmodern defines itself.

Modern thinking is defined by the project of finding the truth. That in itself is hardly distinctive, of course. Premodern civilizations sought the truth as well. But premoderns characteristically sought truth by looking backward, by touching the stones of established traditions, by trusting the authorities who maintain and transmit the ancient ways. Moderns, by contrast, look forward. However they might acknowledge and build on the heritage of the past, their trajectory is toward new information and new understanding that surpass what has gone before.

What is characteristic of modernity, therefore, is the guiding hope that, given enough time and energy, human beings could experience the world, think hard, and come up with reliable answers—*correct* answers—regarding the nature of things. Here was a powerful *confidence* that all persons of goodwill, sufficient gifts (whether in intelligence, aesthetic sensibility, and so on), and appropriate skill can examine the pertinent data and come to the same true conclusions.

It is sometimes alleged against such ways of thinking that moderns thought they had it all figured out. The confidence of modernity, however, is in the *project*, not so much in the (provisional) conclusions. However much confidence modern scientists might have placed in Newton's laws, for example, Einstein's revisions to Newton didn't mean the end of the scientific method nor did it shake modern confidence to the core. Such revisions are typical of the way the project is *supposed* to work: New theories are tested by new experiments and then are correlated with what else we think we know. Newton's famous claim that he merely stood on the shoulders of giants applies to him, too, as scientists build on his work. Science carries on with the confidence that it is coming to closer and closer apprehensions of reality. (And, after all, Sir Isaac's equations still work just fine as long as one isn't dealing with the very big, the very small, or the very fast.)

It is important to note that the same kind of confidence, *mutatis mutandis*, is characteristic of the Romantic movement as well. Romanticism also was entirely confident that people of goodwill (that is, those who sincerely sought the truth), sufficient gifts (in this case, especially intelligence and aesthetic and spiritual sensibilities), and appropriate training (no technical skills were needed, except for expression in, say, painting or poetry, but the skills of observation, concentration, openness to intuition, and so on, were cultivated) could perceive the way things actually are. The Romantics shared their views with each other, whether informally in conversation and correspondence or formally in works of art, with the twofold confidence that they were perceiving reality and that their companions would perceive it the same way. Romanticism was not, that is, a kind of radical individualism, as it is sometimes said to have been. Like the Enlightenment, Romanticism believed that it was perceiving simply reality as it is, and all "right-thinking" people would perceive it properly.

The nineteenth-century moderns had precisely the same confidence. Look at things in Hegel's way, or Marx's way, or Darwin's way, or Freud's way, and you were penetrating to the heart of reality. Details might still need to be worked out, evidence gathered to support this or that unsubstantiated conjecture, or even modifications applied to this or that subpoint (Hegelians, Marxists, Darwinians, and Freudians have been busy in all three tasks), but the basic scheme was sound. This is the way things are.

This modern confidence in knowledge (sometimes called, in the older, broader sense of the term, science) was extended into a confidence in technology (thus, applied science) such that we could shape, and even remake, the world to suit our purposes. *Mastery* and *control* become key implications of the modern mind, whether intellectually (as in "mastering one's field" and "controlling the sources") or much more broadly in all of life via technology ("mastery over disease," "climate control").

Thus whether we speak of Voltaire, Wordsworth, or Marx, we can see here an epitome of the modern project in both science and technology: "We can find out what we need to find out, in order to think what we need to think, in order to do what we need to do, in order to get what we want to get."

It is this confidence that has been lost in postmodernity. Indeed, this confidence has been repudiated. Instead, there is the postmodern recognition that all human perception and thought is necessarily *perspectival*, that is, a matter of point of view. Human perception and thought are profoundly and only *subjective*, and this in two senses: both "from a point of view" (and so *from where*) and also "affected by the one (the subject) doing the viewing" (and so *by whom*).

In the first sense of subjectivity, human knowledge is limited by, restricted to, and characterized by the quality of a particular viewpoint: a certain place, a certain time, a certain light, and so on. There is no absolute viewpoint, no general view of things. There are only particular vantage places that give angles of vision on only particular things. I see the concert from the cheap seats in the second balcony; you see it from the front row; he sees it from the wings; she sees it from center stage. Our reports on the concert will vary because our points of view vary.

In the second place, human knowledge is characterized by the quality of the particular knower—or community of knowers. Gender, age, race, education, physical and mental health, emotional state, prejudices, beliefs, appetites, preferences, and previous knowledge all affect the processes of human perception and interpretation. I see the concert as an envious would-be rock star whose garage band never made it out of the garage. You see the concert as a long-time fan who camped out for two days to get those seats. He sees the concert with the gimlet eye and narrow ambition of a jaded manager. And she is having the time of her life playing her first big concert in her hometown. What happened at the concert and how good was it? It depends on whom you ask. To put this more simply, were all four of us to sit together in a box and watch the opening act, we would *still* report on a different concert experience because we are different people, not just because later on that night we will take up different vantage points around the hall.

There is no neutral, disinterested thinking. There are simply angles of vision on things that offer various approximations of the way things are.

More broadly speaking, postmodernity is the "end of ideology," the recognition of the failure of the grand schemes and comprehensive systems of past cultural efforts. Postmodernity has no confidence in unifying structures, in the "right way" of doing things, whether writing a poem, building a skyscraper, painting a portrait, or educating a child. The "correct way" of doing things was always part of a Great Story of how the world came about and what our place in it now is. Such Great Stories (what in the terms of French postmodernist theory were *grands récits*, translated not-so-happily as "metanarratives") dominated our lives and our culture as those in authority told them to the rest of us to keep things the way they preferred them to be. Marx and Freud tried to unmask such stories (and particularly the Genesis-to-Revelation story of Christianity) as mere ideologies or rationalizations of the powerful. In postmodernity, however, even the metanarratives of Marx and Freud themselves come under suspicion. As one of the most influential postmodernists, Jean-François Lyotard, puts it, the postmodern attitude most simply is one of "incredulity toward metanarratives"—*all* metanarratives.

Thus postmodernity deserves its alternate title of *hypermodernity*, for in this respect it is modernity against itself: The modern emphasis upon the critical role of reason and experience is now directed against every scheme of modern conceptualization that had used those very tools to construct this or that *grand récit*.

Furthermore, the additional category of *history* is also at work. Hegel, Marx, Darwin, and Freud believed that the truth could not be found in the analysis of snapshots of the present, but only in locating present appearances in long historical contexts. So does postmodernity see the narratives of Hegel, Marx, Darwin, and Freud themselves as historically conditioned, as the products of a particular culture at a particular time, not as truths that transcend the ages. Thus postmodernity is inclined to reductionism of a historicist sort: "That's just the sort of thing a white, educated, male, Canadian Christian *would* say!" or, more discreetly, "That's merely the perspective of the ruling class of fifteenth-century Venice, whose mouthpiece this writer clearly was."

So when someone comes along to say, "Here is the Great Story that explains all the other stories," the postmodern person reflexively responds, "Hmph! I doubt it. How could any of us, or even any group of us, pretend to have figured it out, to have seen it whole, to have come up with the Grand Scheme?"

The rules—whether mores, aesthetic standards, or metaphysics— inherited from the past are exposed by typical postmodern analysis as the products of racism, sexism, economic oppression, and superstition. Perhaps more charitably, they are viewed as the products of just one culture at just one time and just one place, and therefore not to be taken seriously as having any universal application.

In this mode of thought, then, "truth" is still discoverable. But there is no longer the modern confidence that truth is open to all. "Truth" (or even "truths") in this more recent mode represents only the particular convictions of particular individuals or groups who examine reality as best they can and make the best interpretations of it that they can. In postmodernity, therefore, there is none of the modern confidence that we are heading for a utopia built on the grounds of our increasingly certain knowledge of reality by means of our increasingly effective technology.

Talk of utopias, certainties, and effective technologies points to the broader cultural patterns of postmodernity and to the social changes that have occasioned its widespread influence in our time. For while postmodernity had its antecedents in the distant past, and its prophets in Søren Kierkegaard, Friedrich Nietzsche, Fyodor Dostoyevsky, and others, it is no coincidence that postmodernity comes into vogue in Europe through the middle of the twentieth century and in North America only in the last quarter of it.

For the mood of disenchantment with Great Stories descends upon Europe through the trials of the two world wars and the intervening Depression. Here the glorious imperial powers of modern Europe are exposed as no more noble than the most bloodthirsty of their conquered colonial peoples. The "long nineteenth century," as some historians call it, ends on August 1914. And no European seriously holds to the blithe "idea of progress" once the camps of Dachau, Treblinka, and Auschwitz come to light, once the saturation bombing of Dresden is reported, and once the smoke of Hiroshima and Nagasaki is seen around the world.

Canadians and Americans, whose countries enjoy a rise in economic and political power through the first half of the twentieth century, do not have a corresponding crisis of confidence until they pass through the turmoil of the Cold War, Vietnam, rapid urbanization and inflation, and the revolution of mores in the 1960s and 1970s.

Thus the debacles and confusions of the twentieth century provide many occasions for Western culture to doubt its modern confidence.

VARIETIES OF POSTMODERNISM(S)

Some people refuse to accept the postmodern critique of modernity, or are oblivious to it, and carry on nicely in modern mode. For all of the postmodern storms in the academies or art galleries, I daresay that Wall Street motors along under the aegis of modernity. And so do most of the sciences, applied sciences, industry, agriculture, and other fixtures of contemporary life. The *mentalité* of postmodernity has not touched them.

Others have seen modernity, and perhaps also postmodernity, and have found refuge from both of these in retreat to premodern ideologies. These refuges usually offer a combination of religion and culture, of both faith and ethnicity. So we see resurgent Islam in Iran, Afghanistan, much of North Africa, and in certain republics of the former Soviet Union; nationalist Hindu movements in India; fundamentalist Christianity in the United States; and so on. To be sure, most of these turns to the premodern are selective. Such movements are often happy to employ up-to-the-minute technologies, whether of persuasion or coercion, in pursuit of their goals, and do not generally long for a return simply to a more primitive society. Instead, they try to blend the premodern and modern in the interest of resisting what they see to be the evils of the contemporary world and particularly of the United States as the bellwether of modern culture.

Postmodernism is the collective array of responses to postmodernity that accept its view of things and then attempt to construct a view of the world, and perhaps an entire way of life, on that basis.

To concentrate again for a moment on the intellectual and cultural elites, it is important to see postmodernism emerging after the early twentieth-century artistic movement known as *modernism*. Modernism was a movement that is really the bridge between the modern project of cultural optimism and the skepticism and even despair of mid-twentieth-century postmodernism.[3]

Modernism shares some of the traits of postmodernity: cynicism regarding nineteenth-century grand narratives; lack of regard for great truths; a fear of empires and other great collectivities; and a distrust of technology and mass man. The talented and tenacious individual artist would turn away from the world as given, and especially from the huge intellectual and social structures imposed on him by culture at large, and would create his own spaces and sounds, even his own language. Think of T. S. Eliot's innovation in verse, James Joyce's novelties and neologisms in *Finnegan's Wake*, and Piet Mondrian's exploration of pure form and color without regard for representation of the world "out there."

Modernism thus turned away from the past and from the metanarratives of the modern project. Yet it still takes pride in its own products as beautiful, good, and true in an absolute sense. Modernism is really a sort of sequel to Romanticism: Those who have the proper ability can read and look and listen to this or that modernist work, and they will "get it." They, too, will see that this composition or that poem just *is* beautiful, good, or true.

It is this last shred of modern confidence that disappears in postmodernity and in the postmodernisms that respond to it. Even the heroism of Modernism will not bring us to the Olympus of absolutes.

Postmodernism got its name first from developments in architecture—a bit surprising, since architecture is not generally in the vanguard of cultural innovation. (One can spend one's own money and time on experimental poetry or painting, but one has to spend lots of other people's time and money in architecture, and that tends to keep things conservative.)

As twentieth-century architecture moved through the modernist Bauhaus and "international" styles, no new style emerged as a clear successor. Instead, architects began to rummage through the past for bits and pieces they would put together in a *bricolage* (to use a term popularized by Claude Lévi-Strauss, itself an ironic term since a *bricoleur* is, literally, a potterer or handyman). Such a conjoining of disparate elements would result in what they hoped would be a powerful mix. Eclecticism became a byword in this new fashion.

Sometimes it was merely a ploy used by interior designers as they desperately attempted to make sense of expensive items collected promiscuously here and there by well-heeled clients who insisted on keeping everything they bought—as the pages of *Architectural Digest* sometimes demonstrated! Often the use of past elements was ironic, as architects reduced or expanded things out of traditional proportions or used surprising materials in their reproduction. Indeed, the first widely recognized postmodern building in America was Philip Johnson and John Burgee's AT&T building in Manhattan, which sported on its roof its signature Chippendale broken pediment in concrete several stories high. The objective was to construct wittily allusive combinations. And sometimes it worked, producing a joyful celebration of the art of various times and places, and wonder at the way diverse artistic elements can begin new "conversations" in new contexts.

The collage of diverse images came powerfully to the mass media in music videos, with their rapidly cut scenes that frequently had only a tangential relationship, if any, to the music or lyrics of the song being performed. Popular music itself borrowed from the past, from the "covering" of popular songs from the 1950s and 1960s, to the much more radical phenomenon of "sampling" from a variety of sources to construct new musical events, a genre pioneered by hip-hop DJs at black urban dance halls.[4]

Advertising quickly picked up on this trend. In the later 1980s and 1990s, television commercials and print spreads often used images that were apparently unrelated to the product in question but were intended to provoke positive particular feelings in the viewer that the advertisers hoped would be associated with the product. Since the information came at the viewer so quickly or obliquely, and since there was no actual argument to be assessed (as in "Buy our product because of the following three advantages it offers . . ."), the commercials were literally irrational. They were sometimes effective nonetheless because of their appeal to other human faculties and drives.

This unsystematic, helter-skelter kaleidoscope is one characteristic experience of postmodernity. As societies have themselves differentiated (to use a sociological term) into largely separate spheres and institutions—financial, religious, artistic, commercial, familial, educational, and so on—so have their inhabitants' minds become unabashedly polymorphic. Not only, that is, do some of us think in an Enlightenment mode while others think in a Romantic mode, but many of us tend to shift from one mode to another, depending on what sphere of our life we are engaging at the moment. Such shifting became typical of modernity as when modern people move from the workplace to home, to church, to social gatherings and so on—each context with its somewhat different outlook and expectations.

Still, in postmodernity (or *hypermodernity*), such rapid shifting has come to entail that we take none of these modes as providing what our forebears thought it provided, namely, truthful and reliable access to reality. More and more of us are comfortable speaking of "your truth" and "my reality." Indeed, it is this easy versatility, this strainless switching among various and even contradictory values and cognitive styles, that is one of the most striking characteristics of the postmodern mind.

The best-known existentialists of the mid-twentieth century brought to wide audiences the idea that the cosmos did not itself have any meaning. Simone de Beauvoir, Albert Camus, and Jean-Paul Sartre agreed that there was no God, no Order, no universal morality. Instead, it was up to each individual to select the values by which he or she would live. For them (unlike their Christian existentialist counterparts, such as Gabriel Marcel) "existence precedes essence." There is no blueprint already provided for our lives: We choose through our living (existence) who we are (essence).

A generation later, deconstruction emerged in the university literature departments now not through novels and plays, as in existentialism, but in arcane works of mostly French criticism. Jean-François Lyotard, Jacques Lacan, Jean Baudrillard, Emmanuel Levinas, and above all Jacques Derrida used the tools of reason and experience to undermine what most people thought of as issues already settled by reason and experience. Which authors and which works belonged on the standard reading list (canon) of literary studies? What were these works about? Who got to decide these things? By patiently and cleverly exposing the ambiguities of language, deconstruction opened up literary criticism to new possibilities and new voices. It showed something of how much our accepted interpretations are open to question by others—indeed (and this was the important political point) how much our accepted interpretations are determined by the powerful in a society, and how those marginalized in society might well read those texts quite differently.

Deconstruction thus dovetailed with the agendas of those seeking liberation and dignity for people who had been silenced or subjugated because of their class, gender, ethnicity, or sexuality. Deconstruction had originated as a rather narrowly intellectual concern to repudiate the *grand récits* not only of traditional interpretation but also of the new orthodoxy of structuralist interpretation that thought it could discern the inherent, universal patterns in all language. Thus deconstruction is sometimes identified as poststructuralism.

Those concerned for oppressed groups, however, saw in deconstruction a tool to level the interpretive playing field, to pull down the canonical authors and their supporters: the "Dead White European Males" (DWEMs, as the argot had it) and the all-too-alive white males who perpetuated this regime.

Some activists have rather cynically engaged in what one might call a "pseudo-postmodernist two-step." This is the rhetorical device of, first, using postmodernist criticism to de-privilege elites and then, second, asserting that the views of one's own group are better than anyone else's. Notice that this is not to claim that one's group's views are just as good as anyone else's, for to say that is to assume a universal standard of goodness, and that is inconsistent with postmodernism. Furthermore, it is politically useless—for if the convictions of privileged white men are just as good as the protesters', why should the former yield any power to the latter? Nor is it to claim that one's group's concerns represent just one viewpoint among many, without grounds for any to be preferred to another in any objective sense. To say that would indeed be truly pluralistic and postmodern, but it doesn't provide the strongest basis for getting other people to change their minds and grant you the power you want. Instead, there is here an exploitation of postmodernism to level the field and then a reversion to modernity (or premodernity) to champion one's own ethos (whether a feminine one, a black one, or a gay one) as simply better. So-called political correctness has been the most obvious manifestation of this sort of thing.[5]

To be sure, truly radical skepticism and its even more radical relative, nihilism, say that there simply is no truth "out there" for everyone. There is only "truth" as whatever individuals or groups find empowering or useful to them. And that's what we should all settle for. But there seem to be relatively few people who hold seriously and consistently to such extremes—notwithstanding the fame of philosopher Richard Rorty and the frequent invocation of Nietzsche nowadays!

One can see in many forms of postmodernism, therefore, a genuine struggle to appreciate and cope with the limitations of the human mind—and of particular human minds located in particular places, times, communities, and circumstances. It is not clear whether postmodernism is a new, coherent paradigm that replaces the modern, or simply the rubble from the collapse of the old. But various forms of postmodernism aim to construct more than a hodgepodge of old and new simply to entertain, or turn a profit, or win a battle. They sincerely aim to liberate the mind and improve the human lot while recognizing how little we actually do know with no certainty that we are heading in the right direction.[6]

MULTICULTURALISM

Other kinds of pluralism and postmodernism confront us on every hand: in aesthetics (what is art?), in politics (which way forward?), and so on. What exacerbates all of this in North America, as in many societies, is the implicit attitude of many Americans and the explicit federal policy in Canada of multiculturalism.

As I understand it, the policy of multiculturalism intends to build stronger, richer communities and countries. It is to do so by encouraging various ethnic groups to maintain something of their inherited character and, out of that tradition, to contribute their distinct strengths to the general project of society. Multiculturalism, that is, resists the melting pot that homogenizes everyone into just one type of citizen and one type of community, and instead encourages diversity of resources for the benefit of all.

Ironically, however, much multiculturalism in both attitude and program has had the effect of encouraging people to concentrate upon their own ethnicity, their own differences, so as to separate them from the whole. As one observer puts it: "The ideal of diversity—of mixing things up, spreading the wealth, creating a new Us—never happened."[7] Instead of a multicultural culture, there has emerged a multiplicity of cultures that strains the unity of the society that comprises them as each focuses upon its own good according to its own lights.

Undergirding multiculturalism and then being reinforced by it has been a widespread relativism, especially among the Anglophone, nominally Christian, white population that traditionally has held most of the power and status in Canada and the United States. A sense of guilt for past sins of chauvinism and exploitation (and much of this sense of guilt surely is justified) has combined with an ignorant sentimentality to produce widespread confusion about just how people of different views on fundamental matters can live together—not just enjoy each other's native costumes, food, and dances.

Multiculturalism thus becomes a vague slogan under which all sorts of people can march: premodern or modern activists promoting this or that group; secular liberal elites who are happy to see their conservative opponents divide into so many disparate and competing groups; postmodern pluralists who don't see why any one group should dominate everyone else; and well-meaning folk who wonder why we can't all just get along. Thus multiculturalism can be seen to be fostering pluralism of all three types.

What is not so clear to many Christians, however, is that multiculturalism and extensive religious plurality can offer an opportunity for Christians to shed the baggage of cultural dominance that has often impeded or distorted the spread of the gospel. It may be, indeed, that the decline of Christian hegemony can offer the Church the occasion to adopt a new and more effective stance of humble service toward societies it no longer controls.

WHAT'S NEW?

The challenges of pluralism—all three kinds of pluralism—and of postmodernity are everywhere. But there has always been a measure of pluralism in every culture, no matter how totalitarian and tightly controlled. There is always some difference, even dissent. What makes our own situation unusual?

First, the *scope* of pluralism is greater than ever. In some societies, there are choices among foods, say, or clothing styles, or even religions (although the last is quite rare in human history). But in our society, it is difficult to think of an area of life that is *not* characterized at least by choices (pluralism in the first sense) and by a sense that having options is good (pluralism in the second sense).

Second, the *amount* of pluralism is extraordinary. Cable and satellite television systems offer more than one hundred channels. Shopping malls testify to the overwhelming variety of consumer goods available. Philosophical and religious options proliferate each year across the continent. There are not just two or three choices in a given area, but often a dozen, or a hundred, or more. To be sure, there is not as much plurality as there could be: I'm still waiting for "The Philosophy Channel" or "The Church History Channel" to appear. Still, there is already an amount of choice virtually inconceivable to people who remember the days of television in the 1950s and 1960s, and it is equally true in a hundred other fields.

Third, the *pace of change* is unprecedented. Options multiply more quickly than one can responsibly assess. Furthermore, not only do choices come faster, they also go faster. Just when you've found the perfect brand of this or that, it disappears. Just when you've settled on a trusted tradesperson or health professional, she moves. Just when you've become comfortable with your computer, it no longer interfaces well with the Internet. Just when you've understood and embraced the fundamentals of this or that religion or philosophy, along comes a new, improved version to consider.

Fourth, widespread *doubt* about whether anyone has the answer, and whether we could recognize it if they did, is new. There have always been skeptics, but not on this scale. Poll after poll show people doubting traditional religions, doubting authority figures, doubting almost everything except their own judgment.

Finally, as we shall see in greater detail in chapter 4, *consumerism* is a lens through which we are all tempted to view everything. So much of contemporary life encourages us to opt in or out as it suits us to do so. So many of the messages we hear are appeals to our choice—from advertisers, of course, but also from entertainment media, pundits, and even political, educational, and religious institutions who traditionally have just *told* us what they thought we needed to hear. To a consumerist culture, everything looks like goods or services to be bought as the sovereign (and perpetually manipulated) individual consumer decides.

We must not exaggerate the uniqueness of the present, as if the past were so different that it can teach us nothing. Yet we must also be aware that we live in a time importantly different from any previous time, and we cannot simply repeat what has served us well before.

3

The Problem of Plausibility

Many Christians are enthusiastic about their faith and excited about discussing it with others. Why, then, do so few of our North American neighbors share our interest? We're all ready to dive into apologetical conversation, prepared to offer impressive answers to any question that comes our way. So why do no questions come our way?

Most apologetics throughout Christian history have been directed at the issue of credibility: "Is it true?" Nowadays, however, we are faced with the prior question, the question of plausibility: "*Might* it be true? Is Christian argument something I should seriously entertain even for a moment?" Without dealing with this prior question of plausibility, apologetics cannot proceed to the traditional task of offering good reasons to believe.

Let's begin with defining plausibility more thoroughly, and then look at a series of cultural realities that together discourage many of our neighbors from any lively interest in apologetical exchange.

THE PLAUSIBILITY GAP

E. E. Evans-Pritchard conducted famous anthropological studies among the Azande of Sudan in the 1920s. He found that the Azande, like many tribal peoples the world over, understood sickness and health primarily in terms of magic and witchcraft. When someone fell ill, it was because he had offended a spirit, or a shaman, or someone else who had enlisted the shaman's aid in retribution. The sensible—yes, the logical—thing to do when faced with sickness, then, was to consult the shaman and make things right with the offended party. Ritual, sacrifice, restitution, and so on all would be entailed, and then one could expect to recover one's health.

Well, we know better, don't we? So, blessed with our superior knowledge, we fly over to Africa in our silver bird. We alight from the plane wearing our priestly garments (lab coats) and greet the assembled Azande.

"O Azande!" we say. "We hear that you understand sickness and health in terms of witchcraft."

The Azande, a noble and patient people, respond, "That is true."

"O Azande!" we say again. "Have you not heard of microbiology, of Louis Pasteur, of bacteria, viruses, and antibiotics?"

The Azande, a noble and patient people, respond, "No, we have not."

"O Azande!" we repeat, thoroughly caught up in our role as saviors, "let us explain to you how wrong you are about illness and how our way of understanding is better."

The Azande, a people whose nobility and patience is now being tried, continue to listen.

"You see," we say animatedly, "there are these *teeny weeny* bugs all over the place. You can't see them; you can't smell them; you can't hear them or feel them—*but they're there!* And they crawl over your skin and into your body through your nose and ears and eyes and mouth and cuts in your skin. Once inside, they breed and breed and breed until there are thousands of them, then MILLIONS of them, then BILLIONS of them all over the inside of your body."

"And that," we conclude with a flourish, "is what makes you sick."

The Azande, a noble and patient people, look at each other for a moment. Then the leader responds: "I think we'll just stick with the witchcraft paradigm, thanks."[1]

One more example, this one literally closer to home, to illustrate how what first might seem implausible to us might be made plausible after all. Let's suppose that at breakfast this morning, I complained to my spouse that I was feeling a bit unwell. I described my symptoms, and as a health professional (which she is) she quickly offered a diagnosis.

"It's because you wear too much blue."

I am incredulous, of course. What she suggests is preposteous. "What are you talking about? How can my wearing too much blue make me feel like I have a cold?"

"Well," she calmly explains, "the most common blue dye used nowadays—Blue No. 3—is extracted from a plant whose juices are mildly toxic to human beings. If you wear blue once in a while, there's no problem. But wearing it as often as you do means that a little bit leaches into your skin each day, and when it accumulates you become sick."

"Oh," I say in a small, respectful voice, overcome by what seems to be irrefutable science. "Maybe I *do* wear too much blue. . . ."

(I must protect my wife's professional reputation by affirming that this story is entirely fictional and as far as either of us knows, we can all safely wear as much blue as we want.)

The amusement we might feel in reading such stories is exactly the point. The implausible explanations offered are not simply unlikely, or difficult to believe. They are *laughable*. They don't count as even *possible* alternatives, worth a moment's consideration. They do not fall within the range of theories that, given one's worldview, one is disposed to entertain seriously.[2] As Thomas Kuhn suggests in his influential analysis of *The Structure of Scientific Revolutions*, when one paradigm, or overarching model, of science confronts over another, it doesn't always denounce it as merely inferior or even bad science: It tends to treat it as *not science at all*. It is simply implausible, and thus not worth taking seriously.[3]

It is this widespread contemporary response to Christian discourse—that Christianity is implausible—that is the primary obstacle to apologetics.[4]

THE PLAUSIBILITY PROBLEMS

General Resistance

The general problem, the problem that faces anyone with a message nowadays, is the broad cultural doubt about absolutes and the authority figures who presume to enforce them. In his surprise best-seller, *The Closing of the American Mind*, Allan Bloom powerfully suggests that an unintended consequence of such widespread relativism is a complacent satisfaction with what one already knows and believes.

> Actually openness results in American conformism—out there in the rest of the world is a drab diversity that teaches only that values are relative, whereas here we can create all the life-styles we want. Our openness means we do not need others. Thus what is advertised as a great opening is a great closing.[5]

If, that is, there are no grounds upon which one can argue that one civilization is superior to another, or that one moral code is loftier than another, or that one way of doing things is just better than another, then why learn about other cultures and philosophies and religions? If I go no further than to think that it's okay for you to do your thing and I to do mine, then where is the incentive to seriously consider whether I should adopt your thing and abandon mine? What begins as a political value of coexisting with differences and resisting authoritarianism that would squelch individuality has become, ironically, a broad indifference to difference and a disincentive to improving oneself by learning from others.

Public discourse, moreover, is dominated by the "information class," which is precisely the class most influenced by postmodernisms, by theoretical arguments directly in favor of such "incredulity toward metanarratives."

I don't need your religious message, therefore, because it isn't any better than mine—or, at least, there's no way to tell that it's better than mine.

The Christian message, however, has a particularly hard time getting across to many of our neighbors today. It's worth looking at a list of several cultural factors to begin to explain why.

Resistance Particularly to Christianity

Most North Americans believe that they do not need to consider your Christian message. They don't want to sit still for extended argument on its behalf. And they *especially* are disinclined to tolerate any sort of call to conversion to Christianity. All this is true, it seems, while the Dalai Lama is a media star, Transcendental Meditation discipline Deepak Chopra packs them in to concert halls for his three-hour talks about spirituality, and Oprah Winfrey features New Age authors in her influential book club. Why don't people want to hear from Christians?

The following sketch sets out three pairs of factors that together weave a powerful fence of resistance to Christian proclamation.

Identity and Ignorance

Let's begin with a fact that is overwhelmingly obvious, but often overlooked by ardent Christians. *Most North Americans believe that they are Christians already.* The Canadian census of 1991—the most recent census for which figures are available at this time—list fully 83 percent of the population as Christians. The 2001 census likely will report a drop. Given poll data taken throughout the 1990s, however, more than 70 percent will probably still identify themselves as Christians. Meanwhile, in the United States, the figures are about 10 percent higher in the poll data.[6]

Devout and observant Christians may well snort at these figures—or grieve over them. It is evident that relatively few of the professing Christians in the general population actually attend church regularly—perhaps 40 percent of Americans, and just over 20 percent of Canadians. Since these people are our colleagues and our customers, our relatives and our neighbors, our friends and enemies, we know many of them well enough to conclude that precious few North Americans are serious practitioners of the religion they claim.

Nonetheless, if someone *thinks* he is a Christian, why would he need to hear from you or me about the Christian faith? Is he likely to welcome someone who says, or even implies, "Well, you're not really much of a Christian, are you? So here's how to shape up." No, with the cultural residuum of Christianity still broadly evident in both countries, it is no wonder that Christian proclamation has trouble getting people's attention.

At the same time, however, it is evident that this majority who see themselves to be Christian really don't understand even the basics of the faith they profess. (To be sure, those who count themselves as ex-Christians might score even lower.) For all of the influence of Christianity on the historical shaping of North America, and for all of those who continue to identify with the Christian religion, there is an obvious and almost general ignorance among *both* those who claim Christianity and those who do not.

I was quietly thunderstruck by this reality once at 35,000 feet. On a flight from Chicago to Minneapolis, I was talking with my seatmate. A young woman on her way to a new job as an executive at a Napa Valley vineyard, she had told me she had been in Chicago to see her boyfriend graduate from the University of Chicago School of Business. That had been her own alma mater, from which she had graduated the year before. I also found out that she had earned her bachelor's degree from Dartmouth College.

She in turn asked me about my work. I told her I taught world religions at a public university, which I did at the time. Then I joked a bit unkindly that some of my introductory students could not place "Jesus Christ" and "the Apostle Paul" in the correct chronological order. Ah, the challenges of teaching nowadays, et cetera.

"Who is this 'Apostle Paul' you're referring to?" she replied, with what I took to be clever, deadpan humor. As I tried to compose a witty comeback, I suddenly realized that she was utterly sincere. And she was completely unaware that this ought to be an embarrassing question for a well-educated North American to ask.

This ignorance among even the elite is a sign of the times. Surveys taken in Canada and the United States have shown again and again how little people actually know of the Christian religion. Ask people in the street how many of the Ten Commandments or the Beatitudes they can name. Forget whether they actually *observe* them: just name them. Bonus points if they can get them in the right order.

Journalist Frederica Mathewes-Green catalogs a number of "Bible bloopers" committed in major publications. A writer in *Harper's*, for example, tells us that "the Bible ranks hope along with faith and love . . . in Psalm 23." (Check I Corinthians 13 instead.) *The Washington Post* urges readers at Christmastime to read "Mark or Luke's narrative at home"—advice that will prompt readers to wonder how the *Post* sees a birth narrative in Mark that no one else does. And *Newsweek* depicts Jesse Jackson holding hands with Bill and Hillary Rodham Clinton and reciting "the fifty-first Psalm, David's prayer for mercy after he had been seduced by Bathsheba"—an unusual interpretation of that story that will comfort only some.[7]

Let's go beyond Bible knowledge per se. You can't talk about Christianity in any sensible way without, for example, dealing with the Trinity, with the Incarnation, and with the Atonement. Now, how many North Americans can offer a good, basic, working definition of these crucial doctrines? Indeed, how many *pastors* can do it?

In sum, we face today a dual challenge from most of our neighbors: They profess a faith they do not understand very well; but because they *think* their understanding is adequate—and thus their practice of it as well—they feel no need to listen to someone who wants to introduce them to Christianity.

Apologists have faced this problem previously in Christendom, of course. Medieval councils routinely adopted resolutions to improve the quality of teaching and faithfulness of practice in so-called Christian Europe. Blaise Pascal and Søren Kierkegaard are only the most famous of a long line of apologists who tried to wake up a sleepwalking culture that comfortably thought itself Christian. So we have resources to draw from in the Christian heritage. And we shall need to do so as long as we continue to face this odd pair of challenges: widespread identity with Christianity and widespread ignorance about that very faith.

Public Stereotypes and Private Pains

In 1989, the Canadian public was appalled as charges were leveled against Roman Catholic clergy serving at the Mount Cashel orphanage in Newfoundland. To the horror of Canadians, whose national history is full of heroic priests, revered members of the clergy were exposed as sinners of the most repellent sort. Mount Cashel, however, was merely the beginning. Soon afterward, hundreds of lawsuits were filed by aboriginal Canadians who had been forcibly schooled—and sometimes physically and sexually abused—in the residential school system. The system itself was operated by the federal government. But many of the schools were staffed and led by clergy and employees of Canada's major churches: Roman Catholic, United, Anglican, and Presbyterian. The stain of scandal was now upon all the mainline churches. And their American counterparts offered up their own sexual and financial scandals in the 1990s, with stories of Roman Catholic priestly pedophilia igniting fresh dismay in 2002.

Meanwhile, the "two Jimmys"—Bakker and Swaggart—gave North American culture new caricatures of fundamentalism and Pentecostalism to shelve alongside Elmer Gantry and the Scopes trial. The opprobrium of the epithet "televangelist" spread even to respectable members of the profession—such as Canadians David Mainse and Terry Winter, and for a time to Billy Graham himself. Bakker and Swaggart were only the most conspicuous, however, of a number of high-profile evangelical clerical disasters on both sides of the border, disasters that involved mainstream evangelical preachers and best-selling authors as well as the "hot gospelers."

Christianity in North America thus suffered considerably from the widely reported, and widely enjoyed, failures of prominent clergy. Yet the ugliness of hypocrisy and betrayal of one's religious profession was not limited to these spectacular cases among a relatively few priests, pastors, and preachers.

Over and over again, talk-radio shows that featured religion were besieged by callers who wanted to report on personal disappointments with people who had called themselves Christians. An abusive father here, a repressive mother there; a flirtatious pastor or a licentious youth leader; a thieving church treasurer or a dishonest employee who loudly proclaimed his faith—over and over again, people of all walks of life reported encounters with repellent Christians. This particular person symbolized Christianity to their victims, and the pain that they caused sticks to the religion they professed.

Perhaps so many experiences of disparity between profession and practice were to be expected in countries in which so many people still claimed to be Christian but knew so little about that faith and apparently showed up rarely in church to learn more. Many of the terrible stories one would hear, that is, could be referred to the so-called nominal Christians whose vice could not fairly be charged to authentic Christianity.

And yet some of the worst stories of domestic abuse have arisen from highly observant Christian homes. I had Mennonite students in southern Manitoba tell me of incest and beatings going on in their small, insular communities. I had social workers among Dutch Calvinist towns in Iowa tell me of the unusually high incidence of such crime in these outwardly pristine and churchgoing communities. No, there are evils that have turned many people away from the Christian Church in North America, within that church as well as within those who falsely claim allegiance to it.[8]

Less dramatically, but no less importantly, are the many people who have been raised as Christians, or who have experienced Christianity in a Sunday school or youth group or camp or small group, and who have found the experience simply unsatisfying. We Christians may comfort ourselves with the thought that what our neighbors encountered was not the whole story, not the entire package, not the authentic heart of the faith. We may hope to introduce them to a better understanding, a better fellowship, a better encounter with Christ. But we need to appreciate how understandably resistant our neighbors will be: Why bother and be burned, or at least disappointed, again?

Challenges New and Old

Some challenges to the Christian faith also have been intellectual. There have always been important questions to ask about the Christian religion, of course. The problem of evil; the nature of the Trinity; the purpose of the cross of Christ; the interaction of God's sovereignty and human freedom—these are perennial puzzles for anyone trying to make sense of Christianity.[9] In modern times, however, three kinds of intellectual challenges have so affected our neighbor's views of Christianity as to make the very idea of Christianity implausible.

The first of these is the so-called warfare between science and religion.[10] The most famous negative incident is the trial and punishment of Galileo Galilei, faithful Christian though he was, by some of the leaders of the Roman Catholic Church in the seventeenth century. Galileo had supported Copernicus's heliocentric theory of the cosmos and in doing so had run afoul of papal politics, despite support for his work among high-ranking officials in the church. The actual story, then, is not merely that of science versus religion, but of a particular public figure at a particular time caught up in politics and propaganda. The stereotype in most people's minds, however, is different and much simpler: Galileo is the bold scientist, the champion of autonomous reason, being bullied by a hidebound, reactionary, and dogmatic church that resists science as a threat to its traditional authority.

The most contentious zone nowadays is not cosmology, however, but biology. Indeed, as it has been for more than a century, the hot spot of conflict is biological evolution. Evolutionary theories had been surfacing throughout the first half of the nineteenth century, but it was Charles Darwin's first edition of *The Origin of Species* in 1859 that helped both to explain and to evidence evolution on a broad—indeed, universal—scale.

Again, there were many religious people who made their peace with evolution in general, and to some extent with Darwin's particular formulation of it. Henry Drummond in Scotland, Asa Gray in the United States, and Sir William Dawson in Canada are just some of the more prominent names among those who have been called "Darwin's Forgotten Defenders."[11] Once again, however, the stereotype is much more stark.

In Britain somewhat earlier—perhaps by the end of the nineteenth century—and in the United States after the notorious trial of science teacher John Scopes in Dayton, Tennessee, in 1925, evolution became a symbol for modern critical thought struggling against superstitious religious dogma. Historian Owen Chadwick points to the implications rippling out far beyond the realm of academic discourse, as he cites George Macaulay Trevelyan, born in 1876, testifying that when he was only 13 years old, he learned that "'Darwin' had disproved the Bible."[12]

Thus a powerful myth emerged that science and religion—and by religion was meant especially traditional Christianity—were intractable opponents. This theme overlaid others in the modern ethos, reinforcing the sense that people now had to choose between intelligence and piety, between tradition and modernity, between their heads and their hearts.

Furthermore, as science enabled the development of technology, it became accepted wisdom in many circles that science has debunked and replaced religion, while technology has made it redundant. Science teaches us what we need to know, and technology helps us do what needs to be done. Modern people, therefore, simply don't need Christianity—indeed, religious faith is the mark of an unsophisticated and probably impaired mind.

The slow rise of science in Western consciousness, therefore, has meant trouble for Christian proclamation. The relatively rapid and recent emergence of world religions—old as they are elsewhere in the world—has posed a challenge that, in some curious ways, complements, rather than contradicts, the purported triumph of science over religion in our culture.

The increasing awareness of and regard for other religions among our neighbors have marked North American society only since World War II. Immigration policies before that event kept North America predominantly white and European in ancestry, with the conspicuous exceptions of aboriginal peoples and descendants of African slaves. With more and more immigration from Asia, we now see mosques, temples, and other religious buildings of a variety and number never before seen in our cities. Devotees of these religions are sending their children to our schools, working with us in business and the professions, and representing us in government. When they knock on our doors, they're not here to proselytize, but to baby-sit our kids or borrow our weed-eater. When they meet us in an airport, they're not selling us flowers but picking us up as our clients.

One of the most powerful upshots of this development is the widespread sense that "they seem like nice people" and that therefore the differences among religions are either not that great or not that important. Even after the cultural convulsion following the events of September 11, 2001, many North Americans are still inclined to believe that all religions really do teach the same basic principles of piety, charity, and decency. ("Terrorism" and "extremism" are simply other categories that don't pertain to this generalization.) Or perhaps their doctrines are quite different, but they are just metaphors for the same basic principles of—again—piety, charity, and decency. Most people still don't know very much about other religions. But the general sense of how their neighbors of different faiths seem just as civilized and pleasant as anyone else, plus a specific symbol or two ("I just can't believe that God would send Gandhi to hell"), make any Christian claim to superiority seem implausible, if not offensive.

Another sort of widespread belief regarding other religions is particularly ironic in the light of the supposed opposition of science and Christianity. Those of our neighbors who are in fact disaffected with science, technology, and modern life in general—and their numbers are growing—often include Christianity in that contemptible package. Western civilization, so this story goes (one might well call it a "metanarrative"), has brought us sexism, racism, environmental degradation, imperialism, and a huge gap between the rich and the poor. Christianity has enabled these disasters with its domineering God, its license to exploit nature, its privileging of males, and its motifs of God's chosen people rising above all other nations. Because Christianity has been part of this destructive complex, it should be set aside in favor of religions that have kinder gods, or none; religions that cooperate with nature, or at least ignore it; religions that make no gender distinction, or perhaps even privilege women; and religions that no longer elevate one nation over another. Thus Christianity is not condemned as the enemy of "good" modernity but is implicated as a conspirator in "bad" modernity.

This argument from recent history is rather striking in the light of a widespread lack of historical consciousness in our culture. C. S. Lewis warned us more than a generation ago that most people are in fact quite ignorant of, and skeptical about, history—all history. Things that happened "long ago" might as well be Aesop's fables or Grimm's fairy tales. To most people, Lewis writes, "the Present occupies almost the whole field of vision. Beyond it, isolated from it, and quite unimportant, is something called 'The Old Days'—a small, comic jungle in which highwaymen, Queen Elizabeth, knights-in-armor etc. wander about."[13] This disregard for history as a continuum that frames our current experience and as something from which we can learn important information is not recognized by apologists nearly as much as it should be. Such *ahistoricism* coincides nicely with both postmodern epistemological doubt and a consumerist focus on immediate gratification: Who cares what some people might say about the past? Let's focus on what we can do and get *now*. Christianity, however, depends fundamentally upon caring about what happened in the past, particularly in the career of Jesus, and what the Bible says about it, so apologists must consider how to respond to this ahistoricism so dominant in our culture.

Even among those who do have a firmer sense that some things in the past really happened and really matter, Christianity frequently comes out badly. The past for most of our neighbors is not a richly complex continuum in which a variety of forces have combined to produce a complicated reality needing sensitive and patient interpretation. Particularly when it comes to Christianity, the past is merely a collection of tableaux that sit fixed in one's mind as stark moral lessons: Christians mounted bloody Crusades against noble Muslims; Christians burned hapless women as witches; Christians foolishly resisted scientists such as Galileo and Darwin; Christians oppressed women and spoiled sex; Christians overran and dominated native peoples; Christians abused the earth. For many of our neighbors, the Christian past is simply a chamber of cultural horrors.

For a religion that takes history as seriously as Christianity does, helping our neighbors understand how to think historically will be high on the apologetical agenda, as it is on the agenda of Christian education in general.

Those Christians who seek, then, to bring the Christian message to our neighbors nowadays face a series of impediments any of which, and especially in combination, make our case immediately implausible in the eyes of many of our neighbors. Such impediments make *us* implausible. As philosopher David Clark puts it, when I engage in apologetic conversations, "I should be aware that . . . *I am not myself*, at least at first. I am whatever the dialogue partner *thinks* I am."[14]

Some of these impediments are genuine obstacles that the apologist will need to treat seriously as such. It makes good sense, that is, for some of our neighbors to be sincerely trammeled by these difficulties and therefore greet our message with indifference or even resistance.

Yet it is also true that we have a peculiar situation to face in that so many of our peers are familiar with at least some aspects of Christianity, and that familiarity has been grounds for contempt. Precisely because our civilization has been so deeply marked by Christianity—by its faults, yes, but also by its gifts and glories—many of our neighbors resist it more vigorously than they do any other religion.

About a century ago, G. K. Chesterton remarked on this problem in late-Victorian Britain. Many people, he noted, and especially the most popular critics of Christianity, were stuck now in a weird twilight zone between Christian faith and outright unbelief. And they were resentful in that zone:

> They cannot get out of the penumbra of Christian controversy. They cannot be Christians and they cannot leave off being anti-Christians. Their whole atmosphere is the atmosphere of a reaction: sulks, perversity, petty criticism. They still live in the shadow of the faith and have lost the light of the faith. . . . The worst judge of all is the man now most ready with his judgments: the ill-educated Christian turning gradually into the ill-tempered agnostic.[15]

We live in a "time-between-the-times," in which people raised in a more or less Christian culture now are reacting against it. This condition especially afflicts Baby Boomers, that generation that has defined itself so centrally as reacting against "the Establishment." Christianity was a part of the regime of Mom and Dad against whom they were reacting—whether the proper Anglican or Episcopal Christianity of certain elite classes; or the dominant Roman Catholicism of Quebec and ethnic neighborhoods elsewhere in Canada and the United States; or the revivalism of the U.S. South; or the conservative Lutheranism of the upper American Midwest. Thus Christianity's unique cultural position has brought it much greater disdain and resistance than other religions that are not so implicated in the *ancien régime*—regardless of whatever blessings Christianity has brought to North American life. If this simple cultural analysis is correct, furthermore, we should see less and less resistance of this sort from younger generations who have been raised without either a personal or cultural framework of accepted Christian influence. My own experience of teaching college students over the last twenty years confirms this sense of things, as does research in this age group conducted by sociologist Reginald Bibby.[16]

Christian apologetics at this time therefore will have to be especially sensitive to this sort of resentment against this particular religion. Indeed, the increasing contact with other religions that is provoking all of us to put our slogans of multicultural acceptance into practice may well come around to prompting our society to afford Christianity a place at least no *worse* than other religions enjoy.

I recall that a Vancouver family publicly protested an advertising campaign for the local amusement park in the summer of 2000. They told one of local newspapers that the campaign cynically and cheaply exploited Christian symbolism (such as the Second Coming, the book of Revelation, and—naturally—hell) to promote its new thrill rides. The story made the front page, and radio talk shows discussed it for a week afterward.[17]

I observed that the vast majority of those calling in to such shows and writing to the newspaper were on the side of the protesting family. What was most interesting is that most supporters were *not* church-going Christians, by their own express identification, but were Vancouverites—that is, citizens of one of Canada's least-churched metropolises—who really did believe that tolerance and respect should be paid to everyone's religion, including Christianity. Perhaps in this most-secular of Canadian communities we see a bellwether of things to come. Christianity can be regarded as just one more option—no better, but also no worse—than any other on the religious smorgasbord.

To use a metaphor such as smorgasbord, however, is to hint at the way all such matters are being interpreted nowadays: through the narrow and distortive lens of consumerism. To this final challenge we now turn.

4

Consumerism

To a man with a hammer, everything looks like a nail. To a consumer, everything looks like a meal.

Everything we have discussed so far—the dazzling array of choices that modern pluralism offers up; the doubt regarding any absolute standard by which we can decide among them; and the resistance to Christian proclamation as a message our neighbors don't want to hear—all of these can be viewed under a single category that defines so much of contemporary life: consumerism. Indeed, a great deal of the secularization/modernization problem that has preoccupied cultural critics in the West for most of this century—that is, the theorizing about what happens to traditional religion when cultures become more and more modern—can be expressed through the terms and dynamics of consumerism.[1] So it is to consumerism that we turn last to add to our outline of contemporary challenges to Christian apologetics and also, in an important sense, to summarize it.

WHAT IS CONSUMERISM?

From a Christian point of view, there is nothing wrong with consumption itself. Indeed, human beings were created by God with the need to consume: to breath air, to eat food, to drink water, and so on. We need ideas as well as vitamins, company as well as oxygen, excitement as well as space. We are intrinsically consumers, according to the Bible, and God pronounced all that "very good."

What we are discussing here, however, is consumer*ism*: an out-look, a way of seeing things, a way of responding to the world, that frames everything in terms of consumption by oneself.

Increasingly, our culture urges us to see ourselves primarily as consumers. In bygone times, people were defined primarily in terms of their jobs: one forged metal and thus was a "Smith;" one made barrels and thus was a "Cooper." The first question you might be asked at a party would be, "What do you do?" You would answer in terms of your job—and, usually, not with a verb matching the question of "doing," but with a linking verb in terms of identity: not "I engineer bridges," but "I *am* an engineer;" not "I fly airplanes," but "I *am* a pilot."

This identity through work still marks us today, of course. But increasingly we enjoy defining ourselves in terms of what we do on our own time, when we don't have to conform to the expectations of the corporation or factory, when we can be "ourselves." We pick clothes, we pick cars, we pick clubs, we pick beverages, we pick entertainments, and we pick companions. We "are" no longer what we do when we're at work, but what we pick, what we consume, when we're at leisure.

Nor does our society encourage us to consider ourselves primarily as citizens or as neighbors—two other traditional identities. Who wants us to act like citizens? Who helps us to do so? As pundit Neil Postman tirelessly has pointed out, our news media don't primarily offer us information to equip us as citizens, but entertainment to keep us interested between commercial breaks. Governments and individual politicians themselves communicate with us to please us and to persuade us to cooperate with them, not to explain what they have done and are doing so as to submit their work to the judgment of an educated electorate.[2]

"Cocooning" has become the way many of us live when we arrive home from work. Through the magic of electronics, we can now have "home theaters"—which is about as odd a term as a "home opera house" or "home sports arena," except that we can indeed view operas and hockey games in our living rooms. My wife and I startled our immediate neighbors in two successive Canadian cities when they found that, within a few months of moving in, we had actually greeted and conversed with other people who lived farther down the same block. So much for neighborhood in the modern city.

To be sure, lots of people defy these patterns. Lots of people work hard to be informed and to act as citizens. Lots of journalists and politicians try to treat us with respect and to help us vote well. Lots of people volunteer their time to improve neighborhood parks, schools, streets, and safety. The question here would simply be, What's the norm? What have we all come to expect of modern life? Mostly, we are encouraged to act as individual consumers—or, perhaps, as individual consuming families—with no strong ties to anyone or anything else that can get in the way of our free choices and the freedom of other people to market their wares to us.

Consuming thus has become a mentality for us. It is the way we tend to define ourselves and to act in the world. As such, it is no longer mere consumption, but consumerism.

THE CONVICTIONS OF CONSUMERISM

A set of propositions—tenets, one might call them—structures the consumerist mentality.

1. The self is both judge of what is good and the primary beneficiary of what is good. In consumerism, the self considers itself to be sovereign. The self is free to decide just what it wants, and to decide what it wants on the basis simply of what it wants. This is not the tautology it appears ("Doesn't everyone in fact have to decide for himself or herself?"), for one might make up one's mind on quite different grounds: because one's deity commands it, or one's prince orders it, or one's beloved prefers it. In consumerism, one might indeed choose to placate one's god, or obey one's superior, or charm one's lover—but the point is that one is utterly free to choose to do so or not on the basis of one's own values, and *no one ought to say otherwise*. There is neither coercion nor even obligation involved. "You pays your money and you takes your choice."

This conviction regarding the sovereign self is in some tension with the second tenet of consumerism:

2. What is good is what the market (of individual consumers) says is good. Some who say this mean "good" here quite cynically. In a cosmos bereft of intrinsic moral or aesthetic standards, all we have left is the financial "votes" of the populace. Others believe instead that the decisions of the market reflect essentially good people making essentially good choices. So the cumulative effect on the market is as good an indicator of "benefit" as we have.

As I say, this conviction does militate somewhat against the ideal of the sovereign self, since the market will listen to a million voices on one side of an issue more readily than it will to the single voice of the dissenter, no matter how loudly the dissenter proclaims his sovereignty. It is not a contradiction, however, at least in the sense that as each of the sovereign selves makes a free decision according to what the market offers at the time, the market registers those decisions and reacts accordingly. The self is then free to choose among the resulting options, and the cycle continues. (In this sense, the sovereign consumerist self is similar to the sovereign democratic self who gets to choose among the options put before it every several years or so—and between elections has to simply cope with the decisions handed down from the higher powers it has helped to appoint.)

There is a further irony here. Consumerism can appeal to two kinds of selves that normally are poised against each other as opposites. The self that is strongly self-directed thus corresponds to the emphasis in point 1. This sort of self is characteristic of modernity. The bewildering anarchy and anomie of postmodernity typically produce a self that is fragmented and thus it takes its cues from various and ever-changing social forces and contexts. This sort of self corresponds to the emphasis in point 2. Consumerism thus flourishes in both modern and postmodern environments. Those who know what they want can look for it in the market. Those who need guidance and validation for their various and transient "selves" can look for them from the market. Only the premodern self—the integrated, single self that chooses to be guided by religious authority, tradition, community, and culture—is resistant to consumerism, as we shall see presently.

3. All else has value only in light of (1) and (2), and therefore properly can be regarded, disregarded, or manipulated in that light. If the individual encounters something—an object, or a philosophy, or a person—then the individual can elect it or not as he or she pleases. The self is the arbiter of what matters for that self. On the larger scale, the market of individual selves all making their decisions determines the only other level of value. If the market likes it, it remains. If the market doesn't, it disappears—either literally (no one produces such unsellable objects anymore) or figuratively (no one cares about, and so no one informs the rest of us about, the now-marginalized item). And if something or someone is attractive enough to receive consumerist attention, that individual might well come under pressure to change to suit consumers' desires even better. The alternative is to face what might be called the wrath—and thus excommunication and annihilation—of the market.

To tone things down a bit from that apocalyptic phrasing, what is striking about consumerism in this respect is its almost blithe disregard for the fate of the "losers" in the marketplace. There is an almost infantile innocence in relegating the now-unattractive or never-interesting object to the dump. If one were to protest, "But you *should* care! You *should* like that thing!" one could expect a sort of round-eyed, blinking stare of incomprehension. "Well, I *don't* like it, and I *don't* care. So that's that." The value of something is what someone is willing to pay for it.

4. Goods (note the pun) can be bought. Perhaps all goods. In a consumerist mentality, there is a sense that everything that matters can somehow be obtained by commercial means in order to be consumed by the interested self. And perhaps the next step is the obverse of this principle: Everything worth having is a "good" or commodity.

Of course pleasure can be obtained this way. Of course power can be obtained this way. Even truth can be obtained this way, if one is willing to pay enough and locate the right media—experts, informants, private investigators, and files. Beauty itself also can be obtained. One can buy beautiful artwork and display it in beautiful homes. One buys beautiful clothes and jewelry to adorn bodies made beautiful by the purchase and use of exercise machines, proper foods and drugs, and the necessary surgery and cosmetics. Even goodness can be obtained by attending the right seminars, reading the right books, supporting the right causes, and choosing the right morals. "Rightness," of course, is entirely in the eye of the consumer: It might be Buddhist rightness, or Pentecostal rightness, or environmentalist rightness—who else is to say?

These dynamics seem so machine-like in some ways that the categories of *technology*, the *technological society*, or, even more evocatively in Jacques Ellul's French, *la technique* ("Technique itself," we might say) have been used to describe us and our culture. What happens to religion, then, and particularly Christianity, in a "technologized," consumerist culture?[3]

CONSUMERISM AND RELIGION

In consumerism, first, religion becomes a consumer good—at best. Religion is something that you add to your life to round it out, to fill in a blank or two, to complement the other ingredients of your lifestyle.

A newsweekly magazine recently called me to ask about Buddhist tantric sex workshops. Not being a specialist in either Buddhism or sex, I wasn't immediately sure why the reporter wanted to talk with me. "Well, you're often good at figuring out why something is happening. So why do you think west coasters are getting into these workshops?"

It suddenly clicked. Most North Americans don't know much about Buddhism, of course, and you can't seriously adopt a religion with just a workshop or two. So the reporter wasn't asking about any great wave of genuine conversion to Buddhism since these people weren't practicing Buddhism the rest of the time. Here's what such workshops can offer instead. You can get spirituality *and* sex *without* guilt. In tantric Buddhism there is a long tradition of probing the intersection of spirituality and sexuality, yet in that religion there is no deity to answer to. So a weekend workshop would be just the thing to perk up a West Coast lifestyle! (I say that, let me make clear, as I reside in Vancouver.)

Second, religions themselves become segmented into items to be picked, and picked over. Traditionally, religions have been offered to us, so to speak, in a "prix fixe" or "table d'hôte" arrangement in which all of the dishes are selected in advance and you opt for either the whole thing or nothing at all. Now we see what Canadian sociologist Reginald Bibby has called "religion à la carte." I want a little Confucianism to organize my life, a little tai chi for strength and balance, a weekend tantric sex workshop for spice, and the twenty-third Psalm when I overdo things and get into trouble.

University of California sociologist Robert Bellah and his colleagues interviewed such people, one of whom has now become famous in social science circles as the originator of the type of religion called "Sheilaism." Her name indeed was Sheila, and she told the researchers how she had put together bits and pieces of various religions in order to construct a way of life that made the most sense to her and brought her the most fulfillment. She didn't claim that she had discovered a path for anyone else but her. It was just what she liked, just what worked best for her. So she called it "Sheilaism."[4]

This sort of religion indicates a third theme of consumerism and religion, namely, that a religion is selected, or even constructed, *by* the self *for* the self. The proof of a religion is not in its authority, or its historical proofs, or its miracles, or its culture-shaping wisdom. The proof of a religion is not what it has done for peoples and cultures across the millennia. The proof is what it says to *me* and what it does for *me*. Religion thus becomes both "do-it-yourself" and "do-it-*for*-yourself."

We need not pick on our friends in la-la land, however. Across our society, people are looking at religion as something they can select or reject as consumers. Christians themselves move to a new city and immediately embark on the quest to find a new church. In the vernacular, they go "church-shopping." They investigate with what amounts to a shopping list: good preaching, good child care, good music, and so on. Increasingly, the denomination of the congregation doesn't matter. The links to one's previous church don't matter. What matters is how the church suits the current needs and preferences of my family and me. Churches themselves can contribute to this mind-set also by their advertising themselves as "the *family* church" or "the *revival* church," as if they are trying to establish a brand in a congested marketplace.

If, as it has for many North Americans, Christianity has come up short, they can turn to the burgeoning choices on the smorgasbord of contemporary religious pluralism. Whole religious traditions are now available as never before, whether Hinduism, Sikhism, or Islam. And parts of them can be selected to suit one's own desires and agenda: perhaps Sufi mysticism in best-selling collections of the poetry of Rumi; or the popular Hinduism-Lite by way of Transcendental Mediation in the teachings of Deepak Chopra; or a lovely candlelit Christmas Eve service when one tires of the frenzy of Yuletide commercialism.

To be sure, North American culture has encouraged a kind of consumerist approach to religion for a long, long time. As historians have noted, since the disestablishment of state churches in the eighteenth century (in the United States), or nineteenth (in English-speaking Canada), or twentieth (in Quebec), all religions and denominations have been "on their own" in the religious marketplace to attract what support they could. The once-ubiquitous, if now almost vanished, "church page" in the weekend newspaper customarily contained a box with the publisher's gentle and interestingly nonspecific exhortation, "Attend the Church of Your Choice."

Religion, furthermore, is an intensely personal matter. And all religions prize individual integrity, the voluntary embrace of the religion by each person, however much cultural expectations and norms frame that decision. So there is an irreducibly individual and volitional element in authentic religion.

Under consumerism, however, everything that does not fit through the window of personal choice and self-fulfillment simply does not appear. Tribal traditions, denominational loyalties, ethnic histories, and community responsibilities can all be shucked off in the name of "it doesn't work for me." Priests do not have any intrinsic authority, but are employees hired to provide certain services on terms that suit the clients—or they are fired. Religious communities—whether a Muslim mosque, a New Age study group, or a Roman Catholic parish—do not deserve any loyalty that lasts beyond their meeting the needs of the individual participants. Once the individual consumers no longer enjoy what they want, they move on.

Indeed, Princeton sociologist Robert Wuthnow has shown how the decades-long trend toward forming small-group fellowships—a way of meeting that was supposed to make up for the lack of strong social bonds among consumers of religion—has not always resulted in what was promised. Small groups can be just as ephemeral as consumerism would suggest. Once they no longer work for a participant—perhaps there's an unpleasant conflict in the group, or someone finds another member obnoxious, or the group just isn't as interesting anymore—she is free to take her leave at any time, and too many leave at the first sign of trouble. (For the record, it is important to note that Wuthnow found that many small groups *do* persist through unhappy times to provide a lasting community for those who persevere.)[5]

Ironically, then, when religions are processed through the machine of consumerism, they end up reinforcing the deep secularity that is pervasive in modern society. Whatever the actual beliefs this or that person might hold regarding God, the supernatural, the transcendent, and so on, the actual ceiling of decision making and accountability is low indeed. I pick the gods I want; I pick the rules I want to live by; I pick the rituals that suit me best. No higher authority and no higher power tells me what to do.

All of these themes characterize religion in the private sphere of contemporary life. That is the sphere to which religion has largely been relocated in modern times. When it comes to *public* importance, religion has nothing useful to say from a consumerist point of view. Indeed, genuine religions are a threat to the values and order of consumerism. They are an enemy to the consumerist ethos.

How so? Religions tend to tell people that there is more to life than buying and selling. Religions, even attenuated ones, tend to encourage people to lift their eyes above the roofline of the shopping mall, to listen beyond the din of the television commercials, and to plug into something more serious and substantial than the Internet. Worse, religions tend to bind people together and to encourage them to take their cues in life from texts, traditions, and teachers that often contradict the imperatives of consumerism. Hindu asceticism, Amish traditionalism, Islamic teetotalism—these are just particularly clear examples of religion getting in the way of full-bore consumerism. These "lumps" of religious people sticking together for religious reasons impede the free flow of advertising to the atomized individuals who are most amenable to consumerist manipulations. They are literally countercultural, and thus a menace to consumerism.

Thus consumerism tries to co-opt religion, to make religion fit into consumerist patterns and convictions. What it cannot make fit, it then opposes—with ridicule from comedians, loss of privilege from governments, and ruthless counterprogramming every hour of every day. One doesn't have to imagine paranoically an actual conspiracy of arch-consumerists, of course. One simply has to see the way modern life tends to flow, and what consumerism cannot carry along in its current, it tends to erode.

Consumerism is, of course, not at all confined to capitalist or democratic cultures, and to discuss it is not to implicitly deride either capitalism or democracy. China, Cuba, Russia, Singapore, Egypt, and Zimbabwe all manifest powerful signs of consumerism. It also is not a new challenge in our own civilization. To regard everything and everyone simply as commodities that might be selected for one's own enjoyment is an attitude manifest throughout history especially by the powerful.[6] Consumerism as a widespread cultural phenomenon is simply most obvious and advanced in societies that are most prosperous and individualized, and thus it is most obvious and advanced in our own.

It is more than a little ironic, in this regard, that Marx saw religion in general, and Christianity in particular, to act as the opiate of industrial capitalism. To be sure, modern Christianity has often served merely to facilitate and legitimate forces that were, at root, antithetical to human flourishing and to Christianity's own ideals.

Christian preaching in the modern world has often sought to keep the poor, the female, and the enslaved in their "proper stations."

Yet, as has been the case precisely with the poor, with women, and with the institution of slavery, it may be that authentic Christianity can continue to provide the smelling salts to awaken cultures rendered somnolent and subservient by the blandishments of modernity. To that possibility we now turn.

PART TWO

CONVERSION

5

Defining Conversion

The apostle Paul described his vocation thus: "It is he [Christ] whom we proclaim, warning everyone and teaching everyone in all wisdom, so that we may present everyone mature in Christ" (Colossians 1:28). In this phrase, "mature in Christ," Paul epitomizes the goal of the Christian life. We are, as Jesus said at the end of the Sermon on the Mount, to "be perfect": that is, whole, complete, fully formed and fully functioning versions of ourselves.

Apologetics, as a form of Christian discourse, thus must find its purpose within this overarching imperative of contributing toward people's maturation in Christ—what Christian tradition has sometimes called *conversion*. Misunderstandings of conversion, therefore, will misshape apologetics. So in this chapter we consider the nature of conversion as part of the groundwork for a proper understanding and practice of apologetics.

THE MYSTERIOUS PROFESSOR SACK

I was raised in a sectarian Protestant church in northern Ontario, Canada. We knew that we were Christians, of course. We were confident that other, very similar sects were Christian also, even if it was unfortunate that they did not entirely agree with us. So the conservative Baptists, the Christian and Missionary Alliance, and a few other churches clearly resided with us in the sheepfold.

We were spiritually generous to some of the mainstream Baptists and Presbyterians we met at evangelistic rallies or student clubs. But their denominations were much too tolerant of theological diversity (which is to say, they were tolerant of theological diversity), so they were all tainted. The United Church of Canada was, by the same logic, beyond the pale—people were true Christians in that church only by accident, and were wise to leave it. Anglicans were confused crypto-papists, and Catholics were full-blown idolaters—however pleasant they were as neighbors or schoolmates.

One of the crucial divisions in this tradition that saw most things in binary terms was the division between the Gospel and the alternative, false religion of *liberalism*. The Gospel taught that we were sinners who could never please God; therefore God must save us by his own free grace. Liberals taught that we were sinners who nonetheless should strive to please God; God would then graciously reward our sincere efforts. The Gospel taught that Jesus was God incarnate who died to take away the sins of the world. Liberals taught that Jesus was a very good man who lived to teach us how to take away the evils of the world. The Gospel offered life. Liberalism offered false hope and eventual destruction.[1]

Years of higher education and Christian experience softened the edges of this outlook somewhat. But as I began to pursue my doctoral degree at a doughty bastion of liberal Christianity, the Divinity School of the University of Chicago, those basic categories remained largely intact.

And so I met Professor Frederick Sack (not his real name, but the story that follows is true). An expert in the history of Christian thought, he became a favorite of mine. He also, however, became a considerable theological nuisance.

As an English teenager (Professor Sack told me once), he had converted to serious, personal Christianity through the witness of evangelical peers. He began to attend church services regularly, including some at one of the mainstays of British evangelicalism, Westminster Chapel in London, where he sat under the preaching of the estimable Dr. Martyn Lloyd-Jones. From London he went up to Cambridge and participated in the Cambridge Inter-Collegiate Christian Union (CICCU)—what North Americans would recognize as the local chapter of the Inter-Varsity Christian Fellowship.

As he anticipated graduating from Cambridge, he was drawn to pastoral ministry in the Presbyterian tradition. His evangelical friends urged him to study at an evangelical college. But the confident young Sack—as he related the story to me—chose instead to confront theological liberalism on its own turf. So he stayed in Cambridge and trained at the Presbyterian seminary, Westminster College.

While there, his theological views began to shift. He still dutifully hung up posters for CICCU events. But he was no longer comfortable with evangelicalism. Further study at Columbia University in New York added grist to the mill, and several decades later, when I met him at the crown of his career, he had spent the rest of his life teaching in decidedly nonevangelical schools.

The evangelical background surprised me, but Professor Sack was obviously yet a liberal. He was happy teaching at Chicago, for one thing. For another, he was an expert on the father of liberal theology, F. D. E. Schleiermacher, and I noticed a portrait of Schleiermacher on his office wall. Professor Sack was delighted to talk about Schleiermacher, whom he invoked as one of his patron saints—inasmuch as Presbyterians have such benefactors, he allowed with a small smile.

So far, so good. The categories were working nicely. But what then was I to make of the portrait that hung beside Schleiermacher's? For there in this den of liberalism was the unmistakable visage of John Calvin—no one's idea of a theological liberal. Professor Sack was delighted to talk of Calvin, too, as another subject of his professional research and another patron saint. Indeed, over much of his career he had labored to show the theological threads that connected Calvin and Schleiermacher.

Connected them? I was immediately perplexed. How could someone maintain both allegiances? It was like cheering for the Montreal Canadiens and the Toronto Maple Leafs at the same time. (Americans will have to translate that cultural reference: perhaps cheering for the Red Sox and the Yankees?) It was absurd.

So I began to probe a little further into Professor Sack's convictions. One of the ways one can do that with some delicacy in theological circles is to ask someone to pick sides in a historic dispute. I brought up the classic conflict between Martin Luther and Desiderius Erasmus in the sixteenth century over the extent to which our salvation depends on God's free gift or on our response of faith and obedience. Luther, of course, despaired of human potential and placed salvation entirely in God's hands. Erasmus, considerably less gloomy about himself and the world than Luther was, believed that authentic Christianity consisted of following the moral example of Christ. So, I asked Professor Sack, whose emphasis was most correct?

I knew, of course, that as a liberal he would champion Erasmus. Liberalism was all about doing one's best. But to my surprise, Professor Sack immediately sided with Luther. It is only by God's grace that we are saved, he affirmed. We have nothing of our own to bring. We are saved only through God's work in the Redeemer.

I was nonplussed. But I persisted. Who, then, is this Redeemer? I mean "Jesus," and he meant "Jesus," but what did each of us mean by Jesus as Redeemer? If he was giving the good Gospel answer regarding salvation, perhaps he was a Christian after all.

Jesus was one who was entirely transparent to God, was the reply. He is the one in whom we see God at work reconciling the world to himself. All of this, I thought, was close to the mark, but what about the Trinity? Was Jesus a great man who shows us God, or God showing himself as a man? Professor Sack, who had given such a heartwarming answer regarding Luther and God's grace, now replied that he agreed with Scheiermacher: The doctrine of the Trinity was not a mystery to be believed but a contradiction to be dispensed with. Jesus the Redeemer is the mystical person (as in the classical sense of *persona*, I concluded—rather like an identity God offers us) through whom we see and relate to God. Jesus is not the physically resurrected Son of God now sitting in heaven in human form, as orthodoxy has affirmed.

I finally put the question that for evangelical Christians, at least, is at the very heart of the matter—as it is for missionary-minded Roman Catholics, Orthodox, and other Protestants. Say that one met a pious Muslim from Arabia, I suggested. Should the Christian hope and try to convert that Muslim to Christianity?

No, Professor Sack replied. He stood with the early twentieth-century theologian Ernst Troeltsch on this one. Christianity is the authentic form of religion for us in our culture, but Islam is the authentic form of religion for them in theirs. Conversion would thus be unnecessary—indeed, inappropriate.

Getting to know Professor Sack meant straining my neat theological categories past the breaking point. He seemed clearly (fatally?) liberal on many crucial questions. But he said so many of the right things as well about the Gospel. And I thought liberals were all pseudo-Christians who trusted in their own good works to earn God's favor. How could he offer answers on both sides of the great gulf fixed between authentic Christianity and liberalism?

And then the vocational question emerged. How should I treat Professor Sack? Yes, of course I should treat him primarily as my instructor. But he is also a fellow human being who needs salvation, as we all do. Should I pray for him? Should I pray *with* him? Is he saved, or not, or what?

CONVERSION IS THE GOAL

Professor Sack remained a conundrum to me right through my studies at Chicago. I have since read further work of his on the history of Christian thought with great profit. But what of his soul? What of his destiny?

It was dealing with him and his apparently incoherent ideas (they were not, of course, incoherent to him!) that compelled me, more than anything else in my life, to reconsider the whole paradigm of conversion and mission I had inherited. In that paradigm, everyone needed to have a conversion experience. That experience must result in both orthodox conviction and holiness of life. The Christian's task toward his neighbor began with ascertaining whether the neighbor was a Christian. If he was not, one tried to evangelize him and walk with him to the point of conversion. If he crossed over to authentic faith, or was already a Christian, then one's responsibility was to help him understand correct doctrine and live a correct life.

Clearly much depended on discerning the spiritual state of one's neighbor. In my case, I needed to figure out whether Professor Sack was truly a Christian. And I realized that his views were not lining up nicely on my grid. The readings, so to speak, were ambiguous.

So I propose instead a new way of looking at conversion that then entails a new way of looking at the Christian mission to one's neighbor. In this new model—at least, new for me, although it in fact is deeply rooted in Christian history—apologetics can find a more appropriate place.

For in the old one, apologetics could easily become a form of intellectual browbeating. It was warfare waged on behalf of the neighbor's soul by mowing down his resistance and presenting the Gospel with irresistible argument in hopes that he would relent and believe. If he was already a Christian, however, then apologetics took an entirely different tack: It became simply a part of Christian education to confirm his faith and help him evangelize others.

So let us consider now what is, in fact, the goal of the Christian mission. And let us begin by distinguishing it from alternatives.

Our task is not to persuade someone of the superiority of the Christian religion per se. The central goal of Christian mission, that is, lies well beyond getting someone to change one religion for another. (Several reasons could be adduced for this, but the most crucial and obvious is simply that no one will be saved merely by practicing a religion, even Christianity. Our own Christian theology reminds us that the basis of salvation is faith in the work of God on our behalf, not correct observance of a religion.)

Our missionary goal, furthermore, is not just to introduce someone to Christ. Real evangelism, so much evangelical teaching has asserted, lies in bringing people to the point of actual encounter with Jesus. Now, such introductions can well be made, of course, and it is a glorious privilege when God brings such an occasion to pass in one's life. But we must see that making such introductions is only part of the Christian mission.

Instead, our objective as those called to love God and our neighbors—to seek their best interests—is to offer whatever assistance we can to our neighbors toward their full maturity: toward full health in themselves and in their relationships, and especially toward God. Our mission must be as broad as God's mission, and that mission is to bring *shalom* to the whole world. In short, when it comes to our neighbors, our goal is to help our neighbors to be *fully converted* into all God wants them to be.

"So then, whenever we have an opportunity, let us work for the good of all" (Galatians 6:10).

WHAT IS CONVERSION?

Two Binary Aspects of Conversion

The New Testament speaks of conversion as *metanoia*: literally, a change of mind. But this is not merely to alter one's opinion on this or that matter. *Metanoia* is a redirection of one's fundamental outlook—what we might call one's mind-set or mentality. It means more than intellectual revolution, furthermore, as it entails change in one's affections and will, the very core of one's self. So conversion is a very serious matter. It is literally radical: from the Latin *radix*, for root.

This organic metaphor points to the next consideration. Conversion, like the new life of plant, can be seen binarily, and in two senses.

First, the plant is either dead or alive. This emphasis is characteristic of evangelical proclamation. As the Sunday School jingle puts it: "One door and only one / and yet its sides are two. / Inside and outside: / On which side are you?"

The Bible supports such a view of conversion. "You must be born again," Jesus proclaimed (John 3:7 NIV). "[God] has rescued us from the dominion of darkness and transferred us into the kingdom of the Son he loves," Paul announced (Colossians 1:13 NIV). Only "those whose names were not written in the Lamb's Book of Life" would go to heaven and the rest to hell, prophesied John (Revelation 20:15 NIV).

Christian theology also speaks in this way, as it uses the category of *regeneration* for the fundamental work of the Holy Spirit in the life of the sinner.

This "in or out" language, finally, appears also in the terminology of contemporary sociology of conversion. But the complexity of this terminology—of conversion, yes, but also of *alternation, transference, renewal, affiliation, adhesion*, and other terms for religious moves one might make—points to biblical and theological counterparts that indicate also that there is more to conversion than just "getting in."[2]

For the second sense of conversion is also organic, and now denotes the sense of becoming fully what one has begun to be. The seed matures into the ripe plant. The baby grows into the adult.

Jesus calls upon his disciples to "be perfect, as your heavenly Father is perfect" (Matthew 5:48 NIV), but he also promises that they will have the help of the Holy Spirit to grow into the fullness of fellowship with God and each other (John 13–17).[3] The Apostle Paul encourages his flocks that "he who began a good work in you will be faithful to complete it . . ." (Philippians 1:16 NIV).[4] In fact, much of Paul's writing in the New Testament follows a form familiar to Bible scholars: Since you have this status and identity in Christ, then grow up into it and act appropriately. "If then there is any encouragement in Christ, any consolation from love, any sharing in the Spirit, any compassion and sympathy, make my joy complete: be of the same mind, having the same love, being in full accord and of one mind. . . . Let the same mind be in you that was in Christ Jesus" (Philippians 2:1–2, 5 NRSV).[5]

To be converted (*metanoia*) does not mean to immediately have a fully converted mind, but to begin with a fundamentally reoriented mind (so the first sense) that is then on its way to complete maturity in this new mind-set (so the second sense). Thus Paul can urge the Roman Christians to have their minds constantly renewed: "Do not be conformed to this world, but be transformed by the renewing of your minds, so that you may discern what is the will of God—what is good and acceptable and perfect" (Romans 12:2 NRSV).

Theological nomenclature has developed through the centuries to explain this more fully. Let's illustrate it by pedestrian example. Well, not pedestrian, perhaps: Let's drive.

Suppose we intend to drive from San Francisco, in northern California, to San Diego, in the far south. I insist on driving, since I've actually visited San Francisco once or twice and I never, ever get lost. You graciously concede the wheel, and off we go.

The miles and hours go by. You begin to feel uneasy, however, when we pass what looks for all the world like a sign welcoming us to state of Oregon. I insist that "Oregon" must be a region of California, and that Los Angeles surely must be coming up soon. As we drive through Portland, however, you are convinced I am heading in exactly the wrong direction. And as the Washington state line comes up, you become rather insistent on the point. In fact, you want very much to convert me to your opinion.

What is it, exactly, that you want when you want me to convert? First, you want me to recognize my error. I can't take any further steps until I have agreed that I am, in fact, heading north instead of south. But let's suppose I do that—"Yes, by golly, this sure looks a lot more like Pacific rain forest than Californian coastland!"—and yet I *don't care*. "Hey, Washington is a beautiful place, too. Almost as nice as British Columbia!"

Surely true *repentance* is what you seek from me. Merely recognizing my mistake is not enough. I must *regret* that mistake. "I'm heading in the wrong direction, and I'm sorry."

Then I must take further action. I must abandon the path I'm on (taking the next exit ramp); turning the car around by crossing over to the other side on the bridge; and get a new start (by getting on the entrance ramp in the opposite direction).

Suppose I do all this. Are you now satisfied? Have I fully converted? No. Not until I drive us all the way to San Diego, which was the objective of the exercise. It's good that I'm properly reoriented. In fact, that binary move is indeed the essential move that has to be made if I'm first heading in the wrong direction. But turning around is not enough. Getting to the goal is all or nothing; it is also a binary matter. I'm not *there* until I'm *there*.

Theologians thus speak of conversion as having multiple stages: repentance (recognition and regret), regeneration (a new start), sanctification (getting closer and closer to the goal), and glorification (arriving at the final destination). Full conversion is all of this.[6]

Single-Point Conversion Experiences?

Many evangelicals have emphasized that true conversion begins with a single, obvious, transformative experience of conversion. This fundamental reorientation and renewal marks the true believer's transition from resistance toward God (whether active or passive) and spiritual death, to faith in God and spiritual life. Whether for certain eighteenth-century preachers or twentieth-century theologians, the dramatic and specifiable conversion experience has been the hallmark of evangelical piety.

Thus evangelicals in particular, and many other missionary-minded Christians, have sought to promote such experiences as authentic conversions. They therefore have marshaled apologetical arguments with one clear goal in view: to help bring someone to that crucial point of decision. And such Christians often have asserted the complementary proposition that those who cannot testify to such conversion experiences—no matter what else is involved in their religious profession—probably are not truly converted.

The paradigm case of such experiences in our day, perhaps, is conversion at a Billy Graham Crusade. Surely these rallies, and Billy Graham's own sermons, promote exactly this understanding of conversion and the normativity of such single-point conversions.[7]

Except that they don't. And it turns out, upon closer inspection, that the Graham meetings and the teaching of Graham himself point to a significantly different understanding of conversion and so-called conversion experiences.

For one thing, the Graham organization never reports "conversions." They report "decisions," whether decisions to become a Christian, yes, but also decisions to "rededicate" one's life to God, decisions to live a more pious and disciplined life, and so on. The Graham team never presumes to know just what has happened in a person's life when he or she testifies to this or that experience. The team can, at least, report that people themselves reported decisions—

much as pollsters and sociologists can report what people say has happened to them, being careful (if they *are* careful) not to equate that simply with what *in fact* has happened to this or that person.

Graham himself preaches at such meetings that it doesn't matter whether or not one has been an active member of a church. Nor does it finally matter whether one has made a "decision" at a previous rally just like this one. What matters, Graham affirms, is whether one is right with God *now*, whether one is a disciple of Jesus Christ *now*. If not, Graham says, it is time to reorient one's life toward God.

Is that reorientation a conversion experience? Graham, in fact, is careful not to say. It could be a death-to-life transition, yes. But it might also be the rekindling of an almost-extinguished but genuine faith.

According to his several biographers and his own memoirs, Billy Graham has experienced what amount to at least three, and perhaps four, major spiritual turning points in his life. More than one of them some might call conversion experiences.

His stereotypical conversion experience came as a teenager who went to a revival meeting in his Carolina town to raise a ruckus and walked the sawdust trail instead. As subsequent weeks passed, however, the young Graham was frustrated in his attempt to live out his dramatically new faith: He had been a good lad before, so no one noticed the difference.

He then went off to Bible school in Florida, but during that time he felt confronted by God over the shallowness and worldliness of his outlook and ambitions. He responded with repentance and fresh resolve. But was this his authentic conversion, while the previous one had perhaps been simply a Southern evangelical rite of passage?

Graham reports two more dramatic decisions early in his career as a preacher, each of which open him up to new vistas of discipleship and ministry. So what are they?

Perhaps more indicative of Graham's fundamental theology of conversion is his declaration that some genuine Christians may not have any such precisely specifiable experiences at all. The two Christians who arguably have influenced Graham the most have been his mother, Morrow Graham, and his wife, Ruth Bell Graham. Both of these women were raised as Presbyterians and thus in a tradition that emphasizes growing up in God's covenant of grace, rather than seeking and expecting a radical conversion experience. Graham points to his mother and his wife as Christians whom he admires for the quality of their faith while allowing that neither of them testify to a particular conversion experience. And lest one think that such remarks arise out of a more mellow, more ecumenical Billy Graham in mature years, one need only consult his very first popular book, *Peace with God*, to find him making this very point in the 1950s.[8]

Graham thus shares with evangelicalism and, indeed, with all orthodox Christianity the belief that sinners need to pass from death to life by the regenerating power of the Holy Spirit. There is indeed this binary element to conversion. But we remark two points in summary: (a) Just when that line is crossed may not be evident to anyone but God—including the subject himself or herself; and (b) having once embarked on the path of discipleship, one must press on to the fully converted life, not daring to rest on one's status as "already saved," but rejoicing in that status as the grounds for cooperating with God so as to "become saved" in the sense of final maturation.[9]

More than Changing One's Mind

Conversion therefore involves the whole person as one transits from one sort of existence before knowing Christ to walking consistently in the Spirit of Christ in every respect.

Intellectually, one believes propositions one did not before: about God, about the world, about oneself, about the purpose of things, and so on. Christianity is not merely a metaphysic or a metanarrative, to be sure, but it involves both of these elements. Christian discipleship properly takes place within these intellectual convictions.

Morally, one has a different sense of what counts as good and evil, what one ought or ought not to do. Some favorite thoughts, words, or actions are now seen to be empty or even wrong, while thoughts, words or actions that in the past seemed vacuous at best and perverse at worst now shine with holiness. Sexual purity, for example, now is blessedly imperative whereas before it might have been quaint at best and repressive at worst. Forgiveness is now seen as divine strength, whereas before it might have seemed subhuman weakness.

Emotionally, one loves what one used to hate or ignore; one shuns former pleasures as toxic and wasteful. One cares about God, other people, the rest of the planet, and oneself in a way one didn't before. Indeed, the fundamental laws of both Christianity and its Jewish antecedent rest on love for God and for one's neighbor, and love entails correct emotion along with correct activity.

Aesthetically, one finds beauty where one once saw nothing worthwhile at all, or perhaps even something repellent. Wizened nuns are no longer objects of callous humor but angels of radiant simplicity and joy. One also now turns away from what used to fascinate and impress. The hottest car, clothes, and condo now look merely garish and silly.[10]

Spiritually, one is sensitive and open to God, yes, but also to the spiritual needs and gifts of other people. One takes seriously the spiritual dimension of earthly struggles and blessings. One responds to challenges with prayer as well as with whatever else is required.

Finally, one treats the physical world differently, valuing it highly as God's good creation, caring for it as a creation that has suffered from human sin, and regarding it as nonetheless secondary to the surpassing worth of God and God's concerns. Thus one tries to keep one's own body healthy, to keep one's property as sound and as lovely as one can, and to support the care of other parts of creation, without elevating any of these good creatures over God himself.

We can note in passing, and follow this up in Part Three, that Christian apologetics can contribute to conversion in all of these aspects, not merely on intellectual matters of fact—what I'm calling metaphysics and metanarrative. Precisely because conversion does involve all of these aspects, conversely, an apologetic that aims only at one of these aspects (as many apologetics do) thus is only somewhat helpful, rather than sufficient in itself.

All of these changes, furthermore, are changes that take place within the individual, within one's own consciousness. But conversion entails more than that. There is a *relational* conversion as well: toward God, of course, but also toward the self, the world, and the church. One might have had little to do with the church before; one might have idolized or exploited the world before; one might have had, and probably did have, an improper and unhealthy self-image before. Christian conversion ultimately means drawing into proper line and balance all of these relationships in the beautiful complex of shalom.

Christian conversion, therefore, amounts to a new *outlook* on *everything*; a new *attitude* toward and *motivation* in *everything*; and a new *relationship* toward *everyone*. Conversion doesn't mean an *entirely* new way of life, of course, as if non-Christians know nothing of truth, goodness, and beauty, and nothing of God. Christians share with their neighbors many overlapping values and concerns because God has been generous with his gifts to everyone. And the Christian carries over into her new life all of what was truly good in her life before. But the core of one's life is now oriented directly toward the worship and service of God in the person of Jesus Christ. Thus the Christian is, in that fundamental sense, a new person.

In one of the most profound metaphors in the Bible, conversion is described fundamentally as the call to *change families*. When Jesus himself was asked to leave the company of his disciples by his mother and his brothers, he responded, "Who are my mother and my brothers? . . . Here are my mother and my brothers! Whoever does God's will is my brother and sister and mother" (Mark 3:33, 34b, 35 NIV). The apostles Peter and Paul tell the early churches that they are now part of a new ethnic group—literally, a new *ethnos* (people) in which the old divisions of Jew and Gentile fade away (Galatians 3:28; cf. I Peter 2:9) and the convert is introduced into a new set of social practices, allegiances, beliefs, and even language.[11]

When one considers, therefore, how firmly we tend to hold onto our opinions about even trivial matters; when one considers how difficult it is for us to embrace significantly new ways of looking at things even when it is obviously to our advantage to do so; and then when one considers all of the aspects of Christian conversion beyond the "merely" intellectual—conversion is a huge matter indeed.

Moreover, Christian theology speaks of the deeply complicating factor of sin in our hearts. As difficult as it might be to change our minds even when we would like to do so, it is almost impossible for us when we fundamentally do not want to do so. Given the basic disposition of fallen humanity to ignore God or to rebel against God in our pride or despair, how can anyone possibly be expected to convert in either sense: to somehow become completely reoriented toward God having been "bent" away from God; and to then proceed to mature on all fronts into a whole and complete person, entirely conformed to God's standards of human perfection? And what, then, are Christians to try to do for their neighbors in the light of this reality?

WHAT WE CAN AND CANNOT DO

We must begin by acknowledging that conversion in either respect—either in terms of fundamental redirection or in terms of full maturity—cannot be accomplished by our own powers of persuasion.

John Newton, a spiritual leader among evangelicals in eighteenth-century England, recalled an account he had read of Luther's lieutenant Philip Melancthon:

> With such sanguine hopes Melancthon entered the ministry at the dawn of the Reformation. He thought he had only to speak and to be heard in order to convince. But he soon found himself mistaken, and that the love of sin, the power of prejudice and the devices of Satan were such obstacles in his way that nothing less than the mighty operations of the Spirit of God could break through. And all who preach upon his principles and with his views have known something of his disappointment.[12]

It was Newton, furthermore, who penned the famous lyrics to "Amazing Grace" that underscore this point in the second stanza:

'Twas grace that taught my heart to fear,
    And grace my fears relieved;
How precious did that grace appear,
    The hour I first believed![13]

Francis Xavier, George Whitefield, and Billy Graham, to consider three of the most widely heard preachers in history, certainly did not make converts of everyone in their sometimes vast audiences. The Apostle Paul himself did not convince everyone he addressed. The Lord Jesus Christ was crucified by people among whom were those quite familiar with his teaching, and even on the mount of the Great Commissioning there were some who doubted (Matthew 28:17). Apologetics and all other such Christian speech cannot in fact accomplish very much when it comes to conversion. We can pause to recognize that we cannot effect conversion *even in ourselves*. Spiritual adepts throughout the ages warn us that mere argument accomplishes little even within our own hearts.

Among the most distinguished commentators on matters of the spirit was the eighteenth-century American pastor Jonathan Edwards. In his classic discussion of spiritual well-being, his *Treatise on the Religious Affections*, he writes:

> Great use may be made of external arguments; they are not
> to be neglected, but highly prized and valued; for they may
> be greatly serviceable to awaken unbelievers, and bring them
> to serious consideration, and to confirm the faith of true
> saints: yea they may be in some respects subservient to the
> begetting of a saving faith in men. [Yet] . . . there is no
> spiritual conviction . . . but what arises from an apprehension of the spiritual beauty and glory of divine things.[14]

And such a direct apprehension is a gift mediated only by the Holy Spirit of God.

When Simon Peter exclaimed that he knew that Jesus was the Messiah, the Son of God, when his fellow Jews could reach only as high as their available category of "great prophet" to describe him, Jesus pronounced: "Blessed are you, Simon son of Jonah! For flesh and blood has not revealed this to you, but my Father in heaven" (Matthew 16:17).[15] Jesus warned the sincere and faithful Nicodemus that his righteousness, even the righteousness of a Pharisee, was woefully inadequate. To Nicodemus's consternation, Jesus said, "You must be born again . . . by the Spirit" (John 3:3–5). The apostles follow their Master in this teaching: Conversion is a divine work only, effected by the Holy Spirit of God (1 Corinthians 3:5–7).

One of the most famous conversions of the twentieth century is also among the most mysterious. The brilliant Jewish philosopher Edith Stein was visiting colleagues during the summer of 1921, her thirtieth year. One morning she happened to pick up a copy of the autobiography of St. Teresa of Ávila and began to read. She stayed immersed in the book for the rest of the day and into the night. The next morning she announced, "This is the truth." She was baptized a Roman Catholic Christian the following New Year's Day. No biographer of Stein's has unearthed a single account that explains this event: no letter or remark to a friend, let alone a published memoir. Patricia Hampl simply writes: "What we know: she read Teresa of Ávila—and recognized there 'the truth.' And so she followed it."[16] What could produce such a change? Christians would say it was obviously and only the Holy Spirit.

Therefore our human responsibility and opportunity is twofold. First, it is to bear witness, to demonstrate in our living and to articulate in our speaking the good news of new life under God's reign. We are to show and tell what God has done, is doing, and will do in the world. And second, we are to offer all we can to help each other in moving toward the goal of full conversion, the goal of full maturity and everlasting shalom. (Part Three will offer detailed suggestions for observing these principles.)

For this is what we owe each other according to the great commandment: "Love your neighbor as you love yourself." You are not content to give *yourself* the mere necessities of existence, surely, but instead you prefer to give yourself the very best life has to offer. I feel the same way about myself, too. And in the Christian religion, there is nothing wrong with this attitude. Jesus never suggested we not seek the best for ourselves. To be sure, sometimes what is truly best for us requires sacrifice: "Whoever does not carry the cross and follow me cannot be my disciple" (Luke 14:27). Yet Jesus himself "endured the cross" in order to secure "the joy that was set before him" (Hebrews 12:2). The key is to realize that securing what is best for oneself takes place within the overarching goal of pleasing God and serving God's world—especially in the form of our neighbor, the "near one." Christianity is not some "zero-sum" ethic, but a "win-win-win" ethic by which God is pleased, our neighbor is served, and we each grow into completeness and joy. So we are obliged by our generous Lord to care for each other as we would have them care for us.

The Christian mission, therefore, is basically simple, even radical. We are to do what good we can, and *all* the good we can. This conception of mission thus avoids the unhappy dichotomy that has afflicted so many churches, especially in the twentieth century: the choice between merely "getting them saved" (the stereotypical evangelical mission) and merely "doing them good" (the stereotypical liberal mission). John Newton puts it beautifully:

> A Christian has the mind of Christ, who went about doing good, who makes his sun to shine upon the good and the evil, and sendeth rain on the just and the unjust. His Lord's example forms him to the habit of diffusive benevolence; he breathes a spirit of good will to mankind and rejoices in every opportunity of being useful to the souls and bodies of others, without respect to parties and interests. He commiserates, and would, if possible, alleviate the miseries of all around him. If his actual services are restrained by want of ability, still all share in his sympathy and prayers.[17]

Furthermore, we are to do what is our part to do, with faith in the Spirit of God and in the rest of God's Church to do *their* parts to achieve the universal goal of shalom. Thus we do not each have to try to accomplish everything that is good to do in any situation. Rather, we each must serve *this* neighbor according to his or her particular need, according to the limits and opportunities of *this* particular occasion, and according to our particular ability to truly help.

We can conclude, then, with some questions that Christians shouldn't ask, and a question we should always ask instead.

"Is he saved?" I don't know, and I cannot know until "the roll is called up yonder." The actual condition of another's heart is mysterious, even to that individual. So from the outside I certainly cannot presume to know, and therefore I do not need to try to know. The whole agenda of some Christians to figure out "who is in and who is out" is therefore mistaken.

"What can I do to convert him?" Nothing. God's Spirit alone can truly convert. Again, God does not call us to do what we cannot do. So we need not, and must not, try to convert anyone—including through what we might pride ourselves on as being impressive apologetics.

"Does he need to hear the gospel?" Of course he does. We all do, again and again, until we see Christ face to face. That's one of the reasons Christians take the Lord's Supper regularly: to hear in it the gospel once again, the gospel of everlasting forgiveness and empowerment to overcome evil and enjoy the good. If we therefore have any opportunity to tell the gospel to another, we should tell it. No one outgrows it.

The good question to ask instead is simply this: *"How shall I treat him? How shall I treat her?"* And the answer is just as simple: with love. Until all of our neighbors are fully mature in Christ, there is something left for serious Christians to do, and when we have the opportunity to assist that neighbor somehow, then we should take it. I daresay that will keep us all plenty busy until the Lord Jesus returns.

As for Professor Sack? Well, I think we did each other the good that we could do in that academic relationship. And since our paths have diverged widely over the years, I simply must entrust him to the ongoing care of Christ and his church—as I hope Professor Sack has done with me.

6

Deciding about Religion

Christians engage in apologetics because they want their neighbors to take Christianity more seriously than they otherwise might. Christians hope that their neighbors will decide to follow Jesus Christ, or to follow him more closely, as a result of such conversations. So how do people make such decisions?

People make religious decisions in much the same way as we make all decisions. So this chapter begins by looking at some basic principles of epistemology, the philosophy of knowledge. Then it outlines the distinct question of making decisions about religion—both in one's mind and also in the rest of one's life. Knowing how people make such decisions thus aids the apologist in considering how he can best communicate good news to his neighbor.

HOW WE THINK

Hypothetical Thinking

When we think about things, we usually are quite particular. We ask particular questions and expect particular sorts of answers.

Q: Why is the sky blue?

A: Because of the way light reflects off it, and refracts through it, to our eyes and because of the way our eyes and brains then interpret that light.

Q: Why do people offer incense to buddhas and bodhisattvas at the local Buddhist temple?

A: Because those beings enjoy receiving such devotion and generously respond with supernatural favors.

Q: Why am I constantly short of cash?
A: Because I am not paid what I'm worth in this philistine society that refuses to recognize true genius.

These answers satisfy the questioner, of course, only if he shares with the answerer a considerable number of assumptions about the world. Each of these answers (and, indeed, each of the questions) assumes a particular understanding of the universe: of physics and biology in the first case; of religion in the second case; and of both society and my abilities in the third case.

Not sharing this understanding will lead to very different answers, and even a breakdown in communication:

Q: Why is the sky blue?
A: Because the occupying alien forces are cloaking their massive armada of spaceships that are currently in orbit around the earth with this opaque blue screen.

Q: Why do people offer incense to buddhas and bodhisattvas at the local Buddhist temple?
A: Because Satan has blinded their eyes to the existence of the true God, and they erroneously believe they can earn the favor of nonexistent spiritual beings.

Q: Why am I constantly short of cash?
A: Because society infallibly rewards only industriousness and talent with financial success.

An answer "works" only within a set of assumptions about the subject in question, and each of these assumptions could well be examined for its own warrants. When we answer a question, we are in fact advancing what scientists sometimes call a hypothesis, an intelligent guess as to what is the case in any particular instance. We then try out such guesses on the world and see how they fit. Each of these guesses in its turn is located within (and makes sense within) a larger structure of hypotheses that is itself a large hypothesis to be tried out on the world. At the most comprehensive level we encounter worldviews, or religions, or philosophies, which attempt to explain everything. We must see that they, too, are hypotheses—intelligent guesses—that are always subject to further tryouts to see how they fit our experience of the world.

We are wise to recognize that all human thought is conducted in this way. We encounter a situation; we compose our best guess as to how to understand it (based on our prior knowledge and our assumptions about the way the world works); and then we see how well our guess (our hypothesis) works in that situation. So let's suppose we have encountered a flock of sheep and we conclude that "sheep are white." We later encounter a similar situation, apply our hypothesis, and see how it works then. If it works perfectly, we are pleased. "Here's another flock of sheep, and behold, they are all white." If it works pretty well but doesn't quite fit the new circumstances, we tinker with the hypothesis and improve it—or perhaps we just store away this oddity for future consideration. "Here is a black sheep. But that must be some sort of exception to the rule." If it works badly, we consider whether the new situation really is similar to the previous one. "Hmm. Here are a lot of grey and black sheep. Maybe these aren't sheep at all, but some other species. Or, perhaps, someone has deliberately dyed the sheep's natural white wool." Maybe the hypothesis is still just fine, and we need, instead, another hypothesis to suit a different challenge. "This flock over here are indeed sheep, and they are white. Those mottled ones over there turn out to be goats. Sheep *are* white." But perhaps we conclude that this new situation really is like the previous one, and yet the hypothesis doesn't work satisfactorily. So we consider a radical change in our hypothesis, or abandon it for a new one. "Sheep naturally occur in a variety of colors after all."

Therefore, when we are thinking about things, we are always assessing particular elements within systems of explanation, rather than brute facts or discrete notions. If I assert, for example, that "this computer screen is blue," I am simultaneously asserting other ideas as well, only some of which I can give for examples here: that the screen appears blue to me via the interpretation of sense experience by my mind, which is trained to label such data as "computer," "screen," "blue," and so on; I can normally trust such experiences and interpretations; I expect that other people see things in similar ways so that my claim that "this computer screen is blue" will make sense to them and correspond to their own experience were they to sit here now and look in this direction at the object before me; and so on.

Thus the simple and rather uninteresting assertion that "the computer screen is blue" implicitly asserts an entire model of human perception and interpretation. (And here is where things get more interesting for the apologist.) Arguments with my proposal that "this computer screen is blue" could take place *within* the model, as in "Well, *I* believe the screen is actually *green* and that you therefore must have an idiosyncratic visual disorder—let's call some other people over to take a look." The general model of "perceiving computer screens" is accepted by both of us in this argument, and the disagreement remains within the model.

Someone else, however, could challenge my contention regarding a blue computer screen from *outside* the more general model of perception and interpretation I hold: "You believe that you see a blue computer screen. Such a belief, however, is just another illusion in the common human confusion of believing in a world of particular objects. Ultimate reality instead consists in the cosmic Oneness of all being. It would be better for you to get past this preoccupation with particulars and concentrate upon experiencing the unity of all."

When we are trying to discern "right and wrong," or "true and false," or "beautiful and ugly," therefore, it would be more accurate for us to speak of "better and worse" *hypotheses* to explain our experiences. "This assertion or this larger model of explanation," we should say, "is the best we have formulated so far to explain what we understand to be the pertinent data." In the midst of disagreement, then, we can properly abandon simplistic assertions of this or that to more accurate and appropriate comparisons of the relative strengths of this hypothesis and that one. Indeed, those who make their living as negotiators realize that often the parties in conflict don't agree even on what count as the main issues, or on how to proceed in dialogue, or on the criteria for what will count as a good idea. These differences must be articulated and resolved if the parties have any hope of agreeing on the particular point in question.

This reference to negotiation underscores a pluralist, postmodern recognition that the Christian will accept as evidence or good reason some things that others will not. Sense experience, intuition, scriptural teaching, church tradition, mystical experience, and rigorous logic, among other resources to which a Christian might refer, have each been rejected by one or another alternative ideology or religion. A helpful semantic move, then, can be made away from loaded terms such as *evidence* and *reason* to the more generic terms of *grounds* or *warrants* or *justification*. This lets us put the question, in any given case, as follows: What *grounds* do you have to believe what you believe?[1]

Someone might well then be able to appreciate that *within* a given system of thought, her neighbor indeed has sufficient grounds for him to give it assent. A sympathetic and imaginative Christian can see how a Buddhist could aim at achieving nirvana as the highest good available, while the Buddhist could see why his Christian friend looks forward instead to the New Jerusalem. The Christian will still disagree, however, with important elements of her neighbor's overarching system of belief (that is, with Buddhism), and thus find the grounds for desiring nirvana (that is, measured according to her own *Christian* system) to be less than convincing. And the Buddhist likely would return the favor.

Critical thinking in a postmodern context, therefore, appreciates that disagreements are not always over particular propositions A or B, but over entire complexes of ideas, whole models of explanation that in turn reside within worldviews—however coherent or incoherent one's worldview might be! In such cases, disagreement is not so much a matter of whether A or B is the case as of whether one model is more effective in explaining all of the relevant data than another. If there is too much variance in their larger models of explanation, two observers cannot come to agreement on A or B because, among other things, their criteria for evaluating the validity or value of A and B are too different.

Many Christians still do not recognize this principle. They focus their disputes instead upon only "*A or B*." For example, they believe it is sufficient to ask, "Did Jesus rise from the dead or not?" They fail to recognize that some people don't care about historical evidence and argument; others freely believe in all sorts of bizarre supernatural events from which the Christian would want to distinguish the resurrection of Christ; and still others are so secularist in their views that *any* alternative explanation is preferable to the implausible assertion that a deity resurrected an ancient Jewish teacher in order to make him Lord of the universe. Failure to see just how differently our neighbors can think and believe will doom our conversations to frustration, whether between a Christian and a Hindu, say, or between an Enlightenment-style thinker and a postmodernist.

Ideally, we ought to appreciate that each hypothesis is, by definition, only a provisional, working model, rather than a statement of absolute truth, right here, right now. As provisional explanations, furthermore, we should be open not only to comparing our hypotheses with others in order to judge their relative merits but also to improving or even replacing our hypotheses, since they are only humanly devised instruments to help us make sense of something. We thus should distinguish between our understandable loyalties to particular thought-systems that have helped us in the past and critical openness to new hypotheses that might well be of greater assistance in the future. In what follows, let's explore that distinction further—the distinction between commitment to a model and openness to another, which is obviously vital to the apologetic enterprise.

Reality, Interpretation, and Truth

"Hey, you have your reality, and I have mine."
"That may be true for you, but not for me."

There is a lot of nonsense clouding our current vocabulary about truth. I'd like to offer some clarity by defining three terms and showing their relations to each other: *reality*, *interpretation*, and *truth*.

Reality is whatever it is. Reality is the way things are. Perhaps there is just One Thing, whether that be the universe, or Brahman, or

God. Maybe there are lots of things. But whatever is actually real, that is what we should mean by reality.

We perceive things, and we interpret them. We name them, or paint them, or represent them in some other way. These *interpretations* of ours, then, are our attempts to "re-present" reality in some approximate form. So a map re-presents the streets of Chicago, say, by showing them in relation to each other, to Lake Michigan, and to the points of the compass.

Now our interpretations are not exactly like the reality they represent. If we were trying to re-present reality in an exact one-to-one way, we would simply have to duplicate it. To produce such a map of downtown Chicago, we would have to construct a parallel Loop— Sears Tower and Chicago River, and all—down to the subatomic level. So our interpretations always give up certain aspects or dimensions of the reality they represent in order to get a particular job done. A typical street map helps us drive around the city. An unusual street map shows the structure of the subterranean conduits for water, gas, electricity, sewage, and so on. A map you'll never see shows all of the people who happened to be on those streets on a particular moment on a particular afternoon. And so on. No map shows everything.

Now, to what extent can we call a map true? *Truth*, I suggest, is a quality, not a thing. There is no Truth anywhere in the cosmos, by which I mean an actual thing one could conceivably visit and witness—as Plato apparently thought one could in the realm of the perfect Forms. (I realize Plato's interpreters have argued for centuries about just what he meant: Their "maps" of his thought don't all agree!) Truth is a quality of an interpretation as follows: To the extent that the interpretation corresponds to the reality it represents, it is true. So if my hand-drawn map of downtown Chicago does in fact position the Art Institute correctly relative to the John Hancock building (such a map would consist of a single line running more or less north and south along Michigan Avenue—I'm pretty good at drawing such maps), then it would be a true map.

Now a map can be true *more or less*, and in two respects. In an absolute sense, every map is not completely true as it does not exactly represent every detail of the reality it describes. My map does not include the famous sculpted lions on the steps of the Art Institute, nor does it depict the trademark gridwork on the face of the Hancock. To the extent that our interpretations of anything fall short of complete correspondence with the reality they represent, they are less than fully true.

That fact, however, doesn't usually bother us because we usually apply a relative standard—technically, a pragmatic standard—instead. We expect interpretations to perform certain limited tasks, and they are true to the extent that they perform those tasks. If my map really does guide you from one Chicago landmark to another, then it is true ("as far as it goes," we might say). If Newton's laws of motion helped NASA put Apollo 11 on the moon, they were true ("true enough," we might say)—even though we know that Einstein & Company had complicated Sir Isaac's laws several decades before the space program began.

So *truth* is a quality of *interpretations* or *representations* by which we denote the extent to which they resemble *reality*—both in an absolute sense (technically, according to their *correspondence*) and in a relative sense of their usefulness in that task (technically, according to their *pragmatic value*). It is obvious that a map is more or less true in these ways.

(What is not so obvious is what we mean when we use "true" to describe things that don't seem obviously interpretive or representational. We might speak of a true friend, and we can use the same definition, albeit with a little stretching. Your friend isn't perfect and sometimes lets you down in this or that minor way, but on the whole, she is steadfast and companionable as a friend ought to be. We might, then, call her a "re-presentation" of "friend-hood," and as she represents it well, she is a true friend.)

It is fashionable in some quarters nowadays to say that "there is no absolute truth." Such statements are obviously self-contradictory: "There is no absolute truth, including the categorical assertion that 'there is no absolute truth.'" But there is also a strictly semantic problem. Yes, there is no "truth" in the sense of an entity called "Truth" floating somewhere in the heavens; but there is indeed absolute truth in the sense that a numeral (say, "four") can exactly represent the reality of the number of letters in the call-sign of my favorite TV station: four. Moreover, to say that "you have your reality, and I have mine" is to speak, at best, poetically. It is really to say, "you have your *interpretation* of reality, and I have my *interpretation* of reality, and those may not agree."

Perhaps people don't use the latter phrase, though, for an important reason that may not come fully to consciousness but is operative nonetheless. (Apologists do well to pay attention to this phenomenon.) If our interpretations disagree, then it is at least possible that we can argue over them and one might emerge as superior to the other. In that event, the person with the inferior interpretation might well feel obligated to change his mind. But if the difference between us is radical, right down to our interpreting what are literally different realities, then argument is pointless: We inhabit different worlds, and that's that.

In this regard, let's recognize that, having said all this, it could yet be entirely rational, sensible, and important to say, "That's your reality, and it's not mine." Suppose I say, "Chicago is a great city. It's sophisticated, energetic, welcoming, and fun." That is the way I have experienced it.

Suppose someone else, however, says, "Chicago is a nightmare. Illegal drugs, violence, poverty, and racism—that's Chicago."

If that person did not experience the parts of Chicago that I did when I lived there (as a middle-class white student living in Hyde Park while attending the University of Chicago), but experienced instead a childhood in the horrors of the Cabrini Green or Robert Taylor Homes projects, then we are literally talking about two different realities. Our mistake is not in using the term *realities*, for we really did experience very different things, and our interpretations are each true as far as they go. Our mistake instead is to generalize from our limited experience of only a select part of that city to the city as a whole. We should say more carefully something like this: "My experience of parts of the huge and complex and variegated city of Chicago was as follows. . . ."

The parallel with religious differences in considering apologetics, then, is probably obvious, but worth spelling out. It may be that we disagree religiously because one of us has a superior interpretation of the same reality we're all talking about. It may also be, however, that we disagree because we are talking about different parts of a complex reality. And it may conceivably be a matter of both problems. The skillful apologist tries to sort that all out with her neighbor as well as she can.

To that end, we can at least make more sense to each other if we will be circumspect about the terms *interpretation*, *truth*, and *reality*, and not just run them together. Religion is fundamentally about truth: trying to figure out what is real and how best to represent it.

Further Complications

No human being in any situation has perfectly certain knowledge. Human knowledge is like human beings: finite and fallen. First, our knowledge is finite. We normally do not know all of the data relevant to an intellectual problem. Even if we did, we could not know for sure that we had acquired all such data: Maybe some of it lurks just out of sight in a location it hasn't occurred to us yet to investigate. We sometimes do not interpret the data properly: Sometimes we compute the measurements incorrectly or hit the wrong keys on the calculator. And even if we normally do analyze things correctly, we could not know for sure that we had infallibly interpreted the data on this particular occasion: Maybe we were very drowsy; maybe someone slipped a hallucinogenic drug into our morning coffee; maybe we are afflicted with a reason-diminishing brain tumor. Contemporary analytical philosophy of knowledge is embroiled in such issues.[2] Nonspecialists probably can settle for the commonsense conclusion that nobody knows it all, and that our best ideas are merely our best guesses—not certain knowledge.

Second, human beings are fallen as well as finite. Christians believe that what theology calls "the Fall" and the "original sin" that descends to us from it have affected our ability to think, as well as our ability and inclination to make moral choices. Even our neighbors who do not believe in a Fall or original sin, however, likely would agree that our morality affects our cognition. (Marx thought so; Nietzsche thought so; Freud thought so; as do their epigones among us.) We tend to see what we want to see and to believe what we want to believe. Even scientists—our contemporary standard for rational integrity—are inclined to do this. After all, if you've spent most of your adult life believing that X is the case; and your research program is built on the belief that X is the case; and your career success depends upon continuing to show that X is the case; then you clearly have a compelling interest to continue to find that X is the case.

Now, reality has a way of undermining certain beliefs about the world. People don't believe just any old thing and then hold to that belief in the face of all contrary evidence. And we retain some of our beliefs with a remarkable resistance to change if they have served us well. (How often, for instance, do we really think and act as if the world is round and not flat?) This habit holds, moreover, for beliefs that don't just work intellectually, but work in what we perceive to be our interests as well: Of course we believe that our race, or nation, or region, or city, or university, or company, or department is better than theirs, and—*voilà!*—here's the "proof."

So we see that none of us knows everything, and none of us knows anything for certain and with perfect clarity.

Graduated Assent

It is at least theoretically possible, in fact, that we are mistaken about even obvious and important things. Yet there are many things about which we doubt very strongly that we are mistaken. There are propositions and experiences about which we are, instead, virtually certain. "Two plus two equals four," I assert, with considerable assurance. "I am now looking at a book," you might affirm with (almost as much? greater?) vigor. Then there are propositions and experiences about which we have absolutely no confidence. "two plus two equals five," for instance, or "I am now looking at a book that is playing the piano."

In between these extremes, however, there is a range of propositions and experiences about which we have more or less confidence. "The square of the hypotenuse of a right-angled triangle is equal to the sum of the squares of the other two sides" seems to nonmathematicians to *sound* like the so-called Pythagorean theorem. We were always *taught* that it is true. And we might even have measured a couple of triangles to test it. But unless we have undertaken considerable and informed investigation into the matter, we probably wouldn't affirm this theorem with the same intensity with which we would affirm other items of our mathematical knowledge, such as "two plus two equals four." Furthermore, about still other propositions of mathematics and logic—say, "The square root of 456,891 is 297"—we might have no immediate opinion at all.

What is true of propositions is also true of experiences. I am pretty sure I'm looking at a computer screen right now as I type these words. I am equally sure I am *not* looking at an Academy Award-winning movie, *The Computer Screen*. In between these two convictions, however, are others about my experience about which I am not so confident. I think I hear the murmur of the building's ventilation system, but it could also be the sound of construction on campus a distance away, or the muffled roar of a jet overhead. I'd have to listen for a few more moments to acquire more data in the hopes of settling this fascinating matter more firmly. And even if I did listen a while longer, I might still not be as sure about what I'm hearing as about what I'm seeing. (Indeed, maybe I'm just so excited about this whole question of background noise that the blood is rushing in my ears and I'm in an otherwise completely silent room.)

Every chemistry laboratory contains long glass tubes that stand upright on a desk and have little marks running up their heights with numbers at regular intervals. These devices are called graduated cylinders, as perhaps you will recall with fondness from your high-school days. If one takes a cylinder marked for 100 ml and drops precisely 1 ml of water into it, is the cylinder now "wet" or "dry"?

The question, of course, is improperly posed. The whole point of a graduated cylinder is to make possible a "graduated" answer: The mostly dry tube yet contains a relatively small amount of water. (Scientists likely would be more precise, of course.) So have philosophers for years advocated a graduated response from us in the case of each proposition or conviction we hold to be true. Rather than see everything in binary terms of black-or-white, true-or-false, all-or-nothing, they suggest that we ought to proportion our assent to the amount of proper evidence or valid reason we possess.

We, too, need to "graduate" our *assent* to ideas we encounter. We need, perhaps more self-consciously than we do, to measure out our agreement in strict proportion to the grounds we have for such agreement. If my Aunt Tillie tells me that she loves me, I believe her statement because I have a lifetime of warrants for that proposition. If my Aunt Tillie offers an opinion about the mass of the star Betelgeuse based on something she thinks she heard on a bus the other day, I will accord her statement less than full credibility. And my Aunt Tillie, being a reasonable person, will not take offense at my action in this case. Indeed, she would be the first to admit that perhaps she mis-heard or misunderstood what was offered on the bus (although since she works as a secretary at Caltech and was taking the bus there that day, maybe she is entirely justified in her claims about Betelgeuse!).

So we need to qualify our assent to things in our own minds—and in our speech. Other people should not have to ask us, "How sure are you about that?" because we ought to have told them already (at least, we should have on any subject in which this qualification would matter). We ought to volunteer just how confident we are—and perhaps on precisely what that confidence is based—that these directions will get you to the next town, or that this wrench is just right for the job, or that your coworker really is scheming to steal your proposal, or that the best way to discipline children is to make them watch MTV. Furthermore, we should be aware for our own sakes of just how much doubt we really do have, or at least *ought* to have, especially about the ideas that shape our lives. Finally, we ought to investigate particularly the basic ideas (the hypotheses) we have about ourselves, about the world, and about God or the gods, and what grounds we have for those beliefs. Perhaps an alternative set of beliefs offers better grounds, and we should consider them seriously.

Some philosophers have said that the best definition of truth is what fits the evidence best (correspondence), while others have said that the truest ideas fit most smoothly and cooperatively into a system (coherence). Still others have said that both external (correspondence) and internal (coherence) virtues ought to be weighed in the balance. And the testing of ideas in the crucible of actual use—to consider what practical difference it makes to believe this or that—is the legacy of the philosophy of pragmatism. (The pragmatic definition of truth goes back much further, of course: At least, one might observe, as far back as the ancient proverbs of the Hebrews, the *Analects* of Confucius, the fables of Aesop, and the Upanishads of the Hindus!)

The bottom line in each case, however, is the same. One ought to hold ideas according to the worthiness of their grounds.[3] One also ought to hold them according to their *importance*, since it clearly would be foolish to cling tightly to a trivial idea, and equally foolish to be indifferent to issues of great moment. And there are no more momentous issues to consider than the issues raised under the category of *religion*.

HOW TO THINK ABOUT RELIGIONS

What Is a Religion?

A thing or an idea must be evaluated according to its kind and purpose. A horse can be assessed in terms of its strength for pulling, or its speed for running, or its intelligence for roping, among other virtues. Different horses will score higher on these various tests—a Clydesdale versus a thoroughbred, for example, on strength versus speed. An automobile can be prized for different reasons by different people: as a conveyance, as a racing machine, or as a status symbol. Minivans, dragsters, and limousines each have their place. (There is no place, however, for luxury SUVs. But I digress.) A person earns regard variously for her wisdom, her beauty, her generosity, her strength, her enthusiasm, and so on, depending on who is evaluating her. How, then, does one begin to consider a religion?

Scholars of religion define religion in two different ways. The first way is perhaps the more typical. A religion is a particular system of beliefs, practices, and (for want of a better term) passions—what is sometimes referred to as "affections." We normally identify such systems with names such as Judaism, Shinto, and Buddhism. Islam, for example, teaches particular ideas to be true ("There is no god but God, and Muhammad is his prophet"), prescribes certain actions (such as the Five Pillars of Islam), and encourages the cultivation of particular concerns and emotions (especially submission to God: the word "muslim" means submitted one). Religions thus are described in terms of what they *are*, and so this is called the *substantive* definition of religions.

The *functional* definition instead considers what religions *do*. A religion, in this view, is what orients, motivates, and structures the central zone of life. Our religion is our fundamental beliefs and values. It is whatever functions as some individual's, or some group's, ultimate concern, the core of one's existence around which everything else is wound.

Clearly Christianity, Hinduism, and Daoism function in this way and are recognized as religions. But so do Marxism, secular humanism, and pragmatism. So does hedonism, status-seeking, and other forms of egotism. Some objects of devotion are unusual: "He looks after that car religiously," we might say. I remember a television segment featuring a middle-aged man living in Oklahoma whose religion was (although neither he nor the interviewer put it this way) supporting the University of Oklahoma Sooners football team. This man wore only clothes patterned in Sooners red and white. His house was red and white brick on the outside, and red and white throughout the interior. His phone rested in a plastic football. His walls were covered by Sooners posters. His work schedule was arranged around the Sooners's schedule—from spring camp to bowl games. And for a while, he said, he sported red letters spelling S-O-O-N-E-R-S across his front top teeth until his wife made his dentist remove them. This man reminds us that "fan" is an abbreviation for "fanatic."

Whatever it is that gives meaning, and purpose, and direction, and intensity to life; whatever gets us going in the morning; whatever drives us forward; whatever consoles us in misery; whatever stands at the center of our lives—functionally speaking, that is our religion.

Investigating Religions

How would someone properly investigate a religion, not just as a matter of intellectual curiosity but as a genuine possibility for guiding one's life?

Students in my courses on world religions would sometimes come privately to me and ask just this question. "I'm interested in Baha'i," they might say. "How would I go beyond the introduction given in this course?"

I recommended they consult at least the following three resources. First, they should read a good introduction to the religion written by a reputable scholar who is trying neither to praise nor condemn the religion. No such observer is completely unbiased, of course, but some are more disciplined and conscientious than others about trying to be as accurate and even-handed as possible. Major publishers of textbooks try to find such authors and books because the less controversial and more objective they are, the more professors normally will opt for them. So one should look to such houses first.

Second, inquirers should read the holy scriptures of the religion in question and recommendations of the religion by its leading apologists. One has to hear the religion in its own voices, and these are particularly important voices. Clergy and professors of this religion are probably the best guides to such literature.

Third, one should try to encounter the religion in the persons of its most loyal devotees. It's easy to make a mistake here: One might visit, for example, one or another of the many declining or moribund Christian churches in North America and come to false conclusions about the religion as a whole. So one should try to find the most faithful mosque, or temple, or synagogue one can—one that is most vitally living out the mainstream of that religion—and get to know believers who can help the inquirer understand the plausibility and attraction of this religion.

The attitude with which one approaches this investigation is crucial. One must be both open and critical. If one is not sufficiently sympathetic, not sufficiently vulnerable to changing one's mind, not sufficiently willing to entertain the idea that these people might just be right—then it is most unlikely that one will enter into that religion far enough to understand its essence. If one is not sufficiently critical, however, one will fail to assess the religion properly, missing its incongruities, contradictions, and perhaps even pathologies. Scholars of religion cultivate an attitude of "analytical sympathy," and so should every other serious observer.

The prudent inquirer also will clarify the goal of such investigation. She is looking for the best option of those that currently interest her—as we will see in the next section, she cannot possibly hope to weigh up all of the world's religions and find the "best" one. Furthermore, she recognizes that whatever conclusion she comes to will be just a "hypothesis," her best judgment on the matter to date. She may well embrace that conclusion with fervor, but she ought to do so while maintaining a critical openness in the future just in case a better option comes along.

This attitude perhaps sounds like consumerism and a lack of full commitment. But (as the last section in this chapter argues) unreasoning commitment, completely closed off from any possibility of correction or improvement, is not faith, but fanaticism. Wisdom recognizes the limitations in all of our thinking, including our thinking about religion.

Comparing and Assessing Religions

When we are assessing a particular religion, therefore, we do well to consider it according to what a religion is supposed to do. Fundamentally, I suggest, a religion does two things: It tells us the way things are, and it tells us how to respond best to the way things are. In short, it offers us a map and a guidebook.

How well, then, does this or that religion serve as the center of human life? How well does it explain the world and our place in it? How well does it recognize our highest good? How well does it diagnose what keeps us from that good? How well does it prescribe the solution to our problems? And how much help does it give us in reaching that highest good?

In attempting to compare and evaluate religious options (I include comprehensive philosophies and other worldviews in this category—they are *functionally* religions also), we must recognize several conceptual difficulties. Religions, after all, are often deeply complex things, with complicated inner workings, bewildering varieties within each species, and customs of speech and conduct that usually take years to understand and master. How can one set about to compare them when merely learning about them, merely gathering adequate data, seems daunting in the extreme? I know scholars who have taken a lifetime to thoroughly understand a single religion, and I know a few who have thoroughly understood two and even three. I know no one who claims to be an expert in more than three. Most religions are just that difficult to fully comprehend.

To complicate things further, even if one could gather an appropriate amount and kind of data on two or more religions, how would one decide what data are in fact appropriate? On what basis would one confidently collect one sort of data (say, about basic doctrines) and set aside as relatively unimportant other data (such as the way believers dress for worship)? Isn't there an implicit value judgment involved here ("beliefs are more important than clothes") that is simply presupposed by the inquirer? It does not "naturally" emerge from the study itself. Or perhaps it does, in the sense that perhaps neither religion A nor religion B seems to take clothing as seriously as it takes ideas. Yet even then another inquirer comes along who is deeply interested in how a religion views and treats the body, and thus sees this lack of interest in clothing as in fact significant. Perhaps such an inquirer might then judge both religion A and religion B to be deficient, and move on to the next options available for consideration.

Finally, of course, the data to be explained—namely, all of reality, which might include supernatural beings and even a God whose nature, thoughts, and actions transcend our complete understanding—appear to be rather numerous and complex. Given that our cognitive abilities are compromised by both our finitude and fallenness, the "mapping reality" part of comparing and assessing religions is, frankly, impossible to undertake with hope of a comprehensive conclusion.

What universal standard of ultimate goodness, of the *summum bonum*, furthermore, can one consult in deciding among religious options? It is relatively easy to decide what an automobile is for in any particular instance and then make a decision as to which candidate fulfills that purpose best. It is less easy, but still possible, to decide what a person is for in a particular instance and adjudicate candidates accordingly: Who jumps the highest? Who plays the violin best? Who writes the tightest computer code? In the case of religion, though, what definition of religion's ultimate purpose sets the standard—since there are so many?

Is the primary objective of religion to eradicate suffering? Is it to achieve individual bliss? Is it to provide social order? Perhaps it is to keep the workers docile and compliant. Or is it to introduce select individuals to ultimate truth? Is it to rescue spirits from their material prisons? Is it to form a people for fellowship with a Supreme Being, leaving the rest for destruction? Who can say for certain, and for everyone?

Most religions recognize that each of us must say for ourselves, according to the wisdom we have learned and the inclinations of our hearts. As a Christian, I believe that God makes clear to people in some elementary, but important, way what really matters in life, and people choose either to honor that wisdom or to elect their own alternative paths. Each person must decide for herself or himself what really matters, and then try to find a way to secure it.

So is the quest for certainty, especially about the ultimate questions of life and death, good and evil, the sacred and the secular, the eternal and the temporal—is that quest doomed? Are there no real answers, just personal preferences? Is there no way to intelligently decide?

I see a middle course—epistemologists sometimes call this view "critical realism." I believe, on the one hand, that human beings cannot know things with absolute certainty—how could we? Each of us, as limited as we are, could well be wrong about *anything* we think we know.

I also believe, however, that God has given us reason, our five senses, memory, conscience, the heritage of the past, each other's company, and other good gifts. In particular, making more or less good use of these gifts, we run up against reality every day—at least, we run up against *something* every day—and it needs explaining. The thoughtful person will then try to find out what explains it best—all of it. Yes, we see the world through intellectual models, through patterns of conscious and unconscious assumptions, impressions, and conclusions. We cannot see things purely objectively. But we do see things, including ourselves, and the best we can do is to keep refining our hypotheses—however particular, however general—to make the most sense we can of what we experience.[4]

Furthermore, we should not reject an option (such as Hinduism, or existentialism, or Shinto) merely because it cannot offer us perfect knowledge that answers all our questions to our complete satisfaction. No religion or philosophy—at least, none of the great ones that have endured the test of time—claims to do that. Each person, after all, has his or her own limitations that keep him or her from certain kinds of understanding. And the cosmos itself is in some respects inexplicable to any human being. So waiting until one has every doubt erased and every question answered is to wait for something that never comes. Our real choice is among real options, and the wise person selects the best of those available. Then she stays alert for opportunities to refine that option or even "trade up" to a significantly better alternative.

"Making sense" of experience, let's be clear, is not limited to "figuring things out." It's not just a matter of assessing and then assenting to a particular metaphysics. At a profoundly basic level, the religious challenge also includes making an art of *life*, of constructing our entire existence in beauty and integrity so that it is not a chaos, but makes sense. *That's* what we ought to seek, and not be satisfied until we find.

Religions are about all of life and demand the allegiance of the whole person. So we have to be both open and critical, not only intellectually, but also morally, aesthetically, emotionally, socially, and so on. Morally, for example, we must ask ourselves whether we are open to a new, better way of understanding what it means to live a good life, while also being ready to go to the trouble of *thinking* hard about this or that ethic, and tracing out its true implications.

Someone might tell us, for instance, that denying the physical body in the interests of elevating the spirit is the best way to live. Are we open to that option, at least a little? And are we also prepared to consider carefully whether that view *is* true and helpful?

Considering religion with the seriousness it deserves means taking one's life in one's hands. Philosopher Thomas Morris chides us: "Many people who spend weeks mastering a new video game, months learning a tennis serve, or years perfecting a golf swing will not invest a few days, or even a matter of hours, in the effort to understand better some of the deeper questions about life."[5] One has to love the truth to find the truth. The most important things in life rarely come to those who do not press hard after them: not music, not literature, not athletic skills, not wholesome relationships.

Religion is about the very deepest questions of our existence, so it offers the greatest challenge of venturesome thinking: of investigating, and weighing up, and living without certainty—and perhaps even living without a religious "home" for a while—as we decide. *That's what it costs* to adequately consider the most important decision one can ever make: the direction of one's life, and whatever life there is to come.

So what then? Suppose we have come to some conclusions in our religious quest. Suppose our neighbor has done so, as we discuss Christianity with him or her. We now have decided upon this or that religious question, to the best of our knowledge. Where does religious commitment come in? What about faith?

COMMITMENT, FAITH, AND KNOWLEDGE

Knowledge as a Condition for Faith

In the movie *Miracle on 34th Street*, a little girl recites her mother's wisdom: "Faith is believing when common sense tells you not to." Even more problematic is the typical story of the bright-eyed kid in Sunday School who responds to the request to define *faith* with "Faith is believing something you know isn't true!"

Two mistakes about the concept of faith are common. The first is to think that faith is a peculiarly religious word and has nothing to do with everyday life. The second is to presume that faith has no relationship to knowledge, that the two stand as utterly separate categories of assent.

In fact, however, everyday life constantly presses us beyond what we know (or think we know) and requires us to exercise faith. As proper as it may be to proportion our assent to the strength of the warrants and importance of the matter, we frequently find ourselves compelled to trust beyond what we're sure of, to make commitments that go outside our sense of safety. And yet these moments of trust and commitment—these acts of *faith*—are intrinsically and importantly related to knowledge.

Faith is what we do when we cantilever our lives out over what we do not and cannot know, while anchoring our lives upon what we think we do know. Faith relies on knowledge even as it moves out from knowledge into the unknown. Steve cannot know for certain that this canoe bobbing by the dock will still float once he gets in it, but he cannot be "mostly convinced" and stay with most of his weight committed to the canoe while reserving some of his weight for the dock. To enjoy the canoe, he has to get all the way in. He has to make a commitment. He has to exercise rationally based faith.

No one, that is, exercises "blind faith" in anything—or anyone. Everyone has a reason to be believe what he or she believes—even if someone else thinks it to be an insufficient reason, and even if it turns out in fact to be a poorly grounded belief. The relationship of knowledge and faith holds in matters large and small, impersonal and personal. I would be a fool to refuse to sit in a chair until its adequacy had been conclusively demonstrated. Parents of small children can never have an evening out if they refuse to trust any baby-sitter. A woman would be a fool to refuse to marry her beloved until the marriage had been somehow guaranteed. Life for us humans means risk, and the wise person is the one who does not seek certainty, but seeks instead *adequate* reason to believe the best alternative available. Then he or she ventures forward in faith, trusting something or someone because of what she thinks she knows about that thing or person.[6]

Faith as a Condition for Knowledge

There are important respects in which the relationship between faith and knowledge is reversed. Faith, that is, can be a condition for acquiring knowledge.

Let us begin by considering a scientific laboratory. A scientist, Dr. Alpha, is attempting to convince another scientist, Dr. Beta, that she has found something important in her research that contradicts some of Dr. Beta's work. Dr. Beta is skeptical, and that's perfectly all right, we should think, especially for a rigorous scientist. But poor Dr. Beta also happens to have paranoid tendencies. He has reached the conclusion that other scientists are constantly trying to trick him or humiliate him. He no longer trusts them.

Now, how successful will Dr. Alpha be in convincing Dr. Beta? She can show him her lab notebooks. "Hah!" he responds. "Fictions!" She shows him the computer printouts. "More fictions!" he replies. She runs a videotape of the actual experiment. "It's amazing what they can do with computer-generated graphics nowadays, isn't it?" he slyly remarks, to Dr. Alpha's mounting exasperation. She calls in technician after technician as eyewitnesses. "They're all in your pay," he stubbornly observes.

Finally, Dr. Alpha levels what she thinks will be a crushing blow. "Then do the experiment yourself and see!"

"And be made a fool of?" he retorts. "Never!" Dr. Beta storms out of the lab. He cannot trust, so he cannot learn.

The same would be at least as dramatically true of a woman as she gets acquainted with a new boyfriend. If she presumes the worst, or even simply keeps him at a skeptical arm's length indefinitely, she will learn only a little about him. Some initial skepticism is healthy, of course. But if she cannot believe anything he says without corroboration of, say, a legally adequate kind ("How do I know you really have the job you say you have? Can I come to the place where you say you work and interrogate the other employees?" "How can I *know* that you're not a pimp or a bigamist? Can I hire a private detective to watch you for the next month?"), then most of us would pronounce their relationship doomed. For she will never be satisfied as long as she has these extreme suspicions. She can always twist the evidence to fit her dark fantasies.

Worse than this, however, is the probability that in the face of this suspicion her boyfriend can, and probably will, decide not to reveal any more of himself to her. He simply walks away. He feels insulted, treated with less faith than he thinks he deserves, and wants therefore nothing more to do with this strange woman who must decide upon everything for herself. That's what happens in personal relationships. The "investigated" party can choose whether or not to reveal more to the "investigator." And if the investigator fails to move forward in appropriate increments of faith in her new friend, then she risks losing the friendship entirely under the crushing weight of her arrogant demand to know it all on her own terms.

So in some sorts of knowledge, ranging in these examples from the most objective to the most subjective, faith of an appropriate sort is necessary to learn and to understand.

Religious Faith

Religious faith is not completely different from the faith we have discussed so far but is simply the variety of faith proper to its object. Just as putting faith in a chair is similar to, but also different from, putting faith in a spouse, so is putting faith in a deity, or several deities, or in a religion with no deities both similar to, and also somewhat different from, the other two. We have different warrants for trusting a spouse than for trusting the God of the Abrahamic religions, for instance. As those religions affirm, God is normally invisible to us, and so divine activity must be inferred from its results, or believed in on the basis of reliable testimony, while spouses perform a great many actions that we can readily sense. Different stakes are involved in each relationship as well. We trust a spouse with our lives, while we trust a religion to guide us reliably for our eternities.

So we might arrive at two crucial propositions about the quest for religious certainty: It is impossible, but it is also unnecessary. We already are accustomed to taking the greatest of relational risks in this life, whether trusting a spouse, or trusting a surgeon, or trusting a rescuer. All we can do is to perform the same exercise of trust in religious matters as well, as human beings who recognize that we do not and cannot know it all before deciding—on *anything*.

To be sure, in many of our personal relationships—with friends, coworkers, family members, and so on—we are wise to trust people neither too much nor too little. We ought to *graduate* our faith, as well as our assent, according to the warrants available. In ultimate relationships, though, we have to make more radical decisions. A fiancee cannot strictly calculate what faith she can put in her groom-to-be and then act proportionately. She cannot decide to enter marriage at 60 percent confidence and therefore get only "60 percent married," with the understanding that she will proceed to marry her husband "more thoroughly" as their relationship goes along and her warrants presumably increase. At the altar she has to decide: "I do" or "I don't." She cannot know what her husband will be like in the future. She does not even have complete or certain knowledge of what he has been like in the past. (Indeed, when one considers how little one did know at the time of one's wedding . . . !) She must, however, enter into a lifetime's commitment, all or nothing, on the basis of what she does know. She must commit herself to trusting her husband. She must exercise faith that day.

She must, furthermore, continue to exercise faith every succeeding day of her marriage, for she will never arrive at full knowledge either of her husband's character or of his activities when he is not in her presence. And we would normally say that she is entirely right to keep trusting him on the basis of her increasing knowledge of him. She ought to do so, that is, at least until the sad day, if it ever comes, when the warrants *against* her continuing to trust him overwhelm her faith. Strange perfume on his shirt, unknown female callers on the phone, loss of affection when he is with her: Such data eventually add up. Then, we would conclude, she must indeed change her mind, and her life, accordingly.

So such faith does not mean the suspension of critical thinking. And it doesn't mean that in the religious sphere, either. You might be entirely entitled to believe in religion X, given what you have learned in life to that point. But if you run up against challenges (what contemporary philosophers call "potential defeaters"), the intelligent person is obliged to pay attention to them. You don't need to throw your faith aside at the first sign of trouble, of course. That would be as silly as a scientist trashing his years of research whenever a lab result came up "wrong." The truly critical thinker, however, pays attention to such difficulties. She tries creatively to see if they can be met within her current scheme of thought, or whether she needs to modify her views, or—in the extreme case— whether she needs to abandon her theory (about this chemical process, about this spouse, or about this religion) for a better one.[7]

So we face the final question. Can I believe? This book, and others like it, can provide at best only *intellectual* warrants. Those warrants, furthermore, can at best provide only reasonable support for faith. They cannot prove the truth of Christianity or of any other religion beyond a reasonable doubt since (a) some of the most basic matters discussed in most religions are complex beyond any total explanation, let alone complete proof; (b) most of us don't have the expertise to assess the finer points of such matters; (c) other religions with different claims offer their own warrants that deserve respectful acknowledgment; and (d) we each are influenced by what we perceive to be in our own best interest to believe is the truth.

As philosopher Alvin Plantinga warns, "In religious belief as elsewhere, we must take our chances, recognizing that we could be wrong, dreadfully wrong. There are no guarantees; the religious life is a venture; foolish and debilitating error is a permanent possibility."[8] Black activist and theologian Cornel West agrees, as he testifies,

> Of course, the fundamental philosophical question remains whether the Christian gospel is ultimately true. And, as a Christian prophetic pragmatist whose focus is on coping with transient and provisional penultimate matters yet whose hope goes beyond them, I reply in the affirmative, bank my all on it, yet am willing to entertain the possibility in low moments that I may be deluded.[9]

The best one can hope for is warrant sufficient to believe—which is precisely, let's remember, all one hopes for in any other exercise of faith.[10]

Believing, Willing, and Loving

Let us observe, finally, that deciding among various understandings of God and evil is ultimately not a matter of the intellect: "Let's add up the arguments and evidence in columns A, B, and C and calculate which religious option comes out best." Deciding about religious faith goes beyond analysis by the intellect to action by the will.

When it comes to most things, to be sure, it seems that the will is irrelevant. One does not in fact "choose" to believe something. One is either convinced by its warrants or not—or (in the spirit of "graduated assent") we would say that one is more or less convinced by the warrants at hand. Yet the will is operative in every human decision to trust rather than merely to "conclude." One finally has to decide whether to get in that canoe, or marry one's beloved, or commit oneself to this or that religion.

To be committed, body and soul, to someone or something, one need not be certain in the strictly epistemological sense of "knowing I am right about this and knowing, furthermore, that I could not possibly be wrong." And it's a good thing, too, since we finite and fallen human beings *cannot* be certain of anything in that sense.[11] But we can commit ourselves to a cause, or a religion, or a deity without holding anything back. We can follow that particular road as best we can, moment by moment, day by day, until it gets us where we want to go or turns out to be a false trail. That's all we can do. And we cannot walk any such path without being willing to take each step—steps of faith.

The will figures in religious decisions in a more specific way, according to Christian doctrine. The fundamental human problem is not ignorance (a deficiency in the intellect), or deprivation (a deficiency in our environment), but sin (a defect in the soul). We are alienated from God, even resistant toward God.

We might think we would gladly choose the right path if God would just become visible and speak to us audibly. If we ourselves don't think so, we probably have had conversations with people who claim that if God would just give them a sign, a miracle, an indubitable proof of his presence, they would believe. And *until* God comes across this way, they imply, they will not believe.

Well, that was the actual experience for a whole generation of Israelites in the wilderness of Sinai. Philip Yancey has pointed out that the ancient Israelite nation, after its exodus from Egypt, enjoyed the direct guidance of God every day through Moses. Not only did the Israelites witness the thunder and lightning of Mount Sinai, but as they traveled on from there, God was right in their midst, in the "tent of meeting." Moses would go in to consult with God "as a man speaks with his friend." With all of these warrants, did these witnesses to the presence of God therefore become especially devout?

On the contrary. They became whiny, greedy, impatient, and disobedient children who wanted God to perform *now* according to their immediate whims, or they would huffily march back to Egypt. God's immediate and evident presence was apparently no guarantee of spiritual goodness or wisdom. God's proximity was not the solution. It only made more obvious the real source of trouble, the hearts of the people themselves.[12] And if we aren't convinced by this truth, we might consider how people responded when God later took human form and lived among us in the person of Jesus Christ for several decades. No, the problem is rarely that God is far away. (I say "rarely" because I respect such phenomena as the "dark night of the soul," a temporary sense of divine abandonment reported by believers at least as far back as the Psalms.) The problem for most of us, most of the time, is what we tend to do with God whether God is distant or near.

The fundamental problem of religious allegiance, then, is not about what we think, but what or whom we love. And if we see that, we will see again one of the fundamental affirmations of this book: that Christian apologetics cannot convince anyone to become a Christian. Apologetics cannot do so, in this case, because argument cannot produce affection. The Apostle James sarcastically warns his flock that rational assent to truths about God are nowhere near enough: "You believe that God is one; you do well. Even the demons believe—and shudder" (James 2:19 NRSV). No, the question is whether one *loves* God, and no one does that without conversion— the exclusive activity of the Holy Spirit.

What, then, can apologetics do? If it can't convert people, what's the point of it? These questions take us to our next chapter.

7

Defining, Directing, and
Defending Apologetics

DEFINING APOLOGETICS

"Apologetics" is "telling someone why you're sorry you are a Christian." So the word can sound, linked as it is with our everyday word "apologize." And clearly apologetics is a positive enterprise, not a regretful one!

There is more than a little irony in another whimsical definition: "Apologetics" is "making someone *sorry he asked* why you are a Christian!"

Avery Dulles begins his magisterial history of apologetics by observing that

> today the term apologetics carries unpleasant connotations. The apologist is regarded as an aggressive, opportunistic person who tries, by fair means or foul, to argue people into joining the Church. Numerous charges are laid at the door of apologetics: its neglect of grace, of prayer, and of the life-giving power of the word of God; its tendency to oversimplify and syllogize the approach to faith; its dilution of the scandal of the Christian message; and its implied presupposition that God's word should be judged by the norm of fallible, not to say fallen, human reason.[1]

It is this penchant of apologists to turn people off and away, to annoy and repel rather than to engage and attract, that acts as a foil for much of what this book promotes instead.

Apologetics instead is discourse (broadly speaking) aimed at quite particular objectives. Apologetics deals with questions of the virtues of a particular thing—in the case of this book, the Christian religion. Typically, Christian apologetics has been preoccupied with the question of the truth of Christianity. Is there a God? Is Jesus divine? Does the Bible tell the truth? And so on. But the history of Christian apologetics shows that apologetics can best be seen more broadly, and in two respects.

First, apologetics deals not only with the virtue of truth, but also with the virtues of goodness and beauty. These are, to be sure, categories more commonly associated with the ancient Greek philosophical tradition. But many Christians—most of whom until the twentieth century, after all, have been shaped by Greek civilization to some extent—have gladly deployed these categories to articulate their conviction that Christianity offers not only an accurate metaphysic, but also the most excellent ethic and aesthetic as well. Apologetics therefore asks, Is Christianity not only true, but also good and beautiful? Does it give the best map to all of reality?

Second, since the very thing to be discussed in such apologetics is more than a matter of mere intellection—namely, the virtues of the Christian religion as a guide to human life—apologetics itself must extend beyond the merely intellectual. Usually, of course, apologetics has been understood to be a branch of theology or philosophy, of rational investigation and argumentation. In this book, however, I want to explore apologetics beyond these modes since, again, Christianity itself speaks to much more than the intellect. Thus I suggest that *anything* that helps people take Christianity more seriously than they did before, *anything* that helps defend and commend it, properly counts as apologetics, and should be part of any comprehensive program of apologetics.

Apologetics, furthermore, can be conducted according to two vectors. An arrow pointing from the outside world into the Christian Church images what we might call *defensive* or *reactive* apologetics. Without meaning anything pejorative by these words—while recognizing that some apologetics can indeed manifest negative traits of each!—let's recognize that this form of apologetics arises when provoked by questions from outside the faith. This form of apologetics, that is, responds to queries, wards off attacks, and in general aims to maintain the structure and integrity of Christianity against challenges that threaten it. In less abstract terms, this form of apologetics tries to *keep a conversation going* when such conversation might be terminated by a devastating assertion ("There's no way to believe in an all-good and all-powerful God and also believe in the reality of evil") or unanswerable question ("How can you believe that Christianity is better than all of the other religions?").

The second vector, an arrow pointing from the Christian religion outward, can be called *offensive* or *proactive* apologetics. Again, this book does not recommend "offensive" conversation in the sense of "off-putting"! Instead, properly offensive or proactive apologetics renders the valuable service of *initiating conversation* where there isn't any.

Christians make a mistake about their faith that is common in other respects as well. We simply assume that since *A* is obviously interesting and important to us, it will be interesting and important to other people. We forget that someone who is uninformed about *A*—about what it is, and why it is significant—will not pay attention to it. We're like math teachers who get carried away with the beauty of an elaborate proof, scribbling delightedly on a chalkboard while the class behind them sits gaping with both incomprehension and inattention.

Offensive apologetics tries to arouse interest. And such conscious attempts to arouse interest among our neighbors is notably lacking among Christians both individually and congregationally. How many of us try to open up spiritual matters in conversation? How well do our churches reach out to people in neighborhoods or even already in our pews and try to show them why they should care about what we're saying and doing?

William J. O'Malley is a Jesuit educator in New York City and recognizes our problem. In desperation, he makes the following suggestion:

> Let me play the game of "what if." What if every bishop,
> every priest and deacon, every parish minister, every cat-

echist were to put aside *everything* else (perhaps for a time even the Christian gospel and the Catholic Church) and focus *only* on one question: How can I touch and enliven that hunger for the divine that lurks confusedly in the people I truly want to serve?[2]

By introducing people who are currently unfamiliar with Christianity to its essence; by warning those who are committed to paths that Christianity teaches are dangerous; and especially by commending Christianity's virtues to these audiences of the unaware or the uninterested—in each of these modes, Christian apologetics reaches out to offer Christianity's blessings to its neighbors.

DIRECTING APOLOGETICS

What is the objective of apologetics? For many, especially those who are keen on apologetics and also, ironically, those who find it distasteful or worse, the purpose of apologetics seems to be obvious: to win the argument! But why would Christians want to do that?

I'm afraid that many of us are attracted to apologetics for reasons that have more to do with our own gain than with God's glory or our neighbor's benefit. I myself was first attracted to apologetic literature to avoid the embarrassment of being bested by my high-school English teacher in front of my classmates. Some of us engage in apologetics to fight our own fear that perhaps Christianity *isn't* true after all, and those well-spoken critics may, in fact, be right. Others of us might conduct apologetic campaigns to assert, or reassert, Christian power in our society: to get (our) religion back in the public school system, for example, or to see it portrayed properly in mass media entertainment and news.

Avoiding shame is a typical human concern, and not always to be despised. Moreover, some doubts about the validity of the Christian faith can, indeed, be met through apologetic research and reflection. And wanting our society to treat the Christian religion and Christian believers seriously is obviously a defensible agenda.

Christians must beware, however, to use the right tool for any job we're doing. And apologetics is best deployed toward two basic goals, which we might distinguish as *internal* and *external*: (a) to strengthen and to mature the faith of Christians; and (b) to remove obstacles, and clarify issues, and offer winsome inducements to those who are not (yet) Christians.[3]

Apologetics, first, ought to be a part of every program of Christian education, whether in the home or the church. Doubts about Christian affirmations arise naturally in the course of living in this world, whether about the reliability of the Bible as revelation, the goodness of the Christian sexual ethic, or the unique and supreme authority of Jesus Christ in a world of religious alternatives. Apologetical arguments properly can help strengthen a Christian's confidence, since we are to serve God with our minds as well as with the rest of ourselves, and intellectual needs are as worthy of Christian response as any other. It is important to affirm this aspect of Christian education, since some Christian communities try to spiritualize or moralize such difficulties away: "Just pray for more faith" or "If you were a more devout Christian, you wouldn't entertain such questions."

Christian faith, then, can be strengthened through internal apologetics. It can also be sophisticated through it. As Christians consider the questions raised in the culture at large or within our own communion, we can reconsider just what the best Christian response really should be. As we do so, we may find that we should refine our understanding of this Bible passage, or that doctrine, or this approach to evangelism, or that approach to political activity. One Christian might find that he doesn't have to go to the wall defending a six-by-24-hour-day creation of the world as he probes the history of Christianity and finds many faithful Christians interpreting Genesis 1 and 2 more figuratively than he had previously thought was tolerable. Another Christian might find that she doesn't need to continue any longer with a militantly aggressive approach to political action, since she has now discovered alternative Christian traditions on this matter. A third Christian might find his views on gender changing as he discovers the Bible is not nearly as protective of male superiority and power as he had previously thought. And so on.

Under the probing of good questions, even fiercely antagonistic ones, Christians thus can find their conception and practice of their religion become more nuanced, more careful, and more mature—without becoming one bit less passionate. Indeed, the commitment to the Christian way might well grow as we see more of its complexity, its beauty, and its ability to respond to the strongest and most subtle of challenges.

Even if one's understanding of Christianity doesn't change, furthermore, responding to apologetical challenges can help one become more articulate about one's faith and one's reasons for having such faith. Such clarity enables one to communicate one's faith and one's reasons for faith more easily to others. And one can more easily spot areas of one's religion that are less well developed than others, and attend to them as such. So engagement in apologetical discussion can be salutary for Christian education itself.

The other, and more typical, direction of apologetics is toward those who are not Christians, or *external* apologetics. Apologetics isn't going to convert any of these people to believers—only the Holy Spirit can do that. But apologetics can help in these three ways. First, apologetics can remove obstacles that keep people from coming any closer to Christ. If Christianity is seen by some as sexist, or homophobic, or imperialistic, or unintelligent, then many of our neighbors will want nothing to do with it or with the figure at its center. By showing that Christianity is not as problematic in these respects as our friends think, we lower the barriers to their moving inward for further consideration.

Second, apologetics can help by clarifying issues. It can do so by literally helping people understand the best way to put their questions. For example, instead of asking, "Why did God create evil?" when Christianity suggests that there is no such thing as "evil" as an entity, then we can ask, "Why did God create a cosmos in which some agents are free to commit evil, and in which he himself sometimes seems to bring evil?" Putting it this way opens up a much more helpful avenue for exploration, since God might have a good reason to create beings who are capable of evil, while it is hard to imagine why God would create *evil* itself.[4]

For another example, when someone asks, "Why do Christians think their religion is right and everyone else's is wrong?" the Christian can respond that this is not really what Christians are saying when they are affirming the uniqueness of Jesus and his central role in the economy of salvation. Other religions do have elements of truth, goodness, and beauty in them that Christians can (and should) affirm. And many believers in other faiths are more admirable than many of us Christians. The zone of contention, then, has to do with more fundamental questions of how God reveals himself to the world and how God is saving the world, and what the roles of the world's religions might be in these activities of God. As long as our friends see the issue in the extremely exclusive way of "Christianity alone is good and everything else is bad," however, they cannot move any further toward encountering and embracing Jesus.[5]

Finally, apologetics can not only perform the "negative" act, so to speak, of clearing away impediments and the "clarifying" act of establishing a helpful framework for conversation, but apologetics also can perform the positive act of offering winsome inducements to the inquirer. The Christian religion, after all, offers many good things to those who walk in the path of faith. For almost two thousand years, the world has witnessed millions of people, across many cultural barriers, convert to Christianity—not just grow up in it. Why did they all do so? Apologetics can set out their reasons, as intelligibly and attractively as possible, in order to help our neighbors see just why they, too, should contemplate the decision of conversion and the demands of Christian discipleship.[6]

So apologetics can perform all of these functions for the benefit of both Christians and their neighbors. It perhaps seems odd, therefore, to feel obliged to defend such an apparently salutary activity as apologetics. But many readers will recognize that in circles both Christian and otherwise, today, apologetics is in disrepute as old-fashioned and quaint, at best, and as offensive to both God and our neighbors at worst.

DEFENDING APOLOGETICS

In societies that pride themselves on being "multicultural" nowadays, apologetics (in the traditional sense of religious argument) is often seen to be in bad taste, and even as offensive. Many Christians who are eager to commend their faith to their neighbors perceive this resistance but don't understand it. Worse, they feel frustrated by it: "If I have found Christianity to be so terrific and I want to tell you about it, why aren't you glad to listen? *What's wrong with you?*"

Avoidance of apologetics does make sense in our culture, however, and from a Christian point of view can even be commendable in several respects.

First, such resistance expresses an epistemological condition. There is a genuine humility among some of our neighbors who simply don't believe that their beliefs, or practices, or mores are better than everyone else's, and so they cannot understand why anyone else would believe such a thing, let alone try to persuade other people to change their minds. Christians who do engage in such attempts at persuasion need to consider this question, or else we will unwittingly and unwillingly appear naive and even foolishly dogmatic.

Second, a moral concern extends from this attitude as some of our neighbors want to extend the gift of tolerance to those who are different. Attempts to persuade other people of the superiority of one's religion is thus seen as not only intellectually implausible, but morally odious. How dare we try to impose our views on others? How dare we imply, or even declare outright, that other people's traditions are inferior to ours? Such behavior is impolite at best, and oppressive and imperialistic at worst. Indeed, it smacks of the authoritarianism that our culture has increasingly resisted since the 1960s.

Third, there is a practical side to this that we Christians can recognize as valid. Just as previous generations were told to avoid discussions of politics and religion at parties in order to avoid unhappily vehement conversation, so the bracketing out of religious argument can help in the everyday concern to ease the strains of pluralism, to avoid needless controversy as we try to live as neighbors. Christians can agree that there are indeed circumstances in which it is best to accentuate our commonalities and set aside our differences for the common good. And we can recognize that the onus may well be upon us to justify at the outset of any apologetic conversation just why we are "disturbing the peace."

Still, our different value systems do bump into each other frequently in public and in private: at school board and city council meetings, in the entertainment media, in family courts, in romantic relationships, and so on. So it is simply not possible to bracket out our religious differences indefinitely, relegating them to some private zone that will never interfere with someone else's.

It remains true, furthermore, that religions typically aren't content to let people believe whatever they like. Religions insist on their views of ultimate matters because it *ultimately matters* what you believe. We live in the world as we think the world is.

Philosopher and Buddhism scholar Paul Griffiths has expanded upon this latter point in *An Apology for Apologetics*. He suggests that the very nature of the religious sense of human beings requires apologetics—at least, among some people on some occasions. This contention is set out in technical language as what he calls "The Necessity of Interreligious Apologetics" (NOIA):

> If representative intellectuals belonging to some specific religious community come to judge at a particular time that some or all of their own doctrine-expressing sentences are incompatible with some alien religious claim(s), then they should feel obliged to engage in both positive and negative apologetics vis-à-vis these alien religious claim(s) and their promulgators.[7]

Essentially, Griffiths contends that from time to time, and especially (we might say) in the increasingly pluralistic cultures of modern societies around the world, religious believers encounter the ideas of others that challenge some or all of their beliefs. Those believers who are called to be "representative intellectuals" must respond to these challenges, and such a response takes the form of apologetics—not of merely ignoring the challenges, or seeking force to simply destroy those putting the challenges, since the challenges are in the ideas themselves and must be dealt with as such. (Griffiths's categories of *positive* and *negative* are parallel to my categories of *offensive* and *defensive* apologetics.)

Not every one is obliged to engage in apologetics, since not everyone has the time, talent, and opportunity to meet such challenges. But at least, Griffiths says, those who are charged with intellectual leadership must do so.

Now, why does he think that? Griffiths offers two imperatives that are rooted in the very nature of religious interest. The first is the *epistemic* duty to seek out, believe, and defend the truth as far as possible. Religions are fundamentally maps of reality, and the serious religious person wants to know which map is best. One cannot ignore a serious dispute of this sort, nor can one resolve it by coercion—as if a fistfight over competing roadmaps would solve the question of their accuracy. Unless we are indifferent or fanatical, we want to know what is the best map, and apologetical argument is one way to confront and evaluate the competing alternatives.

The second imperative Griffiths offers for apologetics is the *ethical* duty to discern what may conduce to one's own good and (perhaps—it depends on the religion as to whether this second consideration obtains) the good of others. Serious religious people want not only to believe what is true, but to enjoy the best life has to offer and, in most cases, to offer that also to others.

Put negatively, to abandon apologetics is to abandon the enterprise that animates religious people the world over: to find the truth and to live in its light as best we can. It is to abandon honest and searching dialogue that might result in someone actually changing his or her mind for the better, and to settle instead for mere understanding, or at least tolerance, of others' views while, indeed, remaining generally unmoved by them—since one has not taken them on as serious alternatives to one's own view.

It is likely that we will have to make clear with our neighbors in such conversations just how religions can indeed contend with each other over their differences. What data do we examine, and according to what standard do we evaluate them? Nonetheless, we can agree with Griffiths that to persistently avoid interreligious disputes is to stick one's head in the sand. It is to hypocritically avoid the possibility of improving one's understanding of reality in the name of fidelity to the cause of understanding reality!

Resistance to apologetics has arisen not only from outside the Christian Church, however, but also from within it. The resistance has taken many forms, but reduces to a kind of passivity or quietism that sometimes, but not always, is reinforced by a more general disparagement of the intellect.

Apophatics and Presuppositionalists: We can't engage in apologetics. One stream of Christian spirituality and theology emphasizes the transcendence and uniqueness of God to an infinite extent. Since God is "wholly other," as one common phrase has it, human beings cannot predicate anything about him directly, but only suggest what God is by negating what God is not. Apologetics is useless, therefore, as it wrongheadedly tries to offer reasons why Christian belief makes sense. This *via negativa* (way of negation) is typified by many within the Eastern Orthodox communion, and in the Western churches by figures as disparate as the sixteenth-century monk St. John of the Cross and the great twentieth-century theologian Karl Barth, particularly in his younger years.

In the stream particularly of modern Calvinist thought has emerged the idea that since the Christian worldview alone rests on divinely revealed truth, it shares no important common ground with other worldviews that do not have this foundation (or set of presuppositions—hence the term *presuppositionalists*). There may, of course, be this or that similar feature between Christianity and some alternative view. But the fundamental orientation of Christianity is toward God, while every alternative is oriented away from him and thus is hopelessly riddled with errors. There is no sufficient common ground upon which one can invite one's neighbor to move from her position to the Christian one. Apologetics has nowhere to conduct business, since only a chasm lies between Christianity and other religions and philosophies. There is, to be blunt, no way to get "here" from "there." One can only pray for God to work spiritual transformation so that people will believe and embrace the essential Christian "package."

Predestinarians and Mystics/Charismatics: We don't need to engage in apologetics. Christians with a strong belief in God's utterly sovereign will—particularly from the Lutheran and Reformed traditions and those influenced especially by Augustine in Roman Catholicism—can sometimes sound as if there is no point in human apologetical effort, or even evangelistic enterprises. Since sin has corrupted human beings to the extent that no one will choose to repent unless God transforms the will in an act of sovereign grace, what is there for the human apologist to do?

Most predestinarian Christians, to be sure, respond to this question by saying that God has called Christians to be his instruments, and he has chosen specifically to make grace available to many through Christian proclamation. So however unclear the importance of apologetics or evangelism might seem to us, we are to engage in it anyway as God uses us to make his grace operative in others. But there have been predestinarians who have gone further, to the point of surrendering to God entirely the initiative for such work. The young would-be missionary William Carey was notoriously cautioned by a Calvinist elder, "If God wants to save the heathen, he'll do it without your help or mine."

Many (but not all) mystical and charismatic Christians also opt out of apologetics on the grounds of God's sovereignty, but with a different sense of what happens in the economy of salvation. Since the fundamental problem, again, is human sinfulness and the only remedy is the transforming work of the Holy Spirit, these Christians see no point in the labor of intellectual engagement. Rightly grasping that conversion is fundamentally spiritual and therefore the province of God's Spirit, they go on to conclude (less rightly, I might say) that apologetical conversation is, strictly speaking, beside the point and therefore a waste of time.

Sectarians and Chiliasts: It is not our job to engage in apologetics. Sectarian Christians believe that God has called them out of the world's societies into separate, holy fellowships. Their role is to remain unstained by worldly contact and to bear witness to the gospel by their fidelity to what they understand to be the patterns of the New Testament. It is not for them to grapple with the sinful confusion of contemporary society, the devil's realm, but instead they are to abandon any compromising association with it. Therefore apologetics—with its requisite study of the world's ideas and concerns, and its attempt to speak in the world's categories in the interest of intelligibility—is obviously a shocking entanglement with worldliness.

Chiliasts—those who believe that the end of the world is upon us—tend to view the work of apologetics as too little, too slow, too late. The *Titanic* is sinking, and having a learned discussion on deck about the integrity of watertight compartments, the likelihood of encountering icebergs, and the theoretical capacity of lifeboats is preposterous, even obscene. The world is about to end, and only loud announcement or faithful withdrawal to await the end makes sense in the circumstances.

Each of these Christian groups has a case to make against apologetics that has convinced many others through the centuries. My sense is that in every case there is a good Christian idea pressed too far, to the point that it is made to run over, or away from, complementary Christian ideas. For example, mystical and charismatic Christians are clearly correct to give pride of place to the converting work of the Holy Spirit—that is one of the main themes of this book also. But they are wrong if they thereby denigrate other good gifts of God, gifts—such as intellectual argument—that are often used by the Holy Spirit precisely in his work of conversion.

It perhaps is not necessary, however, to criticize each of these positions point for point. In brief reply, one can appeal instead to the pattern of ministry of the Lord Jesus and of the pillars of the apostolic church. Jesus performed signs precisely to both clarify and add plausibility to his preaching. Peter's first sermon in Acts 2 is an apologetic directed to his fellow Jews that seeks to convince them of Jesus' messiahship. Paul is recorded in Scripture as devoting himself to many learned disputations with both Jews and Gentiles—perhaps most obviously on Mars Hill, but in many other instances as well (e.g., Acts 17; 28). Among the Corinthians, perhaps, he adopted a deliberately simple message (1 Corinthians 2:1–5), but even here Paul has reasons to adapt his discourse to the need of the moment in order to make it most plausible and effective. In other circumstances, he presents the Christian case quite differently (so before Felix and Festus, Acts 24–25).

Paul also takes pains to explain the logic of the Christian religion to churches in the canonical epistles (with Romans as Exhibit A), rather than simply imposing religious tenets and practices by apostolic fiat. He wants his churches to mature on the "meat" of serious theological understanding (1 Corinthians 3:2). And John writes his gospel account explicitly in order to give grounds for belief in Jesus as "the Christ, the Son of God" (John 20:31). It is not hard to see these as apologetic in the internal sense of strengthening and sophisticating the belief of Christians.

The majority of Christians ever since have followed this pattern of constructive engagement with the ideas and minds of their day, in order that "by all means I may save some" (1 Corinthians 9:22). Indeed, it would seem odd that in a religion whose God tells us to love him with our minds (Mt. 22:37) as well as with the rest of our being, and who gives his people a highly complex set of sacred writings in the Bible, intellectual explanation and defense would not play at least some part in helping at least some audiences come to faith and then grow up in it. I conclude that the various forms of Christian resistance to apologetics have resulted from over-emphases or misconstruals of the nature of the Christian faith, leaving no serious reason for Christians to avoid or disparage apologetics.

If that conclusion is valid, therefore, it remains to be seen just what sort of apologetics should be offered to our neighbors today. The rest of this book takes up that agenda.

PART THREE

COMMUNICATION

8

Principles of Christian Communication

And the Word became flesh and lived among us, and we have seen his glory, the glory as of a father's only son, full of grace and truth. (John testified to him and cried out, "This was he of whom I said, 'He who comes after me ranks ahead of me because he was before me.'") From his fullness we have all received, grace upon grace. The law indeed was given through Moses; grace and truth came through Jesus Christ. No one has ever seen God. It is God the only Son, who is close to the Father's heart, who has made him known.

John 1:14–18

Apologetics typically has been undertaken in what some nowadays would call a "logocentric" fashion: *words* have been the primary means of communication, and *truths* have been the primary freight of that communication.

Christianity, however, is much more than a set of propositions to which one might or might not grant intellectual assent. It is, at its heart, a path of life, a following of Jesus Christ as disciples and as members of the worldwide Church. If apologetics consists entirely of words and truths, therefore, it will literally fail to communicate Christianity, but instead necessarily distort it by shrinking it to what words and truths can portray.

Christian communication instead takes its pattern especially from the ministry of Jesus Christ himself. Just as we have located apologetics, then, in the context of God's overarching project of conversion, so we must also see apologetics in the context of basic principles of all communication worthy of the name of Christ.[1] The famous opening of John's gospel provides two helpful pairs of categories to frame out a more appropriate pattern of Christian communication and therefore of apologetics.

WORD AND FLESH: MESSAGE AND LIFE

Christians, whether individually or in groups, tend to find it easier to concentrate our witness to the gospel either upon proclaiming the message of good news or living it out in faithful obedience. Some of us, that is, tend to be "talkers" and others of us "doers." This dichotomy sometimes shows up in churches in discussions of priorities in Christian mission, as "evangelism" is pitted against "social action" or "charity."

Problems, however, clearly attend any opting of one over the other. If one attempts to convey the message without incorporating it into one's way of life, one will find oneself frustrated by two impediments: There will likely be no opportunity to share the gospel message, and if there is, there will be no context in which it can be interpreted and received properly.

An earnest Christian woman once spoke up at a prayer meeting of the small Chicago church to which I once belonged. She worked as a clerk in the university bookstore, and had done so for years. As a lifelong church member—indeed, as a lifelong Southern Baptist—she was convinced that she ought to be speaking about the gospel to her workmates. But she confessed at this meeting to her complete frustration. She never had opportunity, she said, to speak a single word of spiritual truth to her fellow clerks, and she didn't know what to do.

After expressions of sympathy were offered by members of the group, someone finally asked her a direct and pertinent question: "Lois, how many of the clerks would you say are friends of yours?"

Lois looked a bit stunned. The conversation had taken an unexpected turn, a turn that seemed to strike her as irrelevant. "Well, none of them. I'm white and they're mostly black. And they're mostly younger that I am."

The questioner gently persisted. "How often do you have your breaks with them, go for coffee or lunch with them?"

Again, Lois looked a bit blank. "I always take my breaks by myself to have coffee and read my Bible. And I usually take my lunch in the park across the street on my own."

The rest of the group then tried to help Lois see that with no friends or even cordial acquaintances among her workmates, she would literally have no natural opportunity to speak of spiritual things in the course of ringing in sales in a bookstore. Furthermore, if she *were* to broach the subject, her surprised colleagues might well respond with resistance: "Why should I listen to you? Who are you to talk to me about such things?" Or they might simply deflect her well-meant initiative as irrelevant, since it is unlikely that Lois would know any of them well enough to speak to a zone of genuine need in their lives.

Lois doubtless came across at the bookstore as a decent, responsible coworker. And that consistent morality is not to be despised. But without sharing more of her life with her workmates, her message simply would either never emerge, or would likely not emerge in a way that would be understood and received.

Offering a consistently friendly and honorable life without ever articulating the Christian message, however, is problematic also. For one thing, in cultures still bearing the impress of Christian morality, most people continue to adhere to many values shared with Christians. Some Christians abide by a strict code of behavior that does indeed mark them out, but primarily as negative in the sense that they are distinguished primarily by what they do not do: smoke, drink, dance, swear, and so on in the familiar list of fundamentalist taboos. To be sure, in an age of widespread casual and often cynical dishonesty, predatory business practices, abuse of both legal and illegal drugs, and highly confused sexuality, consistent Christian morality can shine out in contrast. But most of day-to-day life among our peers will show consistent Christians to be, at best, somewhat more virtuous than the norm.

Moral excellence is, of course, a good thing in itself and does not need to be justified instrumentally as a means to some other end. But in terms of apologetics, we must recognize that behavior is not self-interpreting. A "good person" in our culture might be a Christian, but might also be a faithful Buddhist, or Baha'i, or secular humanist. Our friends might see the conspicuous "dots" of our distinctive behavior, but it is not to be assumed that they will "connect" them in a line that leads to Christianity.

Furthermore, we must recall that just as the Christian religion is not to be reduced to "good ideas," it is also not to be reduced to "good morals" or "positive feelings" or "charitable acts." The gospel bears fruit in all of these respects, to be sure. But the gospel is primarily the salvation message of God's love for us and his caring for us especially in Christ. And that very particular content cannot possibly be inferred from mere good Christian behavior.

Jesus Christ set us a good example in this respect. If we put it in terms of what historians sometimes call a *counterfactual*, a "What if things had been different?" exercise of the imagination, we can see clearly how important it is to offer both a way of life and a message that articulates it.

To put it starkly, if "message without life" was sufficient, Christ didn't need to perform signs, nor did he need to form personal relationships in which to teach the gospel to those who would believe him and spread the word. He could simply have hired scribes to write down his message and distribute it. Furthermore, to an important extent Christ's life was a crucial *part* of the message. Thus the gospels are accounts of Jesus' deeds as well as words. So Christ invested years of his life in relationships that would give both credibility and interpretive context to his message, yes, but also actual complementary *content* to his message.

If, to consider the contrary, "life without message" was adequate to the need, then Christ didn't have to preach and could have stayed home in Nazareth, an unusually good and honorable carpenter—or perhaps a faith healer. It is difficult to imagine, however, that anything like the Christian gospel or Christian church, much less the Kingdom of God, could have been established in this way.

Preacher John Stott writes that God has always both acted and provided interpretation of his actions: Deed and word go together in God's revelation of himself and his work.

How could such events be beneficial to those not involved in them unless there were witnesses to record and interpret the events? For example, many tribal migrations were taking place in the Middle East at the time of the exodus. How could anybody have known that Israel's exodus from Egypt was special, unless God had raised up Moses and the prophets to say so? Again, many crucifixions took place during the years that Rome occupied Palestine. How then could anybody have known that the crucifixion of Jesus was special, let alone the turning-point of human history, if God had not appointed and prepared the apostles as witnesses?[2]

Today, as in the first century, people need to know what happened and what it means for them—and what it *can* mean for them. Many of our neighbors also—speaking particularly of apologetics now, and not just evangelism—need warrants to believe that this (Christian) interpretation of the past is the one to which they ought to commit themselves. And those warrants will be offered most convincingly by those whose lives demonstrate the vitality of their message.

Stott warns us, then, about integrity in just this respect. He echoes the Apostle's warning to Titus: "On the one hand, inconsistent Christian conduct gives people cause to 'malign the word of God' and so hinders evangelism. On the other hand, consistent Christian conduct 'will make the teaching about God our Savior attractive' and so will promote evangelism (Titus 2:5, 10). More briefly, bad behavior discredits the gospel, while good behavior adorns and so commends it."[3]

Therefore we are to offer, as God Incarnate did, both word and flesh, both message and life, to our neighbors in apologetics. And it is striking to consider, in the history of Christian mission, how these elements in combination have impressed people with the credibility of the gospel. Augustine, for example, testifies that he was converted by the integrity and charity of other people, not merely by their Christian intelligence. His long-suffering mother Monica and his admirable mentor Bishop Ambrose stand out in this respect. In our own time, collections of spiritual testimonies by Christian philosophers present the recurring motif of kindness and moral integrity impressing these intellectuals at least as deeply as apologetic argumentation. In our own day, philosopher Linda Trinkhaus Zagzebski has affirmed, "The experience of knowing holy people is still the most important evidence to me for the truth of Christianity."[4]

This emphasis, then, shows up in the advice of Peter himself to the early church, advice that contains the classic apologetic text about "making a defense" and that nicely qualifies that text in terms of Christian behavior:

> Now who will harm you *if you are eager to do what is good*? But even if you do suffer for doing what is right, you are blessed. Do not fear what they fear, and do not be intimidated, but *in your hearts sanctify Christ as Lord*. Always be ready to make your defense to anyone who demands from you an accounting for the hope that is in you; yet do it with *gentleness* and *reverence*. Keep your *conscience clear*, so that, when you are maligned, those who abuse you for your *good conduct* in Christ may be put to shame. (I Peter 2:13–16; emphasis added)

GRACE AND TRUTH

As the early church viewed the progress of God's revelation through the ages, Moses—symbol of the Old Covenant—brought the gift of God's law. The law of God is necessary to teach us who he is and who we are, and to show us, as we fail to keep it, how far apart we are. Grace and truth then comes through Jesus the Saviour who reconciles us with God, bridging in his person and work the great chasm between fallen humanity and our holy Creator.

Christ not only brings us God's message of grace and truth in his work of revelation. Christ not only truly and graciously actualizes that message in his work of salvation. But Christ models for us how Christians are then to be in the world: "full of grace and truth."

Apologists are not well known for their emphasis upon grace, but rather upon truth. Other Christians reverse the balance. Yet offering one without the other is both relatively easy and actually harmful to the gospel: truth without grace ("I tell the truth and let the chips fall where they may") or grace without truth ("I serve everyone and offend no one"). Instead, we are to live in the same way that the Apostle Paul tells us we are to speak: "Let no worthless word proceed from your mouth, but only such a word as is helpful for edification, according to the need of the moment, that it may give grace to those that hear" (Ephesians 4:29). Our words, and our deeds as well, of course, must always be positive, always building up, always appropriate to the situation, and always—here is the fundamental point—a grace, or a gift (the two words have the same root in Greek: *charis*) to the recipient.

We cannot communicate the truth of the gospel without graciousness, without love. One entails the other. No one wants to listen sympathetically, or at least openly, to a message delivered without love. If you don't communicate to me that you care about me, that your message is somehow going to benefit me rather than just you, then I'm going to resist it—whether you're telling me life-changing gospel news or selling me a magazine subscription. So in terms of basic human communication, Christians are foolish to try to speak without love.

Furthermore, the truth of *this* message especially will be harder to understand and receive without the simultaneous communication of love. The gospel is about the starkest, most challenging truths there are: about death and life, corruption and resurrection, self-denial and self-realization. Imagine the (in-)effectiveness of the following truthful message delivered with no context of regard for the other person: "You know, Ashley, the Bible says you're a terrible sinner and you're going to hell if you don't repent and convert."

At the same time, loving *entails* truth-telling. I recall young men of my acquaintance telling anyone who would listen just why they refused to be honest with women they were dating. Perhaps you have met them, too: "I didn't want to hurt her, so I didn't tell her about the other woman I was seeing." Yet whose feelings were they sparing? Whose interests were they protecting? Love *often* means telling truth that hurts in order for healing to come and protection to be afforded. A true friend will say, "I think you've made a mistake here." A proper parent will warn her child, "Don't play in the street because it is dangerous." A conscientious physician will announce, "The test results are in and I'm afraid there's bad news."

The gospels portray Jesus as "full of grace and truth," although just how those qualities emerge and combine cannot always be easily predicted or understood. Sometimes Jesus is severe; sometimes he is tender. Sometimes he is confrontational, and sometimes he apparently avoids confrontation. In every case, he tells what is true and does so in such a way that he gives a gift to the audience. He offers something the other person particularly needs, and he does so clearly out of love. Jesus is prepared for his gift to be rejected. He is prepared even to be rejected himself. But if there is a breach, it is not because he has stinted in his offering of either truth or love.

Novelist Larry Woiwode offers us a glimpse of what a Christian apologist can be in his brief portrait of the Russian martyr Aleksandr Menn (1935–1990). Menn was an immensely popular preacher in Moscow under the Soviet régime and baptized numerous high-profile converts. He was spiritual adviser to Aleksandr Solzhenitsyn and Nobel Prize–winning physicist Andre Sakharov.

> Parishioners and friends . . . described him as a man of joy with unusual gifts of discernment; he seemed to sense spiritual needs intuitively and conveyed to others the love of Christ—a light-hearted spiritual healer. In nearly every photograph he is smiling the broad clear smile of one whose joy springs straight from the heart.

Menn was not only a superb pastor, however, but a bold and winsome apologist.

> His books, circulated in *samizdat* (the underground press), undid the Soviet claim that atheism was a science; they advanced Christianity as the true intellectual Way. These writings . . . breathe out the appealing person of Christ. They brought about revival in the Orthodox church; thousands of young people were converted through them.[5]

Fundamentally, of course, grace and truth intertwine even more tightly in the gospel, since the truth of the gospel is, at heart, the grace of God. Thus we are to "speak the truth in love," as the Apostle exhorts us (Ephesians 4:15). And we especially are to do so in the act of defending and commending the faith in apologetics:

Apologetics
by Rich Carl

A pologist strode forth one day
   in search of dragons for to slay,
his sword like diamond hard and clear;
   thus armed with truth he had no fear.
the heathen dragons he did find
   and left a bloody trail behind
and those who died not by his blade
   soon cursed the day it had been made.

the pologist then met a man
   who led a dragon by the hand.
"slay not this beast," the man did cry,
   "we're bound for Castle in the Sky."
the pologist replied, "beware—
   for dragons may not enter there."
the man then said, "oh do not fret;
   the dragon need not know that yet."

a wizard, likewise, that day walked
   and, meeting dragons, stopped and talked;
but he too had a sword with him
   and cut the dragons limb from limb;
yet with the sword he was so skilled
   that very little blood was spilled
and when the limbs were rearranged
   the dragons lived but they were changed.
for magic was the wizard's trade
   and, when he forged his mighty blade,
he used a metal from above:
   an alloy made of truth and love.[6]

APOLOGETICS AS AN ACT OF LOVE

"'You shall love the Lord your God with all your heart, and with all your soul, and with all your mind.' This is the greatest and first commandment. And a second is like it: 'You shall love your neighbor as yourself.'" (Matthew 22:37–39 NRSV)

Love to God

Apologetics, like any other Christian activity, must be undertaken first as an act of love to God. In particular, we must be sure not to compromise God's mission, God's law, God's message, or God's love in our zeal.

First, we must not compromise God's mission. We must not restrict it so that it becomes narrower than God wants it to be: not merely "souls" being "saved," or "minds" being "changed," but whole people being adopted into God's family and cooperating with him in the global work of redemption.

Second, we must not compromise God's law. We must not manipulate or deceive, and particularly not use the "bait-and-switch" tactics that show up occasionally among evangelicals, and particularly in work with students: "Come and find out how to have great sex!" "Come to this talk and your grades will go up!" We must not use fear tactics, or success tactics, or *any other* tactics that are not congruent with the message we are offering and the Lord we serve.

Third, we must not compromise God's message. Throughout the history of the church, well-meaning apologists have trimmed the gospel to make it fit a little easier with the presuppositions and preferences of the audience. Christianity seems too Semitic and not classically sophisticated? Let's make it look and sound like Platonism, as some of the earliest apologists tried to do, or like Aristotelianism, as some medievals undertook to make it. Too much mystery in Christian theology? Let's render *Christianity Not Mysterious*, as John Toland wrote in 1696. Too many references to the superstitious and supernatural? Let's edit the New Testament to make Jesus look more enlightened and sophisticated, as Thomas

Jefferson did (at least twice) literally with scissors and paste. Too much ancient strangeness and especially Jewish elements? Let's follow the lead of modern liberal theology and strictly separate the New Testament's "essential" message from its old-fashioned husk.

No, the gospel will appear foolish to sophisticates in every society. Too much editing of the message to suit the categories and interests of our neighbors can result in our merely echoing them, rather than giving them the gift of something wonderful they don't already have. Apologetics must always maintain fidelity first to the sacred tradition.

Fourth, we must not compromise God's love. Apologetics must always look like God's love at work. People should be able to tell we love God and that we speak and act in the name of God's love. Any apologetics that falls short of this standard falls badly short of the glory of God.

Love to Our Neighbor

Apologetics is not, primarily, about me. I can read apologetics in order to strengthen and sophisticate my faith, yes. I can engage in apologetics and that can benefit me in various ways. But I ought to be commending the faith to my neighbor primarily for her benefit, to the glory of God. I ought *not* to be engaging in apologetic conversation out of some need of my own, whether a need to save face, or show up an enemy, or congratulate myself on my fervor. Apologetics, again, is a form of Christian speech, and as such it is always and only to offer a gift to the recipient—not aggrandize the speaker.

Fundamentally, then, apologetics is about winning the friend, not the argument. We offer apologetics in the service of Christian friends, to encourage their faith. We do so also in the service of those who are not Christians, to encourage their interest. Sometimes, to be sure, apologetics has been undertaken simply to protect the Church under attack, and we might do the same in our cultural contests today. Whatever the situation, however, we engage in apologetics for the same reason we engage in anything as Christians:

to glorify God and to help our neighbor—whoever the pertinent neighbor might be in a given moment.

God cares about people more than he cares about "truth" in the abstract. Jesus didn't die on the cross to make a point. He died on the cross to save people whom he loves. We, too, must represent our Lord with love to God and our neighbor always foremost in our concerns.

COMMON GROUND AND
AUDIENCE-SPECIFIC APPROACHES

With love for God and love for our neighbor guiding and motivating us, therefore, when it comes to apologetics we will take each audience seriously on its own terms. We will not, that is, present apologetics to discharge a duty to our own satisfaction and then depart. In particular, we will not devise an apologetic that impresses *us*, but an apologetic that meets the needs of the particular audience we are addressing.

The deeply pluralistic situation of our culture reinforces the requirement of sensitivity to each person and each group. We must undertake the necessary investigation to establish just what common ground we have with the audience and then try to discern and to meet *that* audience's needs as we have opportunity to do so. Some have termed this concern "person-specific" or "ad hoc" apologetics. The principle is the same: We cannot assume that everyone else thinks as we do and cares as we do. Thus we cannot manufacture a "one size fits all" apologetic and expect it to communicate well with every audience. Fortunately, of course, we are not called by God to address "every audience." Instead, our vocation is to meet the needs of the audiences to which we are particularly called—to love our neighbors.

Chapter 10 outlines a number of practical applications of this principle. For now, we can concentrate on just one, upon which hang all the rest.

Many Christians, and particularly those in the evangelical tradition to which I belong, are typically better at speaking, at proclamation, than at these two necessary skills: asking questions and listening to answers. Yet we must begin by asking questions. Who am I dealing with? What are their questions, their cognitive style or styles, their concerns, and their criteria for deciding about religious matters? Before I rush in with my package of stirring apologetic arguments, I need to ask just what my audience cares about, and how they will likely hear and respond to what I have to say.

John Wesley, who knew a thing or two about effective Christian communication, recommended the following question: "Have I, before I spoke to any, learned, as far as I could, his temperament, way of thinking, past life, and peculiar hindrances, internal and external?"[7]

To do this well, of course, requires me then to listen carefully to what is said in reply to the questions I have asked. I need to listen, furthermore, to *all* of what is being said; to *how* it is being said; to what is *not* being said; to what is *really* being said; and to *why* it is being said.

Professors run an occupational hazard in precisely this case, so let me pick on my own profession to illustrate it. Students ask questions in class, and listeners raise questions after public lectures. We professors, alas, tend to listen just long enough to conclude that we know what the question is and then rush to answer it. Asking a good question is hard to do, however, and particularly about a difficult topic, in front of other people, when one is passionately interested in the subject. Wise and considerate professors wait for a questioner to ramble and meander his way to the end of his question, for it is toward the end, sometimes, that the real question emerges. And the meandering itself sets a context for the professor to discern just what is motivating the question—if the speaker will love the questioner and the rest of the audience enough to patiently attend to the whole question.

I remember being shocked when listening to a recording of a well-known Christian apologist taking questions from a university audience. He had delivered a speech that could accurately, if uncharitably, be called "canned," and did so with evident self-satisfaction. When the floor was opened for questions, however, his smoothness became quite ruffled. He condescended to friendly Christian questioners, cutting them off to re-pose their questions in a way he thought improved them. And any critical questioner was met with palpable impatience and a long-winded reply, with no opportunity for rejoinder. It was, in my view, a disgraceful example of a speaker egocentrically out of touch with his audience.

Alan Bede Griffiths testifies that his friend C. S. Lewis was such a great apologist because he combined rational intelligence and poetic imagination with psychological insight. Lewis was able "to speak to the common man and see into the hidden motives in the heart of everyman," and without such sensitive analysis and connection, Lewis's brilliance would have remained remote from most of his millions of grateful readers.[8] Only by paying careful attention can I possibly get to know the real person or persons before me. Only then can I hope to communicate with that audience in a way that will give them a gift they can recognize and accept as such.

Perhaps the Apostle Paul, genius that he was, could become "all things to all people, so that by all possible means I might save some" (I Corinthians 9:22 NIV). Even he, of course, didn't believe he should offer the same approach to each audience—that's the whole thrust of this passage in I Corinthians, and certainly consistent with what we see of Paul's variegated career in the New Testament. J. Budziszewski observes in this regard:

> Not even the Bible demands starting every conversation with the Bible. To pagans, Paul quoted pagan poetry (Acts 17:28), talked about the weather (14:17), and commented on their own secret suspicion that their idols could not save (17:23).[9]

You and I likely do not have Paul's versatility. But that's okay, of course. We need to become just whatever we can be, say whatever we can say, and do whatever we can do out of our limited repertoires, in order to serve the particular neighbors God places in our way.

So what kinds of audiences can we expect? And what can we offer them? Chapter 9 details how very different both our audiences and approaches can be.

9

Audience-Specific Apologetics

In trying to match the kind of apologetic we offer to the audience we face, we need to consider at least the following two questions: How open is our neighbor to the gospel, and to what kind of apologetic is she most open?[1]

A SPECTRUM OF OPENNESS

In a lecture I enjoyed hearing many years ago, Os Guinness pointed out that the New Testament portrays listeners as widely varying in their openness to receive the gospel. When Paul and Silas refuse to leave a Philippian prison after an angel bursts it open in an earthquake, the jailer drops to his knees and asks, "What must I do to be saved?" As Guinness points out, the response of Paul, as recorded in the Book of Acts, is briefer even than the so-called Four Spiritual Laws of gospel tract fame. He simply says, "Believe on the Lord Jesus Christ." To be sure, Paul accompanies him home and the whole household comes to faith, doubtless under further instruction from the Apostle.

The jailer has seen what he needs to see and has heard what he needs to hear. He is convinced that these men are emissaries of heaven. Now he simply needs to know how he can accompany them there. He finds out, accepts it, and is on his way.

At the other end of the continuum is a surprising group. The gospel did indeed meet resistance from Roman dignitaries, envious magicians, nervous businessmen, priests of rival religions, and other predictable enemies. But perhaps the most intransigent opposition to Jesus himself came from the Pharisees, the most rigorously religious, God-fearing group in ancient Judaism. They are first intrigued by Jesus, then dismayed by him, and finally conspire with other leaders to destroy him.

To them Jesus tells provocative, even embarrassing stories that highlight their refusal to accept him as Messiah. As the relationship deteriorates through the gospel accounts, Jesus is less and less communicative with them until he finally lapses into silence. "Unless you tell us whether John the Baptist's ministry was from God or not, I will no longer answer questions about my own" (see Matthew 21:25–27).

Only conversation that probes and tests, that questions and listens, will divulge how open someone is to receiving the gospel. And it will take time, in many instances, to determine whether the degree of resistance is primarily intellectual, moral, spiritual, or along some other dimension or combination of dimensions.

It could be that someone really does need simply a nagging question answered before she can take the first step of faith. Is Christianity really sexist? Is it homophobic? Is it callous about the fate of those who have never heard the gospel? Does it support the exploitation of nature? If Christians can offer good answers to these questions that are central in some people's lives, they may well be able to undertake the path of discipleship.

Others, however, resist Christianity for motivations that no amount of apologetics can touch. Perhaps, as Jesus implied about the Pharisees, they are deeply committed to a religiosity of self-congratulatory righteousness that refuses to admit the need of a Savior. Perhaps, and especially in our own time, they are committed to something else just as basic, just as self-centered, and just as impervious to the gospel.

Woody Allen, for example, incurred the wrath of public opinion when he began a romantic relationship with his adopted daughter. In the face of unrelenting criticism as his behavior contravened most North Americans' sense of morality, he famously declared, "The heart wants what it wants."

Hugh Hefner, as readers (not just oglers) of his magazine know, fancies himself a philosopher of sorts—a latter-day Epicurean, or outright hedonist. Suppose I spend an evening conversing with Mr. Hefner about the relative strengths and weakness of the Playboy philosophy versus the Christian religion. Suppose that, after several hours, my arsenal of apologetics has prevailed, leading Mr. Hefner himself to concede that I have had by far the better of our exchange. As the evening draws to a close, I silently congratulate myself on my involvement in what surely will be one of the great conversion stories of our time.

Mr. Hefner, however, has one last question: "Will adopting your philosophy, instead of mine, provide me with even more sensual pleasure than I enjoy now? Put most directly, will I be able to enjoy the affection and sexual intimacy of even more beautiful women than I do now?"

This question is one that I do not recall being addressed in any of the apologetics handbooks I have read. "Well," I stammer, "I suppose not. Christianity actually frowns on that sort of approach to life. In fact, it defends pretty strict rules regarding sex and monogamy. But it says that in the long run, this is all for the best."

"Ah," says Mr. Hefner, smiling his famous smile as he sits back in his armchair and lights another pipe. "I thought so. Well, thanks for the interesting time. Good night."

Mr. Hefner, like Mr. Allen, simply does not want what Christianity has to offer. And there is very little that apologetics can do about that. We can maintain that people who share his views are making a bad choice: They are trading carnal gratification for spiritual delight; they are privileging this world instead of the next; they are ignoring good arguments for the truth of Christianity. But if they don't want what we offer, then that is that. Only the Spirit of God can penetrate to the heart where such decisions are made.

It is not only the self-righteous or the hedonistic, of course, who may be closed to the gospel. As Mark Heim points out, serious devotees of other religions naturally will also be firmly resistant to Christian evangelism:

> One will not view [the Christian portrayal of] salvation as the true religious end unless one believes in the triune God and desires communion with that God. Therefore, with a different view of the ultimate or from the standpoint of a specific alternative religious realization, salvation does not appear a . . . higher end at all.[2]

Let us suppose, however, that our audience is at least somewhat open to Christian proclamation, as far as we know. What sort of apologetic should we deploy? Are some forms of apologetics—as the champions of those forms have maintained through the centuries—intrinsically superior to others?

THREE KINDS OF APPEAL

One of the more regrettable aspects of the history of apologetics has been the championing of one or another form of apologetics as superior to the rest, as alone truly Christian. To be sure, some forms of apologetics seem more dubious to some of us than others, and perhaps some need to be ruled out entirely according to basic tenets of the faith. (Appeals to the unquestionable authority of a single leader, for example, or the promise of unending riches, seem far more cultic than Christian.) When it comes, however, to forms of apologetics developed and used by bona fide Christians over the centuries with apparently good effect, the sensible thing to conclude is that each can be useful with certain people at certain times. These various approaches, that is, have been deployed because they are both consistent with the Christian religion and effective in communicating some of its virtues to an interested audience.[3]

Before encountering what I believe are the three main types of apologetic approaches, it is worth observing that all three types submit to three common tests of truth. The first is *coherence*, the extent to which the various elements of a hypothesis fit together and confirm each other. The second is *correspondence*, the extent to which the hypothesis fits the data to be explained. And the third is *pragmatic value*, the extent to which the implementation of the hypothesis makes a difference in actual practice.

We might pause for a moment to observe further that perhaps the first and third of these tests can be seen as versions of the correspondence test. Coherence is supposed to mark true hypotheses because the world itself is supposed to be a coherent place, and ideas that represent it properly can be assumed to be coherent as well. Pragmatism is a useful test in a world in which true ideas make a difference, and the right sort of difference, because of the orderly, sensible place the world itself is. They work, that is, because they represent the way things are.

The rise of postmodernity does not necessarily undermine these tests, but it does at least qualify them in the sense that we recognize as postmoderns that we are only guessing, only offering hypotheses about how things appear to be, without claiming too much for those guesses. (Radical postmodernists, of course, claim to be entirely skeptical about all such tests, but it's not clear what they offer instead as a way to negotiate life.)

Let's look, then, at the three main types of apologetics and assess the usefulness of each. And let us realize that each of these can be deployed to make any one of three claims, in ascending order. First, the apologist might assert that the Christian possesses warrant to hold her views rationally. Christianity is at least plausibly worthy of a responsible person's allegiance. We might call this the *protective* claim.

Second, the apologist might assert that the Christian possesses better warrant to hold her views than does anyone else in the conversation to hold his or hers. Christianity, that is, shows up comparatively better than the available alternatives on the grounds in question. We might call this the *comparative* claim.

Third, the apologist might assert that the Christian alone possesses adequate warrant for her views. Christianity as a whole, or the Christian take on issue *x*, is the *only* rational position one can take. We might call this the *imperative* claim.

I do believe that after the Second Coming, the situation of absolute rational clarity will obtain. The evidence that God exists, for example, or that Christ was resurrected, or that the Christian revelation is dependable as a guide to reality and to salvation, will be overwhelming, rendering every other position untenable. But I do not believe that this situation obtains today. It seems obvious to me (although not to others, and particularly not to some other apologists) that there are good grounds to claim that Buddhism is rational, or that naturalism is, and so on. So I recommend we consider whether we want to make the first or second sort of claim in any particular situation, while I agree it would be thrilling to make the third sort of claim and make it stick. [4]

Appeal to Subjective Experience

"Taste and see," the ancient Psalmist invited his audience (Psalm 34:8). "Try it for yourself," we might say today. A powerful apologetic appeal has been to one's intuitive sense of things, to one's immediate apprehension of spiritual reality.

Blaise Pascal, the great seventeenth-century scientist and public debater, believed that reason was a great gift. He drew on his considerable supply of that gift in many causes, from developing the barometer and early calculating machines to disputing over the nature of Christian doctrine and piety with the finest minds of his society. Yet Pascal himself recognized that "the heart has its reasons that reason does not know."[5] He did not mean anything sentimental by this oft-quoted statement. Instead, he meant that the inner self, the very core of a person, can apprehend the intrinsic validity of something or someone in a way not always open to rational analysis. Uneducated and unintelligent people, this great intellectual declared, can be more certain of the fundamental truths of our existence than the subtlest philosophers and most learned theologians. They are open to such truths, and God impresses them gladly on their hearts.

Pascal is famous for his own "night of fire" in which he experienced a life-changing mystical encounter with God: "not the God of the philosophers," he wrote, but "the God of Abraham, Isaac and Jacob." It would be to mistake Pascal's teaching, however, to suppose that he meant that only such overwhelming experiences count as "the heart's reasons." Instead, he meant something much broader than spiritual experience per se. He meant something more Romantic, we might say: something more intuitive, more wide ranging, in which the heart of a person simply grasps the truth of something or someone by encountering it without the aid of inferential reason.[6]

Søren Kierkegaard possessed of a brilliant intellect that he wielded in public disputations and learned books, nonetheless he also championed a view of apprehending truth, and especially truth about divine things, that was not based upon reason. Kierkegaard has been understood variously on this question, to be sure, but I think he meant that since religious truth is not just a matter of belief, but also of experience and all of life, it must be considered and embraced by the whole person: feelings, attitudes, and actions, as well as by the intellect. Repelled as he was by the arm's-length, formalistic religiosity of his fellow Danes, Kierkegaard emphasized the affective, experiential, and volitional dimensions by contrast—leading some to suppose that he despised reason entirely, despite his many and complex writings![7]

Learned Christian philosophers in our own time—notably Michael Polanyi, William Alston, and Alvin Plantinga—have sought to explain and justify the subjective, personal, and even mystical dimensions of human knowledge in the face of the rationalism that dominates intellectual life. They, too, paradoxically use highly sophisticated rational arguments to try to persuade their readers that there is more to learning about the world than solitary reason. Indeed, they defend "personal knowledge" (Polanyi), or "mystical perception" (Alston), or "basic beliefs" (Plantinga) as being at least as important, and perhaps even more fundamental, than the deliverances of reason per se. Moreover, when considered in the company of reason and tried out in the practice of life, such Christian experiences can strengthen the cumulative case, as it were, for the validity of Christian commitment.[8]

Alston is eloquent on this theme:

> The final test of the Christian scheme comes from trying it
> out in one's life, testing the promises the scheme tells us

God has made, following the way enjoined on us by the Church and seeing whether it leads to the new life of the Spirit. Admittedly, it is not always clear exactly what this involves; it is not always clear whether we are satisfying the conditions laid down for entering the kingdom; it is not always clear where we are at a given moment in our pilgrimage, whether, for example, an apparent setback or regression is a part of the master plan or a failure on our part. And then there is the inconvenient fact that not all members of the body of Christ agree as to just what is required and just how the payoff is to be construed. But with all this looseness and open texture, the fact remains that over the centuries countless Christians who have set out to follow the way have found in their lives that the promises of God have been fulfilled, that their lives have been different, not 100 percent of the time and not as quickly and as dramatically as they may have wished, but unmistakably and in the direction the tradition predicts.[9]

What the philosophers preach, many Christians gladly practice. "You ask me how I know he lives?" they sing. "He lives within my heart." One doesn't need to be an intellectual to testify to one's experience of God and the difference it has made. Moreover, Christians rightly emphasize that only a genuine spiritual encounter with God, facilitated by the Holy Spirit, can occasion genuine conversion. For such encounters all Christians pray—for themselves and for their neighbors. This approach has the further merit of avoiding the classic apologetic reductionism of narrowing Christianity down to a mere system of belief to which one should now assent, or to a subculture one should now join.

Some enthusiasts have gone so far, however, as to commend experiential apologetics as impervious to rational criticism. Indeed, many interpreters have seen the apologetics of Kant, Schleiermacher, and those who follow in their train exactly as attempting to shield Christianity from modern intellectual challenges by reducing its essence to spiritual experience and thus removing it to a safe, nonrational plane—immune to historical, scientific, and at least most philosophical criticism.[10] The same dynamic afflicts less sophisticated forms of Christianity as well, particularly in Pentecostal and charismatic communities and in some forms of Protestant fundamentalism and Roman Catholic pietism, as the mind and heart are split apart, contrary to Jesus' own command to love God with both. Thus this approach risks truncating Christianity in its own way, reducing it to an anti-intellectual, individualistic experientialism.

Nonetheless, this tradition of apologetics remains indisputably important. It puts emphasis where it belongs: on an actual, personal encounter with God at the most basic level of the human person. Any apologetic that ignores this dimension ignores too much of the Christian view of things.

There is yet an intrinsic limitation to this approach. What if your friend says, "Your experience might be wonderful, but how do you know it's based on anything outside your own head? How do you know it's not just wishful thinking?"

Or what if she says, "I can't agree to seek a similar experience, because I can't believe in a God who would permit so much suffering in the world *or* I don't believe Jesus was anything other than another great prophet *or* I don't think the Bible is anything other than another book of religious myths and ethics"?

Or what if she says, "My experience leads me to believe that this alternative religious or philosophical viewpoint is valid"?

Our neighbor then might need another kind of testimony, another kind of apologetic.

Appeal to Evidences and Reasons

Whether the famous "Five Proofs" of Thomas Aquinas in the thirteenth century, the compendium of evidences compiled by William Paley in his *Natural Theology* in the nineteenth century, or the bestselling *Evidence that Demands a Verdict* by Josh McDowell in the twentieth century, the combination of evidences and rational arguments is what most people think of when they think of apologetics.

I recognize that there has been considerable ink spilled over whether evidentialist or empiricist approaches are somehow superior to purely rationalistic ones. Sometimes this argument parallels the dispute over the relative merits of correspondence versus coherence theories of truth. But since this sort of discussion goes back at least as far as Descartes versus Locke and is really a discussion entirely within a modern framework to which all parties give assent, and since rationalist arguments clearly depend to a certain extent upon experience and no evidentialist can argue without using reason, I find the dispute rather unhelpful for apologetic purposes. Why not embrace and employ both, as far as they are useful? Thus I lump them together in this typology.[11]

In the light, however, of our previous discussion of pluralism and epistemology, it should now be clear that such an approach assumes that you share beliefs with your friend that point (somehow) to the virtues of Christianity—or, at least, to the validity of Christian claims versus claims to the contrary. *Which* beliefs are shared, of course, depends on the interlocutors involved. And if the requisite set of presuppositions is not in fact shared, the arguments cannot proceed. There is, in short, no "one size fits all" universal apologetic.

Apologists who work this vein often don't take this point into consideration. They thus are tempted to attribute resistance to their arguments either to stupidity (the audience *cannot* see the force of the argument, so I had better explain it more slowly and simply) or sinfulness (the audience *will* not grant the force of the argument, so I shall have to pray for them). It is possible in any apologetic situation, of course, that the audience truly is either insufficiently intelligent or insufficiently spiritual to agree with the apologist. But the epistemological reality of widely varying cognitive styles, worldviews, and so on can entail simply a barrier of unintelligibility that is not going to be breached by simpler explanations or more fervent intercessions.

Still, we *do* often share relevant common ground with various neighbors. Thus we can deploy various kinds of evidentialist or rationalist apologetics, but we should do so, in the light of postmodern cautions, with something less than triumphalist claims for their power. We should offer them as our best hypotheses so far, as probably true, and thus deserving of a good look by an interested party, rather than demanding a verdict from an overwhelmed inquirer.

So if your friend enjoys the quasi-mathematical precision of analytical philosophy (although not everyone, alas, finds this to their taste), you can argue over the philosophical problem of evil, perhaps with guidance from Alvin Plantinga. If your friend instead is open to the possibility of supernatural explanations of historical occurrences (while other friends might find this idea simply fantastic) and is genuinely interested in historical investigation (again, while many are not), you can argue, with the aid of William Lane Craig, for the historical fact of God raising Jesus from the dead. If your friend is a theist of some sort and simply has never encountered a solid presentation of the authenticity of the Bible as revelation, then set out the case for it in the company of a wide range of philosophical, theological, and biblical scholars—from N. T. Wright to Stephen Evans.[12]

The evidentialist and rationalist approach has the considerable merit of corresponding to the Christian conviction that there is evidence for the truth of Christianity all around us. We should not want to allow certain forms of postmodernism, fideism, mysticism, or other views to force us away from appreciating that there are in the world as we experience it, and in our conceptions of the world as we think about it, various elements that point to the truth of the gospel—however little we grasp of reality, and however much sin clouds our cognition. To the modest extent that we can appreciate the warrants available to us, we should receive them gladly and offer them to our neighbors.

Reason and experience can be grounds we do share with neighbors who otherwise have little use for Christianity. So we gladly exploit them to see if we can pry open the closed minds of our neighbors to the possibility of something more. Particularly with those of our neighbors who are secularists, or "hard-headed agnostics," or atheists, or naturalists—all those who trust primarily in what their senses and brains tell them is true—offering rational arguments can open the door to their considering Christianity seriously. As Jean Hampton testifies:

For reason is what these naturalists celebrate and it is the basis for any criticism of science that they will respect— that is, to the extent that a scientific theory loses its grounding in reason and allows bias, prejudice, and emotional commitments to influence the content of its theorizing, to that extent the naturalists themselves are committed to rejecting that theory. Hence, using reason to develop arguments for moral objectivism and certain religious tenets is a way to get a naturalist who is deeply committed to reason to listen to these arguments. Indeed, in my experience naturalists actually *will* listen to them, in ways that result in minds getting changed and new ideas getting formed.[13]

In this light, this approach also has the advantage of meeting the situation of some people who have particular, limited difficulties with the Christian religion. Perhaps they are inquirers or perhaps already Christians, but they are temporarily stymied by the difficulty of reconciling the doctrine of creation and the scientific theory of evolution; or are frustrated by the contradictory deliverances of modern biblical scholarship on the life of Christ; or are perplexed by Christian efforts to convert other people who seem just as spiritual and noble as anyone else. Such discrete problems sometimes can be cleared up with some straightforward explanation, evidence, and argument, and they should be.

Again, however, this approach is useful only if the apologist shares with her friend enough beliefs about evidence, arguments, and proof to demonstrate her case. Suppose, however, she is in conversation with a Hindu neighbor who does not believe that the world we experience is actually real. Suppose instead she is talking with an atheist friend who simply finds any explanation of creation or miracle or resurrection by divine action simply more incredible than any other naturalist alternative. Suppose she is disputing with a learned Muslim who believes that Christians are just badly confused about their own religion because they regrettably trust in a hopelessly corrupted Bible and a perversely distorted tradition—both of which need correction by the Qur'an. What if, that is, the conversation lacks sufficient common ground for the Christian's arguments to make sense to her neighbor?

Appeal to the Christian Worldview

Theologians in the Reformed tradition of Christianity typically have been especially leery of the forms of apologetics described so far. Because of their strong sense of the effects of sin upon us all, theologians as otherwise diverse as Cornelius Van Til and Karl Barth have been dubious that appeals either to subjective experience or to reason will be all that useful, except as God may graciously use them as means to touch and change the heart. Because of their strong sense of the corruption of all systems of thought that do not give God his proper place and therefore are fatally distorted, Reformed thinkers have suggested that only one sort of apologetics takes seriously enough the radical disjunction of Christianity and every other form of thought.

Now, one doesn't need to be a member of this tradition to appreciate that there are situations in which the difference and disagreement really are about fundamental matters, rather than about details within basically similar outlooks. Indeed, the Reformed emphasis does properly remind us of the basic Christian conviction that there really is a radical difference between giving glory to God and not doing so, and this difference does indeed work out into differences of worldviews.

Still, "ad hoc" or "piecemeal" apologetics of the evidentialist or rationalist sort can have a useful role to play as they deal with particular issues in dispute. And subjective experience is indubitably key for any authentic apprehension of the gospel. What this thrust can direct us toward, in fact, is a sort of global combination of these two approaches (although few would put it this way!). Christians invite their neighbors to line up their preferred philosophy of life over against the Christian religion and then decide which one, on the whole, comes away better in the comparison. For the record, we should note that Roman Catholic apologists—such as the nineteenth- and twentieth-century theologians Louis-Eugène Bautain, Maurice Blondel, and

Pierre Teilhard de Chardin—also have frequently engaged in this sort of apologetic precisely because of their tradition's parallel emphasis upon Christianity as an all-encompassing world-and-life view.[14]

This exercise is not all that easy to undertake. G. K. Chesterton once wrote, in a similar regard,

> It is very hard for a man to defend anything of which he is entirely convinced. It is comparatively easy when he is only partially convinced. He is partially convinced because he has found this or that proof of the thing, and he can expound it. But a man is not really convinced of a philosophic theory when he finds that something proves it. He is only really convinced when he finds that everything proves it. And the more converging reasons he finds pointing to this conviction, the more bewildered he is if asked suddenly to sum them up.
>
> Thus, if one asked an ordinary intelligent man, on the spur of the moment, "Why do you prefer civilization to savagery?" he would look wildly round at object after object, and would only be able to answer vaguely, "Why, there is that bookcase . . . and the coals in the coal-scuttle . . . and pianos . . . and policemen." The whole case for civilization is that the case for it is complex. It has done so many things. But that very multiplicity of proof which ought to make reply overwhelming makes reply impossible.
>
> There is, therefore, about all complete conviction a kind of huge helplessness.[15]

In some instances, however, this kind of exercise is what is required. We're asking our neighbor to consider the best alternative or alternatives within his horizon of plausibility, and then consider how well the Christian religion compares with them. How do things look from points-of-view A, B, and C? One hopes that one's neighbor will find the Christian viewpoint most satisfactory, as philosopher Brian Leftow did when he decided to convert from Judaism to Christianity: "If you see things as they are from the place where you're standing, you're standing in the right place."[16]

One of the advantages of this approach especially in postmodern times is that one does not have to posit a single starting point for each option. One does not, that is, have to begin with the deliverances of science, or the Bible, or common sense, or "what all right-thinking/ rational/educated/sensible people believe." The ideological playing field, so to speak, is level, with no particular rationality or philosophy occupying the high ground. One can begin anywhere one wants, with whatever presuppositions one likes, and then spin out a worldview as best one can.

This approach does not leave us helpless in a total relativism, however, as some fear it does. We then apply to the ideologies before us the three tests of truth in play: Which of the options appears to meet best the tests of coherence, correspondence, and pragmatic usefulness?

We can recall that choosing among horses, or cars, or jobs, or homes can be relatively easy if it is clear what each of these is *for*. So with religion it is crucial to keep clear that a religion is *for life*: It provides a map of reality and directions for making one's way in it. The fundamental question in such a comparison of worldviews, then, is just this: How does religion A or B or C help you make sense of life and negotiate it well?

Again, the apologist can work in either defensive or offensive mode, either simply maintaining a place for Christianity among plausible options, or going further to assert Christianity's superiority among the available options. Such comparative, critical discussion indeed can help to expose both weaknesses in other views and strengths in the Christian view: "How do you explain the natural world?" we can ask. "How do you explain the efficacy of science? How do you explain beauty and our sense of it? How do you explain altruism? How do you explain feelings of guilt and gratitude? How do you explain longings for, and beliefs in, immortality?"[17] A sufficiently broad range of questions, if not exhaustive, can serve to remind us that the religious choice, finally, is a choice of the best option of those available that fits the full range of pertinent evidence with the most coherence and most practical value. This exercise can keep discussions from too tight a focus upon this or that particular matter (science, say, or history, or morality) when really the issue is as large as the meaning of life itself.

The Christian who takes up this apologetic approach, however, must remember what we have discussed about our epistemological and spiritual limitations. Despite what the Christian may believe to be the evident superiority of Christianity in any such comparison, some people really will think that Buddhism, or hedonism, or nihilism makes more sense and suits them better. They will do so typically for a combination of reasons that fit two crucial facts: We think differently partly because we experience different aspects of reality (my part of Chicago is not your part of Chicago) and partly because we have different cognitive styles. We also think differently, however, because serious decisions are resolved by the whole person, not merely by the intellect, and my aesthetics, and ethics, and fears, and hopes are not the same as yours. There is always a blend of powerful intellectual, moral, spiritual, physical, sociological, and psychological, and other kinds of factors at work in assessing something as literally cosmic as religious options.

So we cannot count on any particular outcome in this exercise. We do not undertake it in the hope of convincing someone by overwhelming him or her with the superiority of the Christian religion. Instead, we do so in the hope of presenting our neighbor with a clear enough picture of the Christian religion that the Holy Spirit can find it useful to employ in his dialogue with the neighbor's heart.

A wise missionary friend of mine, Bob Brow, once memorably asked me, How does a jeweler convince a young couple to buy an expensive engagement ring? Brow's answer: He can talk about the glories of the diamond, invoke the "4 C's," and present certificates of quality. All this can be helpful. But what really makes the sale? Training a high-powered light on the diamond set against a black velvet cloth—and shutting up. The clients either fall in love with it or they don't.

In a sense, then, we cycle back to the first of the three approaches. At this global level, one either "sees" it or one doesn't. And whether one sees it or not depends, fundamentally, on whether one has eyes to see, eyes granted sight by the Holy Spirit of God.[18]

10

Guidelines for Apologetic Conversation

In these last two chapters, it's time to get specific about a way to engage in apologetics that is consistent with the observations and principles set out so far. This chapter offers a dozen guidelines for apologetic conversation. The following chapter offers examples from the history of Christian mission that go beyond the typical theological and philosophical discussion that most of us associate with apologetics.

FIRST, LISTEN AND UNDERSTAND

In a rapidly pluralizing and already widely diverse society, we must speak to people as they are, in their variety, not just trot out our "20 surefire answers to 20 common questions." To do so will mean listening and learning so that we can truly understand people's needs and pressure points, and the common ground on which we can then communicate what we have to give them in Christ's name.

We will listen and understand much better if we deliberately cultivate sympathy for our neighbor. Indeed, it is doubtful that we will listen well, or understand much, if we do not sympathize. A primary condition of historical and social scientific study is analytical sympathy. The observer of another person, or tribe, or civilization must aim to be sufficiently open to the plausibility of the subject's way of life that she can finally say, "Here is the world, according to them, and I can see how they can believe and act accordingly." I recognize now in my own process of historical research that I do not really understand whom I am studying if I continue to say to myself,

"How can someone possibly think *that?*" As long as the other person seems alien, literally nonhuman to us, we cannot presume to know who he is, how he thinks, what he wants, and how he is going to be reached best in conversation.

We should have sympathy also because of our recognition of the immensity of conversion. We literally are talking about "God, the world, and everything" when we are discussing the gospel. Ernest Becker puts the point most sharply:

> Each person nourishes his immortality in the ideology of self-perpetuation to which he gives his allegiance; this gives his life the only abiding significance it can have. No wonder men go into rage over fine points of belief: if your adversary wins the argument about truth, *you die*. Your immortality system has been shown to be fallible; your life becomes fallible.[1]

So we ought to sympathize with our neighbor when he questions, hesitates, and even resists our well-meaning efforts to prod him along the trajectory of faith. (We ought to be all the more sympathetic as we remember to our shame how we ourselves resist God's efforts to assist us along the same path toward complete conversion.)

Third, we should have sympathy as we appreciate the strangeness of Christianity. It is, let's be honest, an odd religion. When I teach the world's religions in a survey course, there are two religions I least look forward to explaining: Hinduism and Christianity. Hinduism is incredibly complex, with its multitude of traditions that seem to have virtually nothing in common beyond the generic Indian framework of the cycles of birth, death, and rebirth according to karmic justice; respect for the tradition of the ancient scriptures, the Vedas; and preservation of the social hierarchy of caste. Hindus are monists, monotheists, dualists, tritheists, polytheists, and more. Hinduism, that is, virtually defies the kind of elementary description required in an introductory course.

Christianity almost defies it, too, but not because of such basic diversity. Instead, most Christians, despite the thousands of denominations that have arisen over the centuries, agree on the basic tenets and practices of the Christian religion. The problem is that some of those tenets are literally inexplicable, such as how God can be both three and one in the Trinity; or how this God became truly human in Jesus Christ; or how the suffering and dying of this one individual on the Cross can possibly atone for the sins of the world. Why in the world would anyone believe such a set of propositions when even the greatest theologians do not claim to understand them?

Furthermore, those tenets or practices that we *can* explain a little better, such as prayer, put one in a position whose awkwardness seems not to have occurred to many Christians. We earnestly commend the practice of prayer to others, and we claim its validity in our own lives. Yet consider the following ordinary claim about Christian prayer: "I talked to Jesus this morning." Now substitute the name of any other figure of the past: "I talked to Julius Caesar this morning" or "I talked to Confucius this morning" or "I talked to Napoleon this morning." The stark reality is that either Christian prayer really is communicating with a resurrected being, as our theology claims, or we are *psychotic*—literally delusional (as Freud, for one, thought we were).

The familiarity Christians enjoy for our own religion, especially given its privileged place in North American culture, keeps us from seeing, in the light of other worldviews, how weird it really is. Yet, as G. K. Chesterton advises,

> I think it a piece of plain justice to all the unbelievers to insist upon the audacity of the act of faith that is demanded of them. I willingly and warmly agree that it is, in itself, a suggestion to which we might expect even the brain of the believer to reel, when he realized his own belief.[2]

I sat in a pew on a Sunday afternoon recently, awaiting the start of my sons' piano recital. Their teacher had rented a church for the occasion, and the families of her pupils—some of whom had apparently not been in a church for some time, if ever—were staring at the images all around them. As a father and daughter behind me began to remark on the pictures they saw, I was struck again by this basic principle of Christianity's strangeness.

"Isn't Christianity weird?" the teenager said to her father in a stage whisper. "I mean, all these pictures of a dead guy on a cross. All this blood and suffering and stuff."

"Yeah," her father replied with a nervous chuckle. "It's gross, isn't it? I don't get it."

Figuring out why this man and his daughter don't get it is the task of the listening Christian friend. This friend works hard to understand them. She has learned enough theology and psychology to help her discern what are their fundamental concerns and needs. And only then does she try to offer what she can as a gift to help them move toward this religion that currently seems to them so bizarre.

OFFER, DON'T DEMAND

A friend of mine and I were enjoying our biweekly lunch together at a restaurant near the university campus. My friend worked as a staff member for a well-known student ministry. He told me, as we awaited dessert, that he was flying out that evening to commence a series of lectures at several universities in Ontario. He then leaned toward me and said, "You and I both know that no matter what subject I speak on, I'm going to be asked about why I think Christianity is better than all of the other religions. You're a professor of religions. So tell me."

I copied his body language and tone, and replied, "Sure. I'll just hook up these cables I always have with me, and I'll upload my Ph.D. into your head while we have our cake."

Having once again proven I am a smart-aleck, I then attempted the more challenging task of proving also that I can be helpful.

"Roger," I said, "you don't have to answer that question. You're entirely off the hook."

"How so?" he asked dubiously.

"First," I said, "I agree that this question comes up all the time nowadays. But to answer that question in the usual sense of 'empirically based comparison,' let's realize that you would have to (a) have a Ph.D. in the study of each of the world's religions in order to feel confident that you understood it properly as an analytical outsider, and yet no one has time to do that; (b) convert to each of them in turn, so as to understand it properly as a sympathetic insider, and yet it's impossible to convert at will like this, let alone have time to experience each religion in turn; and (c) evaluate the religions according to a universally valid, objective standard, and yet no human being can possibly be sure that he or she either has such a standard or is evaluating with exact fairness according to it."

"So what can I say? I *do* think Christianity is the best religion of all."

"That brings up my second point. You may think that, and I agree that you have good reason to think that. But you don't *know* that 'Christianity is the best religion' in the sense that you have weighed all the options and Christianity came out on top. So what kind of a claim can you make?"

"Well," Roger replied, "I can say how my life has been changed since my conversion."

"Yes, that's good: It's sincere, personal, and true. What else?"

"I can give the various reasons I have for believing that Christianity isn't just wishful thinking, or some other psychological or sociological crutch. I can tell people why I think it is actually true and in fact the truest understanding of God there is."

"Good. After all, the Christian faith does claim a supreme uniqueness for Jesus' person and work that renders secondary every other religious figure and tradition. And Jesus called us to make disciples throughout the world—'of every creature.' So the implication is clear that following Christ is better than following anyone or anything else, and Christianity offers grounds to believe those claims that millions have found convincing. Anything else?"

"I suppose I can point out why I'm not attracted to other religions or philosophies that I know something about. But I really don't know much about them, so I'm not sure how much I should say."

"Why say anything at all, beyond what you know? Just give people what you have, not what you don't have. And especially don't bother sweating over answering a question that *no one* can answer in any final, comprehensive way."

Roger and I, having thus dispensed with the vexing question of religious pluralism, turned our attention appropriately to enjoying the rest of our cake.

Lest anyone wonder whether there is some sleight-of-hand here that illicitly lets Christians off one of the most important apologetical "hooks" of our time, let's consider two supporting testimonies from two apparently quite distinct sources: the New Testament, and postmodern epistemology.

Let's hear first from what tradition tells us is the voice of the wise old Apostle John, as he provides a model of the sort of testimony an early Christian could offer to the religiously pluralistic Roman world:

> We declare to you what was from the beginning, what we have heard, what we have seen with our eyes, what we have looked at and touched with our hands, concerning the word of life—this life was revealed, and we have seen it and testify to it, and declare to you the eternal life that was with the Father and was revealed to us—we declare to you what we have seen and heard . . . (I John 1:1–3)

John did not pretend to have catalogued the religious and philosophical options of the ancient world and to have judged Christianity somehow superior to all the others. Instead, he offered what he had: what he knew from what he had experienced, thought about, and lived. He offered it with conviction, yes, because it had changed his life and seemed overwhelmingly true, good, and beautiful. But he didn't do anything more than offer what he had.[3]

Postmodernity concurs. No human being knows anything for certain. So we don't argue with our neighbors as if we have "evidence that *demands* a verdict," so to speak. Instead, no matter what the question—whether it is about religious pluralism, or Christianity and science, or sexism, or whatever it might—we simply offer what reasons and stories and aspirations we have. As Rodney Clapp puts it, such an approach means "proposing rather than imposing Christ."[4] And we do so in the hope that one or more of offerings will be interesting and helpful to our neighbors as they make their way toward their destiny.

Such a guideline does not, to be sure, get us off the hook of our proper responsibility. If we are called to engage neighbors who are, like ourselves, scientifically interested and trained, then we ought to be prepared to offer a scientifically plausible account of our faith. If we work among artists, we should have an aesthetic apologetic at hand. Because we cannot know everything and prove our case with certainty does not mean we can be content to know little and demonstrate even less.

All this means, instead, is that we are called simply to do the best we can do given the actual limitations of the situation, including our own. We need not try to answer questions that no one can answer, or even questions that we ourselves could never answer. We are to offer what we have, and hope it is a good gift.

TAKE IT SERIOUSLY

Blaise Pascal, one of Christianity's most impressive apologists and one of the great intellects of the seventeenth century, was vexed not so much by his sworn opponents, as by those who cared nothing about the great issues of life.

> Being unable to cure death, wretchedness and ignorance, men have decided, in order to be happy, not to think about such things.
> We run heedlessly into the abyss after putting something in front of us to stop us from seeing it.[5]

In the next century, the brilliant Swiss preacher John Fletcher—born Jean de la Fléchère—suggested that the two greatest hindrances to authentic Christianity were a widespread lack of knowledge of the true gospel and an equally widespread lack of self-knowledge: "They know not (or rather, feel not) that they are blind, naked, leprous, helpless and condemned—that all their works can make no atonement, and that nothing they can do will fit them for heaven."[6]

John Newton agreed: "It is a proof of the weakness and disorder of their minds that they are capable of being satisfied with such trifles."[7]

It might be worth pointing out, before proceeding, that the neighbor who is giving you a particularly rough ride about the Christian religion is at least paying you, and it, the compliment of noticing Christianity. Many of our neighbors, like Pascal's and Fletcher's and Newton's, slight the whole issue by deflecting it with a casual remark or ignoring it entirely.

If we are indeed going to discuss the fundamental questions of existence, it is worth being clear with our neighbors that we should do so seriously. This requirement is especially necessary in this cultural moment that prizes ironic, self-possessed distance over genuine, vulnerable engagement. "Serious" does not mean "humorless," of course, but rather a sense of appropriateness, treating these matters with the respect they deserve. Several particular guidelines follow.

First, agree to concentrate on one matter at a time, avoiding the tactic of shifting ground as an attempt to avoid any sort of decision, let alone resolution.

An engineering student once brought his best friend, a buddy since childhood, to hear a Christian apologist speak. The engineer, himself a Christian, had been frustrated and embarrassed to the point of helplessness by his quick-thinking, fast-talking agnostic friend, who was majoring in philosophy. When the apologist began to engage the young philosopher, the apologist fairly quickly and adroitly answered his first two questions. The student then seemed to switch gears, speaking more quickly and frequently interrupting the apologist before he could conclude his response. It became clear that the student was, with increasingly obvious desperation, trying to keep the apologist at bay by switching to another question as soon as it looked like the question at hand might actually be answered.

The apologist brought a halt to the conversation and simply said, "I used to enjoy this sort of thing. But I don't anymore. If you'd like to actually see if there might be answers to your questions, then let's keep talking. But if you just want a verbal fencing match, I've got to move on."

The student was momentarily stunned. But, to his credit, he realized he had been unfaithful to his own sense of intellectual integrity, and he resumed the conversation in a much more patient and open way.

Second, declare the strengths, limitations, and weaknesses of one's own warrants. If an argument seems very strong, go ahead and advertise it as such and see how it fares with your friend. But if it isn't as strong, or perhaps you have no good argument at all to advance in the face of a particular question, then say so. The quest in such conversation is to uncover as much as possible that is of value in what we jointly bring to it, not merely to score points.

Part of declaring honestly what we have to offer is to be careful not to exaggerate our status or sources. Professional apologists, alas, often set bad examples here, as they (or their publicists) exaggerate their academic accomplishments. Those who like to list themselves as "Dr." when the title is honorary, or who claim "further studies" at some distinguished university when no degree was earned, perhaps do not exactly lie. But they can mislead audiences regarding their actual scholarly authority and open themselves up to damaging charges of grandiosity at the least.

G. K. Chesterton similarly warns against invoking academic authority to impress a lay audience when such sources would not, in fact, pass muster with genuine scholars. Yet I have heard or read Christian apologists cite out-of-date materials, quote dubious authorities, and fail to address pressing questions because they either had not done their homework or were cynically ignoring countervailing warrants. As Chesterton scathingly writes, "The sophist plays to the gallery, as he did in ancient Greece. He appeals to the ignorant, especially when he appeals to the learned."[8] Each of us must be careful not to claim more for our information and ideas, let alone for ourselves, than we ought.

Third, the complement to this principle is to show genuine appreciation of the other person's good points. Indeed, one must be begin by being able to summarize accurately the other person's position—to that person's satisfaction—or one cannot proceed with serious conversation. Then you can find that some of your neighbor's points are enlightening to you as you consider them, and are genuine gifts from your friend to you. Indeed, it may be that you will have to ponder just how your friend could make such a good point at the expense of your Christian view of things, and you may conclude that it is your Christian view that needs to change—probably in part, but perhaps as a whole. That's the risk we run in any serious intellectual exchange.[9] Furthermore, by acknowledging the virtues in another position, you are setting an appropriate example for your friend whom you hope, after all, will give due consideration to the points *you* want to raise. In short, this is simply the principle of fair play, and it is crucial to genuine dialogue.

Fourth, practice sincere modesty to the extent that you are willing to utter the three words that many apologists loathe the most: "*I don't know*." Surely your friend should not expect the world religion of Christianity to depend upon *your* ability to defend it in every respect! (If he acts that way, perhaps it is a sign that he is interested instead merely in upsetting or embarrassing you, or breaking off the conversation about religion, or some other ulterior motive.) And we ourselves should be exposed as arrogant if we were to take upon our shoulders, Atlas-like, the defense of the church universal.

Richard John Neuhaus, himself no intellectual shrinking violet, cautions us:

> Few things have contributed so powerfully to the unbelief of the modern and postmodern world as the pretension of Christians to know more than we do. In reaction to unwarranted claims of knowledge certain and complete, modern rationalists constructed their religion of scientism, and postmoderns, in reaction to both, claim to know that nothing can be known.[10]

Indeed, the admission of limitation, or even ignorance about *some* things, can be winsome, especially in the postmodern situation. (To be sure, there isn't much that is attractive to most of our neighbors about utter ignorance, so we should be able to answer *some* of their questions!) While some of our neighbors do indeed seem to enjoy being dazzled by an "Answer Man," many instead distrust a know-it-all, someone who presumes to have the great story that explains all the others.

A friend of mine is a highly competent professional apologist. Trained in philosophy and theology, he is a well-published scholar and a well-polished speaker. Having enjoyed a number of his public presentations, however, I once suggested something to him over coffee that seemed to completely perplex him.

"Jim," I said (no, this isn't his real name), "I'm afraid you come across sometimes as a bit, well, mechanical. You know, you're so well prepared and you look so good and you smile so well—you're almost *shiny*. You act like you're still captain of your college debate team, afraid to lose any points at all in case the tide turns later and you'll need those points to come out on top at the end. You're kind of a RoboApologist who seems to just mow down the opposition. And I know you're a much more pleasant, much more humble guy than sometimes comes across."

"Well," he said, rather dumbfounded that anyone would suggest he *shouldn't* try to win all the arguments in an exchange. "What do you suggest?"

I smiled and replied, "How about writing the words 'I don't know' into your script—even if you think you *do* know! Just a few, you know, to look humble to the audience as a fellow seeker!"

He grinned at my cynical advice to tell lies in the cause of Christian apologetics.

"Well, okay," I continued. "Don't lie. But how about honestly admitting when not everything goes your way in one of these debates?"

Such conversations demand that participants submit their egos and even their particular causes to the transcendent objective of following the truth where it leads, to honor the highest morality wherever it appears, and to delight in the most glorious beauty however it emerges. Otherwise, we are not truly engaging each other's ideas: We are simply battling.

We demonstrate our partnership with our friend sometimes precisely in the admission of personal weakness and struggle. "Yes, that bothers me, too," can mean much more than "No problem: Here's the answer to that one." One powerful example particularly comes to mind in regard to C. S. Lewis. Over and over again, people have commented that Lewis's analytical treatment of the question of God and evil, *The Problem of Pain*, doesn't speak to them nearly as importantly as does his later reflections on his wife's death, *A Grief Observed*.[11] Some go so far as to suggest that Lewis wrote the second book differently from the way he did the first because now, at last, he had truly suffered and could speak from experience—this about a man who, before he wrote the former book, had lost his mother as a child, fought and was injured in World War I, and cared daily for his best friend's widow and his own alcoholic brother! The difference is that, for whatever reason, Lewis adopts a much more personal voice in the second book than in the first, and that while both books have much to offer the inquirer into this question, the second appeals to so many because of the personal connection formed by Lewis's admission of personal struggle.[12]

Finally, there is the larger question of the integrity of thought and life. It is true that losing a particular argument doesn't entail that one instantly convert to the winning side. Perhaps another day will reveal the losing side to triumph. Perhaps a third option will emerge.

Refusal to be moved at all, however, by how the conversation ends up needs to be examined honestly. It is worth asking oneself and one's neighbor, "Are you willing to live by what you acknowledge to be true—or, at least, the best answer you have found to date? If not, then why not?"

I remember hearing a brilliant philosophical colleague present a dazzling presentation titled "Rationality Isn't a Rational Concept." It was a tour de force of radical postmodernism, full of wit, wordplay, and penetrating logic. When his hour-long lecture concluded, he handled the first few questions with aplomb. And then someone he knew raised his hand and spoke:

"Richard," he said, "you are the father of an 11-year-old son, are you not?"

"Yes," the philosopher replied.

"Do you raise him to believe that there is no sense to things, that morality is arbitrary, and that we really don't know anything about reality?"

The normally glib professor was quiet for a solid minute. The audience was frozen with concentration upon him as he stared into the middle distance. Finally, he focused upon the questioner and said, "No, I don't. When he's older, we can talk about these things. I do believe them as a philosopher. But I can't live this way, and especially not as a father."

Richard might look like the fall guy in this illustration, but I want to commend him instead for recognizing the situation he was in. Intellectual seriousness demands that when we discuss religious questions, we are willing to take them on as what they actually are, full of moral and aesthetic implication, and not just diverting intellectual puzzles. Richard couldn't resolve his personal incoherence, but he had the considerable courage to admit there was a problem.

One way, in fact, to cut through what might be mere intellectual swordplay can be to ask the following question, a question I learned from a wise pastor who is himself a skilled and compassionate apologist: "If I can indeed answer this question to your satisfaction, are you prepared to then commit yourself to Christ?" Again, someone might well reply in the negative without contradiction or hypocrisy: Why should she convert on the spot just because someone has answered a difficult religious inquiry? At some point, though, it is worth everyone's while to consider what really are the key questions and obstacles at stake, the impediments that truly do stand in the way of someone moving forward in faith.

TEACH FIRST, PREACH SECOND

For the sake of making this point clear, I am radicalizing the difference between teaching and preaching in terms of "information" versus "motivation." In all good teaching, of course, there are elements of inspiration and exhortation, and in all good preaching, there is the affirmation of truth that anchors and drives the call to passionate obedience. For the moment, though, my point is simply that the task of informing our neighbors about the basics of Christianity is necessary before we undertake the task of persuading them about Christianity's virtues.

The well-known English preacher and author John R. W. Stott testifies to this crucial principle. His best-selling introduction to the Christian faith, *Basic Christianity*, no longer serves well as an evangelistic or apologetical book, he says, because the target audience has changed so much:

> The British students for whom it was primarily written in the fifties still had a veneer of theism. One could assume belief in God; the deity of Jesus was the issue. Today one can assume nothing; one would need to begin elsewhere. . . . Because *Basic Christianity*, even in its second edition, still takes too much for granted, it is now used less as an evangelistic book than as a primer for new converts.[13]

It is foolish to try to convince people of the truth and importance of something they don't first recognize or understand. In the light of the widespread ignorance and misunderstanding of Christianity in our society, we must not assume that our neighbors know *anything* important about the Christian faith. We must assume, furthermore, that they probably *do* have ideas about Christianity that are negative: whether stereotypes that need correcting; sins committed by Christians that need putting in context, without excusing them; or the truly "offensive" aspects of the gospel that need clarifying and defending.

So we need to make sure in our conversation that we are talking about the same things when we are discussing such loaded and variously understood terms as *religion*, *spirituality*, *God*, *Jesus*, *Christianity*, *faith*, and so on. Asking our companion, in fact, what he means by such terms is often a good way to open up a discussion of the heart of the Christian faith, since we can hear him out, see what he thinks, and then respond with whatever correction or complement would be helpful in that moment. We shall have to be prepared, of course, to defend our definitions as something more than merely our own preferences. Otherwise, we'll be left with the stalemate of "You have your view and I have mine." Knowing the basic creeds of the Church as well as key passages of the Bible will be essential to help our friends see that these terms have definitions that are not merely up to each individual to devise: The Christian Church in its central documents has actually set out some universal definitions. One is free to posit one's own definition of these terms, of course, just as one is free to define *hippopotamus* as "a long-necked mammal living on the veldt that eats leaves from tall trees." As Chesterton remarked in a similar vein, however, if one wants to *communicate*, one must use words as the community understands them.[14] And the definition of *Christianity*, as of *giraffe* and *hippopotamus*, is already fixed by centuries of common use.

This point seems to need making quite often nowadays in a society that prides itself on fostering individual freedom sometimes to absurd lengths—literally, in this case, to the freedom to use words any way one likes. It is not the most admirable feature of certain forms of postmodernism that they remind us of Humpty Dumpty in *Alice through the Looking Glass*:

> "When *I* use a word," Humpty Dumpty said, in a rather scornful tone, "it means just what I choose it to mean—neither more nor less."
>
> "The question is," said Alice, "whether you *can* make words mean so many different things."
>
> "The question is," said Humpty Dumpty, "which is to be master—that's all."[15]

It is not sheer individualism, however, that is always at fault here. Many of our neighbors simply don't know any better. In a culture that is becoming less and less familiar with Christianity, more and more people will need to know, and many will want to know, just why Christians celebrate this holiday in this manner, or what makes this particular event significant for them—in the same way our neighbors increasingly show interest in the other cultures and religions in our midst.

In fact, we can use a more attractive "voice" in our public dissemination of Christian convictions if we are primarily offering them as information to our neighbors in the true spirit of multiculturalism:

"This is what it is we believe and do, and this is whom we worship. We just want to keep the public record straight, and to offer to you as our neighbors the best fruit of our particular tradition." All we're doing is explaining ourselves to our fellow citizens in a multi-culturally appropriate way—just as our Jewish friends do, and our Muslim friends do, and our feminist friends do, and our homosexual friends do.

We will do this best, of course, if we are actually in touch with people's areas of ignorance and curiosity. Yet many Christians are in touch only with other Christians, and usually only those of their own stripe. Ironically, this is a particular occupational hazard of seminary students, clergy, theological professors, and other full-time "religious" people. So how can we become more aware of the pressing questions and interests of our neighbors so as to acquaint them better with authentic Christianity?

To "read the culture," one does—perhaps for the first time in a programmatic way—what any good anthropologist, or marketer (!), or newcomer does: One reads, and watches, and listens, and partici-pates, and befriends. And one does so by paying attention particu-larly to the culture of the neighbors one is called to reach. No one, nowadays, can pretend to understand "contemporary culture" in its entirety and complexity. There are too many subcultures, too many TV channels, too many Internet sites, too many gathering places, and too many different languages for anyone to claim knowledge of it all. So we do not have to try to know it all.

Instead, we should pay attention to the main things to which our neighbors pay most attention. What are the information and enter-tainment media they enjoy the most? Is it MTV, the *New York Times*, or *Cosmopolitan* magazine? Who are the heroes, the symbols of good-ness and success, and who are the villains, the symbols of evil and failure? Movie stars, entrepreneurs, soldiers, athletes, politicians, activists, drug dealers—who personifies the values of this subcul-ture? Where are the gathering places and what are the community activities of this group? Ethnic community clubs? Raves? "Neigh-borhood Watch" or PTA meetings?

Most of us will not have to watch a great deal of the relevant television, or read much of the relevant literature, or visit many of the social centers to get useful background knowledge of the neighbors in view. To be sure, the more different this group is from our own, the greater the likelihood of misunderstanding or simply not understanding, and only a sustained and critical engagement could provide us with deep understanding. Still, to begin to connect with our neighbors in an intelligible and interesting way, we do not have to spend all of our time "studying their culture," so to speak. A relatively little effort, aimed at the key points of communication and community, can open up their world to us in suggestive and helpful ways. And if one can get access to survey data (such as is available in Canada from Statistics Canada) on one's locale—whether its religious makeup, its economic profile, its demographics regarding ethnicity, family structures, and so on—one can put one's impressions of the neighborhood into a useful broad context.

Clearly, pastors and other leaders will have professional use for this kind of information. It remains to be seen whether seminaries will train such leaders in how to find and use such information domestically in the way that seminaries are accustomed to training cross-cultural missionaries to do so. Still, all of us can benefit from information that explains and clarifies the impressions and intuitions that we each might have about where and among whom we live.[16]

Christians also can access Internet websites and periodicals that specialize in interpreting our culture, and particular aspects of it, from a Christian viewpoint. Mass-market movies (arguably the last remaining common ground in our society—what else can you count on being able to talk about at a party with strangers?)—recently published books, television shows, popular music, and so on all now receive critical scrutiny—some of it thoughtful and useful—from various Christian groups and individuals. Christian bookstores are notorious for the superficiality of their offerings, but many valiantly continue to stock substantial literature, and managers of such stores as well as literate pastors sometimes can be good guides to the few books you'll have time to read to help orient you to your neighbors and our times. Finally, continuing education programs offered by schools of Christian higher education can give us a considerable boost, particularly through summer offerings that many of us can make time to attend.

We simply cannot assume that most people think as we do, know what we do, and care about what matters to us. The pluralism all around us requires Christians to study, to devote ourselves regularly to the analysis of our culture and to a clear understanding of our own religion. We need to do so both as individuals and as churches in Christian education programs that include adults as well as children. We must undertake the sometimes laborious, but necessary, task of building bridges of understanding before we can encourage our neighbors to cross over.

DO AS LITTLE AS POSSIBLE:
A MINIMALIST APPROACH

A crucial mistake in apologetics is to distract and confuse an audience with arguments that either are not central to the issue at hand or somehow inappropriate to the audience's interests and limitations. C. S. Lewis, who was arguably the most effective and most popular apologist of the twentieth century, occasionally allowed himself a remark or illustration that really was not vital to his main discussion, and therefore risked diverting or even alienating his readers. For example, in his best-read apologetic *Mere Christianity*, Lewis intrepidly discusses gender roles in Christian marriage. He decides that there must be a "head" in terms of resolving disagreements between the spouses (itself a highly problematic idea, whether logically, politically, or theologically!). When he asks, then, why it should be the man, he responds:

> Well, firstly, is there any very serious wish that it should be the woman? As I have said, I am not married myself, but as far as I can see, even a woman who wants to be the head of her own house does not usually admire the same state of

things when she finds it going on next door. . . . There must be something unnatural about the rule of wives over husbands, because the wives themselves are half ashamed of it and despise the husbands whom they rule.

It is not at all clear what Lewis is doing here in the thicket of gender relations when he is supposed to be explaining "mere Christianity," but he boldly adds another reason for his championing men as heads of households:

The relations of the family to the outer world . . . must depend, in the last resort, upon the man, because he always ought to be, and usually is, much more just to the outsiders. A woman is primarily fighting for her own children and husband against the rest of the world.[17]

Many people continue to read and enjoy this book without pausing over such things. My point is not to take issue with them or with Lewis on gender questions. It is instead to indicate simply that many others in our day would be so offended by such a passage that it would put them off the whole book. And the most regrettable truth here is that Lewis's views of gender and marriage are simply not part of "mere Christianity" and could therefore have been kept out of sight without cost to his main line of argument.

Christian apologists therefore ought to stick to the main points we want to make and try hard to avoid needless offense. Lawyers will "stipulate" to various facts in a case to avoid spending time proving things upon which everyone involved in the case already agrees. Christians certainly should follow a similar practice in conversation, but should go beyond it by prudently bracketing out everything that is not central to the case to be made. "For the sake of argument, let's agree that p," we might say, as philosophers sometimes do. "I'm not saying that I think p is the case. I'm just saying that I don't think we need to sort it out in order to get done what we have agreed is the most important task before us. Okay?"

In short, concede all you can, affirm all you can, and argue as little as you need to. Economy of discussion is important both intellectually and rhetorically.

For example, if one is trying to argue for the general historical reliability of the New Testament portraits of Jesus, one need not wrangle over whether every detail is exactly correct and harmonious with every other detail. "How many angels were at Jesus' empty tomb?" (a matter over which the gospels do not speak with one voice) is not nearly as significant as the agreement *that* the tomb was empty (a matter over which, significantly, they are entirely agreed).

To be sure, if enough anomalies crop up, the entire argument may be crushed by particulars. One cannot simply ignore inconvenient warrants to the contrary. But if only a few emerge along the way, and none central to the argument, it is hardly responsible to get stuck on them and miss the larger patterns. A good sense of judgment is required, therefore, as to what are the main issues and how to marshal the best warrants on their behalf without either dismissing or overemphasizing matters of lesser importance.

OFFER AS MUCH AS POSSIBLE:
A MAXIMALIST APPROACH

The corollary principle to the foregoing is to offer all the warrants you think might interest your friend. Who knows what might speak to the central issue in his heart? Only God knows. So our role is to be simply as useful as possible by deploying what we believe—through listening and understanding our friend—might be of help to him.

We cannot master the entire apologetic repertoire, of course. But we are not called, any of us, to do so. You are a particular individual, as I am, and each of us has a particular calling to serve particular people. The warrants you or I can most naturally articulate and most persuasively offer therefore will fall normally within a zone in keeping with our identity and calling.

I am not called to offer much help to professional athletes, since there is little that is distinctive in their world to which I, as a decidedly nongifted athlete, can authoritatively or even relevantly speak. You may not be called to serve highly educated representatives of other religions in point-by-point philosophical, theological, and historical argumentation. You can leave that sort of thing to those who are trained in it. But if you happen to find yourself next to someone who is a superior athlete or remarkable intellectual, God may nonetheless call you to witness to him or her precisely on the basis of our generic humanity. All of us experience disappointment, disillusionment, confusion, fear, joy, hope, and love. Any vital Christian can bear witness, in her life and in her words, about the relevance of Jesus Christ to those universally important realities.

Still, within whatever is our natural zone of life and thought, we ought to try to offer all we can to our neighbors. Indeed, as Pascal suggests, we should do all we can to "make [the faith] attractive, make good people wish it were true, and then show that it is."[18]

We can begin by articulating our own faith as thoroughly as we can—to consider, that is, just what we do believe and how we really ought to live. While we do so, we ought to beware of narrow apologetic approaches that imply a narrowness in you, your friend, or your religion. Some people can offer only an appeal to religious experience, which can imply that there is little more to Christianity than yet another interesting experience in a world full of interesting experiences. Other people argue for their faith in a highly rationalistic way, thereby running the risk of implying that Christianity is simply an answer to an intellectual problem, rather than an entire way of life. Still others commend the Christian religion on the basis of its noble morality, thus perhaps implying that Christianity is simply an impressive way of decently governing our behavior, and not also a metaphysic, a community, and supremely a relationship of love for God and his world.

So let us consider all of the reasons we find Christianity to be true, good, and beautiful. Let us enjoy listing the blessings we have received in following Christ. Let us work to articulate the virtues of our religion in accurate and winsome speech, and to embody them in lives of integrity. We represent a generous God, and we need to be generous especially in our offering our friends everything we can offer to help them along their particular paths.

At the same time, let us offer the warrants we have with appropriate circumspection. Some apologists through the centuries have erred by hitching their argumentative wagons to the shooting stars of passing intellectual trends. Plato was "in" for a good long while in the early church and well into medieval times, but apologetics based on one or another sort of Platonism ran into difficulty when the fashion shifted to Aristotle in the high Middle Ages. Aristotelian arguments looked much less impressive when the fashion shifted again to Enlightenment modes. Apologetics that try to show that current scientific theory and discovery support Christian teaching end up forlorn when science moves in a different direction. Apologists who have a good sense of intellectual history thus properly advance any arguments based on current intellectual findings with considerable care—not allowing themselves to be impressed too deeply either with the approval or the disapproval of "contemporary scholarship" regarding the great truths of the gospel.[19]

We also recognize that other religions and ideologies have their own warrants to offer and that many of these warrants overlap with ours. To select three such warrants with a heritage reaching back to the early church: Christianity has been a great missionary success, winning many converts around the world—but so have Islam and Buddhism; Christianity displays a morality that many people have found admirable, but so do most of the great religions and a number of secular philosophies; Christianity offers a rich intellectual tradition, but so do many alternatives.

It is not true that every claim made by Christian apologetics can be paralleled by others. One of the ongoing tasks of apologetics is precisely to clarify what is and isn't parallel in the offerings of contemporary religious options.[20] The point here simply is that Christians must beware of claiming too much as we try to offer all we can to our neighbors. We should indeed offer all we can, but all we *legitimately* can.

CLARIFY WHAT ARE THE MOST IMPORTANT QUESTIONS

Jesus' encounter with the Samaritan woman at the well of Sychar (John 4) has often been remarked as richly illustrative of how we should encounter our neighbors with the gospel. There are other fruitful ways of understanding this story, but let's note a few aspects of it for our present purposes.

> So he came to a Samaritan city called Sychar, near the plot of ground that Jacob had given to his son Joseph. Jacob's well was there, and Jesus, tired out by his journey, was sitting by the well. It was about noon.
>
> A Samaritan woman came to draw water, and Jesus said to her, "Give me a drink."(His disciples had gone to the city to buy food.)
>
> The Samaritan woman said to him, "How is it that you, a Jew, ask a drink of me, a woman of Samaria?" (Jews do not share things in common with Samaritans.) (4–9)

Jesus reaches out to this neighbor, heedless of the social taboos that would separate him from her. Gender, race, and religion are all set aside in the surpassing interest of sharing the gospel.

> Jesus answered her, "If you knew the gift of God, and who it is that is saying to you, 'Give me a drink,' you would have asked him, and he would have given you living water."
>
> The woman said to him, "Sir, you have no bucket, and the well is deep. Where do you get that living water? Are you greater than our ancestor Jacob, who gave us the well, and with his sons and his flocks drank from it?"
>
> Jesus said to her, "Everyone who drinks of this water will be thirsty again, but those who drink of the water that I will give them will never be thirsty. The water that I will give will become in them a spring of water gushing up to eternal life."
>
> The woman said to him, "Sir, give me this water, so that I may never be thirsty or have to keep coming here to draw water."
>
> Jesus said to her, "Go, call your husband, and come back."
>
> The woman answered him, "I have no husband."

Jesus said to her, "You are right in saying, 'I have no husband'; for you have had five husbands, and the one you have now is not your husband. What you have said is true!"

The woman said to him, "Sir, I see that you are a prophet." (10–19)

Jesus intrigues the woman by using the immediate context to stimulate interest in eternal matters. The concrete particulars of drinking water at noon on a hot day become the materials by which Jesus constructs a message of everlasting refreshment. His startling request for water from a Samaritan woman becomes an even more surprising discussion of water that quenches thirst forever.

Then when Jesus prompts the woman regarding a sore point in her life, she answers with integrity, and he commends her. All seems to be going well. But the woman now shows that Jesus' incisive comments have cut through her comfort. She apparently tries to divert the conversation away from herself and toward, of all things, matters of religious and ethnic controversy. It is indeed instructive for us that secondary questions of religion can be used as a shield against primary ones.

> "Our ancestors worshiped on this mountain, but you say that the place where people must worship is in Jerusalem."
>
> Jesus said to her, "Woman, believe me, the hour is coming when you will worship the Father neither on this mountain nor in Jerusalem. You worship what you do not know; we worship what we know, for salvation is from the Jews. But the hour is coming, and is now here, when the true worshipers will worship the Father in spirit and truth, for the Father seeks such as these to worship him. God is spirit, and those who worship him must worship in spirit and truth." (20–24)

Jesus accepts that the Samaritan and Jewish traditions are different, and he briefly underlines the superiority of the Jewish claim. But he radically undercuts the whole matter by placing it in the eschatological context of the inbreaking Kingdom of God. For in Jesus' own career it has become clear that such distinctions do not matter. What matters is the heart of each person: whether he or she will worship God sincerely. Thus Jesus returns the focus of the conversation implicitly to the woman's own heart, to her attitude toward God who requires her allegiance "in spirit and truth."

She then cleverly picks up on the eschatological theme itself and uses it as a delaying tactic.

> The woman said to him, "I know that Messiah is coming" (who is called Christ). "When he comes, he will proclaim all things to us." (25)

In other words, she says, we can defer this rather searching matter for that wonderful (and conveniently distant) day when Messiah will come. Then we can focus upon such challenging religious questions.

Jesus finally bores in to the fundamental reality of her situation:

> Jesus said to her, "I am he, the one who is speaking to you." (26)

To her great credit, the woman drops her defenses. Indeed, she even leaves her water jar behind and goes back to her town, saying to her own neighbors, "Come and see a man who told me everything I have ever done! He cannot be the Messiah, can he?" (29). Many of the townspeople come to faith because of her testimony alone. Others come out and ask Jesus to stay with them, which he does for two days, and many more believe when they meet him.

To arrive at the questions that matter most, it is crucial that apologists understand two sets of questions and then balance them properly: what our neighbors are asking and what the gospel asks of them. Apologists who focus too much on the questions being asked by their neighbors tend to let those questions entirely frame the conversation. Important parts of the gospel, alas, then can be bracketed out because they have not occurred to our neighbors and would surprise them, or they do not appeal to our neighbors and would offend them. Any apologetic method that tries simply to correlate Christian revelation with the categories and questions of the day—

whether the work of the second-century apologists, or of the early modern rationalists (such as Toland and Locke), or certain liberal twentieth-century theologians (such as Bultmann and Tillich)—runs the terrible risk of cutting Christianity to fit non-Christian presuppositions and interests.

Indeed, even scrupulously orthodox apologetics in the very act of arguing for Christianity in the common language of contemporary rational discourse can dangerously reduce Christianity. Even if the Christian view prevails, the Christianity so vindicated can be merely a set of bloodless assertions to which people are asked to assent, rather than remaining a path of life in the train of the Lord Jesus Christ to which people are called to commit themselves, body and soul.[21]

For example, in Western and Eastern civilizations, there are strong currents of thought that describe the essential human problem as ignorance, rather than as sin. We just don't know enough; we're confused; if only we could see things clearly, then all would be well. Christianity agrees that we have, indeed, confused and ignorant minds, but it attributes that serious problem to the even more fundamental pathology of our deranged hearts. We do not think well primarily because we do not will aright. Apologetics that merely speaks, then, to the mind as if people merely lack correct information will never speak to the central problem that the gospel says we face.

Christian proclamation that emphasizes the gospel tradition with too little regard for contemporary concerns, however, risks the charge of throwing the gospel at our neighbors "like a stone"—in the powerful indictment of Karl Barth's work rendered by Tillich.[22] We may congratulate ourselves on our fidelity, but our neighbors will look back at us with incomprehension and ingratitude—*and it will be our fault*. Jesus took pains to speak intelligibly and attractively to those who wanted to hear him and his divine message. He used whatever common ground was available to instruct and appeal to his audiences. So ought we to extend ourselves to meet our neighbors, to come alongside them and offer them what we can in the way they can best appropriate it.

Such a gift, however, may lie in our reframing the issue at hand, posing a different question from the one on the table, challenging our friends to look at things another way. Blaise Pascal constantly remarks in his apologetic reflections, the *Pensées*, that our neighbors prefer to be distracted especially from the sober fact of death and the possibility of eternal judgment. We do them a kindness, he insists, when we rouse them from their self-imposed stupor. We give them the gift they need when we acquaint them with the realities of their situation and the possibilities of their destiny. This is a theme common to much of Kierkegaard's anguished writing, and C. S. Lewis echoed this counsel when he advised Christians that "it is our painful duty to wake the world from an enchantment."[23]

Many evangelical Christians are familiar with the recommendation of twentieth-century apologist Francis Schaeffer to "tear the roof off" of our neighbor's intellectual and spiritual domicile to let in the driving rain of reality, to expose them to the true implications of their delusion. This act must be undertaken "with tears," as Schaeffer recommended, since it violently bereaves people of what shelter they have enjoyed heretofore.[24] To do so, one would have to be confident that the Holy Spirit had placed one in just the right relationship and at just the right moment to engage in such drastic intervention. To continue Schaeffer's metaphor, most of us, instead, more commonly will have opportunity to dislodge a shingle or two, or offer a concerned opinion about the structural integrity of the roof rather than undertake its wholesale demolition. This striking image, however, does graphically reinforce the priority of gospel categories and the need, at times, for us to help our neighbors come to grips with those categories when they might initially prefer to keep things safely in less threatening terms.

When I began research toward a book on the problem of God and evil, I began with the project of theodicy in view. That is, I began with the project of explaining God's ways to human beings such that Providence, and especially Providence's relationship with evil, would be made both clear and consistent with the teaching that God is not only all-powerful but all-good. So I read the Bible with this project in mind. I read all I could of the great philosophers and theologians on this subject through the ages. And I read numerous novelists, poets, biographers, and autobiographers who had wrestled with the issues as well.

I found some ideas that were truly enlightening and helpful on this dark, terrible subject. But the most important discovery I made was that I was asking the wrong question. "Can we figure out what God is doing in order to satisfy ourselves that God is both powerful and good?" is not the fundamental question of religious inquiry. The fundamental question is, "Whether we can figure it all out or not, do we have grounds to trust God anyway?" Answering the former question can forever remain a mere intellectual pursuit, a great dispute of everlasting point and counterpoint. Answering the latter question confronts us with the existential question of trusting God: the question that really matters, right now.[25]

A group of businessmen had met early on Friday mornings for a year to discuss religious questions with their Christian host in his office's boardroom. One day, after two hours of serious conversation about the claims of Christ in a world of religious alternatives, one of the participants breezily remarked, "Well, I guess we're just going in circles, aren't we? We're like those little wind-up cars that bounce into walls and furniture, back up, and keep on running around without actually getting anywhere."

There were rueful grunts of assent from several quarters, and the meeting seemed to be breaking up without much progress having been made.

Then another member spoke up. "I refuse to believe that we have just talked for two hours for nothing. We *have* clarified some of the issues. We *have* seen that Jesus is not like any other religious leader and that Christianity makes claims for him that no other religion makes for its founder. So we really have come to a new place, the place of deciding whether these claims are true."

"Yeah," replied the first speaker. "But since we can't ever know for sure about these things, we're just stuck, aren't we?"

His friend replied, "We are in fact deciding all the time. When we leave this building and go to work in a few minutes, we are going to live by *some* religion, by *some* worldview with particular values and not others. We can't claim to be absolutely certain about that worldview, either, and yet we're living our entire life according to it. So it's bogus to say that we can't accept Christianity until we have every question answered, every doubt removed, and every argument squarely in place. The only thing any of us can do is look at what we think we know and then make the best decision we can on that basis."

He looked around at the rest of the group. "We are not going around in circles unless we are simply refusing to drive straight ahead."

This kind of confrontation can happen helpfully only when there is sufficient trust, goodwill, and respect among the participants, of course. But this exchange, I have been told by several of the members of this group, struck them as important and constructive. No one converted on the spot, to be sure. But the defensive efforts to keep the gospel claims at bay were overcome by this refocusing on the fundamental questions, as Jesus overcame the diversions of the woman at the well.

Focusing on the most fundamental issue of all—as Jesus did in that encounter at Sychar—is the subject of the next guideline.

FOCUS ON JESUS

Since the heart of God's revelation of himself is the figure of Jesus Christ, and since the heart of the Christian story of salvation is the career of Jesus Christ, Christian apologetics—like everything else in the Christian religion, from worship to mission, from prayer to almsgiving—rightly focuses on Jesus Christ. The heart of the Christian religion is personal relationship with Jesus Christ, and it is this to which apologists hope to point their neighbors. Whenever we can, therefore, we aim to focus on Jesus Christ: not on Christian metaphysics, or Christian morals, or Christian church membership—although each of these can help the case as Christ is truly known through them.

We don't talk about the Christian religion, furthermore, as a means to something else: social cohesion, perhaps, or moral uplift, or personal satisfaction. People should become Christians primarily because they want to follow Jesus as the Way, the Truth, and the Life (John 14:6). Christianity can be judged as beneficial in this or that way, yes, but Christianity matters fundamentally because it is *true*. And it is true—in a way no other religion is—precisely as it puts Jesus Christ at its center where he belongs.[26]

So we leave aside secondary matters if we can. To put this another way, and perhaps too simply, we should avoid the popular apologetic zones located at the beginning and end of the Bible—"creation versus evolution" at the one end, and apocalyptic themes of judgment and rescue, heaven and hell, at the other—if our neighbor is willing to look with us at the heart of the Bible: the gospel testimony to Jesus. And we should eschew airy abstractions about "spirituality-in-general," "religion-in-general," "God-in-general," and even "Christianity-in-general" if we can possibly move to consider the specific, particular, and supremely important person of Jesus Christ.

Philip has encountered this rabbi named Jesus and has become convinced that he is the promised Messiah. He goes to his friend Nathanael to urge him toward faith in Jesus as well. But Nathanael is comfortable right where he is and is dubious of Philip's enthusiasm for this preacher from the no-account town of Nazareth. As he famously remarks, "Can anything good come out of Nazareth?" (John 1:46).

Philip's response is instructive. He replies, "Well, there are at least fourteen good reasons to believe that something good can come from Nazareth. Let's begin with historical precedents; move on to strictly logical matters; and conclude with some mystical intuitions I and others have had."

No, Philip does not respond that way. Instead, he simply says to the inert Nathanael, "Come and see."

Jesus himself rarely called on people to buy his whole package on the spot. Instead, his typical invitation was, "Come, follow me." Walk with me, listen to me, watch me, and see what sense you make of me—and what sense I might make of you. As in his dialogue with the woman at the well, every important question eventually comes round to this: What do you think of Jesus?

To say this, however, is to appear to cheat a bit. It is one thing for Philip to challenge Nathanael to see for himself when Jesus is only a short distance away. What good does it do, two thousand years later and Jesus dead and gone, to encourage people to "focus on Jesus" nowadays? Yes, it's fine to focus upon Jesus as a subject matter, in the sense that the biblical and theological testimony about him is fundamental to Christian thought and life. But apologetically what difference does it make to insist on focusing upon Jesus?

There are at least two respects in which we can focus on Jesus apologetically. The first is, indeed, intellectually. Various apologetic problems change when referred to the subject of Jesus. The importance of some questions diminishes. Does it ultimately matter whether science and Christianity are in easy harmony with each other? Does the fate of the world, or even a single human life, rest on the archaeological verification of biblical history? These questions, to be sure, can impede a person's willingness to take the Christian package seriously, and thus they deserve serious answers. Remembering the figure of Jesus and his significance for revelation and salvation, however, puts them properly into less-than-ultimate perspective.

Other questions can be radically changed by remembering to include Jesus in their consideration. The problem of God and evil, for one, changes dramatically when the discussion changes to "God-as-presented-in-Jesus and evil." One might, for instance, be quite willing to imagine a Supreme Being who is loftily indifferent to human suffering. But can anyone imagine Jesus so impassive?[27]

The question of Christianity and other religions also takes on a different color when it shifts to "Jesus and other religious leaders." Christianity may look more or less like other world religions in many generic respects: Christianity offers salvation, as do others; Christianity teaches high moral values, as do others; Christianity encourages regard for the neighbor, as do others. But Jesus himself does not look like every other religious leader. No other such figure is said to be God Incarnate; no other suffers for the sins of the world; no other rises from the dead as the firstborn of a general resurrection to come; and so on.[28] (To be sure, Gotama Buddha doesn't look quite like anyone else, either; nor does Muhammad or Lao-Tse.

"Mere uniqueness" isn't especially interesting or important. What ultimately matters is whether these special claims about Jesus, or anyone else, are *true*.) The point here is that as one examines the personalities and careers of these quite varied leaders, it becomes more and more difficult to easily maintain that all religions ultimately amount to the same thing and that it doesn't matter whom you follow. Apologists therefore will want to focus upon the claims Christians have made about Jesus, rather than abstractions about religion, theism, or even Christianity. The particular claims about Jesus lie at the heart of the matter.

Christian apologetics, however, wants to encourage our neighbors to go beyond discussion of Jesus to actual encounter with him. They want people to "come and see," to "come and follow." Yet Jesus is, indeed, dead and gone—even as Christians affirm that he is also resurrected, ascended, and coming again. What about this interim time when he is simply not apparent?

It is true, as Rudolph Otto observed early in the twentieth century, that modern seekers actually have considerable advantages over first-century disciples: There is an entire Bible to read; two thousand years of Christian reflection to consider; millions of Christian testimonies to explore; and the record of the Church itself through the ages. Aside from immediate personal contact, those investigating Christianity have many more resources at their disposal than perhaps anyone else in history.[29]

The question of immediate personal contact is nonetheless crucial, however. So consider that Jesus' disciples got to know who Jesus was by listening to him, and watching him, and traveling with him, and working with him. That means, literally, that they were in proximity to, and paid attention to, his body. Just as you and I get to know each other, the disciples never had direct access to Jesus' mind and heart. They got to know him only as he mediated himself to them through the life of his body.

The New Testament makes one of its more astounding pronouncements when it declares that the Christian Church is metaphorically the Body of Christ. One crucial claim implied therein is that people today can indeed listen to Jesus, and watch Jesus, and hang around Jesus by listening to, and watching, and hanging around *Christians*—each Christian as an individual, yes, but especially Christians in our life together as congregations. And just as the Holy Spirit cultivated faith in the hearts of the disciples as they observed Jesus in the first century, so the Holy Spirit cultivates faith in the hearts of people today who walk in company with the Christian Church.

This principle requires our churches therefore to be our partners in apologetics. Inviting people to come to church to see for themselves is a great way to move beyond the "I say/you say" deadlock of personal discussion. But if our friends do finally pay a visit and the congregation itself has little to offer, if the church is not in fact living a life that reflects the life of Jesus, then what else can we do? I believe, frankly, that the generally dismal state of the churches in the West (not universally dismal, thank God!) continues to be the single most important factor in the difficulty we face as apologists.

It is also true, however, that those same churches, when they truly live out the Christian ideals of faith, truth, hope, and especially love, are also among the very best arguments in favor of Christianity's claims. And some churches are just that. As Stanley Hauerwas and William Willimon put it, "Epistemologically, there is no substitute for 'saints'—palpable, personal examples of the Christian faith."[30]

Philosopher William Alston speaks of his own return to faith in terms worth quoting at length:

> It was primarily a process of responding to a call, of being drawn into a community, into a way of life. . . . I found God as a reality in my life through finding a community of faith and being drawn into it. That's where the message was being proclaimed, and if I had not been able to see, eventually, that He Who was being proclaimed was Himself at work in those proclamations and in those proclaimers, I would, no doubt, have continued to turn a deaf ear.
>
> . . . I am as keenly aware as anyone of the many failings of institutionalized Christianity. . . . Nevertheless, the new life of the Spirit is being lived there, and my experience, for

what it is worth, confirms the New Testament picture of the new life as essentially a life lived in the community of the faithful.[31]

The experience of encountering a group of otherwise ordinary people in which the Christian faith is taken for granted as true and life-giving powerfully helps it to make sense to newcomers. In such communities, Christianity becomes plausible because it is lived with integrity. As Jesus promised, "By this everyone will know that you are my disciples, if you have love for one another" (John 13:35; see also Matthew 5:16; I Peter 2:12; 3:15–16).

Such communities become "plausibility places," zones in which the obstacles to faith can seem smaller or even irrelevant in the face of such authentic commitment. This particular phenomenon of plausibility, to be sure, is true of any attractive religious community. So it makes good sociological sense, as well as spiritual sense, to invite our neighbors in to meet Jesus Christ in the company of the church.

READ THE BIBLE

Apologists often have to talk about the Bible before they can invite people to read it. Some of our neighbors doubt its wisdom because of what they suppose is its conflict with science: "Darwin has disproved the Bible" is a common way of putting this misconception.[32] Others reject it because of its purported sexism: from its almost exclusively masculine language for a God who is not male, to its accounts of male leadership and status from cover to cover, to its apparent support for gender hierarchy in both Old and New Testaments. Still others have read the deliverances of the Jesus Seminar and other critics of the Bible's historical reliability, and wonder how much they can believe when they read some of the extraordinary stories the Bible contains. Some of our neighbors don't see why they should read *any* ancient literature to deal with contemporary problems. Their counterparts don't see why they should read *this* collection of religious writings when there are so many others now easily available from the world's religions from which to choose. So there is a lot on the apologetic agenda when it comes to this crucial resource of the Christian religion.

Suppose, however, we can indeed invite our friend to read the Bible—read it alone, read it with us, read it at church. Then we should! Many Christians, in fact, seem reluctant even to suggest Bible reading to their friends for fear, perhaps, that they will be seen as "pushing too hard." Yet students of any religion know that reading the primary text of a religion is a necessary part of one's acquaintance with it. So of course we should recommend Bible reading.

We do so also on theological grounds. Christians believe that God has specially inspired the Bible and continues to bless people through it in a way God seems not to do so regularly through any other writing. Indeed, God's Holy Spirit characteristically impresses the truth of the Bible on people's minds such that they just *believe* it to be the very Word of God. I have become convinced that no set of deductive proofs or inductive arguments go very far in establishing the Bible's status as divine revelation. People come to believe that the Bible is the Word of God by encountering it and then simply *seeing* that it is such. (Thomas Aquinas and John Calvin described and defended this phenomenon in the language of their day; philosopher Alvin Plantinga has done so in our own.[33])

The Bible isn't magic, to be sure. Reading it won't necessarily help anyone spiritually, let alone cause her to be convinced of its divine provenance. The Word of God comes to each of us through the Bible as the Holy Spirit uses it to communicate with us. If one resists the Holy Spirit, the Bible remains a closed book to that person, whether she is a casual reader or a professional scholar. But the Christian can offer to put it before an inquiring friend and help her to appropriate its benefits more and more. What else happens is, as in other dimensions of the larger project of conversion, a matter between the Holy Spirit and that friend.

The Bible's own variegation is a help in all this, by the way. As we take seriously the specific peculiarities of each audience, we have in the Bible a diverse library to meet different tastes and needs. One audience prefers history; another is moved more deeply by poetry;

yet another enjoys straightforward theological discourse. Consider just nine books of the Bible—Genesis, Ezra, Psalms, Proverbs, Song of Solomon, Isaiah, John's Gospel, Romans, and Revelation—and one faces a dazzling array of literary riches. Wise Christians guide their audiences to the parts of the Bible most immediately resonant with their need.

The Christian apologist thus should try to *quote* Scripture from time to time as a natural touchstone of Christian discourse (we will, therefore, have to develop the disappearing art of memorization in order to do so!). She should also *refer* to Scripture, again as the benchmark by which representations of the Christian religion are validated. And she should try to get her friend to *read* Scripture for himself, to open himself up to whatever light God would give him in that encounter.

PRAY WITHOUT CEASING

If we have agreed that the Holy Spirit is the primary agent of conversion; if we have agreed that his guidance is essential to us as we question, listen to, and care for our neighbor; if we have agreed that our neighbors will receive the gifts we offer only as their hearts are drawn by the Holy Spirit; and if we have agreed therefore that apologetics can be useful only if it is undertaken with these principles in mind; then we must pray.

If we remember the reality of sin: how it confuses and distracts the mind; how it distorts the sense of what is beautiful and good; how it attracts us to evil and repels us from good; how it urges us away from obedience and love toward God; how it afflicts, therefore, both apologist and neighbor potentially even to the subversion of the relationship; then we must pray.

If we recognize that potent media are employed by commercial and political interests to entice people to spend their money and time in worldly ways; if we acknowledge that influential individuals—family, friends, lovers, employers—may have their own reasons for keeping our neighbors from advancing in authentic faith; if we discern that there are malevolent spiritual powers at work to retard and corrupt the work of God's kingdom; then we must pray.[34]

Ora et labora —"pray and work"—was the motto of the medieval monks, and it should be the motto of every Christian. Prayer offers us several benefits as we seek to cooperate with God in the work of apologetics:

- Power: the power to think hard and well when we are engaged in apologetics; to listen carefully to our neighbors; to discern what is truly at stake; to speak an apt and useful word; and to offer what other resources we can in love to meet that neighbor's need.
- Poise: to keep focused on the needs of the other and avoid defensiveness, irritation, inappropriate attraction, and other complications and distractions; to take time to deliberate properly before speaking; and to know when to quit, to know when it is time for a break and adjourn the conversation for another time.
- Perspective: to recognize that God is with me; to reinforce that Christ is the focus; to remember that the Holy Spirit is the agent of conversion, not me; and to recall that I don't know, and cannot know, how this conversation is supposed to go, according to God's own agenda, so I am only to do my best to love my neighbor and leave the ultimate results with him.
- Positive feelings: self-giving care; genuine sympathy and even affection; sturdy loyalty to God and the Church; and other "affections" that orient us properly to the task at hand.

If we see apologetics for what it is—an aspect of Christian witness that cannot accomplish much on its own but can be used by God to affect our neighbor's eternal transformation—then we must pray. So the advice of lawyer-turned-preacher E. M. Bounds (1835–1913), the great teacher of prayer:

> No learning can make up for the failure to pray. No earnestness, no diligence, no study, no gifts will supply its lack.
> Talking to men for God is a great thing, but talking to God for men is greater still.

> Without this unction on the preacher the gospel has no more power to propagate itself than any other system of truth. . . . Without the unction, God is absent, and the gospel is left to the low and unsatisfactory forces that the ingenuity, interest, or talents of men can devise to enforce and project its doctrines.[35]

Let's remember, too, to ask Christian friends to pray for us. Each day is an opportunity to demonstrate the light and love of Christ in all sorts of ways. We dare not take it up without the support of Christian brothers and sisters who love us, who care about our work, and who bear us up before God in prayer.

REMEMBER *PROCESS* AS WELL AS *CRISIS*

Having spent a little while considering prayer, let us now transit smoothly to our next subject: hockey.

One of the mistakes even skilled hockey players sometimes make is to try to shoot the puck hard, rather than shoot it quickly. In particular, when a puck arrives on a player's stick and he is in scoring position, some players wind up to shoot the puck with maximum velocity (a "slap shot"). Yet the best scorers know that only rarely do such shots succeed. Most often, the successful shot is the quick flick of the wrist that fires the puck at the goal with minimum set-up time. "Just get it on the net and get it there quickly" is the heart of scoring wisdom.

The moral here for apologists is simple: Don't try to overwhelm; take the opportunity you're given.

For those unfortunates who are bereft of hockey knowledge and thus are struggling to grasp the deep implications of the previous illustration, let us turn to another sporting analogy, this time from baseball.

A few players can make a living trying to hit home runs. Most players, however, even in the big leagues, wisely try to "hit for average." They try to get on base any way they can. Indeed, were most players to try to hit home runs each time, they would simply increase their number of strikeouts as they wildly swing and miss.

Furthermore, baseball can ask players literally to "sacrifice" their individual success for the good of the team: through bunts that likely won't get the batter on base but will help a teammate move from one base to another; through "taking a strike" that the player might otherwise have tried to hit, in order to let a teammate attempt to steal a base; and through the aptly named "sacrifice fly ball" that might turn out to be a home run, but usually will instead be a guaranteed "out" for the batter while allowing a teammate to advance a base or two.

The moral here for apologists is like unto the first: Don't try to do it all yourself; just try to contribute to the team effort.

The Bible says that Christians are "God's coworkers" in his great project of cosmic shalom (1 Corinthians 3:9). This phrase does not mean that Christ is our "resource person" to provide us with what we need to perform our individual tasks so much as it says that Christ is himself the primary "doer" of the task and we are his assistants. When it comes to anything important in life as a Christian, and particularly in apologetic conversation that aims to benefit the neighbor, we remember this cardinal principle: You can't do it all, no matter what you do, so don't try! We are part of the Church, which itself is only one corporate player in God's great mission of global peacemaking. We must do just what we each can do, and trust the rest of the Church and God himself to do their parts as well.

A different angle on this point is worth considering. It would be irrational for your friend to rest his personal decision about the world religion of Christianity entirely on whether you happen to be able to defend it to his satisfaction. There are so many other resources for him to access if he really wanted to learn and assess Christianity in a responsibly thorough way. It therefore is equally irrational for you to think the same way, as if it is all up to you. You are there, in that situation, to do something, but not everything. So the question is simply this: What is it that you can do to help your neighbor?

Consider our hapless hockey and baseball players once again. If they reach beyond their ability, trying to shoot the puck *through* the goaltender or swinging for the fences every time, they will be grace-less failures. Rodney Clapp warns us about this problem in much of our Christian witness:

> Much of our difficulty in being Christians is due to awk-wardness, a deficiency of skill in deploying our heartfelt dis-positions—in more than one sense, a lack of gracefulness. . . . And so our fumbling attempts at love come off as intrusive or maudlin. Our desire for peace becomes bland toleration or an overwhelming enforcement of our own will and way.[36]

By all means let us stretch ourselves to improve our skills in the arts of Christian living, including apologetics. But let us also work within our limitations and do what we actually can do, rather than forfeit opportunities for some considerable success in God's work by des-perately trying to do it all. Sensitivity, aptness, precision, gentleness—none of these important qualities will mark our witness if we simply aim to overwhelm by brute force, even if the force is kindly meant.

It helps to think about all of this in terms of *process*, especially over against the emphasis on *crisis* in some forms of popular evange-lism. Yes, at any given moment, someone might be encountering the Holy Spirit in a true moment of *krisis*, a true moment of decision, from which she will continue on one path or another with everlast-ing consequences. But we cannot know whether such a moment is now upon our neighbor. So we must not act as if we do know it is, and press for an ultimate decision as if we could be sure that this moment is indeed a crisis moment. Such knowledge and action are, again, the province and prerogative of the Holy Spirit of God. And our exces-sive pressure might well harden our friend against us and our mes-sage, rather than help them forward.

Our task, instead, is to contribute what we can as our neighbor makes her way along. And we should do so with the long view in mind, remembering that no matter how literally critical this mo-ment may be for her, she is still embarked, as are we all, on a lifetime of transition.[37]

A few considerations emerge from this basic point. First, let us cultivate sympathy once again for our neighbor. Simply because we happen to be enthusiastically convinced of the merits of Christian faith, we cannot expect her to throw over her own worldview without considerable effort. It is entirely rational, after all, *not* to abandon one's "paradigm" at the first sign of difficulty, or even after multiple signs, if that view of things has commended itself with significant warrants in the past. And let us also turn the tables to recognize that *you* aren't about to convert on the spot if she happens to get the better of the argument, are you?

(Apologists would do well to keep this reality in mind before they scorn members of their audience for not immediately giving in to their putatively superior arguments. It is one thing to challenge a neighbor to reconsider her position in the light of a particular discussion. It is another thing—an odious thing—simply to pronounce her intellectually or morally deficient for not immediately granting the superiority of our views.)

A second consideration should encourage apologists to trust God to govern such encounters and make something good of them—no matter what. An experienced TV producer once greeted me after I had taped an apologetical debate and stepped off the set. I was discouraged because I felt I had not always been clear or cogent. She said, "Don't ever judge your performance by how you feel when you finish. Wait to see the tape. You're never as bad, or as good, as you first think you are."

A friend of C. S. Lewis heard him speak during the Second World War to servicemen. He writes:

> I know that he had a profound effect. It was neither striking nor startling; he was not that kind of person. There were, so to speak, no headlines in the morning papers, but as a result of hearing Lewis there were handfuls of young people all gaining quite new concepts of how they fitted into the life that immediately lay before them. I had this [information] direct from a friend who commanded a large training school.[38]

So we should resist the temptation to "over-read" the apparent results of our apologetic encounters—whether bad *or* good. Experienced pastors have learned that they cannot accurately assess the quality of their sermons. Authors are notoriously bad judges of what is best and worst in their own writing. None of us can know fully what effects we are having on other people at any time, much less the effect on them wrought by God's Spirit as he uses our work to further his hidden work of transformation. In fact, as David Clark reminds us, "Overheard conversations persuade effectively."[39] The most influenced audience in an exchange may not be your direct interlocutor, but someone sitting at the next table or in the seat behind.

Third, we must heed Jesus' warning not to cast pearls before swine (Matthew 7:6). This teaching, harsh as it sounds, reminds us that many of our neighbors currently care no more for the gospel truths than pigs care for indigestible jewels. If they can't consume it, they don't want it. And they will resent the one who wastes their time by offering it. As we have opportunity to do good to these neighbors, we certainly should do it—and then move on. Indeed, we must be especially careful not to expend too many of our resources of time, money, creativity, and concern on those who disregard them while neglecting those who would receive them gladly.

Everyone needs the gospel, of course. I do not mean we should neglect everyone who happens to be rich, glamorous, and apparently blithely indifferent to spiritual matters. Many outwardly successful people have become successful in these terms precisely because they are driven by unsatisfied longings that can be filled only by God. I do mean, however, that we must not chase after the attention of those who, to all appearances, really do not care, and particularly not at the expense of those who do. Prayerful discernment will be crucial in sorting out our priorities here. We do what we can for any neighbor on the occasion God presents to us and trust God and the rest of the Church to carry on from there.

Fourth, to allow our neighbors to process things according to their own timeline is to recognize their true freedom before God. This allowance is not to be granted condescendingly, but humbly, as we recognize that each person works things out before God in his own time and his own way. God grants each of us this privilege, and it is arrogant for the eager apologist to try to take command of a situation that is progressing under the providence of God.[40]

Finally, we should not feel it imperative to share some sort of digest of the Gospel in every conversation that touches on spiritual things.[41] Some churches have so instilled the urgency of evangelism in their members that those members feel a terrible pressure to force a basic presentation of "salvation" into every conversation even remotely connected to religious matters. One prominent campus Christian organization until quite recently required all of its speakers to conclude every public lecture on any subject with at least a five-minute presentation of its version of the gospel message.

Such wrenching of discourse in order to "get the gospel across" gets across a lot of debatable theology instead: (a) This gospel digest is all that really matters; (b) what we have just been talking about is actually only a setup for this all-important message; (c) if you were to die immediately after this conversation and not have heard this message and accepted it immediately and sincerely, you would go to hell; and so on.[42] We mean well, but by such a jarring, disjunctive move, we can end up merely undercutting the good that we have accomplished in the preceding conversation. And we will do so forgetting that the Gospels portray Jesus himself as *never* offering a terse, formulaic summary of his message.[43]

We must not reduce God's mission to the world, and to our neighbor in particular, simply to the verbal articulation of a gospel digest for them to accept or reject. Instead, let us love our neighbors as best we can each moment according to the need and opportunity. And let us then trust "the team" to pick it up from there and carry God's plan forward.

WORSHIP GOD

The idea of worship perhaps seems out of place in considering apologetics. To be called upon to worship God *while* engaging in apologetics can appear almost comical: "I'm trying to talk to someone right now, Lord. Can I sing or pray a little later?"

Worship, however, is precisely the context in which faithful apologetics must be undertaken. Fundamentally, worship is giving

God his due. So when we recognize the very limited place our efforts have in God's great program of conversion, and we act accordingly, we give God worship. When we treat another person respectfully as someone whom God loves, even if he happens to annoy us or challenge us, we give God worship. When we pray as we listen to our neighbor, asking the Holy Spirit to help us hear this person well, we give God worship. When we hesitate before we reply, pausing to collect ourselves before God and to reaffirm our trust in him to help us, we give God worship. And when we part from our neighbor and commend him to God's care in our absence, we give God worship.

We worship God also in our recognition of the Scriptural principle that God can use our weakness and even our failure to advance his purposes. And we are willing to acquiesce in such humiliation for the greater good of God's kingdom. Sometimes it is salutary especially for us professional talkers to fail: to run out of responses, to have to admit our limitations, to agree with our neighbor that we, too, don't have all the answers and perhaps can never answer this or that question. We worship God as we remember that the conversation that really counts is *not* the one between us and our friend, but between our friend and the Holy Spirit.

Finally, the nexus of worship and apologetics should be considered from yet another angle. Inviting our neighbor to witness Christians at worship—whether in a church service, in a home fellowship group, or even in an individual's personal devotional time—can itself be apologetical. Our neighbor can see and hear us as we encounter God, and in such a situation can perhaps understand better just why we believe as we do, and act as we do, and love as we do. Some churches nowadays hold meetings for seekers that are largely evacuated of worship so as to let the visitors feel most comfortable. There is, indeed, some good sense in such projects. But seekers also can be invited to witness the richest possible worship, to come alongside us as we enjoy God's company and each other's fellowship in the glory of authentic encounter. Such experiences can also be profoundly apologetic as they can help our friends take Christianity more seriously than they had before, and perhaps provide an occasion for them to meet God in a new way.

Worship, then, is not only something we do before and after we engage in apologetics. It is itself the context for, and even a mode of, apologetics.

TRY THE SIDE DOOR

All of the suggestions offered so far have been in a "frontal" direction of straightforward encounter. Our society, however, often resists such directness.

It is a society in which we fear religious controversy as a threat to our current peace more than we fear the ultimate issues at stake in such controversy. It is a society suffused with the dynamics of irony and humor, keeping oneself from any final commitments and subverting the obvious, the standard, and the traditional so as to leave everything in play and nothing fixed, objective, and authoritative—except the freedom of individuals to pursue their own goals as they see fit. It is a society in which most people do not want to hear any simple, straight talk about Christianity: They already are Christians, or they "have heard it all before," or they even fear Christianity as sexist, homophobic, anti-environmentalist, imperialist, and other bad things. And it is a society in which we consumers are bombarded with attempts to claim our attention for this or that message, whether to eat at this particular restaurant in a couple of hours or to trust ourselves to that particular religion for all eternity. Our society, in sum, is leery, dubious, distracted, and jaded. Is there anything we can do?

If we cannot come in the front door, we should explore for other entrances. The next chapter suggests some "side doors" we might try.

11

Other Modes of Apologetics

Let your light shine before others, so that they may see your good works and give glory to your Father in heaven.

Matthew 5:16

Apologetics normally has been defined as a branch of Christian theology and its cousin, philosophy of religion. Standard histories of apologetics assume this apparent truism.[1] Great figures in the history of Christian thought agree—figures as diverse as F. D. E. Schleiermacher, B. B. Warfield, and Paul Tillich.[2] So it might appear presumptuous to suggest that to define apologetics merely as a branch of Christian theology and philosophy is to drastically narrow the scope and effectiveness of apologetics. It might even appear impertinent to suggest that such narrowness thus compromises the witness of the church.

In the light of what else I have suggested in this book so far, I must risk both charges. In fact, I shall presume that in our time, as in every time, only a minority of our neighbors is interested in theological and philosophical conversation. Yet a larger number do concern themselves, at least on occasion, with the question of the truthfulness of religious claims. I shall presume, furthermore, that the church is to meet that question—indeed, even to provoke that question—in a manner appropriate to each person's authentic need, and that doing so is the essence of the apologetical task. I shall go on to presume that God furnishes the church with the resources necessary to accomplish this mission.

I delight to find, therefore, that the history of the church renders up a wide range of intriguing and exemplary modes of apologetics if we will but look beyond the confines of theology and philosophy.[3] Instructed and encouraged by these examples, we can go on to consider their relevance to apologetics in our time and place.

ARCHITECTURE

The people who produce the Merriam-Webster dictionary doubtless represents the common mind of our culture when it gives as its first definition of the word *church* "a building for public and especially Christian worship."[4] Many Christians know, however, that the primary definition of this word according to the New Testament is the congregation of Christians, the people themselves: the *ekklesia* or assembly. Yet the public image of the church in general and of individual congregations very much is defined by their physical plants.

Christians throughout history, therefore, wisely have paid both attention and money toward the erection of structures that would convey a particular message to the surrounding community. Medieval cathedrals and other grand church buildings spoke eloquently of the devotion of princes, clergy, and townspeople to God—and, it must be allowed, to civic and personal pride. The images in carved stone, paint, and stained glass were the "books of the illiterate," joining with sermons and with seasonal mystery and miracle plays to educate the masses in the Christian faith.

Such education was necessary as it is in every Christian community. But the great churches played a crucial apologetic role as well. The populace of Europe needed to be impressed deeply with the authority and power—and thus the credibility—of the Church by every means possible. This was because, as Jean Delumeau and others have argued, medieval Europeans clung to their tribal religions while understanding little and observing less of the Christian faith until well into the Reformation period.[5] So these buildings bore witness to the grandeur of the medieval God, his majesty Son Jesus, and Jesus' glorious mother Mary. They thus testified also to the spiritual authority of the Church, the Church that figuratively (and usually literally) occupied the high ground in a society.

A similar motive inspired Protestants to erect their own versions of cathedrals closer to home. In nineteenth-century Ontario, Canada, for example, Anglicans joined with Presbyterians, Methodists, and even Baptists in constructing church buildings that asserted the moral leadership of Christianity in that culture. Each of these groups drew heavily on the symbolism of the medieval cathedral, thus together producing what Westfall calls a distinctive architecture, "Ontario Gothic."[6]

In the United States, Christian institutions have used architecture to impress themselves and others with their place in the culture. Many Christian colleges as well as churches, for instance, have used Colonial or Gothic architecture to assert that they are, so to speak, pillars of society. Oral Roberts University in Tulsa, Oklahoma, and Robert Schuller's Crystal Cathedral in Garden Grove, California, dramatically exemplify a different approach, declaring in their "space-age" architecture of sharp-angled steel, concrete, and glass that they are at America's sophisticated cutting edge. Willow Creek Community Church in suburban Chicago, to select just one more example, has deliberately chosen a physical plant that looks like the well-manicured office park in which its target audience spends much of their week.[7]

These large structures provide vivid examples. But the same principle obtains for more modest buildings as well that are themselves more appropriate to their environment and ministry, whether the urban storefront church or the suburban church "bungalow." In each case, the Church speaks to all who pass by. "Take us seriously," it says. "Don't discount us as eccentric or irrelevant. See? We belong here."

This realm of architecture draws us to consider the broad issue of physical space, and the even broader issue of visual presentation. We do not have to explore semiotics very far to agree with the axiom that every artifact is a text, is a sign.[8] What, therefore, are we saying by the physical spaces in which we present the Christian message? What is the floor plan, the lighting, the furniture, and the decor?

What is the message we are sending about what we believe about the beauty of worship, the comfort of people's bodies while in our company, the importance of clearly reading music and words during songs and prayers, and so on? Some of us have churches that assert that we belong—even that we belong at the center of society. Others of us have chosen instead to signify our difference by resistance to symbols of mere cultural success. Still others are trying to show, somehow, both that we belong and yet remain distinctive.

This concern extends to the physical appearance of the human presenters as well. Clothes, haircuts, jewelry, and so on all speak—and quite powerfully, sometimes—about class, profession, authority, sophistication, one's presumed relation to the audience, and so on. We might think we can ignore such matters, but our audiences and neighbors do not—indeed, cannot—ignore the clues we give off in these ways.

Consideration of architecture also points us to the vexed question of the interpretation of signs, the ambiguity of symbols. However glorious cathedrals might appear to some, for instance, others see in them only expensive European stone or Californian glass that was paid for as indulgence for the rich instead of in relief of the poor. If apologetics matters to Christian individuals or groups, we will try to ascertain carefully what crosses, ICTHUS-fish, mahogany paneling, ecclesiastical robes, business suits, tapestries, or earrings may signify—or *not* signify—to each of the neighbors we are trying to contact.

LITERATURE

Apologists love to speak and write: Words are their stock-in-trade. Yet some of the most eminent apologists have realized that straightforward, prosaic argument may well be inferior to other genres of literature in making a way for the gospel in the hearts of many. Stories and poems can be allusive, suggestive, implicative, polyvalent, and surprising. They can arouse interest, offer an alternative viewpoint, even create a longing, in more people than discursive argument can.[9] They can conceal as well as reveal—as Jesus said his own parables did. And they can let people gradually enter into the truths they depict as the characters, plot, motifs, and other devices do their work over time.

Many contemporary Christians know at least some of the works of C. S. Lewis. Lewis was a noted scholar of English literature whose international fame yet rests largely on the wide range of fiction he wrote as well as his popular theological apologetics. Lewis composed children's stories in *The Chronicles of Narnia* (1950–1954), a science-fiction trilogy (1938, 1943, 1945), and a retelling of Greek myth in *Till We Have Faces* (1956). He addressed theology more directly, but still in allegory and metaphor, in *The Great Divorce* (1946) and, perhaps his best-read book, *The Screwtape Letters* (1941). Lewis also was a master essayist, and his popular *Mere Christianity* (1952) and other collections of essays are in print to this day, more than 30 years after his death.

One of Lewis's most trenchant observers was theologian Austin Farrer. In an essay reflecting upon Lewis's career as an apologist, Farrer makes this striking point:

> His real power was not proof; it was depiction. There lived in his writings a Christian universe that could be both thought and felt, in which he was at home and in which he made his reader at home. Moral issues were presented with sharp lucidity and related to the divine will and, once so seen, could never again be seen otherwise. . . . Belief is natural, for the world is so. It is enough to let it be seen so.[10]

More recently, English novelist Susan Howatch has published a string of best-selling psychological novels that show Christian clergy—of all people!—in a positive light, and therefore the faith they represent as at least plausible for our contemporaries. Indeed, the very foibles and failures she exposes in their lives help to portray them as more truly heroic than any plaster saints.[11] And on the other side of the Atlantic, Flannery O'Connor and Frederick Buechner have depicted real Christians in real situations of life and death with both startling candor and undeniable appeal.[12]

The heritage of writing Christian apologetics in a variety of genres stretches back centuries, however. One can see apologetics as a prime motive in Eusebius's *Ecclesiastical History* (323); in Augustine's autobiographical *Confessions* (397–98) and historical *City of God* (417–427); and in Desiderius Erasmus's satire, *The Praise of Folly* (1511). Søren Kierkegaard wrote some of the most profound philosophy of the nineteenth century, but he also addressed the masses of his native Denmark through his provocative journalism. For some minds, Christianity has become more plausible because of sublime poetry that speaks a Christian worldview. In English, for example, there is a very rich tradition, in the works of Edmund Spenser, John Donne, George Herbert, John Milton, William Cowper, Gerald Manley Hopkins, and many more.[13] And what can be said of word-artists can be said, *mutatis mutandis*, of artists in other media as well—paint, sculpture, dance, music, and so on.

Perhaps no single apologist was as versatile as G. K. Chesterton (1874–1936). He did write direct apologetics, some of which can profit readers a century later: *Heresy* (1905), *Orthodoxy* (1908), and *The Everlasting Man* (1925) particularly come to mind. But Chesterton also wrote history that lifted up Christian themes and ideals, notably in his biographies of Francis of Assisi (1924) and Thomas Aquinas (1933). He wrote explicitly Christian verse, some of it doggerel but some of it still quite moving and republished to the present. Chesterton wrote sprightly and frequently savage commentary in column after column of newspaper.[14] And he wrote very popular fiction, particularly in the unlikely genres of thriller (*The Man Who Was Thursday* [1908]) and mystery story (featuring his Roman Catholic priest/detective, Father Brown).[15]

The heritage of literary Christian apologetics, then, reaches far beyond the discourse of the theologians and philosophers. These various genres of literature prompt us therefore to consider the broad issue of rhetoric, and the even broader issue of communication theory and strategy. However cogent our arguments, they cannot effect anything if no one listens. Are there other ways to proclaim the Christian message that will attract a wider hearing?

In many Christian circles, more to the point is the question of whether we will support artists in poetry, fiction, television, movies, music, and other media—and these will be our own congregants, and spouses, and students, and children. Will we instead continue to suspect and denounce them as worldly, compromising, and superficial compared to the solid, stolid work of preaching, teaching, and writing Christian theology? If we do not foster such creative and, yes, unsettling expression in our communities, then our communities may be rendered mute in many sectors of our culture today.

Yet another consideration that arises in this context but pertains also to other of these modes, is the question of the usefulness of one or another piece of literature in a particular situation. Just as rigorous philosophical apologetics have value only in certain cultures and among certain people, so a particular poem, or novel, or song, or picture might well convey an appropriate Christian message in some cases but might alienate people in others. The motif of the crusading knight, to pick an obvious example, had a significantly more popular appeal in Victorian Britain than it has had in missionary work among Middle Eastern Muslims. Attitudes toward gender roles that might have seemed proper to most people as late as the mid-twentieth century nowadays strike many of us as sexist, and apologetics containing such attitudes will be off-putting to such audiences.[16]

Humor is wonderfully helpful or terribly dangerous, depending on the context. Sometimes it is entirely healthy to reply to certain extreme views with hearty laughter, as in "Oh, come on! Who really can live like that?" Satirical fiction is an especially apt genre for deflating the pretensions of rival ideologies, and it is one that is seldom taken up nowadays by Christians while it has been commonly used to disparage Christianity. But humor also can appear to be an illegitimate expedient to dodge genuine difficulties. Sarcasm in particular can occasionally cut to the heart of the matter, but more often merely cuts nastily into one's opponent. Once again we must keep clearly before us not only what message we think we are sending, but also what message is likely to be understood by its recipients.

WORLDLY KNOWLEDGE AND WISDOM

This sort of apologetics makes contact with people's immediate, secular concerns. In the case of knowledge and skill, Christians offer expertise in some area that others find valuable. On the basis of this positive association, those others might then consider more seriously what Christians have to say about spiritual matters. A marvelous example of this is retold by Jonathan Spence about the Jesuit missionary Matteo Ricci:

> In 1596 Matteo Ricci taught the Chinese how to build a memory palace. He told them that the size of the palace would depend on how much they wanted to remember: the most ambitious construction would consist of several hundred buildings of all shapes and sizes; "the more there are the better it will be," said Ricci. . . .
>
> In summarizing this memory system, he explained that these palaces, pavilions, divans were mental structures to be kept in one's head, not solid objects to be literally constructed out of "real" materials. . . .
>
> The real purpose of all these mental constructs was to provide storage spaces for the myriad concepts that make up the sum of our human knowledge. To everything that we wish to remember, wrote Ricci, we should give an image; and to every one of these images we should assign a position where it can repose peacefully until we are ready to reclaim it by an act of memory. . . .
>
> The family that Ricci was seeking to instruct in mnemonic skills stood at the apex of Chinese society. Governor Lu himself was an intelligent and wealthy scholar who had served in a wide variety of posts in the Ming dynasty bureaucracy. . . . Now he had reached the peak of his career, as a provincial governor, and was preparing his three sons for the advanced government examinations; he himself had passed these exams with distinction twenty-eight years before, and knew along with all his contemporaries

that success in the exams was the surest route to fame and fortune in the imperial Chinese state. Thus we can be almost certain that Ricci was offering to teach the governor's sons advanced memory techniques so that they would have a better chance to pass the exams, and would then in gratitude use their newly won prestige to advance the cause of the Catholic church.[17]

So-called tent-making missionaries go beyond mere self-support in precisely this way, using their special abilities to bring plausibility to their convictions about the Gospel. Christian scientists, soldiers, musicians, explorers, and industrialists all have used the platforms they have earned through their particular worldly successes to testify to their Christian faith. Indeed, these are the forebears of today's Christian pop heroes, athletes, and singers, who do the same thing.

Sophisticates may grimace at this sort of thing as so much heroworship. Many people, however, have claimed that they were encouraged to take Christianity more seriously when these "winners" gladly endorsed it. As I write this chapter, in fact, I remember a conversation I had with a prominent businessman just last week who said that his own return to serious Christian commitment came as he watched the televised funeral of his favorite professional golfer, Payne Stewart, and listened to testimony after testimony to Stewart's faith—not his athletic prowess. This thoughtful and obviously sincere businessman, whose life is now marked by extensive volunteer work and devotion to his previously estranged family, said exactly this to me, albeit with a smile: "I figured if Christianity was good enough for Payne Stewart, it was good enough for me."

A similar testimony is offered from a different point of the cultural compass by the influential twentieth-century Canadian social critic George Grant. He says he was first roused from being what he himself called "a sharp, ambitious little pragmatist" by enjoying himself in the company of attractive people who conversed about religious matters without embarrassment. "For the first time in his life," biographer William Christian writes, "he was hearing the language of transcendence, a language he had never heard before, being spoken articulately by people whom he admired."[18]

C. S. Lewis applied this principle of the apologetic usefulness of publicly valued knowledge to the crucial genre of popular scholarship. It is worth quoting him (as it usually is) at length:

> I believe that any Christian who is qualified to write a good popular book on any science may do much more by that than by any directly apologetic work. The difficulty we are up against is this. We can make people (often) attend to the Christian point of view for half an hour or so; but the moment they have gone away from our lecture or laid down our article, they are plunged back into a world where the opposite position is taken for granted. As long as that situation exists, widespread success is simply impossible. . . . What we want is not more little books about Christianity, but more little books by Christians on other subjects—with their Christianity *latent*. You can see this most easily if you look at it the other way round. Our Faith is not very likely to be shaken by any book on Hinduism. But if whenever we read an elementary book on Geology, Botany, Politics or Astronomy, we found that its implications were Hindu, that would shake us. It is not the books written in direct defense of Materialism that make the modern man a materialist; it is the materialistic assumptions in all the other books. In the same way, it is not books on Christianity that will really trouble him. But he would be troubled if, whenever he wanted a cheap popular introduction to some science, the best work on the market was always by a Christian.[19]

Writing such books, or teaching such subjects in schools and universities, or engaging in academic research in these areas are all activities that God blesses as part of his work of shalom. They are not to be undertaken merely for the ulterior motive of apologetics, just as any other worthy work is undertaken for its own sake to the glory of God. Lewis's objective and mine is simply to urge Christians to consider how the intellectual resources of the Church can best be deployed particularly with an eye toward apologetics.

Wisdom is a second dimension of this apologetical theme. Christians contribute as they can to the public conversation—in neighborhood associations, in the workplace, on school boards, in mass-media forums, and in government. Such Christians bring the wisdom of the Christian tradition to bear on matters of societal concern, and they do so in such a way that those who do not share Christian presuppositions nonetheless can appreciate and benefit from this wisdom. Education, financial responsibility, marriage and childrearing, conflict management, ecological stewardship, racial justice, and a host of other generically human concerns all have been discussed by Christians in public language. Beyond the important intrinsic benefits of such "salting" and "lighting" of one's culture (Matthew 5:13, 14), Christians hereby construct reputable standpoints from which they can share more specifically Christian convictions.

Among the most prolific and influential Christian voices in America during the middle of the twentieth century was that of pundit Reinhold Niebuhr. In a steady stream of journalism published in such magazines as the *Atlantic Monthly*, the *Nation*, *Commentary*, and the *New Republic*, Niebuhr helped millions of thoughtful Americans interpret their times as a basis for common action. Perhaps no one in North America in that century so easily moved between what Larry Rasmussen calls "the language of Zion and that of regnant secular culture," and no other white Protestant of his day so sophisticatedly modeled the relationship of theory and practice. Niebuhr, interestingly, constantly refused the title of theologian, but he did acknowledge his engagement in apologetics: "the defense and justification of the Christian faith in a secular age." Yet Niebuhr did so in an unusual apologetic mode. He helped his fellow citizens—including major policymakers in the 1940s and 1950s— understand their times and respond to them. And he did so frequently by keeping his fundamentally important Christian convictions implicit, yet nonetheless commending them to those with ears to hear by their formative presence in his thought.[20]

"Worldly knowledge" is something Christians have long appreciated and exploited. We do not have to look only at celebrated "winners," however, to judge the merits of this form of apologetics. Any important work done well is more and more effective as an apologetic as our society witnesses what sometimes seems to be a continual erosion of integrity in service. A Christian plumber who answers calls promptly, fixes problems quickly and thoroughly, and charges a fair price for time and materials makes a powerful impression for good on every customer. A Christian manager who sets out clear expectations, listens attentively to both complaints and suggestions, and responds with evident thoughtfulness and wisdom elicits respect that strengthens any explicitly Christian testimony she might render. Good, skilfull service thus casts threads around others that connect them to us in mutual respect within which spiritual conversation might take place.

The danger always lurks, however, that Christianity will be misunderstood hereby as guaranteeing success in worldly affairs. It can be a short step from the testimonies of local celebrities at a Billy Graham Crusade to the "health-and-wealth" message of the heretics on the evangelical fringe. As Christians thus appeal to worldly talent, wisdom, and accomplishment in order to overcome the prejudices of others, they need deep roots in Biblical teaching like I Corinthians 1:26–29 (NRSV):

> Consider your own call, brothers and sisters: not many of you were wise by human standards, not many were powerful, not many were of noble birth. But God chose what is foolish in the world to shame the wise; God chose what is weak in the world to shame the strong; God chose what is low and despised in the world, things that are not, to reduce to nothing things that are, so that no one might boast in the presence of God.

It may well be, that is, that Christians who have enjoyed success in ways that impress their neighbors must engage in the paradox of exploiting their status in order to win a hearing for a gospel that subverts precisely that status under the grace and glory of God.

POWER EVENTS

The mention of "winners" brings forward a striking tradition in Christian apologetics that is largely obscured in our contemporary context. Indeed, it goes back to Christianity's heritage in ancient Israelite religion and the famous confrontation between Yahweh's prophet Elijah and the prophets of Baal on Mount Carmel. When challenged to display his power, Baal was silent, embarrassingly so. When it was his turn, Yahweh answered with a roar of fire (I Kings 18). Other wondrous signs pointed to God's blessing upon the work of many people in the Bible, most notably the ministry of the Lord Jesus himself.

Subsequent church history treasures its lore of amazing events and dramatic confrontations. The entire genre of hagiography—the lives of the saints—is preoccupied with these attestations of God's power. One of the most effective missionaries in the early church, in fact, became known as Gregory Thaumaturgus (ca. 213–ca. 270), whose surname means the "Wonder-Worker."

Among the most impressive stories of all is the tale of Wynfrith of England, better known under his later name of Boniface, Apostle to the Germans (680–754). K. S. Latourette tells what happened in 723.

> Following the advice of some of the most stalwart of his converts, he went to Geismar and, in the horrified presence of a large number of pagans, began cutting down a huge ancient oak held sacred to Thor. Before he had quite completed the task a powerful gust of wind finished the demolition. The tree crashed to the ground and broke into four sections. The pagan bystanders, who had been cursing the desecrator, were convinced of the power of the new faith. Out of the timber Boniface constructed an oratory to St. Peter. The Geismar episode may well have proved decisive evidence for the validity of the gospel in terms (and this is the key point) which the populace could understand of the superior might of the God of the Christians. Presumably, too, it helped to wean from pre-Christian magical practices many

of the nominal converts who observed the rites of both the new and the old faith.[21]

Such confrontations will seem to many of us not heroic, but horrifying. How can Christians possibly condone such a drastic approach to religious alternatives? I can hardly recommend such a course of action to most readers in our current context!

Other observers have noted, however, that these power events are reported much more frequently by missionaries and others on the edges of Christian evangelistic advance rather than among the populations of settled Christians who have welcomed others to their societies. It may be that on the borders of open religious conflict, in societies who face stark religious choices, a "power encounter" may prove decisive and beneficial. Yet as the "Christian West" itself becomes less and less Christian, this mode of apologetics may become more evident here as well. Indeed, the growing North American interest in the phenomenon of exorcism shows that in the view of many of our contemporaries, open spiritual warfare is not just something that happens someplace else.[22]

The so-called signs-and-wonders movement nowadays champions "power events" as apologetics, implicitly opening up the issue of the miraculous and the even broader issue of power as an appropriate symbol for Christianity. As in biblical times, Christian wonder-workers today face the problem of how to foster the correct interpretation of such signs, such as physical healing or spiritual deliverance. Do the wonders lead people out of preoccupation with their own needs to maturation in discipleship and community? Or do such blessings ironically confirm people's selfish individualism, as in "What's in it for me?" The challenge now, as then, is to use the medium of power to convey the Christian ethic of finding our own salvation in devoting ourselves to the glory of God and the welfare of others, not in a message of "God on call" to serve our whims.

A similar problem regarding power and the gospel comes into focus as we consider a typical form of contemporary apologetics-as-spiritual-contest, the public debate. When the Christian apologist squares off against his opponent, the debate may be advertised as an intellectual dialogue, the purpose of which is to clarify and test various ideas.[23] It seems too often, however, that this is not the actual case. Instead, what we have here is a power encounter between champions. The typical attendance pattern, reported to me from a number of professional apologists, is of enthusiastic attendance at debates versus much smaller attendance at the same apologist's individual lecture the next day. This pattern indicates that something more elementary is taking place than a lofty dialogue of ideas.

Seeing such events this way helps to explain why winning is so palpably important to the participants and their supporters. A mere intellectual exchange could be considered well worthwhile if everyone left with clearer, truer ideas and a fresh determination to inquire further into the subject—as a good class period can be worthwhile. But in power events, there must be "victor" and "vanquished."

The dangers in such a simple dichotomy are several. Since each side is sorely tempted to glorify itself as entirely right and true, and to demonize the other as evil and false, then each side is sorely tempted to cheer without reflection any point made by its champion and to denigrate immediately any idea advanced by the opponent. Bad enough, then, that each side thus is tempted to intellectual polarization and oversimplification. There is little chance therefore to benefit from, or even properly engage, the differing views of the other.

As Jean Hampton points out, furthermore, an attitude of disparagement and ridicule always fails to persuade—presumably the point of the exercise: "Unless [the opponent's] reasons are uncovered and directly addressed, they continue to exercise their sway over the minds of those who are susceptible to them."[24]

Worse, however, is the social polarization, with hostility the only emotion remaining for the other side. Christian communication, characterized by grace and truth, cannot be offered in such a situation. How can a gospel of love be conveyed by people who are full of hate?

Worst of all is the spiritual polarization, with the dualism of "we = good" and "they = evil" leading directly to the deadly sin of pride, with the concomitant contempt for, and dismissal of, the neighbor who opposes us. Jesus had very strong words for such attitudes: "But I say to you that if you are angry with a brother or sister, you will be liable to judgment; and if you insult a brother or sister, you will be liable to the council; and if you say, 'You fool,' you will be liable to the hell of fire" (Matthew 5:22, NRSV).

Dorothy L. Sayers once quipped, "Controversy is bad for the spirit, however enlivening to the wits," but public religious debate seems to be deadly for both soul and mind.[25] It may be that debates do not necessarily have to reduce to these dynamics. The basic question, however, must be faced by each of us: How can any medium of power convey the gospel of grace?

JUSTICE AND CHARITY

To some Christians, cutting down a sacred tree displays courage and power, and perhaps it can help to liberate people from religious confusion. The Christian religion, however, is about much more than that. Missionaries more typically have demonstrated the authenticity of the message of God's love through acts of justice and charity.

In the late sixth century, for instance, Pope Gregory the Great earned lasting respect and loyalty to his office by interceding for the city of Rome against barbarian invaders and by spending church money on massive relief for the poor—when the political leaders of the late Roman Empire failed to help. The generosity of monasteries as places of refuge, healing, and nourishment redounded greatly to the credit of the church in the Middle Ages. The abolitionist campaign of William Wilberforce and his associates in the so-called Clapham Sect in Britain—and the many other worthy causes championed by evangelicals in the nineteenth century on both sides of the Atlantic—burnished the image of the Christian faith in those societies.

Perhaps no movement in church history, however, was as sweeping in its attempt to provide for human needs as was Pietism under the direction of A. H. Francke in eighteenth-century Germany. With the support of Pietist leader P. J. Spener, Francke moved to

Halle and became a pastor and professor of biblical languages and theology. These duties were not enough for the indefatigable Francke. He organized the establishment of the famous Halle *Stiftungen* (institutions), and historian Howard Snyder makes an impressive list of them.

> Most of these institutions were started partly in response to needs in Glaucha and the surrounding area after the plague of 1682–83, which reportedly reduced the population of the town by two-thirds. Francke was so moved by the ignorance and poverty of the children of Glaucha that in 1695 he began a school for the poor which soon grew to over fifty students. This led to the founding of an orphanage in 1696, and eventually to a whole series of interrelated and mutually supportive institutions. These included a *paedagogium* for the sons of the nobility (which the young Count Zinzendorf attended for six years), a Latin school to prepare students for the university, and German schools designed to provide a practical secondary education for boys and girls of ordinary citizens. In addition to the orphanage and schools, Francke founded a home for poor widows (1698), a bookstore, a chemical laboratory, a library, a museum of natural science, a laundry, a farm, a bakery, a brewery, a hospital, and other enterprises. He was instrumental also in founding the Canstein Bible House which was lodged in the new orphanage building, completed in 1698. By 1800 the Bible house had distributed nearly three million Bible and Scripture portions in several languages.[26]

Snyder goes on to describe Francke's explicit objectives for these institutions.

> They were part of a very intentional reform vision. . . . He saw his schools as means for infiltrating all levels of society with Pietist influence. His educational methods and ideas were in fact applied very widely due to the success of the Halle schools.[27]

Second, however, Francke's institutions served as examples of Pietist Christianity that impressed many people well beyond the boundaries of Germany, reaching even to the hinterland of Puritan New England as Francke corresponded with Cotton Mather. As another scholar puts it, Francke was the "originator, founder, and lifelong head of a charitable enterprise which has caught the imagination . . . of people the world over. Nothing like it could be found in the long history of the Christian church."[28]

The apologetic of good deeds was commanded in the Sermon on the Mount (Matthew 5:16), and the history of the Church is full of instances of noble Christian obedience to it. Consider, now, the Salvation Army's image in the minds of contemporary North Americans, as well as people elsewhere. Quaint as their uniforms and brass bands may appear, they have a solid reputation for social service that shields them (so to speak!) from ridicule and gives them a basis upon which to speak. Mother Teresa also acquired such moral capital that gave her a platform for views (such as her hatred of abortion) before audiences (such as that of the Nobel Prize ceremony) unused to such direct moral confrontation. Again, these two examples remind us that love for the neighbor is offered for its own sake in obedience to God, not merely as a means to evangelistic ends. Still, these acts of justice and charity do indeed express the good news of God's love, and they create grounds upon which Christians can go on to set out that message explicitly and with plausibility.[29] As William Placher notes, "It is striking that early Quaker abolitionists and Christian pacifists in different ages had a public impact precisely by witness rather than by argument according to 'publicly acceptable' criteria."[30]

Indeed, in an era that exploits the whirlwind of changing mores to encourage certain types of individual choice (especially consumerist choices), there is yet—and perhaps increasingly—respect for unyielding moral integrity. This paradox shows up frequently in prime-time television and mass-market movies, especially those that feature an outsider—perhaps a child, perhaps an angel, perhaps an alien, perhaps a hero—whose holiness (a word that denotes both separateness and goodness) calls our normal values into question.

Moral apologetics counts for a lot in a culture surfeited with words and images.[31] As Stanley Hauerwas and William Willimon put it,

> the world's cynicism and unbelief make the courage, conti-
> nuity, and conviction of anybody, even ordinary people,
> appear to be adventuresome and heroic. An unbelieving
> world can make a saint out of almost anybody who dares to
> be faithful.[32]

In a culture full of doubt as to whether there is a God who loves and cares for the world, godliness helps to keep alive the plausibility of Christian conviction. The point is put poignantly in the letter of martyr Etty Hillesum written shortly before she was sent to Auschwitz in 1943: "If we just care enough, God is in safe hands with us despite everything."[33]

CHRISTIAN COMMUNITY

If a pragmatic test is applied to Christian claims, it ought to show whether Christianity delivers what it promises. Among the most basic assertions of Christianity is the declaration that Christ established a community of believers that would be characterized chiefly by worship of him and love for each other (John 13–17). The inquirer therefore is entitled to ask whether such communities exist. He may want to know, after he has witnessed all the demonstrations of power and prestige and integrity and charity that Christians can muster, whether Christianity does indeed transform individuals, decisively reorient them toward Christ, and integrate them into a community of love.

Monastic renewal movements understood this point, planting new communities of faith to initiate and sustain Christian testimony throughout Europe. Mass evangelists in our era wisely pay attention to what they call "follow-up" work so that the fire of revival can be sustained in the fireplaces of existing or newly founded churches, once the tents have folded up or the stadiums have emptied. Contemporary theologians of the Church across a very wide range of viewpoints agree that the spiritual health of the Church is a critical factor in the success of evangelistic effort.[34]

John Wesley, the eighteenth-century founder of Methodism, stands as an exemplar of this sensibility. Wesley devoted enormous energy to constructing a system of various kinds of small groups to lead people into the Christian faith and to help them mature once they were converted. For all of the spectacular successes of Methodist oratory, Wesley believed that it was in these intimate meetings of earnest fellowship, rather than in the general preaching services, that the great majority of authentic conversions occurred. Indeed, he early resolved simply not to preach anywhere in which he could not follow it up by establishing such groups with adequate leadership.[35]

Today, the Church in its various forms offers what I call *plausibility places* to those investigating the faith. If congregations, parachurch organizations, house fellowships, and Christian families ourselves are clearly devoted to Christ and Christian fellowship, and live out our Christian calling with integrity (with all of the previous categories of "corollary apologetics" in view), we accomplish something deeply important.[36] These social structures, these environments, are places in which people can consider the Christian truth-claims as if those claims really might be true. Once inside such structures, inquirers now might well attend to theological and philosophical apologetics because they have been welcomed into a context in which those arguments are now at least incipiently interesting, intelligible, and plausible.

The challenge, then, is to complement our proclamation of the gospel with public demonstrations of God's care for the earth, for the financially and socially needy, for beauty and joy, and for the intellectual life. We must demonstrate our worthy citizenship if we are to distinguish ourselves and our message in the welter of other options available, if we are to attract dubious postmoderns, if we are to overcome the plausibility problem, and if we are to challenge as well as appeal to our consumerist neighbors. The examples of Christian endeavor we have considered in this essay can inspire us to do so. And we must understand that it is authentic for Christians to embrace this wide agenda, not as something we take on strategically

in the narrower cause of evangelism and "saving souls," but in cooperation with the God who is at work to redeem the whole world.[37]

This contention might well strike home more powerfully if we
consider the counterfactual situation: What if the church did *not*
deploy these other resources? What if church architecture was non-
descript and merely functional as a meeting space—or instead stood
out oddly, incongruously, in its community? What if the only Christian literature was theology and philosophy? What if Christians had
nothing useful to offer others except Christian ideas? What if Christians entirely avoided spiritual contests? What if Christians spent
all of their energies in theological and philosophical pursuits? What
if Christian fellowship (I speak of a "worst-case scenario") consisted
entirely of academic conferences? As valuable as theological and
philosophical apologetics undoubtedly are, it seems unlikely that
many people would consent to sitting still for them, and especially if
all of these other confirmations were absent.

It may be, in fact, that it is precisely for lack of sufficient "corollary apologetics," as we might call them, that so many people in our
communities today generally are *not* deeply interested in what Christians have to say theologically and philosophically. Since the Christian message fundamentally is an invitation extended to human
beings (not just human brains) to encounter and embrace the person
of Jesus Christ (rather than merely to adopt a doctrinal system or
ideology) it is then obvious that establishing the plausibility and
credibility of that message will depend upon more than intellectual
argument. It will depend instead upon the Holy Spirit of God shining out through all the lamps of good works we can raise to the glory
of our Father in heaven.

Conclusion: Humble Apologetics

From all my lame defeats and oh! much more
From all the victories that I seemed to score;
From cleverness shot forth on Thy behalf
At which, while angels weep, the audience laugh;
From all my proofs of Thy divinity,
Thou, who wouldst give no sign, deliver me.

. . .

Lord of the narrow gate and the needle's eye,
Take from me all my trumpery lest I die.

C. S. Lewis[1]

Apologetics is dangerous work. In an era in which voices from several sides remind us of how problematic are human claims to knowledge; in a culture that increasingly resists and resents anyone who seeks the conversion of another; and in an activity whose stereotype is of rationalistic conceit and intellectual bullying—what sensible, sensitive person would want to engage in apologetics?

If we are going to defend and commend our faith, we must do it in a new mode: with a different voice and in a different posture. Our apologetics must be humble. It must be humble for several reasons, but chief among these is that God himself comes to us in humility, seeking our love and drawing us to him. The Lord Jesus Christ is our model of humility; the Holy Spirit of God is our humble companion who helps us to follow Christ's example as we proclaim Christ's message. As Lesslie Newbigin reminds us, then, "the means by which the good news of salvation is propagated must be congruous with the nature of the salvation itself."[2]

Apologetics, therefore, must be humble in at least three respects: it must epistemologically humble, rhetorically humble, and spiritually humble.

Epistemologically humble: Given historic Christian teachings regarding the finitude and fallenness of human beings and of our thinking in particular, we must be careful not to claim too much for what we believe. We Christians should not need postmodernists to tell us that we do not know it all. We should not need anyone to tell us that all human thought is partial, distorted, and usually deployed in the interest of this or that personal agenda. We can be grateful for those postmodern voices that have reminded us of these truths, but we believe them because our own theological tradition says so.

Thus we are as committed as we can be to what we believe is real, and especially to the One whom we love, worship, and obey as the Way, the Truth, and the Life. We gladly offer what, and whom, we believe we have found to be true to our neighbors in the hope that they also will recognize it, and him, as true. We recognize that there are good reasons for them not to believe, even as we recognize that there can be good reasons for our own doubts. Indeed, we can recognize that God may have given *them* some things to teach *us*, and we gratefully receive them in the mutual exchange of God's great economy of *shalom*.

We recognize, ultimately, that to truly believe, to truly commit oneself to God, is itself a gift that God alone bestows. Conversion is a gift. Faith is a gift. God alone can change minds so that those minds can both see and embrace the great truths of the gospel, and the One who stands at their center.

Rhetorically humble: Given these epistemological realities, apologetics should forgo the triumphalist accents that bespeak a certainty our own theology claims we cannot have. The greatness of the subject matter of our message—the nature of God, the nature of human beings, the salvation of the world, the end of history—should cause us to hesitate and stammer as we remember how little we can claim to know about such things.[3] In particular, we should abandon apologetic presentations that, to borrow from some actual book titles, presume to put things *Beyond Reasonable Doubt*, that tell us to *Be Sure!* or that, perhaps most famously, provide us with *Evidence that Demands a Verdict*.[4]

We should instead adopt the voice of a friend who thinks he has found something worth sharing but recognizes that not everyone will agree on its value. Indeed, we should adopt the voice of the friend who wants to stay friendly with our neighbors whether or not they see what we see and believe what we believe. To put it more sharply, we should sound like we really do respect the intelligence, and spiritual interest, and moral integrity of our neighbors. We should act as if we do see the very image of God in them. We should therefore avoid any attempt to manipulate them into religious decision. And we should continue to love them whatever their response to the gospel might be—as God does.

Yes, such a voice will likely be more attractive and effective in an age of multiculturalism, pluralism, postmodernism, and consumerism. But it is a voice that speaks authentically out of Christian convictions about our own very real limitations and our neighbors' very real dignity, not cynical expediency. We are rhetorically humble because we are *not* prophets infallibly inspired by God, let alone the One who could speak "with authority" in a way no one else can speak. We are mere messengers of that One: messengers who earnestly mean well, but who forget this bit of the message or never really understood that bit; messengers who never entirely live up to their own good news; messengers who recognize the ambiguities in the world that make the message harder to believe; and therefore messengers who can sympathize with neighbors who aren't ready just yet to believe everything we're telling them.

Spiritually humble: Apologists who remain faithful to basic Christian teaching never presume to be accomplishing all that much. It is God who does the crucial work of drawing our neighbors toward his light, giving them eyes to see it and hearts to want it, and then "shedding this light abroad" in their hearts as they enjoy spiritual renewal.

In the apologetical contest, however, we are tempted to lose our perspective—whether in a public debate or across the kitchen table. Dorothy L. Sayers resisted the vocation of "Christian apologist" for several reasons, one of which was that "it fosters an irritable and domineering temper."[5] We become too closely identified with the arguments we are deploying, and too focused upon the apparent outcome of the conversation. It all becomes twisted around our needy, nervous egos, instead of rotating nicely around the Center of all things. Thus we lose our love and find it increasingly easy to objectify our neighbor as an obstacle to be overcome, a prize to be won, an enemy to be vanquished.

If all goes well, furthermore, we face a different and no less insidious temptation. C. S. Lewis concluded an address to fellow apologists thus:

> I have found that nothing is more dangerous to one's own faith than the work of an apologist. No doctrine of that Faith seems to me so spectral, so unreal as one that I have just successfully defended in a public debate. For a moment, you see, it has seemed to rest on oneself: as a result, when you go away from that debate, it seems no stronger than that weak pillar. That is why we apologists take our lives in our hands and can be saved only by falling back continually from the web of our own arguments, as from our intellectual counters, into the Reality—from Christian apologetics into Christ Himself. That also is why we need one another's continual help—*oremus pro invicem* ["Let us pray for each other"].[6]

We can simultaneously congratulate ourselves for our brilliant argument (and self-congratulation is never a spiritually healthy thing) and, ironically, weaken and imperil our own faith by reducing the basis of our faith to that particular argument.

The Apostle Paul, a skillful debater who was happy to wrangle with rabbis and philosophers alike, recognized the perils of linking faith improperly with clever argument. Indeed, Lewis was perhaps thinking of Paul's great words to the Corinthian church:

When I came to you, brothers and sisters, I did not come proclaiming the mystery of God to you in lofty words or wisdom. For I decided to know nothing among you except Jesus Christ, and him crucified. And I came to you in weakness and in fear and in much trembling. My speech and my proclamation were not with plausible words of wisdom, but with a demonstration of the Spirit and of power, so that your faith might rest not on human wisdom but on the power of God. (I Corinthians 2:1–5)

So with all this humility, why would any good Christian undertake apologetics at all? Glenn Tinder reminds us that Jesus taught "a posture of expectancy. The men and women of Israel, and . . . human beings everywhere, were called upon to turn their lives into a concentrated act of waiting for a community that would be created not by political leaders but by God."[7] Our very lack of confidence in apologetic prowess to effect conversion into the Kingdom of God mirrors our lack of confidence in any human efforts to produce that Kingdom.

Yet humility is not only an acknowledgment that we are dependent. As Tinder writes, we are also to be expectant: We believe that God is in fact active in our world, bringing people into his Kingdom and graciously calling us to work with him in his program of global reclamation. So we work in his name, including the work of apologetics, and we expect to achieve his objectives in that work.

Therefore, our humility is dependent, and expectant, and finally *obedient*. We engage in apologetics because it is one way—not the most important way, to be sure, but one way—to serve our neighbors in God's name. We all do have minds that need convincing and satisfying. Christianity meets all of our needs, and it certainly does not deny our need for credibility, for adequate grounds on which to base our most important commitments of faith. God has provided those grounds, and it is a false piety that neglects to enjoy and employ them in his service. Our humility is, after all, not primarily before our neighbors, but before God. And if God has commissioned us to work with him in testifying to the virtues of the gospel, then we must do so with vigor and enthusiasm.[8]

We Christians do believe that God has given us the privilege of hearing and embracing the good news, of receiving adoption into his family, and of joining the Church. We do believe that we know some things that other people don't, and those things are good for them to hear. Above all, we believe that we have met Jesus Christ. If Christians are in fact privileged in these ways, to say it once more, it is not because we are smarter, or holier, or humbler than other people are. It is just because (we believe) God has, in his mysterious generosity, given us this privilege.

For all we know, *we might be wrong* about any or all of this. And we will honestly own up to that possibility. Thus whatever we do or say, we must do or say it humbly. But what we *think* we know does point in a single direction: to the claims of the gospel. And on the basis of what we think we know—the only basis anyone has to believe anything—we offer to our neighbors in apologetics the Truth, the Goodness, and the Beauty we think we have found.

We do so in the firm hope—we *hope* in *God*; we don't rely on our apologetics—that the gospel of life-changing blessing will bless them, too.

Notes

PART ONE: CHALLENGES

1. Puralism

1. Helpful introductions to these subjects with special attention to religion are the following: Peter L. Berger, *The Sacred Canopy: Elements of a Sociological Theory of Religion* (Garden City, NY: Anchor Books, 1969); Os Guinness, *The Gravedigger File: Papers on the Subversion of the Modern Church* (Downers Grove, IL: InterVarsity Press, 1983); David Lyon, *The Steeple's Shadow: On the Myths and Realities of Secularization* (Grand Rapids, MI: Eerdmans, 1985).

2. See Jon Butler, *Awash in a Sea of Faith: Christianizing the American People* (Cambridge, MA: Harvard University Press, 1990); John Webster Grant, *Moon of Wintertime: Missionaries and the Indians of Canada in Encounter since 1534* (Toronto: University of Toronto Press, 1984); Terrence Murphy and Roberto Perlin, eds., *A Concise History of Christianity in Canada* (Toronto: Oxford University Press, 1996).

3. Hick's most accessible introduction to his thought on these matters is John Hick, *A Christian Theology of Religions: The Rainbow of Faiths* (Louisville, KY: Westminster John Knox Press, 1995).

4. Allan Bloom, *The Closing of the American Mind: How Higher Education Has Failed Democracy and Impoverished The Souls of Today's Students* (New York: Simon and Schuster, 1987), 25–26.

5. The following are widely used introductions to modern intellectual history: Franklin L. Baumer, *Modern European Thought: Continuity and Change in Ideas, 1600–1950* (New York: Macmillan, 1977); and Roland N. Stromberg, *European Intellectual History since 1789* [many editions] (Englewood Cliffs, NJ: Prentice-Hall, 1966). See also Colin Brown, *Christianity and Western Thought: A History of Philosophers, Ideas and Movements*, vol. 1 (Downers Grove, IL: InterVarsity

Press, 1990); and Alan G. Padgett and Steve Wilkens, *Faith and Reason in the Nineteenth Century: Christianity and Western Thought*, vol. 2 (Downers Grove, IL: InterVarsity Press, 2000).

6. See Kant's famous essay, "What Is Enlightenment?" reprinted many times.

7. For the influence of the Enlightenment on British evangelicals, see the pertinent chapters of David W. Bebbington, *Evangelicalism in Modern Britain: A History from the 1730s to the 1980s* (London: Unwin Hyman, 1989). The vast literature on Jonathan Edwards agrees at least on this, that he was very much a child of the Enlightenment. See, for example, Sang Hyun Lee, *The Philosophical Theology of Jonathan Edwards*, exp. ed. (Princeton, NJ: Princeton University Press, 2000); and Gerald R. McDermott, *Jonathan Edwards Confronts the Gods: Christian Theology, Enlightenment Religion, and Non-Christian Faiths* (Oxford and New York: Oxford University Press, 2000). And for Edwards himself, see *Scientific and Philosophical Writings*, ed. Wallace E. Anderson (New Haven, CT: Yale University Press, 1980).

8. To be sure, there is a rational sense for the word *intuition* as well. The ability of, say, a talented handyman to fix small engines without being able to explain how he knew what was wrong or how he knew how to repair it is not likely a matter of Romantic insight! Rather, intuition here is an inarticulate but still rational apprehension of a situation and the application of technique based on previous experience and accumulated knowledge.

9. Quoted by David M. Knight, *Humphry Davy: Science and Power* (Cambridge, MA, and Oxford: Basil Blackwell, 1992), 36; cited in John Hedley Brooke, "Science and Theology in the Enlightenment," in *Religion and Science: History, Method Dialogue*, ed. W. Mark Richardson and Wesley J. Wildman (New York: Routledge, 1996), 25.

10. "Epitaph intended for Sir Isaac Newton"; quoted in John Bartlett, ed., *Familiar Quotations*, ed. Emily Morison Beck, 14th ed. (Boston and Toronto: Little, Brown, 1968), 412b.

11. "The Tables Turned," 1798; in William Wordsworth, *Selected Poetry*, ed. Mark Van Doren (New York: Modern Library, 1950), 82.

12. Alfred, Lord Tennyson, Canto CXXIII of "In Memoriam"; in *The New Oxford Book of Christian Verse*, ed. Donald Davie (Oxford and New York: Oxford University Press, 1981), 235.

13. William P. Alston, *Perceiving God: The Epistemology of Religious Experience* (Ithaca, NY: Cornell University Press, 1991); Alvin Plantinga, *Warranted Christian Belief* (New York: Oxford University Press, 2000).

14. This is the dominant motif in Baumer.

2. Postmodernity and Postmodernism(s)

1. For recent reconsidering of Locke, see Nicholas Wolterstorff, *John Locke and the Ethics of Belief* (Cambridge: Cambridge University Press, 1996).

2. The canon of postmodernity and postmodernism, so to speak, includes the recognized works of Jacques Derrida, Jean-François Lyotard, Jacques Lacan, Emmanuel Levinas, Michel Foucault, and their ilk. The literature emergent from and surrounding all things "postmodern" is immense, of course. In addition to the works mentioned in the subsequent notes, I have found most informative and suggestive the following books, dealing as they do with much broader aspects of the postmodern condition than deconstruction per se: George Steiner, *Real Presences* (Chicago: University of Chicago Press, 1989); J. Richard Middleton and Brian J. Walsh, *Truth Is Stranger than It Used to Be: Biblical Faith in a Postmodern Age* (Downers Grove, IL: InterVarsity Press, 1995); Terry Eagleton, *The Illusions of Postmodernism* (Oxford: Blackwell, 1996); Robert Hughes, *The Shock of the New*, rev. ed. (New York: Knopf, 1991); Tom Wolfe, *From Bauhaus to Our House* (New York: Farrar Straus Giroux, 1981); and Tom Wolfe, *The Painted Word* (New York: Bantam Books, 1975).

3. So Norman F. Cantor, *Twentieth-Century Culture: Modernism to Deconstruction* (New York: Peter Lang, 1988). I recognize that modernism is one of the most complex episodes in our cultural history, including as it does contradictory tendencies and products on a vast scale. I therefore, helpless to do otherwise, will focus on what Martha Bayles calls constructive modernism, leaving aside perverse modernism (a term Bayles borrows from Jacques Barzun) and then the less constructive aspects of postmodernism as well. (Ironically—and irony is thick in the air in all of this—I mention deconstruction precisely because I take it to be, especially in Derrida's hands, an attempt to accomplish something good, not merely tear things down and apart.) Bayles herself dismisses postmodernism entirely as simply the continuation of characteristics of perverse modernism: "injunctions to break with the past, to attack aesthetic standards, to shock the audience, and to erase the line between art and life" (385). I agree with most of what she writes about perverse modernism per se: I don't agree, however, that this is all there is to say about postmodernism, so I say more.

For Bayles's terminology, see *Hole in Our Soul: The Loss of Beauty and Meaning in American Popular Music* (Chicago, IL: University of Chicago Press, 1996 [1994]), 32–54. For illustrations just from the world of graphic art of how bewilderingly complex modernism is, see Hughes, *The Shock of the New*.

4. For a helpful introduction to the emergence of hip-hop, see Bayles, *Hole in Our Soul*, 342–46.

5. For examples, see William C. Placher, *Unapologetic Theology: A Christian Voice in a Pluralistic Conversation* (Louisville, KY: Westminster/John Knox Press, 1989), 92–104. Martha Bayles describes this sort of thing as a "fast shuffle" (7–8).

6. Alvin Plantinga acknowledges numerous areas of overlapping concern between postmodernism and Christianity in *Warranted Christian Belief* (New York: Oxford University Press, 2000), 423–25. The rest of his chapter on "Postmodernism and Pluralism," offers some powerful rebuttals to some common arguments against Christianity offered in the name of those two (425–57).

7. Holland Carter, "Beyond Multiculturalism, Freedom?" *The New York Times on the Web* (http://www.nytimes.com/2001/07/29/arts/design/20COTT.html). This incisive article focuses particularly on the art world, but its implications touch on most other aspects of multiculturalism. Cf. Reginald W. Bibby, *Mosaic Madness: The Poverty and Potential of Life in Canada* (Toronto: Stoddart, 1990); and Charles Taylor et al., *Multiculturalism* (Princeton, NJ: Princeton University Press, 1994).

3. The Problem of Plausibility

1. The first account I read of this research was in William C. Placher, *Unapologetic Theology: A Christian Voice in a Pluralistic Conversation* (Louisville, KY: Westminster/John Knox Press, 1989), chap. 4, 55–73. Philosophers Peter Winch and Kai Nielsen touched off a lasting debate in the 1960s over issues arising from this research: Placher's notes include many of the relevant citations. For a clever exercise in viewing a modern society anthropologically, with the problem of plausibility in the foreground, see Umberto Eco, "Industry and Sexual Repression in a Po Valley Society," chap. in Eco's *Misreadings*, trans. William Weaver (London: Picador, 1994), 69–93.

2. On such "control beliefs," see Nicholas Wolterstorff, *Reason within the Bounds of Religion*, 2nd ed. (Grand Rapids, MI: Eerdmans, 1984); and his extension of these reflections in "Theology and Science: Listening to Each Other," in *Religion and Science: History, Method, Dialogue*, ed. W. Mark Richardson and Wesley J. Wildman (New York: Routledge, 1996), 95–104.

3. Thomas S. Kuhn, *The Structure of Scientific Revolutions*, 2nd ed. (Chicago: University of Chicago Press, 1970).

4. Mark Richardson and Wesley Wildman speak to this point when they write, "Still others hold that apologetics is a matter of expressing Christian beliefs so as to render them discussible in a broad variety of communal contexts, which is as efficient a way as exists of justifying them" ("Introduction to Part

Two," in *Religion and Science* [New York: Routledge, 1996], 92). What I think Richardson and Wildman mean is that the task of apologetics is to make Christian beliefs worth discussing in a particular context: that is, to make them plausible.

5. Allan Bloom, *The Closing of the American Mind: How Higher Education Has Failed Democracy and Impoverished the Souls of Today's Students* (New York: Simon and Schuster, 1987), 34.

6. George Gallup, Jr. and D. Michael Lindsay, *Surveying the Religious Landscape : Trends in U.S. Beliefs* (Harrisburg, PA: Morehouse, 2000).

7. Frederica Mathewes-Green, "Psalm 23 and All That," *Christianity Today* 44 (7 February 2000): 82.

8. Nancy Nason-Clark, *The Battered Wife: How Christians Confront Family Violence* (Louisville, KY: Westminster/John Knox Press, 1997).

9. I have offered what help I can on some of these questions in *Can God Be Trusted? Faith and the Challenge of Evil* (New York: Oxford University Press, 1998).

10. For helpful discussions of these matters, see the pertinent essays in Charles E. Hummel, *The Galileo Connection: Resolving Conflicts between Science and the Bible* (Downers Grove, IL: InterVarsity Press, 1986); David C. Lindberg and Ronald L. Numbers, ed., *God and Nature: Historical Essays on the Encounter between Christianity and Science* (Berkeley: University of California Press, 1986); W. Mark Richardson and Wesley J. Wildman, ed., *Religion and Science: History, Method, Dialogue* (New York: Routledge, 1996).

11. David N. Livingstone, *Darwin's Forgotten Defenders: The Encounter between Evangelical Theology and Evolutionary Thought* (Vancouver: Regent College, 2000 [1984]).

12. Owen Chadwick, *The Victorian Church*, 2nd ed., vol. 2 (London: Adam and Charles Black, 1972), 1. The quotation marks around 'Darwin' are in Chadwick.

13. "Christian Apologetics" in C. S. Lewis, *God in the Dock: Essays on Theology and Ethics*, ed. Walter Hooper (Grand Rapids, MI: Eerdmans, 1970), 95.

14. David K. Clark, *Dialogical Apologetics: A Person-Centered Approach to Christian Defense* (Grand Rapids, MI: Baker Books, 1993), 199; emphasis in original.

15. G. K. Chesterton, *The Everlasting Man* (New York: Image, 1955 [1925]), 13.

16. See Reginald W. Bibby, *Restless Gods: The Renaissance of Religion in Canada* (Toronto: Stoddart, 2002), 85-91.

17. Douglas Todd, "Why a Prominent Theologian Will Boycott Playland," *Vancouver Sun*, 22 July 2000, A1, A2.

4. Consumerism

1. For some helpful introductions, see the following: Rodney Clapp, ed., *The Consuming Passion: Christianity and the Consumer Culture* (Downers Grove, IL: InterVarsity Press, 1998); Craig M. Gay, *The Way of the (Modern) World or, Why It's Tempting to Live as if God Doesn't Exist* (Grand Rapids, MI / Carlisle, Cumbria / Vancouver, BC: Eerdmans / Paternoster Press / Regent College Publishing, 1998); David Lyon, *The Steeple's Shadow: On the Myths and Realities of Secularization* (Grand Rapids, MI: Eerdmans, 1985).

2. Alan Bulley, with long experience in the Canadian federal civil service, comments: "Government has so completely adapted to the consumerist model that it describes Canadians not as citizens but as 'clients' for its suite of 'services.' Then the bigwigs wonder why no one is happy with the services 'delivered'—because choice is limited by federal or provincial monopoly!" (personal correspondence with the author, 2001).

3. Two major Christian voices in this regard have been those of Jacques Ellul and George Grant: Among many works, see Jacques Ellul, *The Technological Society*, trans. John Wilkinson (New York: Vintage Books, 1964); and George Grant, *Technology and Justice* (Toronto: Anansi, 1986).

4. Robert N. Bellah, *Habits of the Heart: Individualism and Commitment in American Life* (New York: Harper & Row, 1985), 220–21.

5. Robert Wuthnow, *Sharing the Journey: Support Groups and America's New Quest for Community* (New York: Free Press, 1994).

6. Harry Stout observes that eighteenth-century English Christians faced challenges in similar terms (our experience is a more advanced version of theirs): "Increasingly the logic and structure of the marketplace came to stand as a shaping metaphor for society in general. . . . As the public sphere grew more impersonal and abstract, the private self gained proportionate importance as the repository of spiritual experience. . . .

". . . The critical issue was . . . how to take the old verities and present them through new voices that would speak to the changing circumstances of eighteenth-century society. How, in a word, were they to make religion *popular*, able to compete in a morally neutral and voluntaristic marketplace environment alongside all the goods and services of this world?" (Harry S. Stout, *The Divine Dramatist: George Whitefield and the Rise of Modern Evangelicalism* [Grand Rapids, MI: Eerdmans, 1991], xvii).

PART TWO: CONVERSION

5. Defining Conversion

1. A sophisticated form of this argument was offered in J. Gresham Machen, *Christianity and Liberalism* (Grand Rapids, MI: Eerdmans, 1974 [1923]). Suffice it to say that there was no sophisticated form of this argument offered in my upbringing.

2. For a helpful introduction to the sociology of conversion, see Lewis R. Rambo, *Understanding Religious Conversion* (New Haven and London: Yale University Press, 1993).

3. Cf. I Peter 2:2; II Peter 3:18.

4. Cf. Ephesians 4:13.

5. Cf. Colossians 2:6–4:6.

6. Two classic sermons by John Wesley illustrate several of these points: see "The Scripture Way of Salvation" and "The Marks of the New Birth" in *A Burning and a Shining Light: English Spirituality in the Age of Wesley*, ed. David Lyle Jeffrey (Grand Rapids, MI: Eerdmans, 1987), 209–28.

7. I discuss this matter at greater length in John G. Stackhouse, Jr., "Billy Graham and the Nature of Conversion: A Paradigm Case," *Studies in Religion/ Sciences Religeuses* 21/3 (1992): 337–50.

8. Billy Graham, *Peace With God* (New York: Perma Books, 1953), 110–12.

9. John Newton, author of "Amazing Grace," stands as an indisputable exemplar of evangelical piety in the eighteenth century and thus as a counterpart to Billy Graham. As one of his best biographers notes in this regard, "he understood conversion not only as the inauguration of the spiritual life, but also as the progressive, lifelong transformation of the believer. Union and communion with Christ . . . was the goal towards which conversion was directed, both as an experience of initiation and as a process of incremental growth toward its full realization" (Bruce Hindmarsh, *John Newton and the English Evangelical Tradition: Between the Conversions of Wesley and Wilberforce* [New York: Oxford University Press, 1996], 331). Hindmarsh details Newton's own conversion trajectory along these lines in his discussion of Newton's testimony: "'I Know of No Case More Extraordinary than My Own': The *Authentic Narrative* (1764)," chap. in Bruce Hindmarsh, *John Newton and the English Evangelical Tradition: Between the Conversions of Wesley and Wilberforce* (New York: Oxford University Press, 1996), 13–48.

10. Bruce Hindmarsh offers a suggestive example of the conversion of aesthetics in his discussion of eighteenth-century English evangelicals: "Newton

and Evangelical Aesthetics," in *John Newton and the English Evangelical Tradition: Between the Conversions of Wesley and Wilberforce* (New York: Oxford Unversity Pres, 1996), 280–88.

11. For some contemporary reflections along these lines, see Rodney Clapp, *A Peculiar People: The Church as Culture in a Post-Christian Society* (Downers Grove, IL: InterVarsity Press, 1996); Stanley Hauerwas and William H. Willimon, *Resident Aliens: Life in the Christian Colony* (Nashville, TN: Abingdon Press, 1989); and George A. Lindbeck, *The Nature of Doctrine: Religion and Theology in a Postliberal Age* (Philadelphia: Westminster Press, 1984).

12. John Newton, "The Small Success of the Gospel Ministry"; sermon excerpted in *A Burning and a Shining Light*, ed. David Lyle Jeffrey (Grand Rapids, MI: Eerdmans, 1987), 394.

13. Reprinted in *A Burning and a Shining Light*, ed. David Lyle Jeffrey (Grand Rapids, MI: Eerdmans, 1987), 451.

14. Jonathan Edwards, *Religious Affections* (New Haven: Yale University Press, 1959 [1746]), 307. See also John Fletcher's reflections on the Holy Spirit variously addressing the spiritual "eye," or "ear," or "feeling" in "Letters on the Manifestation of Christ" (c. 1775); excerpted in *A Burning and a Shining Light*, ed. David Lyle Jeffrey (Grand Rapids, MI: Eerdmans, 1987), 368–69.

15. As if he were commenting on this passage, H. Richard Niebuhr writes: "There is no continuous movement from an objective inquiry into the life of Jesus to a knowledge of him as the Christ who is our Lord. Only a decision of the self, a leap of faith, a *metanoia* or revolution of the mind can lead from observation to participation and from observed to lived history" (H. Richard Niebuhr, "The Story of Our Life," in *Why Narrative?* ed. Stanley Hauerwas and L. Gregory Jones [Grand Rapids, MI: Eerdmans, 1989], 41).

16. Patricia Hampl, "Edith Stein," in *Martyrs: Contemporary Writers on Modern Lives of Faith*, ed. Susan Bergman (Maryknoll, NY: Orbis Books, 1996), 204–5.

17. John Newton, "Letters"; excerpted in *A Burning and a Shining Light: English Spirituality in the Age of Wesley*, ed. David Lyle Jeffrey (Grand Rapids, MI: Eerdmans, 1987), 431.

6. Deciding about Religion

1. Without getting too technical, let me signal that Alvin Plantinga's use of the word *warrant* is not the same as mine. His is specially suited to his epistemological agenda of showing what it is that, when added to a true belief, makes it *knowledge* (rather than, say, a lucky guess). He says that warrant is that added

something. (Of course, he is much more specific and interesting than that: see his *Warranted Christian Belief* [New York and Oxford: Oxford University Press, 2000]).

My use is more commonplace. I mean by "warrant" simply whatever it is that gives us the basis to believe this or that. It might be a sense impression, or the word of a trusted friend, or a cogent argument, or something else. My answer to the question, "Why do you believe *p* ?" is my warrant or my grounds or my justification. (I recognize also that the term *justification* is also something of a weasel-word in technical epistemology. I expect that readers of this volume will understand it well enough in context as a generic term.) Some epistemological aficionados might suspect, and they would be correct in so suspecting, that I am using such terms as *grounds, justification*, and *warrant* to avoid using the narrower words *evidence* and *reason*, since part of my concern is to open up the category of grounds-for-belief beyond evidentialism and rationalism.

2. For a technical introduction to the state of the art, see Alvin Plantinga, *Warrant: The Current Debate* (New York and Oxford: Oxford University Press, 1993).

3. For those interested in such matters, perhaps a short comment is in order regarding "basic beliefs" and the agenda of so-called Reformed epistemology, an epistemology identified with the work of Alvin Plantinga, Nicholas Wolterstorff, William Alston, and others and one to which I am greatly indebted. These philosophers have launched various attacks on particular understandings of the ethics of belief in which one is told to proportion one's beliefs to the preponderance of the evidence. Thus it may appear that they are also disagreeing with me in this passage. (An early example of this argument is provided in Nicholas Wolterstorff, "Can Belief in God Be Rational If It Has No Foundations?" in *Faith and Rationality: Reason and Belief in God*, ed. Alvin Plantinga and Nicholas Wolterstorff [Notre Dame, IN: University of Notre Dame Press, 1983], 135–38; a more recent study is Nicholas Wolterstorff, *John Locke and the Ethics of Belief* [Cambridge and New York: Cambridge University Press, 1996].)

I am sure they would yet agree, however, that there remains an epistemic obligation to believe properly, as it were. And believing properly would mean, among other things, to believe according to the legitimacy of the "promptings" or grounds one has to believe this or that.

Perhaps one is inferring *p* from *q*. If *p* really does follow from *q*, then all is well. If not, then not. Perhaps instead one believes *p* in what Plantinga calls a "basic" way: One looks at a tree and just knows that there is a tree—if everything is in proper epistemic order (for his careful definitions and defenses, see his trilogy on "warrant" beginning with *Warrant: The Current Debate*). Again, however, such a belief is open to challenge from "defeaters" and "qualifiers," so one would still properly claim, if pressed, only a particular degree of firmness for one's belief that there is a tree over there. Basic beliefs do not mean certain beliefs, since "basic" refers to the manner in which one forms beliefs, not to how veracious they might be. (As Plantinga writes: "It is worth noting that even if I believe something in the basic way, it doesn't follow that I wouldn't cite various other propositions in response to your question, 'Why do you believe *p*? What is your reason for believing *p*?'" [*Warranted Christian Belief*, 176n11].)

I further suggest that the claim for *p* on the basis of the *sensus divinitatis*, or any other divine revelation, is not privileged beyond dispute, but is in the same boat with any other epistemic claim: How do you know that *p* is in fact a deliverance of the Holy Spirit and not a delusion? One might well have formed the belief that *p* simply on the basis of the operation of the *sensus divinitatis*. The *firmness* of one's belief that *p* should be proportioned, I maintain, to the grounds one has to believe that the *sensus divinitatis* is a valid basis for beliefs; that this particular instance is an instance of its functioning correctly; and so on. (See Plantinga, *Warranted Christian Belief*, chap. 8.)

I affirm, therefore, that one's convictions are always liable to the challenge, "Is the firmness of your belief in *p* properly proportioned to the grounds you have for believing it?" And I like to think the Reformed epistemologists would agree. To claim otherwise, it seems to me, leaves us vulnerable to either dogmatism ("I just know it and that's that!") or confusion ("Who can say? Who can really know anything?").

I hope to offer more on epistemology at book-length before long. In the meanwhile, I present a few more reflections on these matters in "Why Christians Should Abandon Certainty," in *Living in the LambLight: Christianity and Contemporary Challenges to the Gospel*, ed. Hans Boersma (Vancouver: Regent College Publishing, 2001), 33–42.

4. So George Lindbeck: "The reasonableness of a religion is largely a function of its assimilative powers, of its ability to provide an intelligible interpretation in its own terms of the varied situations and realities adherents encounter.... Confirmation or disconfirmation occurs through an accumulation of successes or failures in making practically and cognitively coherent sense of relevant data, and the process does not conclude, in the case of religions, until the disappearance of the last communities of believers or, if the faith survives, until the end of history" (*The Nature of Doctrine: Religion and Theology in a*

Postliberal Age [Philadelphia: Westminster Press, 1984], 131). See the larger discussion regarding postliberalism and apologetics, pp. 128–35.

5. Thomas V. Morris, *Making Sense of It All: Pascal and the Meaning of Life* (Grand Rapids, MI: Eerdmans, 1992), 15.

6. One advance reader wondered if I might be depersonalizing Christian faith here into mere cognitive decision ("On the basis of my knowing *x*, I shall therefore risk in the following way . . .") rather than personal trust. Yet the latter depends upon the former. One never trusts someone without a store of important knowledge on which one bases one's faith. Knowing you to be a kind and responsible person, for example, I entrust my pet to your care while I'm away. The Apostle Paul brings these themes nicely together: "But I am not ashamed, for I know the one in whom I have put my trust, and I am sure that he is able to guard until that day what I have entrusted to him" (II Timothy 2:12 NRSV).

7. For seminal reflections on these issues, see William James, "The Will to Believe," in *The Will to Believe and Other Essays in Popular Philosophy* (New York: Dover, 1956), 1–31; and Thomas S. Kuhn, *The Structure of Scientific Revolutions*, 2nd ed. (Chicago: University of Chicago Press, 1970).

8. Plantinga, *Warranted Christian Belief*, 63.

9. Cornel West, *The American Evasion of Philosophy: A Genealogy of Pragmatism* (Madison, WI: University of Wisconsin Press, 1989), 233; cited in William C. Placher, *Narratives of a Vulnerable God: Christ, Theology, and Scripture* (Louisville, KY: Westminster/John Knox Press, 1994), 96.

10. William Alston gathers up several of these points with characteristic lucidity and integrity:

> The evaluation of explanations is a tricky affair at best. Even in empirical science where predictive efficacy can be factored into the equation it is difficult to show that one competing explanation is superior to all its competitors, not to mention the fact that we usually cannot be sure that we have identified all the (serious) competitors. Standard criteria of explanation like simplicity, economy, scope, systematicity, and explanatory power can be appealed to, but such appeals are far from providing us with effective decision procedures. If the explananda are complex patterns of experience, feeling, thought, and behavior—where there is no possibility of a precise predictive test, where the explanations are not embedded in any rich theoretical matrix, and where the competing explanations have not been developed to the point at which it is clear just what consequences can be derived from them—we are in a much worse position to support any particular explanatory claim. . . . The fact remains that . . . one is not

in a position to repose unqualified confidence in Christian explanations of the Christian life. . . .

—or, one supposes, anything else. See William P. Alston, *Perceiving God: The Epistemology of Religious Experience* (Ithaca, NY: Cornell University Press, 1991), 297. C. Stephen Evans, himself a skilled apologist, has much to offer on the subject of epistemology and apologetics throughout his study of *The Historical Christ and the Jesus of Faith: The Incarnational Narrative as History* (Oxford: Clarendon Press, 1996). While I disagree profoundly with him on many matters, I find that Hans Küng takes up several of these matters with characteristic cogency in *On Being a Christian*, trans. Edward Quinn (Garden City, NY: Doubleday & Company, 1976), 68–88. And Lesslie Newbigin offers a helpful introduction to many of the points discussed in this chapter in two books: *Proper Confidence: Faith, Doubt and Certainty in Christian Discipleship* (Grand Rapids, MI: Eerdmans, 1995) and *The Gospel in a Pluralist Society* (Grand Rapids, MI: Eerdmans, 1989).

11. I argue this point in "Why Christians Should Abandon Certainty."

12. Philip Yancey, *Disappointment with God: Three Questions No One Asks Aloud* (Grand Rapids, MI: Zondervan, 1988).

7. Defining, Directing, and Defending Apologetics

1. Avery Dulles, *A History of Apologetics* (Eugene, OR: Wipf and Stock Publishers, 1999 [1971]), xv.

2. William J. O'Malley, S.J., writing in *America* (18 October 1997); cited without further reference in Martin E. Marty, *Context* 30 (15 February 1998): 7.

3. There are indeed similarities between my categories of *internal* and *external* and Schleiermacher's categories of *polemics* and *apologetics* in his *Brief Outline of the Study of Theology*, trans. Terrence N. Tice (Atlanta: John Knox Press, 1977 [1830]), 29–40. In my view, they don't exactly overlap, particularly regarding the discernment of heresy that Schleiermacher makes prominent, but parallels remain, for what they might be worth!

4. I explore these issues at length in *Can God Be Trusted? Faith and the Challenge of Evil* (New York and Oxford: Oxford University Press, 1998).

5. Gerald R. McDermott, *Can Evangelicals Learn from World Religions? Jesus, Revelation and Religious Traditions* (Downers Grove, IL: InterVarsity Press, 2000); John G. Stackhouse, Jr., ed., *No Other Gods before Me? Evangelicals Encounter the World's Religions* (Grand Rapids, MI: Baker, 2001).

6. For testimonies to the usefulness of apologetic argument as helping position one to accept faith, without such argument actually propelling one into faith, see the autobiographical accounts in Kelly James Clark, ed., *Philosophers*

Who Believe: The Spiritual Journeys of Eleven Leading Thinkers (Downers Grove, IL: InterVarsity Press, 1993); and Thomas V. Morris, ed., *God and the Philosophers: The Reconciliation of Faith and Reason* (New York: Oxford University Press, 1994).

7. Paul J. Griffiths, *An Apology for Apologetics: A Study in the Logic of Interreligious Dialogue* (Maryknoll, NY: Orbis Books, 1991), 3.

PART THREE: COMMUNICATION

8. Principles of Christian Communication

1. Much wisdom on these matters is found in the fourth proposal of P. J. Spener's classic tract on Pietism: *Pia Desideria*, trans. Theodore G. Tappert (Philadelphia: Fortress Press, 1964 [1675]), 97–102.

2. John R. W. Stott, *Evangelical Truth: A Personal Plea for Unity, Integrity and Faithfulness* (Downers Grove, IL: InterVarsity Press, 1999), 39.

3. Ibid., 113.

4. Linda Trinkhaus Zagzebski, "Vocatio Philosophiae," in *Philosophers Who Believe: The Spiritual Journeys of Eleven Leading Thinkers*, ed. Kelly James Clark (Downers Grove, IL: InterVarsity Press, 1993), 239.

5. Larry Woiwode, "A Martyr Who Lives," in *Martyrs: Contemporary Writers on Modern Lives of Faith*, ed. Susan Bergman (Maryknoll, NY: Orbis Books, 1996), 24–25.

6. Rich Carl, "Apologetics," *His* 38 (March 1978), back cover. For a longer portrait of the godly apologist, see John Dryden, "The Character of a Good Parson," in *The New Oxford Book of Christian Verse*, ed. Donald Davie (Oxford and New York: Oxford University Press, 1981), 131–34.

7. John Wesley, "A Scheme of Self-Examination Used by the First Methodists in Oxford" (c. 1730); excerpted in *A Burning and a Shining Light: English Spirituality in the Age of Wesley*, ed. David Lyle Jeffrey (Grand Rapids, MI: Eerdmans, 1987), 230.

8. Alan Bede Griffiths, "The Adventure of Faith," in *C. S. Lewis at the Breakfast Table*, ed. James T. Como (New York: Harcourt Brace Jovanovich, 1992), 17.

9. J. Budziszewski, "Talking Straight," *First Things* n. 95 (August 1999): 72.

9. Audience-Specific Apologetics

1. A helpful book with this concern at its heart is David K. Clark, *Dialogical Apologetics: A Person-Centered Approach to Christian Defense* (Grand Rapids, MI:

Baker, 1993). While I disagree with details throughout this book, I heartily concur with most of its main concerns.

2. S. Mark Heim, *The Depth of the Riches: A Trinitarian Theology of Religious Ends* (Grand Rapids, MI: Eerdmans, 2001), 284.

3. Enthusiasts of various "schools" of evangelical apologetics thus will see that I am not about to pick sides among "presuppositionalists," "evidentialists," "cumulative-case" proponents, and the rest. I thank God for the value of each approach. For a temperate example of polemics among these groups, see Steven B. Cowan, ed., *Five Views on Apologetics* (Grand Rapids, MI: Zondervan, 2000).

4. The intermediate position of offensive apologetics I offer there, namely, one that claims Christianity is the *better* or *best*, but not the *only rational*, option, would complement the otherwise helpful discussion in Stephen T. Davis, "Resurrection and Apologetics," chap. in *Risen Indeed: Making Sense of the Resurrection* (Grand Rapids, MI: Eerdmans, 1993).

5. Blaise Pascal, *Pensées*, trans. A. J. Krailsheimer (London: Penguin, 1966), *pensée* 423.

6. Two helpful introductions to Pascal's apologetic thought are Peter Kreeft, *Christianity for Modern Pagans: Pascal's* Pensées—*Edited, Outlined and Explained* (San Francisco: Ignatius Press, 1993); and Thomas V. Morris, *Making Sense of It All: Pascal and the Meaning of Life* (Grand Rapids, MI: Eerdmans, 1992). A recent, accessible biography of Pascal is Marvin R. O'Connell, *Blaise Pascal: Reasons of the Heart* (Grand Rapids, MI: Eerdmans, 1997).

7. A helpful introduction to the vexed question of faith and reason, and particularly Kierkegaard on this matter, is C. Stephen Evans, *Faith Beyond Reason: A Kierkegaardian Account* (Grand Rapids, MI: Eerdmans, 1998).

8. Michael Polanyi, *Personal Knowledge: Towards a Post-Critical Philosophy* (Chicago: University of Chicago Press, 1958, 1962); William P. Alston, *Perceiving God: The Epistemology of Religious Experience* (Ithaca, NY: Cornell University Press, 1991); Alvin Plantinga, *Warranted Christian Belief* (New York: Oxford University Press, 2000). Rudolph Otto concludes his classic apologetic, *The Idea of the Holy*, 2nd ed. (New York: Oxford, 1950 [1923]), with an appeal to subjective intuition of the truth of Christianity—what his translator calls "personal divination" (168-74).

9. William P. Alston, *Perceiving God: The Epistemology of Religious Experience* (Ithaca, NY: Cornell University Press, 1991), 304.

10. Nancey Murphy offers this scathing indictment of such programs: "If theological meanings are not grounded in theological facts—facts about the

character and acts of God, in particular—then they are mere fairy tales, however comforting they may be. Not the opiate of the masses, but the opiate of the intelligentsia" ("On the Nature of Theology," in *Religion and Science: History, Method and Dialogue*, ed. W. Mark Richardson and Wesley J. Wildman [New York: Routledge, 1996], 153).

11. In my own tradition of North American evangelicalism, I follow E. J. Carnell who sought to blend both approaches, each of which he had learned from purists on both sides: see John G. Stackhouse, Jr., "Pioneer: The Reputation of Edward John Carnell in American Theology" (M.A. thesis, Wheaton College, 1982). Cf. Gary Dorrien, *The Remaking of Evangelical Theology* (Louisville, KY: Westminster/John Knox Press, 1998), 68–75, 81–95.

12. Alvin Plantinga, *God, Freedom, and Evil* (Grand Rapids, MI: Eerdmans, 1974); William Lane Craig, *Apologetics: An Introduction* (Chicago: Moody Press, 1984), 167-206; William Lane Craig et al., eds., *Jesus' Resurrection: Fact or Figment? A Debate between William Lane Craig and Gerd Ludemann* (Downers Grove, IL: InterVarsity, 2000); N. T. Wright, *The New Testament and the People of God* (Minneapolis: Fortress Press, 1992); C. Stephen Evans, *The Historical Christ and the Jesus of Faith: The Incarnational Narrative as History* (Oxford: Clarendon Press, 1996).

13. Jean Hampton, "Feminism, Moral Objectivity, and Christianity," in *Christianity and Culture in the Cross-Fire*, ed. David A. Hoekema and Bobby Fong (Grand Rapids, MI: Eerdmans / Calvin Center for Christian Scholarship, 1997), 116–17.

14. For introductions to Bautain, Blondel, and Teilhard, see Avery Dulles, *A History of Apologetics* (Eugene, OR: Wipf and Stock Publishers, 1999 [1971]), 178–79, 203–6, and 221–25. Sir Norman Anderson suggests this approach also as the concluding recommendation in *Christianity and World Religions: The Challenge of Pluralism* (Downers Grove, IL: InterVarsity Press, 1984 [1970]), 187–192.

15. Chesterton, *Orthodoxy* (Garden City, NY: Image/Doubleday, 1959 [1908]), 83.

16. Brian Leftow, "From Jerusalem to Athens," in *God and the Philosophers: The Reconciliation of Faith and Reason*, ed. Thomas V. Morris (New York: Oxford University Press, 1994), 191.

17. Among these questions, probably the least addressed in Christian history has been that of aesthetics. Perhaps the most ambitious apologetic offered on aesthetic grounds was that of François René de Chateaubriand (1768–1848) in his *The Genius of Christianity; or, Beauties of the Christian Religion*. For a brief introduction, see Dulles, *A History of Apologetics*, 172–74. A much more recent

apologetic on behalf of beauty, drawing heavily on the work of Hans Urs von Balthasar, is Thomas Dubay, S. M., *The Evidential Power of Beauty: Science and Theology Meet* (San Francisco: Ignatius, 1999).

18. William Alston testifies: "It was more like having one's eyes opened to an aspect of the environment to which one had previously been blind; more like learning to hear things in music that one had been missing; more like that than coming to realize that certain premises have an unexpected implication" ("A Philosopher's Way Back," in *God and the Philosophers*, ed. Thomas V. Morris [New York: Oxford University Press, 1994], 28). For a postliberal expression of some of these themes, see William C. Placher, *Unapologetic Theology: A Christian Voice in a Pluralistic Conversation* (Louisville, KY: Westminster/John Knox Press, 1989), chap. 8: "Truth," 123–37.

10. Guidelines for Apologetic Conversation

1. Ernest Becker, *Escape from Evil* (New York: Macmillan, 1975), 64; cited in Ted Peters, *Sin: Radical Evil in Soul and Society* (Grand Rapids, MI: Eerdmans, 1994), 52.

2. G. K. Chesterton, *The Everlasting Man* (New York: Image, 1955 [1925]), 275.

3. "The apostles concentrated on recounting, again and again, a historical event which was intimately known to them, and to which they could give their unqualified, personal testimony: the life, words and deeds, and above all the death and resurrection, of One with whom they had kept close company for some three years. The original Twelve were no philosophers and had had no theological training; but they could not be silenced from 'speaking about what we have seen and heard' (Acts 4:20)" (Sir Norman Anderson, *Christianity and World Religions: The Challenge of Pluralism* [Downers Grove, IL: InterVarsity Press, 1984 (1970)], 176). Cf. F. F. Bruce, *The Defense of the Gospel in the New Testament*, (Grand Rapids, MI: Eerdmans, 1977 [1959]); and Avery Dulles, "Apologetics in the New Testament," chap. in *A History of Apologetics* (Eugene, OR: Wipf and Stock, 1999 [1971]), 1–21.

4. Rodney Clapp, *A Peculiar People: The Church as Culture in a Post-Christian Society* (Downers Grove, IL: InterVarsity Press, 1996), 170.

5. Blaise Pascal, *Pensées*, trans. A. J. Krailsheimer (London: Penguin, 1966), *pensées* 133 and 166.

6. John Fletcher, "Mediations"; excerpted in *A Burning and a Shining Light: English Spirituality in the Age of Wesley*, ed. David Lyle Jeffrey (Grand Rapids, MI: Eerdmans, 1987), 363.

7. John Newton, Sermons on "Messiah"; excerpted in *A Burning and a Shining Light: English Spirituality in the Age of Wesley*, ed. David Lyle Jeffrey (Grand Rapids, MI: Eerdmans, 1987), 419. Newton adds: "For though sin be a grievous illness and a hard bondage, yet one effect of it is a strange stupidity and infatuation which renders us (like a person in a delirium) oblivious to our true state. It is a happy time when the Holy Spirit, by his convincing power, removes that stupor which, while it prevents us from fully perceiving our misery, renders us likewise indifferent to the only means of deliverance" (ibid., 420).

8. Chesterton, *The Everlasting Man*, 279.

9. Philip Clayton and Steven Knapp focus on this point acutely in the dialogue of religion and science: see "Rationality and Christian Self-Conceptions," in *Religion and Science: History, Method, Dialogue*, eds. W. Mark Richardson and Wesley J. Wildman (New York: Routledge, 1996), 131–42.

10. Richard John Neuhaus, "The Public Square," *First Things* n. 86 (October 1998): 83.

11. C. S. Lewis, *The Problem of Pain* (New York: Collier Books, 1962); C. S. Lewis, *A Grief Observed* (New York: Bantam Books, 1961).

12. Lewis's former Oxford colleague John Wain speaks about the "curious impersonality" of most of Lewis's writing in "A Great Clerke," in *C. S. Lewis at the Breakfast Table and Other Reminiscences*, ed. James T. Como (New York: Harcourt Brace Jovanovich, 1992 [1979]), 68–76.

13. John R. W. Stott, "Jottings for a biography," 1993/94, p. 23; quoted in Timothy Dudley-Smith, *John Stott: The Making of a Leader; Vol. 1: A Biography: The Early Years* (Downers Grove, IL: InterVarsity Press, 1999), 459.

14. Quoted in Martin E. Marty, "The Difference in Being a Christian and the Difference It Makes—for History," in *History and Historical Understanding*, ed. C. T. McIntire and Ronald A. Wells (Grand Rapids, MI: Eerdmans, 1984), 43–44.

15. Lewis Carroll, *Through the Looking Glass* (New York: Grosset & Dunlap, 1946), 229–30.

16. John G. Stackhouse, Jr., "Contextualization in Canadian Theological Education: A Friendly Provocation," in *Studies in Canadian Evangelical Renewal: Essays in Honour of Ian S. Rennie*, ed. Kevin Quast and John Vissers (Markham, Ontario: Faith Today, 1996), 34–44.

17. C. S. Lewis, *Mere Christianity* (Glasgow: Fontana, 1952), 100. Lewis's writing regrettably has lots of dubious gender references scattered here and there. *The Problem of Pain*, for another example, has him describing the Incarnation thus: "It has the master touch—the rough, male taste of reality" ([New York: Collier Books, 1962], 25).

18. *Pensée* 12; cited without further reference to the edition used in Thomas V. Morris, *Making Sense of It All: Pascal and the Meaning of Life* (Grand Rapids, MI: Eerdmans, 1992), 145.

19. Such apologists can begin well with Avery Dulles, *A History of Apologetics* (Eugene, OR: Wipf and Stock Publishers, 1999 [1971]).

20. A model of such comparison still is Sir Norman Anderson, *Christianity and World Religions: The Challenge of Pluralism* (Downers Grove, IL: InterVarsity Press, 1984 [1970]).

21. C. S. Lewis warned Christians of this fact in his essay on "The Language of Religion," in *Christian Reflections* (Grand Rapids, MI: Eerdmans, 1997 [1967]), 129–41. For a more recent warning, see Gregory A. Clark, "The Nature of Conversion: How the Rhetoric of Worldview Philosophy Can Betray Evangelicals," in *The Nature of Confession: Evangelicals and Postliberals in Conversation*, eds. Timothy R. Phillips and Dennis L. Okholm (Downers Grove, IL: InterVarsity Press, 1996), 201–18.

22. For Tillich regarding Barth, see "What Is Wrong with the 'Dialectic' Theology?" reprinted in *Paul Tillich: Theologian of the Boundaries*, ed. Mark Kline Taylor (Minneapolis: Fortress Press, 1991), 104–16.

23. C. S. Lewis, "The Funeral of a Great Myth," in *Christian Reflections* (Grand Rapids, MI: Eerdmans, 1997 [1967]), 93.

24. Francis A. Schaeffer, *The God Who Is There: Speaking Historic Christianity into the Twentieth Century* (London: Hodder and Stoughton, 1968), 127–30.

25. John G. Stackhouse, *Can God Be Trusted? Faith and the Challenge of Evil* (New York: Oxford University Press, 1998), esp. chap. 6, "The Fork in the Road."

26. These are themes sounded also in Diogenes Allen's suggestive and useful book, *Christian Belief in a Postmodern World: The Full Wealth of Conviction* (Louisville, KY: Westminster/John Knox Press, 1989).

27. This move was crucial for my own thinking about this question; I have discussed it in *Can God Be Trusted?*

28. See Anderson, *Christianity and World Religions*.

29. Rudolf Otto, *The Idea of the Holy*, 2nd ed., trans. John W. Harvey (New York: Oxford, 1950 [1923]), 169–70.

30. Stanley Hauerwas and William H. Willimon, *Resident Aliens: Life in the Christian Colony* (Nashville, TN: Abingdon Press, 1989), 103.

31. William Alston, "A Philosopher's Way Back," in *God and the Philosophers*, ed. Thomas V. Morris (New York: Oxford University Press, 1994), 27.

32. Owen Chadwick, *The Victorian Church*, 2nd ed. (London: Adam and Charles Black, 1980 [1972]), 1.

33. See Alvin Plantinga, *Warranted Christian Belief* (New York: Oxford University Press, 2000). Cf. Nicholas Wolterstorff, *Divine Discourse: Philosophical Reflections on the Claim that God Speaks* (Cambridge: Cambridge University Press, 1995).

34. So the testimony of El Salvador martyr Rutilio Grande, S. J., as he declared one month before his death in 1977: "It is dangerous to be a Christian in our milieu! . . . precisely because the world which surrounds us is founded radically on an established disorder before which the mere proclamation of the Gospel is subversive" (quoted in Carolyn Forché, "Oscar Romero," in *Martyrs: Contemporary Writers on Modern Lives of Faith*, ed. Susan Bergman [Maryknoll, NY: Orbis Books, 1996], 59). Christians outside Latin America cannot comfort themselves with the illusion that Grande speaks only of his own society.

35. E. M. Bounds, *Power through Prayer / Purpose in Prayer* (Westwood, NJ: The Christian Library, 1984), 24, 72.

36. Rodney Clapp, *A Peculiar People: The Church as Culture in a Post-Christian Society* (Downers Grove, IL: InterVarsity Press, 1996), 117.

37. David Clark puts this point in a particular way: "Skillful apologists ask others to take a step at the edge of their latitude of commitment" (*Dialogical Apologetics: A Person-Centered Approach to Christian Defense* [Grand Rapids, MI: Baker Books, 1993], 224). Asking too much can provoke resistance; asking too little is of no use to our neighbor. Helping our neighbor take another step is the rule.

38. Charles Gilmore, "To the RAF," in *C. S. Lewis at the Breakfast Table and Other Reminiscences*, ed. James T. Como (New York: Harcourt Brace Jovanovich, 1992 [1979]), 187–88.

39. David K. Clark, *Dialogical Apologetics*, 223.

40. See Glenn Tinder, *The Political Meaning of Christianity: An Interpretation* (Baton Rouge: Louisiana State University Press, 1989), 104–5.

41. A nice example of such restraint in ambition is C. S. Lewis's "*De Futilitate*," in *Christian Reflections* (Grand Rapids, MI: Eerdmans, 1997 [1967]), 57–71. Christian analytical philosophers have also set us good examples in their willingness to work hard within tightly circumscribed conversations to establish some good thing, but not everything, about the Christian message. For more popular examples, see Alvin Plantinga, *God, Freedom, and Evil* (Grand Rapids, MI: Eerdmans, 1974); and Richard Swinburne, *Is There a God?* (Oxford: Oxford University Press, 1996).

42. For theological reflections on these matters with which I have considerable sympathy, see Clark H. Pinnock, *A Wideness in God's Mercy: The Finality of Jesus Christ in a World of Religions* (Grand Rapids, MI: Zondervan, 1992); and

several essays in John G. Stackhouse, Jr., ed., *No Other Gods before Me? Evangelicals Encounter the World's Religions* (Grand Rapids, MI: Baker, 2001).

43. For suggestive reflections on the examples set by Jesus and Paul in religious dialogue, see Pinnock, *A Wideness in God's Mercy*, 129–43.

11. Other Modes of Apologetics

1. J. K. S. Reid, *Christian Apologetics* (London: Hodder and Stoughton, 1969); Avery Dulles, *A History of Apologetics* (Eugene, OR: Wipf and Stock, 1999 [1971]).

2. F. D. E. Schleiermacher, *Brief Outline on the Study of Theology*, trans. Terrence N. Tice (Atlanta: John Knox, 1966 [1830–31]); B. B. Warfield, *The Idea of Systematic Theology Considered as a Science* (New York: Randolph, 1888); Paul Tillich, *Systematic Theology*, vol. 1 (Chicago: University of Chicago Press, 1951).

3. It perhaps is worth noting that none of the categories that follow describe resources that are exclusively Christian. Other religions have their counterparts. Yet that reality does not undercut the usefulness of such apologetical resources. Just as in the case of Christian theological and philosophical apologetics that have parallels in other religions, good use of the following suggested resources can be made in comparison with the offerings of other religions.

4. *Webster's Ninth New Collegiate Dictionary* (Springfield, MA: Merriam-Webster, 1990), s.v. "church."

5. Jean Delumeau, *Catholicism between Luther and Voltaire: A New View of the Counter-Reformation* (Philadelphia: Westminster, 1977).

6. William Westfall, *Two Worlds: The Protestant Culture of Nineteenth-Century Ontario* (Kingston, Ontario, and Montreal: McGill-Queen's University Press, 1989), 126–58.

7. Ken Sidey, "So Long to Sacred Space," *Christianity Today* 37 (8 November 1993): 46.

8. For an introduction to semiotics, see Terence Hawkes, *Structuralism and Semiotics* (Berkeley and Los Angeles: University of California Press, 1977), 123–50; and for delightful examples of its use, see Umberto Eco, *Travels in Hyperreality* (London: Pan, 1987).

9. It is striking that C. S. Lewis, whose works exemplify this principle as much as anyone's in the twentieth century, himself was moved toward faith by literature: "Both [Lewis] and I came to religion by way of literature," testifies his friend Alan Bede Griffiths ("The Adventure of Faith," in *C. S. Lewis at the Breakfast Table and Other Reminiscences*, ed. James T. Como (New York: Harcourt

Brace Jovanovich, 1992 [1979]), 15; cf. C. S. Lewis, *Surprised by Joy: The Shape of My Early Life* (New York: Harcourt Brace Jovanovich, 1955).

10. Austin Farrer, "In His Image," in *C. S. Lewis at the Breakfast Table and Other Reminiscences*, ed. James T. Como (New York: Harcourt Brace Jovanovich, 1992 [1979]), 243.

11. The first of Howatch's novels in this series is *Glittering Images* (New York: Crest, 1996). For an introduction to Howatch, see John G. Stackhouse, Jr., "His Majesty's Sacred Service," *Books and Culture* 4 (September 1998): 26–29.

12. Flannery O'Connor, *Collected Works* (New York: Library of America, 1988); Frederick Buechner, *Godric* (San Francisco: Harper, 1983); Frederick Buechner, *The Book of Bebb*, reissue ed. (San Francisco: HarperSanFrancisco, 2001).

13. For examples, see Donald Davie, ed., *The New Oxford Book of Christian Verse* (Oxford and New York: Oxford University Press, 1981).

14. For samples, see Lyle W. Dorsett, ed., *GK's Weekly: A Sampler* (Chicago: Loyola University Press, 1986).

15. Chesterton acquired a reputation also for his art, especially caricatures. See Alzina Stone Dale, *The Art of G. K. Chesterton* (Chicago: Loyola University Press, 1985).

16. If I may use a personal illustration, I deliberately use gender-inclusive language even for God in my apologetic, *Can God Be Trusted? Faith and the Challenge of Evil* (Oxford and New York: Oxford University Press, 1998). I do so, not because I think one always should use gender-neutral language for God, but because such usage is an accommodation to the concerns of many people who might have been put off that book over what is, in that discussion, a secondary matter.

17. Jonathan D. Spence, *The Memory Palace of Matteo Ricci* (New York: Viking, 1984), 1–4.

18. William Christian, *George Grant: A Biography* (Toronto: University of Toronto Press, 1993), 62.

19. C. S. Lewis, *God in the Dock: Essays on Theology and Ethics*, ed. Walter Hooper (Grand Rapids, MI: Eerdmans, 1970), 93. Nicholas Wolterstorff makes the same point: "It seems clear that apologetics (defense of the faith) is not some distinct area of inquiry to be assigned to theologians. The psychologist who rejects behaviorism and works out a psychological action-theory as an option to the pervasive behavior-theories should be viewed as, in effect, engaged in apologetics" (*Reason within the Bounds of Religion*, 2nd ed. [Grand Rapids, MI: Eerdmans, 1984 (1976)], 157n45).

20. Larry Rasmussen, ed., *Reinhold Niebuhr: Theologian of Public Life* (Minneapolis: Fortress Press, 1991), 3. The Niebuhr quotation is from Reinhold Niebuhr, "Intellectual Autobiography," in *Reinhold Niebuhr: His Religious, Social and Political Thought*, ed. Charles W. Kegley, 2nd ed. (New York: Pilgrim, 1984), 3; cited in *Reinhold Niebuhr: Theologian of Public Life*, ed. Larry Rasmussen (Minneapolis: Fortress Press, 1991), 2.

George Grant, it should be noted, played a similar role north of the border in Canada; for an introduction to his life and thought, see Christian, *George Grant*. Grant also often spoke and wrote publicly with his Christian convictions implicit, albeit fully operative. After an early, bruising, and unproductive controversy, he testified that he learned the need to be more subtle. "I knew from that that you had to write fairly indirectly if you wanted to live, particularly in the academic community" (quoted in Christian, *George Grant*, 156).

21. Kenneth Scott Latourette, *A History of the Expansion of Christianity*, vol. 2: *The Thousand Years of Uncertainty* (New York and London: Harper & Brothers, 1938), 92.

22. See the bibliography in Gary S. Greig and Kevin N. Springer, *The Kingdom and the Power* (Ventura, CA: Regal, 1993), 446–50.

23. Literally the only female author I have read who has addressed precisely this issue is Jean Hampton in a section entitled, "How to Fight," of her essay, "Feminism, Moral Objectivity, and Christianity," in *Christianity and Culture in the Crossfire*, eds. David A. and Bobby Fong Hoekema (Grand Rapids, MI: Eerdmans / Calvin Center for Christian Scholarship, 1997), 124–28. This whole essay is chock-full of wisdom.

24. Hampton, "How to Fight," 124–28, 125.

25. Quoted in Barbara Reynolds, *Dorothy L. Sayers: Her Life and Soul* (New York: St. Martin's Griffith, 1993), 82.

26. Howard A. Snyder, *Signs of the Spirit: How God Reshapes the Church* (Grand Rapids, MI: Zondervan, 1989), 87. See also Gary R. Sattler, *God's Glory, Neighbor's Good: A Brief Introduction to the Life and Writings of August Hermann Francke* (Chicago: Covenant, 1982).

27. Snyder, *Signs of the Spirit*, 88.

28. F. Ernest Stoeffler, *The Rise of Evangelical Pietism* (Leiden: E. J. Brill, 1965), 31; quoted in Snyder, *Signs of the Spirit*, 89.

29. Ron Sider tells the extraordinary story of Ed Dobson, former vice president of Jerry Falwell's Moral Majority and pastor of a large evangelical church, and his care for homosexuals in Grand Rapids, Michigan (Ronald J. Sider, *Living like Jesus: Eleven Essentials for Growing a Genuine Faith* [Grand Rapids, MI: Baker

Books, 1996], 167–69). Sider refers to Ed Dobson, *Simplicity: Reconciling Your Life with Your Values* (Grand Rapids, MI: Zondervan, 1995), chap. 6.

30. William C. Placher, *Unapologetic Theology: A Christian Voice in a Pluralistic Conversation* (Louisville, KY: Westminster/John Knox Press, 1989), 167.

31. William Dyrness, "What Good Is Truth? Postmodern Apologetics in a World Community," *Radix* 26:3 (1998): 4–7, 23–26.

32. Stanley Hauerwas and William H. Willimon, *Resident Aliens: Life in the Christian Colony* (Nashville, TN: Abingdon Press, 1989), 58.

33. Quoted in Calvin Bedient, "Etty Hillesum," in *Martyrs: Contemporary Writers on Modern Lives of Faith*, ed. Susan Bergman (Maryknoll, NY: Orbis Books, 1996), 169.

34. Among many examples, see Harry Blamires, *Where Do We Stand? An Examination of the Christian's Position in the Modern World* (Ann Arbor, MI: Servant, 1980); Eric G. Jay, *The Church: Its Changing Image through Twenty Centuries* (Atlanta: John Knox, 1977, 1978); Hans Küng, *On Being a Christian*, trans. Edward Quinn (Garden City, NY: Doubleday, 1974); Richard F. Lovelace, *Renewal as a Way of Life: A Guidebook for Spiritual Growth* (Downers Grove, IL: InterVarsity Press, 1985); Wolfhart Pannenberg, *The Church*, trans. Keith Crim (Philadelphia: Westminster, 1983); W. A. Visser 'T. Hooft, *The Renewal of the Church* (London: SCM, 1956).

35. Snyder, *Signs of the Spirit*, 224, 230. On these societies, see also Howard A. Snyder, *The Radical Wesley and Patterns for Church Renewal* (Downers Grove, IL: InterVarsity Press, 1980), 53–64 and passim; Henry D. Rack, *Reasonable Enthusiast: John Wesley and the Rise of Methodism*, 2nd ed. (Nashville: Abingdon, 1992), 237–50; and Robert G. Tuttle, Jr., *John Wesley: His Life and Theology* (Grand Rapids, MI: Zondervan, 1978), 276–82.

36. On the family as a "mission station," see Rodney Clapp, *Families at the Crossroads: Beyond Traditional and Modern Options* (Downers Grove, IL: InterVarsity Press, 1993), esp. 149–66.

37. Arthur F. Holmes, *Contours of a World View* (Grand Rapids, MI: Eerdmans, 1983); John R. W. Stott, *Involvement*, vol. 1: *Being a Responsible Christian in a Non-Christian Society*, and vol. 2: *Social and Sexual Relationships in the Modern World* (Old Tappan, NJ: Revell, 1984, 1985); Nicholas Wolterstorff, *Reason within the Bounds of Religion*, 2nd ed. (Grand Rapids, MI: Eerdmans, 1984).

Conclusion: Humble Apologetics

1. C. S. Lewis; cited without further reference in James T. Como, "Introduction: Within the Realm of Plenitude," in *C. S. Lewis at the Breakfast Table and Other Reminiscences*, ed. James T. Como (New York: Harcourt Brace Jovanovich, 1992), xxv.

2. Lesslie Newbigin, *The Household of God* (New York: Friendship, 1954); quoted in S. Mark Heim, *The Depth of the Riches: A Trinitarian Theology of Religious Ends* (Grand Rapids, MI: Eerdmans, 2001), 66.

3. See Os Guinness, *Fit Bodies Fat Minds: Why Evangelicals Don't Think and What to Do About it* (Grand Rapids, MI: Baker Books, 1994), 152. This sort of hesitation is a theme running through Glenn Tinder, *The Political Meaning of Christianity: An Interpretation* (Baton Rouge: Louisiana State University Press, 1989).

4. Robert J. Morgan, *Beyond Reasonable Doubt: Evidence for the Truth of Christianity* (Wheaton, IL: Evangelical Training Association, 1997); Brad T. Bromling, *Be Sure! A Study in Christian Evidences* (Montgomery, AL: Apologetics Press, 1995); Josh McDowell, *Evidence That Demands a Verdict: Historical Evidences for the Christian Faith* (San Bernardino, CA: Campus Crusade for Christ, 1972).

5. Quoted in Barbara Reynolds, *Dorothy L. Sayers: Her Life and Soul* (New York: St. Martin's Griffith, 1993), 339.

6. C. S. Lewis, "Christian Apologetics," in C. S. Lewis, *God in the Dock: Essays on Theology and Ethics*, ed. Walter Hooper (Grand Rapids, MI: Eerdmans, 1970), 103.

7. Tinder, *The Political Meaning of Christianity*, 71.

8. The believer . . . doesn't really think the beliefs in question *are* on a relevant epistemic par. She may agree that she and those who dissent are equally convinced of the truth of their belief, and even that they are internally on a par, that the internally available markers are similar, or relevantly similar. Still, she must think that there is an important epistemic difference: she thinks that somehow the other person has made a mistake, or has a blind spot, or hasn't been wholly attentive, or hasn't received some grace she has, or is blinded by ambition or pride or mother love or something else; she must think that she has access to a source of warranted belief the other lacks. If the believer concedes that she *doesn't* have any special source of knowledge or true belief with respect to Christian belief—no *sensus divinitatis*, no internal instigation of the Holy Spirit, no teaching by a church inspired and protected from error by the Holy Spirit, nothing not

available to those who disagree with her—*then*, perhaps, she can properly be charged with an arbitrary egoism, and *then*, perhaps, she will have a defeater for her Christian belief. But why should she concede these things? She will ordinarily think (or at least *should* ordinarily think) that there are indeed sources of warranted belief that issue in these beliefs. . . .

As a result, of course, the serious believer will not take it that we are all, believers and unbelievers alike, epistemic peers on the topic of Christian belief" (Alvin Plantinga, *Warranted Christian Belief* [New York and Oxford: Oxford University Press, 2000], 453–54).

Index

with the proposal for a peace conference and summit talks on Berlin and Germany, with participation by the German Democratic Republic and the Federal Republic of Germany. It did not withdraw the six-month deadline; it chose not to mention it. Eager for negotiations, without the duress explicitly having been withdrawn, the Western powers on February 16 [4] informed the Soviet government that they were prepared to take part in a four-power conference of foreign ministers to deal with the problem of Germany in all its aspects. They likewise agreed that German "advisers" be invited and consulted.

The foreign ministers conference opened in Geneva on May 11, 1959. Thereby the Soviets achieved two gains: first, the conference was beginning within the six-month deadline of the November 27 ultimatum, and, secondly, East Germans were in attendance as if they represented a legitimate government. These Geneva negotiations are a sad story, for the Western powers offered such concessions to the Soviets that, if their proposals had been accepted, the position of West Berlin would probably have been undermined. The following concessions were offered in the Allied proposals of June 16: [5]

1. The Western garrisons were to be limited to their present figure, approximately 11,000, and they would be armed wholly with conventional weapons as at the time. Consideration would be given to the reduction the size of the garrisons "if developments in the situation permit."

2. Free and unrestricted access to West Berlin would be continued under the procedures in effect in April 1959, but these procedures might be carried out by East German personnel.

3. "Activities which might either disturb public order or seriously affect the rights and interests, or amount interference in the internal affairs, of others [propa-

There are many reasons why the Soviets made this decision, holding tenaciously to their position in the Soviet zone and transforming it into a Communist state, the German Democratic Republic (GDR). In the first place, from the standpoint of traditional military thinking, East Germany was a valuable addition to the glacis which thus stretched from the Western frontier of the USSR across Eastern Europe to the Elbe.

Second, the massive Soviet occupation forces in East Germany served as a "cork in the bottle" with respect to the political instabilities in Eastern Europe. When Khrushchev and other Soviet Politburo members descended on Warsaw in October 1956 to attempt to prevent the accession of Gomulka to the top Polish Communist party leadership position, five divisions of the Soviet Army in East Germany fanned out along the East German-Polish frontier to add to the threat of the two Soviet divisions marching on Warsaw from their barracks in lower Silesia. When twelve years later in August 1968 the Soviets invaded Czechoslovakia, major components of the Soviet invading force came from the Soviet Army in East Germany.

Third, East Germany makes a very important economic contribution to the Soviet Union. For many years East Germany has been the number one trade partner of the USSR, having around 20 percent of total Soviet foreign trade—in 1970 it was 23 percent. The GDR provides the Soviets and the Eastern European Communist countries with high quality products: machine tools, electrical equipment, optical and chemical products.

Fourth, a divided Germany is a weakened Germany. However, while West Germany alone is certainly no threat to the Soviet Union, even a reunited Germany would hardly be a serious threat.

Fifth, the Soviets regard their strong position in East Germany as a potential jumping-off place against

West Germany and against Western Europe, both in a military and a political warfare sense. While in recent years the Soviets have muted their aggressive language in view of their efforts to achieve recognition, *de facto* or *de jure*, of the GDR and general acceptance of the *status quo* in central and eastern Europe, nevertheless it is doubtful that the Soviets have abandoned the long-range aim of unifying Germany under Communist control. For this purpose the GDR is a vantage point or springboard. In a speech at the All-German Workers Conference in Leipzig on March 7, 1959, Khrushchev made clear his expectation that Germany will be reunited in the future, when the working class in West Germany also comes to power and brings about "the socioeconomic reforms" which will make it possible to put the two parts of Germany readily together again. He said, "how, on what foundation shall the reunification of Germany take place? We are not for just any kind of reunification . . . one must approach the question of reunification above all from the class standpoint. Those who represent the interest of the working class cannot even permit the thought that by a reunification of Germany the workers and peasants of the German Democratic Republic . . . shall lose all their achievements and agree to live as formerly under the conditions of the capitalist yoke. . . . I repeat we are for the reunification of Germany and the German people will again be reunited. This is only a question of time. In this connection it is naturally very important on what foundation Germany will again be reunited." [1]

In the note of November 27, 1958,[2] the Soviet government declared that it regarded as null and void all the wartime agreements on the occupation of Germany and the administration of Berlin. It demanded the withdrawal of Western military forces from the city and proposed to

make West Berlin a demilitarized "free "the most correct and natural" soluti reunite West Berlin with East Berlin and the German Democratic Republic. If th did not accept this proposal within six viet Union would at that time sign a the German Democratic Republic and East Germans control of all access to Soviets sought to "normalize" the situat "only madmen" would think of "unleash war over the preservation of privilege West Berlin." While Stalin had attack sition in Berlin quietly with practical b Khrushchev attacked the position with bombastic speeches, the illogic of Com tion, and threats of war. Although the viously the aggressors in the block note of November 27 put the West explain why such apparently "reasona ing to eliminate an "abnormal" remr II were not acceptable. More importa were actually to turn over access cont East German authorities and the unacceptable to the Western Allies, t been obliged to take positive actions aggressive in order to maintain free

The United States' reply of D rejected the Soviet allegations and that it could not embark on discuss Union "under menace or ultimatu quiring whether the Soviet Union wo into discussions among the four po of Berlin "in the wider framework solution of the German problem as pean security." Moscow responded ganda and intelligence activities] should be avoided in both parts of Berlin."

These Western proposals caused anguish among the West Berlin and West German authorities, and they were contrary to the views and recommendations of the American authorities in Berlin, and of the British and French there as well. There are two factors which help explain these proposals. John Foster Dulles had resigned as Secretary of State on April 15, and he died on May 26. We sorely missed at this juncture his anti-Communist moralism, his fortitude, his understanding of German views, and his close association with Adenauer. The new Secretary of State, Christian Herter, was by nature a man of compromise, and new in his position, he was more susceptible to the views of the compromise-prone British Foreign Secretary, Selwyn Lloyd. Second, the three Western governments were under the psychological war-crisis pressure deliberately created by Khrushchev, and concessionary proposals could readily be rationalized as an effort to avert major war. Fortunately the Soviets did not accept these Western proposals. Early in July President Eisenhower had invited Khrushchev to visit the United States. He accepted readily, doubtless thinking that a personal meeting might result in even better arrangements on Berlin from the Soviet standpoint. At the meeting in Camp David September 26, 1959, Khrushchev agreed to withdraw the earlier Soviet ultimatum and President Eisenhower agreed to reopen negotiations on Berlin at a four-power summit conference in 1960.[6] This summit conference was subsequently scheduled to take place in Paris in mid-May 1960, but it never really convened. On May 1 an American U-2 plane was brought down on Soviet territory. On his arrival in Paris on May 15, Khrushchev told President De Gaulle that he was unwilling to meet with President Eisenhower unless the

President were to apologize publicly for the U-2 flight and all those in the American government who had been involved in it were dismissed. Undoubtedly Khrushchev had noted a hardening of the American position in public statements during previous months, and presumably therefore decided to use the U-2 incident as a pretext for breaking up the conference. Likewise he had evidently decided to await the outcome of the American presidential elections and the advent of a new administration. From June until December 1960, before and after the presidential elections, Khrushchev declared repeatedly that he would allow the new American President time to take over and study international problems. After January 1961, he made it clear that he still regarded Berlin as an urgent question and began to hint that he would take action on Berlin unless his demands were accepted.

The summit meeting between President Kennedy and Khrushchev took place June 3 and 4, 1961 in Vienna. From the American standpoint, the timing and circumstances could not have been worse. On February 22 President Kennedy had sent a personal note to Khrushchev suggesting a meeting for a direct personal exchange of views without an attempt at negotiations. Khrushchev did not deign to reply for two months. Meanwhile in April the disastrous Bay of Pigs venture took place and the Western position in Laos had sharply deteriorated. On May 4 Khrushchev replied that he was willing to meet with President Kennedy. The President accepted, and as a result, the meeting took place with the President obliged to speak not from a position of strength, but from a background of grievous failure. Under these circumstances it is not surprising that Khrushchev was not impressed with President Kennedy, as the transcript of conversation reveals. At any rate, Khrushchev was not restrained from passing to the President on June 4 an *aide-mémoire*,[7] which demanded a demilitarized neutral status for West Berlin, set a new six months time limit for talks between the two German states, and threatened a separate treaty with the German Democratic Republic. Khrushchev, moreover, talked to the President in bellicose terms; President Kennedy described the talks as "somber."

the East Germans commenced to build the Wall about one o'clock on Sunday morning, August 13, 1961. Actually it was not a wall at first; it was a barbed wire fence with tank obstructions at some critical points. A few days later they began erecting a wall of cement blocks, particularly in the central and populated areas.

What did we know beforehand? There was considerable criticism at the time that Allied intelligence was caught flatfooted, entirely ignorant of the East German intentions. Simultaneously the Allies were accused of foreknowledge that the wall was going to be built. Shortly before his death, Chancellor Adenauer—who should have known better—repeated in Madrid the charge that the United States had known in advance that the wall was going to be built through the middle of the city. The truth of the matter is mixed, as is usually the case. We certainly did not have clear knowledge in advance. We were certainly not informed by the Soviets of the East German intention. The East Germans had cleverly disguised the material preparations for their action; for example, the barbed wire, we learned later, had been stored in the several *Kasernen* (military barracks) in East Berlin; the building blocks for the wall had been stored in part in the *Kasernen* and in part at construction sites, and indeed in part had been taken directly from the materials on hand for construction work in process. We knew that the East Germans were going to do something to seal off the refugee flow which had grown to alarming proportions from their standpoint. During the peak weeks in the three previous months they had been losing between six and ten thousand refugees weekly. Many of us thought that the East Germans were going to seal off the whole of the city by introducing such tight controls for the entry into East Berlin of Soviet Zone Germans that the flow of refugees to the West would be stopped at the border between the Soviet Zone and East Berlin, rather than between East and West Berlin. We had seen the East Germans undertake precisely such controls that July during an Evangelical *Kirchensynod* (church synod) held in West Berlin; we had the impression that this effort was a trial run, that it had been fairly successful, and that the East Germans would be able to perfect these controls so as to diminish radically the refugee flow without disturbing the residual four-power status of the whole city of Berlin. Sealing off the whole city had some obvious disadvantages from the East German Communist standpoint. It would have tended to keep the people of the German Democratic Republic out of their own "capital city," East Berlin. It would have left the inhabitants of East Berlin free to leave, or free to go back and forth between West and East Berlin. It would not have prevented the free movement of Westerners into East Berlin. Hence some observers thought that the East Germans would cut the city through the middle. However, it was more generally believed that despite all the threats and ultimata the Communists would not want to cause international complications by such flagrant violation of international agreements and established practice.

In actual fact, the decision was presumably made ten days earlier at a meeting in Moscow of the heads of government of the Warsaw Pact countries, when Ulbricht may have argued that the measures taken in July to control the population movement were not adequate and that only a barrier through the middle of the city would do the job. On Sunday morning, August 13, a communiqué was issued stating that the Warsaw Pact countries had met and officially requested the East German regime to take the necessary action to "establish order" along the border to West Berlin, to prevent the "subversive activity" which was luring East Germans from their homeland, and to protect thereby the security of the German Democratic Republic and the other countries of the Socialist camp. Heavily armed units of the East German army, with tanks and armored cars, and armed police were concentrated in the center of the city where the major refugee crossing points to West Berlin were located. Troops and police were also deployed along the entire sector border. Other East German troops were deployed on the zone/sector border of the whole city, backed by a ring of three Soviet divisions, including one tank division. These large-scale deployments were obviously designed to cut off the escape of the thousands of prospective refugees in East Berlin that day, to cow any tendency toward a popular uprising, and to deter the Western Allies from the use of force.

Khrushchev took action, but he did not take action along the lines of his previous threats. He did not dare attempt to enforce his ultimatum; it would have been too dangerous—and besides *he* knew that the "missile gap" was a fiction.

Why did the Communists find it necessary in the summer of 1961 to build the Wall? In the spring of 1958, Anastas Mikoyan had visited East Berlin and taken occasion to look around West Berlin at the same time.

Struck by the contrast between West Berlin and East Berlin, he gave Ulbricht "unshirted hell," saying that the East Germans should remove finally the World War II rubble, clean up East Berlin and rebuild the center of the city in order to make it a "show window" of the Socialist camp able to outshine West Berlin, the "show window" of the West. About this time Khrushchev was making his boasts about the Soviet Union's surpassing the United States in per capita production in a few years and Ulbricht was imitating him by claiming that the GDR would surpass the Federal Republic in per capita production of consumer goods by 1961.

What was the situation in East Germany in 1961? The forced collectivization in the spring of 1960 had led to a sharp decline in agricultural production and great resentment in the countryside. Consumer shortages and maldistribution had led to worker apathy and a decrease in productivity. Communist pressure on the church, in education, and in cultural matters had further alienated the intellectuals. In 1960, ten percent of the East German doctors fled to the West. There is a story which is very revealing about the situation at the time in the GDR. The flight of physicians had been so alarming that the East German regime had imposed special controls on, and police surveillance of, doctors. As a result, in one rural district from which five physicians endeavored to flee, four were caught by the police and only one escaped with his entire family. The four who were caught had sold some of their possessions (one had sold his house, another had sold his car) or had withdrawn money from banks or bought diamonds, etc. The one who was successful in escaping with his family was the one who bought a new house, redecorated it, and moved into it three weeks before he left. He was thereafter not watched and he brought his entire family out, albeit with just a few small valises. He left much behind, but accomplished his escape.

There is a certain irony in the fact that the Berlin crisis which had been initiated by Khrushchev in November 1958 in order to drive the Western Allies out of Berlin had the effect instead of driving East Germans out of the Communist German Democratic Republic. Khrushchev's Berlin crisis had increasingly stirred up and worried East Germans who had followed the ups and downs of the ultimatums and threats and quieting statements from November 1958 on. The renewal of Khrushchev's threatening demands in the winter and spring of 1961 once more served to stimulate a high rate of refugee flights. There was a growing *Torschlusspanik*—that marvelously expressive German word which in this context means "panic from fear that the escape hatch would be closed." Press reports about the Berlin discussions at the Kennedy-Khrushchev meeting in Vienna on June 4, the Soviet release on June 10 of the *aide-mémoire* Khrushchev had given to Kennedy on June 4, Khrushchev's television speech on June 15 reasserting his ultimative demands before the Soviet people, and strong accompanying statements by Ulbricht had the effect of bringing on the panic with full force. In July 1961 more than 30,000 East Germans came over as refugees into West Berlin— nearly twice the previous monthly average. The East German authorities made frantic efforts to stop the refugee flight through more frequent checks and interrogations. They introduced measures to oblige some 50,000 East Berliners working in West Berlin to give up their jobs. They supported these measures with an intensive propaganda campaign, ranging from branding refugees as "traitors" to inventing a "polio epidemic" in West Germany. They probably succeeded in blocking or restraining the flight of many thousands, but they could not stem this panic tidal flow. More than 22,000 refugees arrived in West Berlin in the first twelve days of August.

The Wall signified the failure of Ulbricht's "show window" effort, a demonstration that the Communists could not win in open, honest competition with the capitalist West. What did the Wall accomplish for the Communists? It stopped the refugee flow; it broke contacts between East and West Germans; it halted the role of West Berlin as a meeting place for all Germans; and it made easier the economic and political development of the GDR as a separate Communist state in the Eastern European pattern.

Why did the Western Allies permit the building of the Wall? There were many reproaches at the time, and we who were involved there tended to search our souls and reproach ourselves as well. However, we recognized that Berlin had been divided into four sectors by the Four Power agreements going back to 1944–45. The city became effectively divided, albeit without a wall, at the time of the Berlin blockade and the airlift in 1948–49. Thereafter there was a separate currency, a separate administration, an Eastern-oriented economy in East Berlin, the Soviet sector. East Berlin had been under Communist control for sixteen years. On the other hand, it is true that there had been freedom of movement within the city during all this period; even during the Berlin blockade, 1948–49, free movement between the sectors of Berlin had continued unimpeded. Moreover, this freedom of movement within the city was grounded in explicit agreements with the Soviets. On July 7, 1945, in a meeting in Berlin between General Clay and Marshall Zhukov, it was agreed that transportation and movement within Berlin were to be unrestricted between the sectors. This right of free movement had been confirmed by practice, and was likewise supported by interpretation of the May 4, 1949 quadripartite agreement which terminated the Berlin blockade, and by the June 1949 agreement of the Four Power Council of Foreign Ministers. By construction of the Wall and the attendant restrictions on free movement between East and West Berlin, the Soviets and the East German Communists were thus acting in direct violation of Allied rights.

Should the Western Allies have moved in on August 13 to remove the barbed wire? General Clay, who came to Berlin five weeks later and stayed through the winter until early May, thought that perhaps it might have been done successfully within the first twenty-four hours. No one who has ever worked for this extraordinary man would dispute his view lightly. If General Clay had been there on August 13, it *might* have been different, but I honestly doubt it. When General Clay at the time of the Berlin blockade in 1948–49 was the American Military Governor for all of Germany, he reported directly to the Army chief of staff in Washington, and through his political adviser, Robert Murphy, directly to the Secretary of State. In 1961, the United States commander in Berlin, a major general, was at the end of a command line with two headquarters echelons between him and Washington; he reported first to Army headquarters in Heidelberg, from there to the U.S. commander of NATO forces in Paris, and then to Washington. In any case General Clay would have had to seek authorization for any action, and in my opinion he never would have received the authorization, just as he never received the authorization he requested to push an armed convoy through the Soviet zone to Berlin to break the surface route blockade in July 1948.

Furthermore, it must be borne in mind that the barbed wire was not directly on the sector boundary; it was well on the Eastern side. To remove the barbed wire we would have had to cross the sector line into an area which had been under Soviet and Communist control for more than fifteen years. Moreover, the sector line on the Western side was divided into three components: American, British, and French. Any action to be effective would have had to be a joint Allied action. To obtain authorization for prompt action from three governments was hardly possible. The French commandant was under the very strict control of the French Foreign Office; he did not even have authority to send a protest letter to the Soviet commandant without the specific approval of the text by Paris, and there were standing instructions in the Quai d'Orsay that no policy message to the French commandant could be sent without the personal approval of French Foreign Minister Couve de Murville. The British commandant had a little more leeway than the French, but he certainly would have needed authorization from London before taking any action. As a matter of fact, the British commandant was under instructions from the highest authority in London not to move any of his troops out of his sector into another sector without the prior approval of the other commandant. If the British troops were to engage in joint maneuvers with the Americans in our sector, the British had to make a formal request to our commandant for permission for their troops to enter the American sector. The Soviet commandant certainly would not have given such permission—least of all on August 13, 1961.

The East German armed forces and police were at the barbed wire. If we had crossed the line to remove the barbed wire, I am convinced that they would not have sought to resist. They would have moved back two hundred or four hundred yards and commenced to rebuild the barbed wire fence there. They were committed and they would have had to do it. We would then have been obliged to keep moving in farther and farther into the Soviet sector in order to remove the barbed wire, giving thus the appearance of aggression on our part.

There was another factor cautioning inaction on our part, perhaps the most important one. In the center of the city near the main Friedrichstrasse railroad station and the major crossing points into West Berlin, there were thousands of East Germans who had come from the Soviet Zone into the city on that day with the intention of going over to West Berlin. These thousands were milling around behind the East German army contingents. On the Western side, moreover, there were thousands of West Berliners watching what was going on at the sector line. A spark could have caused a conflagration in the form of a popular uprising as on June 17, 1953 which would have brought out the Soviet tanks again—with unforeseeable consequences. The German city authorities and the Allies as well recognized this great danger.

The Allied commandants were criticized very bitterly in Berlin for their failure even to protest on the first day, August 13. Nearly eight months later during my farewell call on Deputy Mayor Amrehn before departing from Berlin, Amrehn spoke with vehemence about our failure to protest the Soviet/East German action on the first day. Under the circumstances I felt obliged to tell him the real story to which he responded with sympathetic understanding: The three commandants and their staffs met that Sunday morning in the American sector since the U.S. commandant was in the chair that month. The chairmanship rotated every month. Mayor Brandt, Deputy Mayor Amrehn, and other Berlin officials joined the meeting for an hour or so. After their departure the commandants continued to meet. Discussion hinged on an immediate Allied protest to the Soviet commandant to be delivered that afternoon. The British and American commandants felt that they had the authority on their own to send a protest letter to the Soviet commandant. The French commandant, however, said that he would have to obtain authority from Paris for a protest letter. He would not only need authorization to send the protest letter, but also the text would have to be approved by Paris. Obviously, this could not be done in one day. Nevertheless the French commandant was prepared, without seeking authorization from Paris, to join his British and American colleagues in the issuance of a public protest statement to be released that afternoon. It was agreed to proceed then on that basis; we political advisers were assigned the task of drafting the protest statement.

The time then being 2:00 P.M., I invited my British and French colleagues to join me for a quick lunch at the U.S. officers' mess during which we discussed the terms of the statement. After lunch we went over to my office and in an hour or two, we had drafted an agreed Allied protest statement, had it translated into German, and arranged for its release in Berlin at 6:00 P.M. The British and French political advisers were to return to their headquarters, obtain clearance from their commandants for the text of the statement, and telephone their clearance back to me. They were preparing to leave my office when we learned that the State Department was calling my superior, the deputy commandant and head of the State Department Mission in Berlin. The head of our Mission talked on the phone with an assistant secretary of state, with the Secretary of State apparently in the room. He reported on events in Berlin, mentioned preparation of the Allied protest statement, and indicated the terms of the statement. He was then told that the Allied commandants were not to issue any statement whatsoever, that this was such a serious matter Washington would issue whatever statements were to be made. We were told that the commandants should proceed to draft a tripartite protest to the Soviet commandant which should be cleared with the three capitals. After telephoning the President, the Secretary of State did release to the press that day a unilateral U.S. statement which was weaker than our tripartite protest statement and which contained the happy thought that the measures taken thus far were aimed at residents of East Berlin and East Germany and not at the Allied position in West Berlin or access thereto. After that, Dean Rusk went to the baseball game. The President was in Hyannisport, and Dean Rusk was playing it very safe. He knew President Kennedy's predilection for handling all particulars himself, a predilection heightened by the Bay of Pigs disaster, and one which earned the President in the ensuing months the comic nickname of "the Berlin desk officer."

At any rate, I had the task of telling my British and French colleagues that on orders from Washington we could not participate in the issuance of the tripartite protest statement we had just finished drafting. They shook their heads and spared me words of comment.

There is another basic reason why the Allied commandants in Berlin did not seriously consider taking forceful action against the erection of the Wall, nor even request authorization for such action. The foreign ministers of the United States, Britain, France, and West Germany had met in Paris August 5–7, primarily to discuss the Berlin situation. The main outcome of the meeting was agreement on three vital issues regarding Berlin over which the Allies were ready to go to war, if necessary. All three vital issues were related to *West* Berlin only. These three vital issues, which were leaked to the Paris *Herald Tribune* at the time, were to uphold Allied rights in West Berlin, to ensure the economic viability of West Berlin, and to maintain free access to and from

West Berlin. The three Allied commandants in Berlin were aware of this tripartite understanding, and this agreed policy explains to a considerable extent their reaction to the Wall, as well as the reaction in Washington, London, and Paris.

Presumably the Warsaw Pact countries had made their decision on August 4 before this Western foreign ministers meeting and the *Herald Tribune* story about the agreement on the three vital issues. However, the Soviets had certainly already noted that President Kennedy in his otherwise strong speech on July 25 used the phrase "West Berlin" throughout, indicating concern about Allied rights in the Western sectors and about the protection of West Berlin, and showing a lack of concern with East Berlin. Also the Warsaw Pact countries on August 4 had the "benefit" of the views of Senator William Fulbright, chairman of the Senate Foreign Relations Committee, who on July 30 over nationwide television in the United States had stated that "the Russians have the power to close it [the sector border] in any case. . . . next week if they chose to close their borders they could, without violating any treaty. I don't understand why the East Germans don't close their border because I think they have a right to close it." [8] Even if the decision had already been made, the Paris *Herald Tribune* disclosure of the Western agreement on the three vital issues was doubtless reassuring to the Soviets and the East Germans on the eve of their August 13th action.

In the ensuing days it became quite clear that some action was required in order to restore the damaged morale of the West Berliners. The protest note which the three Allied commandants had sent to the Soviet commandant in Karlshorst on Tuesday afternoon, August 15, after having been cleared verbatim in the three Western capitals, was hardly sufficient to satisfy the West Berliners. An angry note of protest on the day of the Communist action might have had some palliative effect, but a mild protest two days later was more annoying to the West Berliners than helpful. It was exceedingly difficult to make the Kennedy Administration see beyond its abstract preconceptions and come to understand the actual situation in West Berlin. After five days the Administration was finally prodded into action by the reports and insistent urgings of the State Department mission in Berlin, by the German experts in the State Department and the Pentagon, by a strong report from Edward R. Murrow, the head of the United States Information Agency, who was visiting Berlin at the time, and also by West German reactions and the views of Mayor Brandt. On Friday, August 18, the White House announced that Vice President Johnson accompanied by General Clay was to visit West Berlin the coming weekend, and that the United States garrison in Berlin was to be reinforced by one U.S. Army battle group (around 1,500 men), which was to move to Berlin overland from West Germany on the Autobahn to West Berlin.

Let me digress here to mention an example of the type of legend-building which wittingly or unwittingly permeates historical writing. Jean Smith was an American officer in the Allied staff in Berlin. His book, *The Defense of Berlin,* is regarded as a rather authoritative work on Berlin. In general, it is quite sound and perceptive; however, it is entirely wrong in connection with the role that Mayor Brandt played at the time the Wall was built. The Allied staff was a military staff for the coordination of tripartite battle plans; it was located at the British headquarters. As an officer on the Allied staff, Smith was not in the *Kommandatura* structure; he did not attend the commandants' meetings, nor did he have access at the Allied staff to the U.S. Mission Berlin's political reporting on the situation in Berlin. The paper jacket on his book states that he had a series of exclusive interviews with Lord Mayor Willy Brandt of Berlin. It is not credible to me that the former mayor of Berlin, now the Chancellor of the Federal Republic, gave Smith misinformation. It is possible that Smith misunderstood or misinterpreted Brandt, or more likely he had other sources in Brandt's coterie who painted a false picture. Smith states that "the significance of the East German action in closing the sector border was not immediately apparent to American military headquarters in West Berlin. . . . It was only later in the day, after much prodding from Mayor Brandt that Allied headquarters fully realized the significance of the East German action." [9] He mentions that "the three Western Commandants began a series of meetings which lasted throughout the day. Mayor Brandt attended several of these." [10] Actually the three Western commandants met at 10:00 A.M.; they were joined at 11:00 by Mayor Brandt, Deputy Mayor Amrehn, and other Berlin officials; the mayor and the West Berlin officials remained for an hour or an hour and a half, after which the three Western commandants continued their meeting until around 2:00 P.M. Smith reports that Mayor Brandt "in no uncertain terms advised the military authorities that the entire Western position in Berlin was at stake. . . . The Mayor pleaded for energetic action which would force the Communists to 'cancel their unlawful measures.' Among other things, he asked for an immediate show of force along the border." [11] Smith continues, "Prodded by Brandt's forceful arguments the Commandants began to revise their earlier estimates of the situation. The Mayor's proposals were forwarded to each of the three Western capitals but no action was taken." [12] Smith later cites a list of suggestions which the mayor is supposed to have made "in his earliest conferences with Allied officials in Berlin after the border closure had gone into effect." [13] These include immediate reinforcement of the Allied garrison, with the movement of Allied troops along the Autobahn; the immediate arrival in West Berlin of a prominent American personality, preferably a cabinet minister; the appointment of General Lucius Clay as American commandant, etc.

The fact is that the commandants and their staffs were well aware at once of the seriousness of the situation; they did not need to be alerted or "prodded" by anyone. Mayor Brandt had been out of the city for half the time in the preceding weeks campaigning for the West German parliamentary elections—after the Communists had begun to build the Wall he returned from West Germany to Berlin early Sunday morning—and the commandants were perhaps more familiar with the West Berlin situation in many respects at the time than he. Brandt was a subdued and reflective man at the meeting with the commandants on Sunday morning. He did not plead for energetic action; he did not ask for "an immediate show of force" along the border; he did not put forth proposals which were forwarded to the three Western capitals. His one great concern, and a very legitimate one, which we all shared, was that a popular uprising might break out on the sector border, in which West Berliners would join with East Germans with the result that the Soviet tanks would come out again on the streets of East Berlin as they had in June 1953. In his book entitled *Berlin: Success of a Mission?* Geoffrey McDermott, the head of the British Foreign Office Mission, describes Mayor Brandt at the meeting with the Allied commandants as follows: "He was grave but statesman-like. He never demanded any rash action from the protecting powers nor reproached us for lack of firmness, though some of his colleagues later tried to make scape-

33

goats of us." [14] Perhaps Jean Smith talked mostly to some of these colleagues.

The suggestions cited came spontaneously from many sources, as is usual in critical situations. The reinforcement of the American garrison, with the movement of troops along the Autobahn, was raised Monday, August 14, in the White House staff by military and political officers; it was discussed Tuesday afternoon in the Department of State in an interdepartmental meeting. The State Department Mission in Berlin in a telegram Monday or Tuesday reporting on the Berlin morale situation requested that a prominent American be sent to West Berlin at once, naming several names, but not the Vice-President. It was Margaret Higgins who first suggested that Lucius Clay be sent to West Berlin. Maggie was a close friend of General Clay from her days as a war correspondent; she had a house on Cape Cod very close to Clay's; also she had good contacts with the White House. On Sunday, August 13, she went from Washington to the Cape to discuss with President Kennedy and General Clay the idea of Clay's return to Berlin.

Mayor Brandt's letter of August 16 to President Kennedy depicted the serious Berlin morale problem and proposed: the Western powers should demand the reinstitution of four-power responsibility for Berlin, but simultaneously proclaim their three-power authority over West Berlin; they should reiterate Allied guarantees of continued presence in West Berlin until reunification, and if desired have this supported by a plebiscite in West Berlin and the Federal Republic; a clear statement should be made that the German problem is not settled for the Western powers and that they still insist on a peace settlement which permits the self-determination of the German people and provides for the security interests of all parties; the Western powers should bring the Berlin issue before the United Nations, at least on the grounds that the USSR had flagrantly violated the UN Declaration of Human Rights; and the American garrison in Berlin should be strengthened in a demonstrative way. The last point about the garrison comes at the end of the letter after Brandt expresses his "bitterness" as a result of Allied statements that one refuses to negotiate with the Soviets under duress, yet nevertheless after this example of clear blackmail, one hears that one cannot refuse to negotiate. Although Mayor Brandt's letter of August 16 made President Kennedy furious, it is possible that the letter may have had an influence in the decision to send reinforcements to the American garrison.

These countermeasures, increasing the American garrison by a battle group with movement to West Berlin across the Autobahn and sending Vice-President Johnson and General Clay on a visit to West Berlin, were not real countermeasures against the Communist action. They were not designed to endeavor to undo the Communist action or to retaliate. They were merely an effort to revive the sinking morale of the West Berlin population, and they were remarkably effective in this purpose.

Why were there no real countermeasures? We must seek the answer in the differing appraisals made in Washington of the Berlin Wall. There was a powerful group in Washington seeking a settlement with the Soviets, including Dean Rusk, Adlai Stevenson, Senators Fulbright and Mansfield, and the White House boys, Sorenson, Rostow, and Schlesinger. They were ready and eager to negotiate with the Soviets on West Berlin; they thought that it might be possible to conclude a mutually acceptable arrangement over West Berlin on a long-term basis—perhaps to replace the rights, or reinterpret the rights gained by the unconditional surrender of Nazi Germany. They saw such Berlin negotiations within a framework of larger negotiations with the Soviets seeking an overall settlement, a search animated by a certainly legitimate concern over possible nuclear warfare. The flow of East German refugees through West Berlin was regarded as a hindrance to such a settlement. The Communist move in building the Wall, in effect, removed in their view an issue, an impediment to an overall settlement. It gave a clean Communist-type edge to the East and West frontier on the one juncture where it had previously been lacking in Europe. Perhaps this group was influenced by a false appraisal of post-Stalinist Soviet communism.

Arrayed on the other side were former Secretary of State Acheson, Paul Nitze, General Maxwell Taylor, the Pentagon, and the German desk officers in the State Department. These men regarded negotiations with the Soviets over Berlin as highly undesirable, since in their opinion the West only stood to lose by such negotiations. Moreover, they believed that a failure to react properly to the Communist measures would only have the effect of increasing Soviet demands. The first-named group was, however, definitely in ascendancy in Washington at the time.

The two broad policy alternatives were passive acceptance with verbal protestations, or countermeasures. The dominant group was quite content with passive acceptance, verbal protestations, and some limited measures to maintain West Berlin morale. What were the possible countermeasures? There were four:

1. *Travel Control.* Since East German passports were not recognized by the Western European governments, East Germans had to obtain a so-called T.T.D. (Temporary Travel Document) at the Allied Travel Office in West Berlin. Travel to Western Europe was important for the East Germans for economic and political

reasons. The Allies in West Berlin with the cooperation of the NATO countries could curb the travel of East Germans totally, if desirable, or selectively as might be more pertinent.

2. *Economic Countermeasures.* The West Germans could cancel, or cease to perform, or slow down performance under the interzonal trade agreement with the East German regime. A West German threat to terminate the interzonal trade agreement had been used effectively in the fall of 1960 to bring about a prompt cessation of East German harassment. Cooperation of the other NATO countries would have been required to make a rupture of interzonal trade effective. Another possibility was a selective economic embargo which likewise required the cooperation of all the NATO countries. Mayor Brandt pushed for a selective economic embargo by the West German government on vital goods imported by East Germany, but in the atmosphere of an election campaign Chancellor Adenauer was not inclined to be receptive to ideas broached by his political opponent. Moreover, with the Wall an accomplished fact bringing the same sharp physical division between East and West Berlin which already existed between East and West Germany, the West German government doubtless wanted to maintain the remaining economic bond lest the division become complete in economic as in other respects.

3. *Cultural Countermeasures.* The Allies and the NATO countries were engaged in a diverse cultural exchange with the Soviet Union and the Eastern European Communist countries, and a more limited exchange with East Germany. These cultural activities could be cancelled or selectively curtailed.

4. *The Military Governor's 1949 Reservation to the Basic Law.* A fourth countermeasure, the one with the

most serious implications, would have been a withdrawal of the Military Governor's 1949 Reservation to the Basic Law of the Federal Republic. Under the Basic Law, the Constitution of the Federal Republic, Berlin was named as a *Land* or state of the Federal Republic. The Military Governor's reservation in 1949 made on account of the four-power status of Berlin prevented this article from coming into effect. Withdrawal of the reservation would have affirmed a legal connection between West Germany and West Berlin. On the other hand, it could be interpreted as a violation of the four-power agreements on the status of Berlin upon which the Western Allies were basing their rights in Berlin. Moreover, the West Germans would thereby have acquired powers in West Berlin which, if inappropriately exercised, might have led to more serious complications, indeed to hostilities. Presumably the Western Allies hesitated to give such powers to the West Germans for the same reason that Khrushchev, although he threatened repeatedly to turn over controls on the access routes to Berlin to the East German authorities, refrained from taking such action.

There were some other possible countermeasures suggested, measures that might be taken in other parts of the world where the Allies had a leverage which they did not have locally in Berlin. At Berlin itself the Communists had all the advantages. The State Department Mission in Berlin pressed for countermeasures, *deterrent* countermeasures. Western relations with the Communist countries have been operated predominantly on a tit-for-tat basis, more elegantly called "reciprocity." The Soviets throw an American military attaché out of Moscow and we throw a corresponding Soviet military attaché out of Washington. The Soviets restrict the travel in the Soviet Union of American diplomats, and we restrict the travel of Soviet diplomats in the United States.

This is tit-for-tat diplomacy; it gets rather tedious at times, but I am not sure it isn't necessary. A deterrent countermeasure is a countermeasure which goes beyond the tit-for-tat scale in order to seek to deter the Communists from taking actions that they are threatening. It is pertinent only in situations of stress and pressure from the Communist side. It must be carefully gauged because it must not exceed a proper mass for deterrence; it aims at deterrence without escalation, without inciting the Communist side to take stronger actions. Thus in any particular situation it is not easy to determine what is a proper deterrent countermeasure. The purpose of deterrent countermeasures in our opinion, was not to undo the Wall—we could hardly hope for that—but to deter the Communists from taking further actions which might lead to a dangerous confrontation.

The Kennedy Administration paid no heed to our urgings for deterrent countermeasures. Nothing was done by the Allied side except the minimal measure of controlling selectively the travel of East Germans through the West Berlin Allied Travel Office. The U.S. government presumably did not push for countermeasures because there were too many people at the top who espoused the view that the erection of the Wall might be "good" in the context of overall United States-Soviet relationships. The British and the French were assuredly little inclined to take any measures which might appear aggressive. However, the attitude of the Federal Republic was perhaps governing. In comparison with economic countermeasures, most of the measures considered had a minor significance; they might be useful in association with economic reprisals. However, it became clear for the reasons stated previously that the Federal Republic was most reluctant to take any drastic action with respect to interzonal trade.

In government as in business there is invariably a sharp discrepancy between the viewpoints of the field and the headquarters. A headquarters often discounts the views of the field office as an expression of too close emotional involvement in the local circumstances; it is only the headquarters that supposedly sees things in perspective, the "big picture." We in the U.S. Mission Berlin learned that Washington in those days tended to view our recommendations with a certain suspicion, readily finding in them traces of a malady called "Berlinitis" or "localitis." However that may be, the reaction of the United States government at the time of the Wall was weak. I am convinced that one of the many factors which made possible or led to the U.S.-Soviet confrontation in the Cuba missile crisis was the weak reaction of the United States government at the time of the Berlin Wall. Khrushchev misread the weak reaction to mean an endemic weakness.

Geoffrey McDermott lists "four specific crises which could have led to war. The first was the building of the Wall in August 1961. Then, after Clay's arrival in Berlin, there was the Friedrichstrasse confrontation of American and Soviet tanks in October. In December the *Vopo* stopped the U.S. commandant from crossing to see his Soviet opposite number and tempers flared. In January and February 1962, the Russians interfered with Allied traffic in the air corridors." [15] In my opinion, there was little likelihood of war resulting from any of these instances, even the tank confrontation.

Nevertheless, the tank confrontation was the first time that U.S. and Soviet armed forces had stood directly over against one another in hostile posture. The circumstances leading thereto were as follows: On the evening of October 22, the head of the State Department Mission in Berlin, Minister E. Allan Lightner, Jr., and his wife drove in their U.S. Army-licensed car through the Friedrichstrasse checkpoint on their way to attend an opera in East Berlin. By a long-standing arrangement with the Soviets, both military and civilian members of the Allied occupation authorities traveled freely into East Berlin, without a request for personal identification from the East German police (the *Volkspolizei,* known as *Vopos*), by virtue of the military license plates on their cars. On that evening the *Vopos* stopped Mr. Lightner's car and requested that he show documentation. In accordance with regulations, Mr. Lightner refused to show identification to the *Vopos,* and requested that a Soviet officer be summoned to the checkpoint. The *Vopos* did not respond to this request. After waiting forty minutes for a Soviet officer, Lightner informed the *Vopos* that he intended to drive on into East Berlin as was his right. He roared the motor and drove through the first line of *Vopos,* but was stopped at the second barricade. The irate *Vopos* told him he could spend the night there waiting for a Soviet officer. Meanwhile, the alert platoon of the Second Battle Group and four M-48 medium tanks and two armored personnel carriers had arrived at the checkpoint. The MP officer in command of Checkpoint Charlie, the American checkpoint in Friedrichstrasse, came across the sector line to the Lightner car at the second barricade to deliver a message from headquarters that Mrs. Lightner was to return to the checkpoint. A strong-minded lady from Massachusetts, she told the MP that she preferred to stay in the car and see the affair through to the end. However, some minutes later the MP officer returned to state that General Clay *orders* Mrs. Lightner to return to the American checkpoint. Escorted by the MP officer, she reluctantly walked back to Checkpoint Charlie. After Lightner's car had been at the second barricade more than thirty minutes, with no Soviet officer having arrived, a squad from the alert platoon of the Battle Group, eight men with bayonets fixed, marched crisply to the East Berlin side of the checkpoint, took up positions alongside the car, and then accompanied the car forward beyond the East German barrier into East Berlin, encountering no interference by the *Vopos*. Lightner then drove on for a block or two, turned around and, escorted by the squad, came back through the East German barricade, undisturbed by the *Vopos*. Lightner then decided to attempt to reenter East Berlin again in the normal way. Joined in his car by a U.S. Mission civilian official, Lightner drove forward; when the *Vopos* again demanded a show of identification, Lightner signaled for the eight-man squad to come forward, and the car was escorted into East Berlin and returned, as previously. Meanwhile, Major Lazarev, the acting Soviet political adviser, had arrived on the scene. General Watson had called me at home at 8:00 P.M., informing me of Lightner's detention at the sector frontier, and I had gone at once to the emergency operations room in the headquarters. After some time there, I went down to Checkpoint Charlie. When Lazarev arrived, I walked across into East Berlin in order to confer with him. Lazarev who was quite familiar with the established procedures admitted that the *Vopos* were in the wrong and indicated that remedial measures would be taken. Being informed of Lazarev's statement and in order to affirm demonstratively the right of Allied access, Lightner, followed by two other American licensed civilian cars, then drove his car back into East Berlin and after driving some minutes in East Berlin returned through the checkpoint; this time both entering and leaving East Berlin, the Americans were not disturbed by a request for personal identification.

At the time of the erection of the Wall, the Soviets and East Germans made an effort to give an impression that their measures were not an infringement of Western rights. The Warsaw Pact communiqué explicitly stated that the right of access to West Berlin was not to be affected. Colonel Solovyev, the Soviet commandant, told General Watson and me at a meeting that he had made sure that the East German measures would not affect the freedom of movement of the Allied authorities in East Berlin. For more than a year the East Germans had from time to time sought to make American individuals show identification when driving into East Berlin. They tended to be selective, specializing in American schoolteachers who were not always familiar with the procedures. It is doubtful that the East German *Vopos* on that Sunday evening knowingly chose to stop the head of the State Department Mission in Berlin; more likely they by chance picked the wrong target for their harassment.

On Monday, October 23, the East Germans published an official announcement that all "foreigners" except Allied military officials in uniform, must on entering East Berlin show their personal identification to the East German police. Major Lazarev's assurances had evidently been swept aside by higher authority. The East Germans apparently felt confident enough to press the issue. Had it not been for General Clay's presence in Berlin at that time, there is little doubt that the American military and civilian authorities in Berlin would have been obliged to crawl back ignominiously from the strong position taken on Sunday evening. Washington did not want any trouble, and doubtless regarded the issue as too picayune for a show of force. We were told later that President Kennedy had been annoyed by Minister Lightner's Sunday evening venture, and reportedly said, "We didn't send him to Berlin to go to the opera in East Berlin"—a statement which, if reported correctly, shows how unwise it is for a president to become overenmeshed in details when lacking the pertinent background knowledge; it was and had been for years standing practice for the Allied military and civilian authorities to show their presence in East Berlin by attendance at the opera, theater, art exhibitions, city tours, etc.; after the Wall it was believed particularly important so far as the East Berliners were concerned to maintain this policy. General Clay advised Washington in strong terms that the East German pretensions must not be tolerated and that we had to meet the issue head-on if we were to maintain our position in Berlin and our credibility with the Communists.

On Tuesday evening, October 24, my wife and I gave a black-tie dinner in honor of General and Mrs. Clay which General Watson, the French political adviser, Serge de Guenyveau, and the new British political adviser, Keith Matthews attended . The dinner, of course, had been arranged three or four weeks earlier, but it took place by chance at a time of particular tension, and the after-dinner period was somewhat disturbed by several telephone calls for General Clay and General Watson. Through these telephone calls with the Berlin Command, arrangements were finalized for two American military officers of known probity, dressed in civilian attire, to seek to enter East Berlin early the next morning in a private, Army-licensed American vehicle. Early next morning at breakfast I received a telephone call from the Berlin Command emergency operations room, instructing me to go at once from home to Checkpoint Charlie. The American vehicle with the two "civilians" had been stopped by the *Vopos;* the American Army provost marshal had talked without success to the new Soviet provost marshal and political adviser; as American political adviser, I was to talk to the Soviet in his capacity as Soviet political adviser in order to seek to arrange the cessation of *Vopo* obstruction of the free movement into East Berlin of U.S. Army-licensed vehicles. There were three levels of contact between the American and Soviet military headquarters: the provost marshal level, the political advisers, and the commandants themselves. It was customary to endeavor first to settle issues on the provost marshal level, then to move to the political advisers, and thereafter to the commandants. The same Soviet officer usually served both as Soviet provost marshal and Soviet political adviser.

The new Soviet political adviser, who made his first appearance on that day at Friedrichstrasse, was a Lieutenant Colonel Alexeiev. Alexeiev was probably not his real name. The Soviets had presumably deliberately left the political adviser position vacant for over six months, since Lieutenant Colonel Odintsov,[16] the previous incumbent had left Berlin toward the end of March. In view of the tense situation at Friedrichstrasse, the Soviets apparently decided to fill the political adviser position with a trusted person, fully instructed as to their purposes. Alexeiev was not a Red Army officer. He may have been a Party official, but he was very likely also a KGB officer.[17]

Arriving at Checkpoint Charlie on Friedrichstrasse, I had a talk first with the American provost marshal who told me of the sudden appearance of the new Soviet provost marshal and political adviser and of his unsuccessful discussion with him. The American vehicle with the two military officers in civilian clothes had returned to Checkpoint Charlie. The provost marshal informed me that he had told the Soviet representatives that the American political adviser would be coming to the Friedrich-strasse crossing point. Mr. Firestone, the Army Russian translator in uniform, and I climbed into a jeep driven by a soldier. The jeep moved forward across into East Berlin and was stopped by a *Vopo* barring the way. We noted three Soviet officers standing about a hundred feet away start to walk toward us; we recognized Major Lazarev, the deputy Soviet political adviser and the Soviet officer English translator. Not wishing the jeep's stoppage to create a new issue which might thwart my mission, I climbed down from the jeep, followed by Firestone, and we walked undisturbed through the *Vopo* lines to meet the Soviet officers. Introducing myself to Alexeiev, I spoke of the long tradition of cordial relations between the American and Soviet political advisers and that it was unfortunate hence to be meeting the new Soviet political adviser for the first time in these unpleasant circumstances. Since it was a bitterly cold morning and there were large crowds on the east side of the Friedrichstrasse crossing as well as on the West Berlin side, I suggested that we stroll away from the crossing point in order to discuss more quietly the possibility of settling amicably the issue that had arisen. Alexeiev was agreeable and we walked around together for about a half an hour. Since Alexeiev was new in Berlin, I spoke extensively about the background of freedom of movement between the sectors of Berlin, referring to the original Military Governors' agreement of July 1945 and the agreements of May and June 1949. Specific arrangements had been made with the Soviets some years ago that U.S. Army licenses were sufficient identification both for the vehicle and its passengers. It was accordingly established practice for the East German police at the sector border to wave U.S.-licensed cars through, without requesting further identification. If the Soviets wished to change the arrangements in any way, we were prepared to discuss the matter with them. However, we could not permit the East German police to attempt to assert the right arbitrarily to control the movement of American-licensed vehicles and American personnel. We did not recognize the East German authorities; we looked to the Soviets as the responsible authority in their sector of Berlin. Alexeiev mostly listened though he did interject forcefully that the East Germans had their own government, that identification of persons entering their capital was a proper exercise of authority, and that the Soviet Army garrison in East Berlin no longer regarded itself as an occupation authority. We had been walking away from the Friedrichstrasse crossing point, and at one point in the conversation, Alexeiev abruptly declared that we should turn back, that we were getting too far away from the crossing point; he seemed to suspect a ruse on my part to draw him away from Friedrichstrasse. As we were walking back, I proposed to Alexeiev that he arrange with the *Vopos* that the Army-licensed vehicle with the two civilians be permitted passage into East Berlin under existing agreed procedures and that the U.S. and Soviet commandants should then meet that afternoon to discuss the general issues involved and to seek to arrive at a settlement of any differences. Alexeiev replied that the Soviet commandant would be ready to meet with the American commandant in the afternoon; he did not respond to my suggestion that he arrange with the *Vopos* the unimpeded passage of the American-licensed vehicle.

Returning to Checkpoint Charlie, I found that ten American M-48 medium tanks had meanwhile moved up to the checkpoint and taken positions on Friedrichstrasse facing the *Vopos* and their barriers. From Checkpoint Charlie I reported by phone to General Watson in the Berlin Command emergency operations center, told him of the discussion with Alexeiev, and suggested that we send the Army-licensed vehicle with the two civilians forward again in order to ascertain whether Alexeiev had chosen to arrange its unimpeded movement into East Berlin. This suggestion was adopted; the vehicle drove forward into East Berlin, was stopped by the *Vopos* again as before, and then returned to the West Berlin side. A convoy was then formed, with one army jeep carrying four U.S. military policemen with rifles and bayonets affixed going ahead of the civilian vehicle, and two army jeeps each with four MPs behind. With this military escort, the American civilian vehicle moved through the East Berlin checkpoint without incident. Similarly escorted it returned to Checkpoint Charlie. I reported the unimpeded passage of the escorted civilian vehicle to General Watson and it was agreed that I should go over to the East Berlin side again, seek out the Soviet political adviser, and arrange a meeting of the American and Soviet commandants for 3:00 that afternoon at the Soviet military headquarters in Karlshorst. Walking through the crossing point into East Berlin, I found Major Lazarev. Lieutenant Colonel Alexeiev was not there. Later I learned that, presumably on seeing the ten American tanks drawn up at Friedrichstrasse, Alexeiev and the Russian translator had come through Checkpoint Charlie into West Berlin in a Soviet army car and had driven around in the immediate area behind Checkpoint Charlie in order to discover the strength of the American military force there. Major Lazarev commented with feeling on the impropriety of the use of military force to escort an American civilian vehicle through the East German crossing point. I rejoined that we had sought to avoid it, as he knew, but that the Soviets had not responded to our suggestion. Lazarev was able to confirm three o'clock that afternoon as the time for the meeting of the American and Soviet commandants.

The meeting of the commandants was not productive. General Watson set forth firmly and articulately the American position that the Soviets were permitting the East Germans to obstruct the passage of American vehicles into East Berlin, contrary to established practice and explicit agreements with the Soviet authorities. It was clear that Colonel Solovyev had no authority to deal with the substance of the issue. He rather lamely insisted that the East German authorities were a sovereign government and that the Soviets could not interfere with measures they had taken to control entry into their territory. He termed the U.S. troop escort an "open provocation," adding, "we have tanks too." Meanwhile the American tanks and the military policemen remained at Checkpoint Charlie. Several times later that day and the next day, American cars were escorted through the East Berlin checkpoint by military police, as on Wednesday morning. Early Thursday morning, October 26, thirty-three Soviet tanks came into East Berlin and bivouacked in the center of the city not far from the Friedrichstrasse crossing. Late in the afternoon, Friday, October 27, after an American military escort had again brought a civilian vehicle through the *Vopo* barrier, ten Soviet tanks moved down Friedrichstrasse to the East Berlin side of the checkpoint, thus effecting the tank confrontation.

At 2:15 the next morning the telephone rang in our home. My wife arose out of bed to answer it. She relates that a cheery British voice spoke out as if it were three o'clock in the afternoon. "Oh, Mildred, it's Keith, Keith Matthews [the British political adviser]. Is Howard there?" "Yes, he is. Do you wish to speak to him?" "Tell him please that I am coming over to see him. I have to get my clothes on and I'll come straight away." Thirty minutes later he arrived. "I had to come now," he said, "I have an *Immediate* from the Cabinet in London."

The British Cabinet wanted to know the reasons for

the confrontation of American and Soviet tanks at the Friedrichstrasse crossing point and what American intentions were at Friedrichstrasse. The British government had evidently become alarmed at the American-Soviet tank confrontation. I told Matthews that there was no reason for concern. The East Germans with Soviet approval had been denying us the right of the free movement of our vehicles into East Berlin. In order demonstratively to assert our rights, we had brought up tanks and used military police escorts. We had a fine group of well-controlled officers and men at Friedrichstrasse. There was no likelihood that our men would initiate any shooting, and there was likewise manifest restraint on the other side. Besides, General Clay had accomplished his purpose when the Soviet tanks moved down to the East Berlin Friedrichstrasse crossing. General Clay had wanted to force the Soviets to acknowledge Soviet authority and responsibility in East Berlin. When the Soviet tanks appeared, the fiction of East German responsibility for the denial of our access to East Berlin was destroyed and Soviet responsibility proven. The point having been made, we anticipated that the American tanks would soon be withdrawn—in fact they were withdrawn a day or two later, thirty minutes after the Soviet tanks withdrew.

Many circles in Washington may have been as alarmed as the British government at the Soviet-American tank confrontation. During the confrontation President Kennedy telephoned General Clay. The President was in a cool and relaxed mood; he appeared to accept General Clay's explanation of the course of events, and chuckled a bit during the conversation. General Clay's forceful action may have frightened London and Washington; it did not frighten the West Berliners. On the contrary, it had a decidedly beneficial effect on West Berlin morale. Thousands of West Berliners came down to Friedrichstrasse to see the American tanks in position at the crossing point; with enthusiasm they watched the American military policemen escort the civilian vehicles through the *Vopo* lines; they believed that this was the only language the Communists understood, and it encouraged them to keep faith in American assurances of their security against Communist attacks. The tank confrontation may also have impressed the Soviets as to the dangers of the Berlin situation. They doubtless regarded General Clay as a "dangerous" man—no greater compliment could be paid to him. However, they were also certainly apprised of the widespread Washington view critical of General Clay's action. At any rate, the tank confrontation had no effect on the overall Soviet appraisal of the Kennedy administration, as indicated by the Soviet action a year later in initiating the Cuba missile crisis.

As mentioned previously, Geoffrey McDermott cites as another crisis "which could have led to war" the incident two months later when the *Vopos* stopped the American commandant at the crossing point as he was entering East Berlin to make an official call on the Soviet commandant. This was an incident of relatively minor significance which never could have led to war. After the tank confrontation no efforts had been made by American officials in civilian clothes to enter East Berlin by car on private visits. There had been occasions when I had accompanied General Watson on official calls to the Soviet commandant. Meanwhile a matter was pending which required a call on the Soviet political adviser. Shortly after the erection of the Wall, Frederick Pryor, an American graduate student who was writing a doctoral dissertation on East-West Trade, was picked up by the East German police in East Berlin and detained on charges of espionage. I had discussed his case several times in September and October with Major Lazarev urging that

the Soviets arrange his release from East German detention. Since Pryor was still being detained,[18] it seemed desirable to discuss the matter with the new Soviet political
adviser, Alexeiev. Accordingly, a meeting with the Soviet
political adviser in Karlshorst was arranged for December 22 by telephone as was customary. We realized that
this would be a test case of official civilian entry into
East Berlin. I went in an official U.S. Mission Berlin
licensed car, driven by a soldier in uniform, and accompanied by a Foreign Service officer and Firestone, the
Army translator. When we arrived at the East Berlin
crossing point, we were stopped by the *Vopos* who requested personal identification. It was quite clear that
they were waiting for us. I explained in German who I
was, that I had an appointment with the Soviet political
adviser, and that it was improper for them to request
identification. When the *Vopos* continued to insist on
identification, we returned to West Berlin. The Soviets
play chess in foreign policy; they like best to set up situations in which the opponent stands to lose no matter
which alternative course of action he adopts. If we had
shown our identification, we would have recognized *Vopo*
authority at the sector border; if we refused, we sacrificed
the business at hand and the political adviser channel to
the Soviets.

Immediately thereafter a meeting was arranged for
the next day between General Watson and the Soviet commandant, at which General Watson intended to protest
the *Vopo* refusal to permit me to enter East Berlin for a
scheduled appointment with the Soviet political adviser.
However, when the commandant's car, with myself and
another civilian accompanying General Watson, arrived
at the crossing point the next day, the *Vopos* stopped the
car and demanded that the civilian aides identify themselves. Under the circumstances, General Watson turned

back and returned to West Berlin; later he sent by military messenger a strongly worded protest to Colonel Solovyev. It was, as an American spokesman termed it, a "calculated affront on the part of the Soviets." However, it demonstrated that the Soviets no longer had any interest in maintaining in Berlin the commandant's channel of communication. Perhaps Alexeiev had been sent as the hatchet man for the job. From our standpoint the commandant's channel had become increasingly sterile. As for the Soviets, they abolished the Soviet commandant's office on August 22, 1962, alleging that the Western commandants were trying to use the office "to present unjustified claims to interference of the Western Powers in the internal affairs of the Sovereign and Independent German Democratic Republic and its capital." [19]

Tension in Berlin over the years has brought about a feeling of solidarity among the Western Allies and the West Berliners. There is a special breed of U.S. government military and civilian officials called *Alt-Berliner* ("old Berliners"), numbering in the thousands. Their distinction is that they have all served in Berlin in the American military or civilian establishment sometime after 1945, and their lives have become associated with the people of that city and their survival in freedom. When Berlin is threatened, the old Berliners stir and become active. The measures which the Kennedy administration took to shore up West Berlin morale at the time of the Wall were, assuredly, the result of the obscure and energetic push of the old Berliners scattered in large numbers in key positions throughout Washington officialdom. There is doubtless a similar special breed of old Berliners in London and Paris, smaller in number because the British and French establishments in Berlin have been smaller than the American. One of the unique pleasures of diplomatic work in Berlin was to experience not only the congeniality of British and French colleagues living under the same stress, but also the generally common viewpoints on basic issues. We three political advisers rarely had difficulty in coming to a mutual understanding among ourselves, nor did we often find differences with our superiors in Berlin. The problem was to gain acceptance of a common viewpoint from our respective capital cities, and we each tended to feel ourselves more often in opposition to our own capital than to our Berlin colleagues, experiencing thus the solidarity of field officers obliged by circumstances to work in common, over against separate headquarters, each of which viewed the problems from varying premises and preconceptions.

This sense of solidarity was not limited to the Western Allies, but it encompassed the West Berliners as well. In a sense, we were all in the same boat, or rather in the same trap,[20] surrounded by twenty-three Soviet army divisions. The Allied military forces were token, a trip wire for general war; our security depended on the steadfastness of our government, or rather on the Soviet perception of our government's steadfastness. There is a strong human solidarity born of threat and there can be a transnational loyalty as evidenced by the following. Each October the West Berlin police held in the giant Olympic stadium a *Polizeischau* (a police exhibition). There was marching, acrobatics on motorcycles, demonstrations of police dog training, etc. The stadium was always packed with Berliners, West and East, and one section was reserved for the occupation authorities and their families. The American, British, and French armies each provided a band for the occasion, as did the German police. The army bands first marched separately playing national tunes, followed by the German band. Each band was greeted enthusiastically by the Berlin audience. However, the high point of the day always came when the three Allied army bands marched together with the West Berlin police band playing the tune of "Die Berliner Luft," which had somehow become the anthem of the city. At that moment there was always an emotional stirring which gripped the Berliners and the Allies alike in response to this symbol of their joint resistance to a common threat.

As to be expected of an old Berliner, powered by nostalgia, in May 1967 I returned to Berlin for a visit, the first since we had left at the end of February in 1962. I went and came back on the military train from Frankfurt to Berlin as I formerly used to travel. I spent a week in the city. How different was the atmosphere! So relaxed on the train, at the military headquarters, in the State Department Mission, among the Berlin population. Everything seemed thriving, prosperous. How different the atmosphere in Berlin was then from the time of tension before and immediately after the Wall was built.

The Wall represented the failure of the Communist "show window" policy, but it also represented the failure of the Communist effort to force the Western Allies out. We who were in Berlin when the Wall was built did not then recognize that the Wall meant the end of the crisis, the end of Soviet threats and ultimata. After a period of adjustment to the fact of the Wall, after the initial period of flights and dramatic shootings at the Wall, the situation in the divided city quieted down. By the fall of 1962, the Berlin crisis was over; not over by agreement, the Soviet push just stopped.

Why did the Soviet push stop? Partly the Wall, by halting the refugee flow, bringing about a reluctant acquiescence of the East German population in their lot, and introducing a Communist-type frontier through the divided city, made the continuing presence of a free West Berlin as an enclave in the Communist realm more tolerable to the Soviets; partly the Cuba missile crisis, partly the downfall of Khrushchev and the advent of a less venturesome collective leadership—more importantly, the Soviet rift with Communist China, and the concomitant Soviet fear of conflict on two fronts brought the consequent need to quiet down friction points with the West and to seek a *status quo* settlement on the basis of a divided Europe.

2
The Cuba Missile Crisis

robert Frost, who made a trip to the Soviet Union as a guest of the Soviet authorities in the summer of 1962, was treated with great acclaim and homage as a distinguished American poet. During his visit he had a long conversation with Khrushchev. As reported in the press Khrushchev said to Frost during his conversation: "The Western democracies are too liberal to fight." [1] At the time I was in charge of the Office of Research and Analysis for the Sino-Soviet Bloc in the Department of State. We in that office thought that this comment of Khrushchev was a strange remark; it showed profound misunderstanding. We thought at the time the remark had some reference to impending action directed at Berlin. Later with the benefit of hindsight we realized that Cuba was probably in Khrushchev's mind.

"The Western democracies are too liberal to fight." They are too soft and decadent. Bourgeois democracy is an old decaying form of civilization which will have to make way for the new Communist order. And the bold, adventurous Khrushchev sought to "nudge" the historic course forward a bit on its appointed way.

This is the ideological component of Soviet motivation, a vital element in my opinion. One of the reasons why our National Intelligence Estimates fail so often in their estimate of Communist intentions on crucial issues derives from the failure to understand properly—and it is not easy—the workings of the ideological factor. The view is often expressed that Americans tend to overemphasize the role of ideology as a guiding principle of Soviet foreign policy. This does not seem to me true. I know that it is not true for the practitioners in the field of foreign affairs; on the contrary, more are inclined to emphasize the national interest and power aspects than the ideological. There were many elements in Soviet motivation, and I will discuss them later. My aim here is merely to point out the ideological component which is usually ignored and which may have been a necessary, albeit not a sufficient, condition for the Soviet action of putting offensive guided missiles into Cuba.

Khrushchev sent the missiles to Cuba after personally taking the measure of the new, young American President. President Kennedy met Nikita Khrushchev for the first time in Vienna in June 1961, two months after the disastrous Bay of Pigs venture. As related previously, Khrushchev sought the meeting, responding in May to a proposal made by President Kennedy at the end of February. After the meeting President Kennedy was very much disturbed by the press reports that he had been browbeaten and bullied by Khrushchev. The truth is that he *had* been browbeaten by Khrushchev, as was evident to all of us who read at the time the transcript of the Kennedy-Khrushchev conversations. The Soviets and Communists are prone to browbeat American officials, when they can. Trained in Marxist-Leninist dialectic and in the rough-and-tumble of Communist argumentation, they find it easy to *beat at* capitalist leaders. I recall the reports of an American Cabinet member's conversations when visiting in the Soviet Union which made my colleagues and me nauseous because it came through so clearly that the Soviet officials were kicking and beating the American Cabinet member with words, and he either did not know that he was being beaten, or if he did, he did not know how to respond. The Khrushchev-Kennedy conversation was certainly not that bad. However, Khrushchev took the President over the humps, and it seemed quite evident that he thought the new President was young, inexperienced, and indecisive.

We were in Berlin at the time, having been there four years. The Berlin crisis had been going on for nearly three years, and by then we were pretty sensitized to the events in the outer world which might affect us. We experienced the Bay of Pigs as every American did as a national shame and disaster, but in Berlin we also experienced it as a personal threat. Coming so soon after the Bay of Pigs, the transcript of the Khrushchev-Kennedy conversation made us anticipate a Soviet action against Berlin. We did not have to wait long. The Soviets let the East Germans build the Wall through Berlin in August 1961—to be sure, this was a much less dangerous action than other possible actions. My point is that the erection of the Berlin Wall and the Soviet introduction of missiles into Cuba were direct consequences of Khrushchev's appraisal of President Kennedy. I do not mean to imply that Khrushchev's appraisal was correct; in the Cuba missile crisis he certainly miscalculated.

Let me sharpen this point by a reminiscence. I attended the Moscow Conference of March and April 1947, the first meeting of the four-power Council of Foreign Ministers to consider the German and Austrian peace settlements. General Marshall had become Secretary of State late in January of that year; since I had left Washington early in January to participate in the meetings in London of the deputy foreign ministers preparatory to the Moscow Conference, I had not met him before arriving in

Moscow. Winston Churchill said or wrote once that General Marshall was "the greatest Roman of them all." George Marshall made visibly a tremendous impression on the Russians. He was a big man, of military bearing, a man of choleric nature under great control, a man of awesome presence. He was somewhat inarticulate, could rarely respond at the table unless his advisers passed him notes on pieces of paper, and then he had trouble reading the notes. Among glib foreign ministers used to words, Marshall's inarticulateness may have even been impressive in contrast. I can think of no American leader of the past thirty years who has impressed the Russians in quite the same way as George Marshall. This is a long, roundabout way of making the simple statement that if General Marshall had been President of the United States and met with Khrushchev in Vienna in June of 1961, neither the Wall would have been built in Berlin nor would the Cuba missile crisis have taken place. Neither would the Bay of Pigs, incidentally, have taken place as it did. Of course, we cannot select our presidents by the criterion of the impression that they may or may not make on the Russians. Nevertheless, we might as well accept the fact that the personal encounter of an American president with a Soviet leader may have significant consequences.

The United States Intelligence Board, the highest committee of the American intelligence community, on September 19, 1962, approved an estimate concerning the Soviet arms build-up in Cuba which came to the conclusion that the Soviets would most probably not introduce offensive missiles into Cuba.

Intelligence estimators think primarily in terms of precedent. The Soviets had never previously stationed strategic nuclear weapons outside the Soviet Union, not even in Communist Eastern European countries which they could readily defend. Cuba was not a stable and dependable ally as were the Eastern European countries. Cuba was far away from the Soviet Union; communications between Cuba and the Soviet Union were subject to American interruption. It would be too provocative and risky to put offensive missiles into Cuba in view of the likely strong American reaction. The Soviets had previously provided surface to air missiles (SAMs) to Iraq and Indonesia. At the time of this estimate the U-2 photographs had revealed the presence of surface to air missile sites in Cuba, but nothing more. Given Castro's continuing fear of invasion despite his success at the Bay of Pigs in 1961, it was natural to believe that the Soviets were providing Castro at his request antiaircraft missiles to help him combat any future invasion attempts.

It is curious to note that John McCone, the director of Central Intelligence, who was at that time on a yacht in the Mediterranean on a wedding trip, had a different view from the assembled intelligence community experts in Washington. On August 22 he had expressed this view to President Kennedy, and separately to the Secretary of the Treasury, Douglas Dillon, the day before leaving Washington for the wedding. Apprised by CIA of the views of the estimators in the preparatory stages, he sent a series of messages called the "honeymoon telegrams," in which he argued that the Soviets had not gone to the expense, labor, and trouble to put surface to air antiaircraft missiles into Cuba against a possible United States invasion of Cuba, but that the Soviets must have had more important reasons, namely, to protect the introduction of offensive missiles. He did not, however, from the distance try to make his view prevail.

Klaus Knorr in his article in *World Politics,* April 1964, entitled "Failures in National Intelligence Estimates, the Case of the Cuban Missiles," and Roger Hilsman, the director of the State Department Intelligence and Research Bureau in 1962, in his book *To Move a Nation*, express essentially the same view that it was not the American intelligence community which erred. On the contrary, it was the Soviet intelligence community and the Soviet leadership which underestimated the risk involved in this venture. The Soviets had not expected a strong American reaction. Roger Hilsman writes that the National Intelligence Estimate reached its conclusion in part because it had not been in the Soviet interest to put in offensive missiles, given the high risk of being discovered and "the high probability of a strong American response. After all, intelligence estimators must assume that the opposition is acting in its own best interest or their job is completely hopeless. . . . to be correct, the American analysts would have to estimate that the Soviets would misestimate." [2]

This is a rather neat way of making the American estimators right and the Soviet estimators wrong. However, it misses the essential point that it should be the task of our estimators to think as the other side does. The argument from precedent which naturally misses the *moment* of change, and the inability to think as does the other side are in my experience the two chief causes of intelligence estimate failures on key issues.

As to the inability to think as does the other side, I want to digress with an example on another issue. When returning to Washington in June 1969, from a three-year assignment abroad, I was intensely interested in ascertaining how the intelligence community had fared with respect to the Soviet occupation of Czechoslovakia in August 1968. My former colleagues and friends admitted that they had done very badly. The Cierna Meeting in Eastern Slovakia had put them to sleep and they had thereafter not expected the Soviet occupation. They said to me, "Why should you blame us? The Czechoslovakian leaders who are Communists were surprised themselves." A few days later I happened to visit the Foreign Service Institute, the State Department's institution for training Foreign Service officers. During a conversation with the director of the Area Training Office, the subject of the Soviet occupation of Czechoslovakia came up. He told me that in early August 1968, they had told the members of a course in communism to constitute themselves as members of the Central Committee of the CPSU and to consider as such members, whether the Soviets should occupy Czechoslovakia. The director told me with some pride that of the class of sixteen, thirteen had expressed the view that the Soviets together with the Warsaw Pact Allies should occupy Czechoslovakia since Dubcek was apparently no longer able to maintain the primacy of the party and they recommended occupation with massive armed forces in order to prevent or reduce bloodshed. That is one case of a correct result of the effort to think as the other side does – unhappily it was only a training exercise!

In the Cuba missile crisis, both the American and the Soviet estimators were wrong: the Americans were wrong in their estimate of the likelihood of the Soviets introducing offensive missiles into Cuba; the Soviets were wrong in their estimate of the likely American response to such action. Miscalculation has been an element in the origin of every major war in this century. How dangerous miscalculation can be now at a time of nuclear armaments, the Cuba missile crisis demonstrated.

The Soviet arms build-up shipments leading to the introduction of offensive missiles in Cuba began in July. The Soviet plan of shipment was in two phases: first, surface to air antiaircraft missiles, MIG fighters, harbor defense missiles, and coastal patrol boats with ship-to-ship missiles – all defensive weapons; second, the medium range (around 1,000 miles) and intermediate range (around 2,000 miles) ballistic missiles, and the IL-28 light bombers – the offensive weapons. Four Soviet battle groups armed with nuclear weapons were also to be put into Cuba to give protection on the ground to the missiles. The first shipments arrived in Cuba in late July and hence must have been loaded in the Soviet Union in early or middle July. The first shipment of offensive missiles probably arrived in Cuba early in September. Such a major arms shipment was a very complex logistical undertaking which must have required extensive detailed planning even before being set in operation. If the decision to put offensive missiles in Cuba in this way were made without prior planning, it would have been taken perhaps three or four months ahead, in March or April 1962, in view of the lead time needed to prepare the logistic plan, to select the material, send it to the ports, and arrange for the shipping. Evidence based on an analysis of Cuban-Soviet relations seems to indicate, however, that the final Soviet decision was made, or communicated to the Cubans, in June; the manifest signs of tensions and differences suddenly vanished around June 24. It is possible that the Soviets may have originally thought to satisfy Castro with surface to air antiaircraft missiles of a defensive nature, and hence were already well prepared by June to implement the first defensive phase of the arms shipment. However, it is equally possible, and perhaps more likely, that in the previous months the Soviets had prepared a detailed logistic plan and taken the initial steps in implementation before communicating to the Cubans their willingness to station ballistic missiles on Cuba.

Whose idea was it? Did Castro ask for the missiles, or did the Soviets decide it would be a good move and raise it with the Cubans initially? This is the type of question to which one rarely has a firm answer with respect to Communist regimes. Khrushchev may have inadvertently brought the Cuban request on himself. From November 1958 on, he had frequently brandished Soviet rockets, along with his other threats, in connection with Berlin. On July 9, 1960, three days after President Eisenhower reduced the Cuban sugar quota for 1960 by 700,000 tons, Khrushchev stated that "in a figurative sense, if it became necessary, the Soviet military can support the Cuban people with rocket weapons." [3] On the next day, in a television talk Castro seized upon Khrushchev's statement, claiming that the Soviets had offered real, not figurative rockets. Khrushchev quickly withdrew in the ensuing weeks to a blander statement that "If any armed intervention is undertaken against Cuba, the necessary aid will be forthcoming." [4] Khrushchev and Castro met in September 1960 at the United Nations in New York. There is evidence that the Cubans kept insistently raising the rocket issue, to such an extent that a *New York Times* report from Havana in November 1960, "based on the most reliable diplomatic sources," stated that the Soviets told the Cubans "to quit rattling Soviet rockets." [5] There can be little doubt that the Cubans persisted on this issue. It is possible that Castro posed the rockets as an alternative to protection as a member of the Warsaw Pact or to a bilateral USSR–Cuba mutual defense treaty; while the other two alternatives offered no benefits to the Soviet Union, rockets in Cuba under Soviet command did promise real advantages. Khrushchev reported to the Supreme Soviet on December 12, 1962, that the missiles had been installed in response to a Cuban request. Castro gave diverse and contradictory versions at first but later seemed to clarify the matter. In 1965 he told Lee Lockwood: "Naturally the missiles would not have been sent in the first place if the Soviet Union had not been prepared to

67

send them. . . . We made the decision at a moment when we thought concrete measures were necessary to paralyze the aggressiveness of the United States, and we posed this necessity to the Soviet Union." [6] Our conjecture at the time of the missile crisis was that Castro asked for the missiles, alleging that this arms build-up was necessary to protect Cuba from American invasion. He would have argued that the Bay of Pigs had been a failure, but that the Americans would be likely to try again. The Soviets responded, not for Cuban purposes, but for their own.

Who among the Soviet leaders made the decision? Was it the military? The Soviet military have a reputation for being cautious. Was it the Politburo, and, if so, who among the Politburo were the decisive proponents? Was Khrushchev reluctant, as some reports indicated, accepting the decision finally on the insistence of the military and some of his Politburo colleagues? This is also the type of question about which one rarely has any firm information. My own conjecture is that this was a Khrushchevian move; it fitted in with his character, that of a bold, adventurous innovator. It fitted in with his character to make the effort and to withdraw promptly as he did when confronted with the likely consequences. In May 1960 a shuffle of personnel in the Central Committee Secretariat of the CPSU indicated that Khrushchev may have lost some of his control and that a top-level group was seeking to curtail his authority. Khrushchev presumably took the Cuba action on the basis of a collective Politburo decision; he would want to ensure that his colleagues shared the responsibility. Nevertheless, Khrushchev may have thought that a successful move into Cuba would so enhance his personal position as to disarm his opponents. When his colleagues dumped him in October 1964, one of the charges against him was adventurism. The Chinese spoke of "adventurism" and "capitulationism" in referring to the episode. There were important domestic factors leading to Khrushchev's downfall—the disastrous agricultural situation, five bad harvests after the bumper harvest of 1958 and the failure of the Khrushchevian virgin-land venture, the repeated reorganizations of the economy and the party which Khrushchev undertook, and the impending threat of another Khrushchevian domestic reorganization. Even if these domestic factors were perhaps more important, Khrushchev's failure in the Cuba missile crisis and the consequent damage to Soviet prestige throughout the world was certainly a factor in his downfall.

Cuba was an unexpected gift when it fell in the lap of the Soviets. The Soviets had played no part in the Cuban revolution. The Soviets were at first hesitant to accept this gift at its face value. Castro was in their eyes an undependable figure, and the Communist apparatus did not appear to have control of the Castro revolution. Over a year passed after Castro marched into Havana before the Soviets granted him diplomatic relations or economic aid. Not until after the U-2 incident, May 1960, were diplomatic relations resumed, May 8; the Soviets agreed to supply arms late in June, and after the Chinese in November had committed themselves to buy a million tons of sugar in 1961, the Soviets agreed in December 1960 to purchase 2,700,000 tons of sugar in 1961. During the second half of 1960, Castro had showed by the nationalization of United States property that his anti-American orientation was not a passing phase—this made him more interesting for the Soviets. On the ideological front, the Soviets also displayed caution. Although in April 1961 Castro declared that the Cuban revolution was "socialist," the Soviet slogans for the November 7th anniversary that year greeted Cuba as building "a new way of life," not "socialism." However, in the May 1, 1962 slogans of the Soviet Communist Party, the Cubans were promoted to the stage of "building socialism."

As a result of Castro's economic and political policies, Cuba became more and more economically dependent on the Soviet bloc. The Bay of Pigs revealed to the Soviets the firmness of Castro's control in Cuba and opened up to them the full vista of opportunity which a Communist Cuba offered them. Moreover, the half-way measures taken by the United States during the Bay of Pigs attempt, as well as the world public reaction, lead them to believe that powerful inhibitions had been imposed on the United States with respect to any further actions concerning Cuba. The Soviets may thus have thought that they could move without restraint.

On October 21, 1961, Roswell Gilpatric, the deputy secretary of defense, in a speech before the Business Council at Hot Springs, Virginia, disposed of the missile gap fallacy by making a public disclosure of America's decided superiority over the Soviet Union in nuclear weapons. The exposure of the "missile gap myth" ended a four-year period during which Western confidence in U.S. strategic superiority had been undermined by the spurious picture of a rapid Soviet acquisition of a large intercontinental strike force. Thanks to the U-2 overflights and to the information passed to the Americans and the British by the Soviet Colonel Oleg Penkovskiy, the United States possessed a precise view of the size and location of the Soviet missile force. The Soviet leaders learned from Gilpatric that the United States had not been deceived about the strategic balance.

How were the Soviets to cope with this manifest weakness on their part? Khrushchev was confronted with the habitual resource allocation bind of the Soviet economy. It is likely that the Soviet military pressed for a crash program to build a bigger and better-hardened Soviet ICBM force. Any such program would be very burdensome to the Soviet economy and would make it much more difficult for Khrushchev to meet even partially the growing expectations of the Russian people for better housing and more consumer goods. Likewise, it might cut into the Soviet space program and hamper the extensive military and economic aid programs to India, Egypt, Indonesia, and other developing nations. Certainly, the cheapest way for the Soviets to meet the strategic imbalance was to put into Cuba medium range and intermediate range missiles of which they had plenty on hand. By installing MRBMs and IRBMs on Cuba, the Soviets' first-strike missile capability would be so enhanced that the United States' second-strike nuclear response would be radically diminished—perhaps even the control centers for the second strike might be damaged. As a result, the U.S. nuclear deterrent would be seriously undermined. The potential military gain thus was great, sufficient to justify a high degree of risk. Also there would be an important political gain in the conflict with the Chinese Communists for the leadership of the world Communist movement—how better demonstrate forward momentum in the worldwide struggle against "imperialism," momentum attained under Soviet leadership.

The Soviets evidently believed that they could get away with stationing ballistic missiles in Cuba, without effective challenge by the United States. They may have expected that a well-planned, fast, and secret operation would be completed before being discovered by the United States. Khrushchev used to the hilt habitual Soviet/Russian duplicity in his protestations and assurances to President Kennedy about the "defensive" nature of the Soviet weapons in Cuba: through Ambassador Dobrynin to Robert Kennedy on September 4, 1962, through Soviet Embassy press officer Bolshakov early in October, directly himself to our Ambassador Foy Kohler in Moscow on October 16, and through Soviet Foreign Minister Gromyko to the President himself on October 18. Both these latter "assurances" came after the President knew definitely about the offensive Soviet missile weapons in Cuba, but several days before his disclosure of this fact to the world. The Soviets may have believed that the United States government would wring its hands, sputter, and run to the UN, but would not take decisive action. Doubtless, the Soviets did not want to risk thermonuclear war, and they must have thought that the risk of an immediate U.S. thermonuclear response was negligible.

The evidence indicates that the Soviets did not want these missile bases for immediate military purposes, in order to be able to undertake a nuclear war against the United States. Khrushchev undoubtedly had political purposes in mind. Was it Berlin? For four years he had been threatening Berlin with one ultimatum after another. While it is possible that Khrushchev may have wanted missile bases in Cuba in order to strengthen his hand in Berlin in the ensuing months, it does not seem likely that the Soviets would take such risks for Berlin. The Soviets were undoubtedly seeking to accomplish a major shift in the world balance of power in their direction, which they would subsequently seek to exploit in diverse ways and in various disputes, including Berlin.

Before the President's disclosure of Soviet missiles in Cuba, there were four policy alternatives considered in the U.S. government during the week of October 15 to October 22. They were as follows: do nothing, blockade, air strike to take out the missile sites, and general air attack followed by invasion. Curiously enough, it was the Secretary of Defense who initially argued "do nothing" on the ground that the strategic balance was really not basically altered by the presence of Soviet MRBMs and IRBMs in Cuba. "A missile is a missile," he said, "it makes no great difference whether you are killed by a missile fired by the Soviet Union or by Cuba." After a couple of days he left this position recognizing the political damage to the United States if we did nothing. His military argument was probably unsound too; it was vigorously contested by Paul Nitze and others.

The proposal for the blockade measures had supporters from the start; it had the great advantage of giving Khrushchev a way out. Llewellyn Thompson, the former Ambassador in Moscow, had just returned from there, knew Khrushchev well, and feared the danger of an impulsive response by him if we were to shed Russian blood, as we certainly would have by a surprise air strike against the offensive missile bases. His sagacious advice on dealing with Khrushchev had great influence on the President through the crisis. The air strike proposal had a notable proponent in Dean Acheson and there were other supporters. Acheson expressed his view in the short article in *Esquire*, February 1969, entitled "Dean Acheson's Version of Robert Kennedy's Version of the Cuban Missile Affair—Homage to Plain Dumb Luck." The invasion proposal had its proponents too, particularly among the military; Senator Richard B. Russell of Georgia, chairman of the Senate Armed Services Committe, supported by Senator J. William Fulbright, chairman of the Senate Foreign Relations Committee, also urged an immediate invasion during the meeting with the President held for the briefing of the congressional leadership at 5:00 P.M., Monday afternoon, October 22, two hours before the President's disclosure speech. There were some who thought that we might as well use this opportunity through invasion to get rid of Castro once and for all. Not everyone shared Ambassador Thompson's concern that American military action in Cuba caused by the Soviets putting offensive missiles there would have resulted in a Soviet nuclear reaction against the United States or a military reaction in some other place.

Assuming inaction on the Soviet part, the key issue with respect to the alternative to invade has seemed to me, in retrospect, the possible effect on the Latin American countries. Since the Cuba missile crisis, Castroism has seemed to have lost to a considerable extent its appeal in Latin America. Invasion might have been a grave alienating factor in United States-Latin American relations. Certainly the unanimous support which the United States obtained so promptly in the OAS (Organization of the American States) for the blockade was very desirable and impressive—it doubtless made an impression on the Soviets.

The two weeks, October 15 to October 28, were rather tense. In retrospect, it does not appear that we were as close to nuclear war as many feared. Some of us thought that the Russians had gone way out on a limb and that when they became aware of this, they would withdraw, no matter what the loss. But who could be certain about such a judgment? When stakes are so high, they throw shadows.

There were some lighter aspects of the Cuba missile affair, however. When sure evidence of the presence of offensive Soviet missiles in Cuba became available from U-2 photographs on the evening of Monday, October 15, top level officials were informed that same evening, the President on Tuesday morning. Roger Hilsman, director of the Bureau of Intelligence and Research in the State Department, "cut in" a group of us on Wednesday afternoon. I inquired whether I should leave Thursday evening as planned on the sleeper for Cincinnati to fulfill a commitment to speak Friday evening at a University of Cincinnati weekend student seminar. Roger Hilsman told me at once, "Oh heavens, you must go!" The President, he explained, was keeping all his speaking engagements and he had instructed everyone to go ahead with ordinary business so as not to let the press become suspicious prematurely before the government made up its mind how to proceed. Well, the press would not have noticed it one way or another, I thought, but the University of Cincinnati sponsors would have been annoyed, and it was pleasant duty naturally to participate in this business-as-usual procedure of the United States government. The topic of my talk, appropriately enough, was "Ideology and Conflict."

I attended seminar sessions Saturday morning and then left on the sleeper Saturday night for Washington. Sunday morning I went from the rail station to the Department at eight o'clock in the morning and arrived home from the Department late that night. During that memorable Sunday—it was the day before President Kennedy's television address to the American people and to the world disclosing our knowledge of what the Soviets were doing in Cuba—the press and radio correspondents were prowling the halls of the State Department. Really, it was one of the miracles of present-day Washington that the U.S. government was able to keep a secret of this dimension for one whole week. It was rather clear on that Sunday that the secret could not be kept much longer as the press and radio men had noticed too many strange signs. The NBC correspondent Elie Abel, the author of the book *The Missile Crisis* saw me in the hall on that morning. He said to me, "What are you doing here on a Sunday morning?" "Oh, I just came in on the sleeper from Cincinnati. I had to give a talk Friday night at a University of Cincinnati gathering and I wanted to catch up on the cables and work before going home." He looked at me as if to imply "that's a likely story" and then said, "Maybe so, but there is something wrong; there is something going on; there are too many people in the Department for a Sunday morning, and none of them will see me." By Sunday evening, several newspapers had the story, but they refrained from publishing it at the President's personal request so as not to forewarn the Soviets and permit them to take some initiative which might run counter to the planned U.S. measures.

One other item in a lighter vein: Washington, as you know, is a place for status symbols. During the next week after the President's disclosure, the major status symbol was whether you slept in your office at night. Mc-Namara had a couch in his office. George Ball and Alexis Johnson took turns sleeping in the State Department. This naturally affected a group of us and so we dutifully arranged also to sleep in the Department. A colleague brought in a rollaway bed and three or four of us alternated in sleeping in the Department. During the next ten days, I slept in the Department two or three nights which was minimum performance in compliance with the status symbol.

President Kennedy's disclosure speech [7] on television to the nation at 7:00 P.M., Monday, October 22, was a masterful address, one of the great speeches of the American presidency. The President set forth clearly the nature of the newly discovered Soviet offensive missile sites on Cuba, related in detail the false assurances and deliberate deception of the Soviets, and exposed the introduction of strategic nuclear missiles into Cuba as "an explicit threat to the peace and security of all the Americas," thus putting the threat in a hemispheric context. He termed "this secret, swift, and extraordinary build-up of Communist missiles" as "a deliberately provocative and unjustified change in the status quo which cannot be accepted by this country." He set forth as our objective "to secure their withdrawal . . . from the Western Hemisphere." He then outlined "the following initial steps" being taken: (1) "a strict quarantine on all offensive military equipment under shipment to Cuba"; (2) "the continued and increased close surveillance of Cuba and its military build-up"; (3) "any nuclear missile launched from Cuba against any nation in the Western Hemisphere" will be regarded "as an attack by the Soviet Union on the United States, requiring a full retaliatory response upon the Soviet Union"; (4) reinforcement of Guantanamo; (5) an immediate meeting tonight of the Organization of American States "to consider this threat to hemispheric security"; (6) an emergency meeting of the UN Security Council is being requested to consider our resolution calling "for the prompt dismantling and withdrawal of all offensive weapons in Cuba, under the supervision of United Nations observers"; (7) Khrushchev is urged to eliminate this reckless threat to world peace by withdrawing these offensive missiles from Cuba. This was followed by a reference to previous American efforts to limit the spread of nuclear arms and to eliminate military bases in an effective disarmament treaty and, with a statesmanlike eye beyond the crisis, by announcing American willingness "to discuss new proposals for the removal of tension on both sides." Kennedy's speech not only had the effect of uniting the American people behind the President, but it also openly and effectively challenged the Soviets before the world. Stimulated by a skeptical British press reaction to his speech, the President decided on Wednesday, October 24, to release the missile site photographs to the world press. These were used with telling effect by the U.S. representative at the UN, Adlai E. Stevenson, at his confrontation with the Soviet representative Valerian Zorin during the Security Council meeting on Thursday.

Why did the Soviets offer so promptly to dismantle the guided missile bases? The United States government discovered the presence of the offensive missiles in Cuba before the Soviets had been able, for the most part, to put them in operational readiness. Hubert Humphrey had, you may recall, a phrase for it: "The Soviets have been caught with their rockets down, and their missiles showing." The U.S. method of disclosure was effective in gaining unanimous OAS collaboration, and this unusual demonstration of inter-American solidarity may have surprised as well as impressed the Soviets. Clear support was gained from all the NATO countries so that any Soviet expectations of pressure on the U.S. by some fearful allies against forceful measures proved to be mistaken. Moreover, the photographic evidence, the President's disclosure of Soviet secretiveness and deception, and Adlai Stevenson's courtroom indictment of the Soviet Union before the world forum of the UN Security Council achieved a majority world public opinion support of the U.S. naval blockade measures.

The Soviets learned that we were in earnest with respect to the blockade. Moreover, the blockade measure had the great advantage of not foreclosing the other more forceful measures. Indeed, it was probably not the blockade itself that brought about the Soviet decision to dismantle, but rather the fact that the United States had mobilized in Florida and the southeastern states a formidable military force capable of air strike and invasion of Cuba. After all, the blockade only stopped the Soviets from bringing more offensive missiles into Cuba. Even after Soviet ships stopped in the Atlantic on Wednesday, October 24, and turned back, the Soviets continued feverishly working on the missile bases in Cuba. The United States' problem was to have this work stopped and the missiles in Cuba dismantled and removed.

The Soviet leadership apparently became alarmed when the United States seemed to be preparing for further military action against Cuba. If the United States had proceeded with an air strike against Soviet installations, killing Soviet personnel, or if the United States had gone over to a military invasion of Cuba to destroy the Castro regime, the Soviets would have been faced with the decision of initiating nuclear war against the United States or accepting a greater defeat than mere removal of the rockets. They moved quickly to announce their decision to discontinue further work on the offensive missile bases and to dismantle and return these missiles to the USSR, in order not to be confronted with the foregoing dilemma. They decided, in effect, to cut their losses.

President Kennedy and his advisers have been justly praised, in my opinion, for their restraint in the handling of the crisis, for beginning with the minimum application of force at a blockade level and holding other more forceful measures in reserve as a threat. I do not think Dean Acheson is right when he calls it "plain dumb luck" and when he says that Kennedy was helped "by the luck of Khrushchev's befuddlement and loss of nerve," Khrushchev did lose his nerve, but it wasn't luck; he had good reason to be shaken.

It was apparent in the secret letter from Khrushchev to Kennedy which came in a long four-part cable from Moscow on the evening of Friday, October 26. Roger Hilsman says "The letter was most emphatically not 'the outcry of a frightened man' as some accounts [Elie Abel] would have it." [8] Later Roger Hilsman says that Khrushchev had faced "the prospect of an escalating confrontation squarely, that he was horrified at what he saw at the end of that road." [9] Well, "horrified" or "frightened" — when we read the letter of October 26, many of us thought Khrushchev was frightened and that he was throwing in the towel. In a conversation with a high American official of our embassy in Moscow, on his first trip back to Washington shortly after the Cuba missile crisis, I asked him what the situation had been at Moscow during that week after the disclosure. He told me that among Soviet officials he had seen nothing but "scared" people in Moscow that week. In his speech to the Supreme Soviet on December 12, 1962, Khrushchev admitted that "the smell of burning hung in the air" at the height of the Cuban event.[10]

If Khrushchev was throwing in the towel in that letter of October 26, the question was, of course, how properly to pick it up. It was done by combining the contents of this long, rambling, and emotional letter with the specific proposal made to the United States government by Alexander Fomin, a Soviet Embassy official, through John Scali, the State Department correspondent of the American Broadcasting Company, and by ignoring the second Khrushchev to Kennedy letter that arrived Saturday morning proposing a *quid pro quo* deal in withdrawing missiles from Cuba and Turkey. Fomin who was listed in the diplomatic bluebook as a Soviet counselor of embassy, was regarded by American security officers as a high ranking Soviet intelligence officer in the guise of a diplomat; he was believed to be a KGB colonel and the chief of Soviet intelligence operations in the United States. He called John Scali whom he previously knew, inviting him to lunch on that Friday afternoon, October 26. Fomin asked Scali to pass to the highest level in the State Department the following proposal for resolution of the crisis:

1. The Soviet government would dismantle and ship back to the Soviet Union the offensive missiles in Cuba, and would pledge never to reintroduce missiles into Cuba;

2. The United Nations would supervise and verify the removal;

3. The United States would pledge publicly not to invade Cuba.

That evening Scali told Fomin, as instructed by Secretary Rusk, that the United States government saw real possibilities in this proposal, adding that "time is very urgent." In a letter sent Saturday evening, October 27, at 8:00 P.M. and given to the press at the same time, President Kennedy replied to Khrushchev's first letter of October 26 by expressing general acceptance of "the key elements of your proposals" understood to be as follows:

"1. You would agree to remove these weapons systems from Cuba under appropriate United Nations observation and undertake, with suitable safeguards, to halt the further introduction of such weapons systems into Cuba.

"2. We, on our part, would agree—upon the establishment of adequate arrangements through the United Nations to insure the carrying out and continuation of these commitments—(a) to remove promptly the quarantine measures now in effect, and (b) to give assurances against an invasion of Cuba." [11]

This message was broadcast by radio to Moscow at once. When Khrushchev accepted Kennedy's understanding of these proposals in his reply the next morning, Sunday, October 28, broadcast similarly in view of the time urgency by Moscow radio at 9:00 A.M. Washington time, the Cuba crisis was settled along these lines, except that Castro refused to permit UN inspection of the dismantling of the missile sites on Cuban territory and the verification of the removal of the missiles was obtained by U.S. aerial surveillance and naval observations of the vessels returning to the Soviet Union.

Why did Khrushchev use Fomin as the channel for

negotiating with the United States government in this critical situation? It is not unusual for the Communists to go outside official diplomatic channels; the Communists may not trust diplomatic channels that much. A secretive conspiratorial regime may think that an informal private channel may get more readily to the inner thinking of the other side. Also, such a regime may think it easier to disown an unofficial approach subsequently, if it so desires. Perhaps Khrushchev trusted his KGB chief more than he did Dobrynin; perhaps even his KGB communication channel was faster or better than his official diplomatic channel. At any rate, John Scali played an important role in the settlement of the Cuba missile crisis, particularly when he "exploded" to Fomin on Saturday afternoon that he had been "double-crossed" by Khrushchev's second letter. On Sunday afternoon, October 28, after Khrushchev's letter accepting Kennedy's proposal had been received, Fomin passed to Scali a message from Khrushchev thanking him for his assistance in resolving the Cuba issue. And Fomin added, he thanks you too for your "explosion" of yesterday afternoon — which means that Fomin's report of Scali's "explosion" about being double-crossed by the Cuba-Turkish deal proposed in Khrushchev's second letter and about such a deal being entirely unacceptable to the United States government had helped Khrushchev prevail over those colleagues and advisers who had drafted the second letter and insisted it be sent.

The second Khrushchev letter, it should be mentioned, may well have been suggested to the Soviets by the Walter Lippmann commentary on Thursday, October 25, proposing a Cuba-Turkey deal of this sort. The Soviets probably thought that the United States government was floating a trial balloon by Lippmann's article. Fomin referred to Lippmann's column when Scali was berating him Saturday afternoon. To my mind this Lippmann commentary is one of the good examples of the disservice that American news commentators on occasion pay the American people.

Why was Khrushchev frightened? Was it the well-articulated, well-orchestrated Kennedy administration policy, or "crisis management" in the contemporary gobbledegook terminology? Certainly this was an important factor. However, there is another factor which seems to me more important and which is not mentioned by Elie Abel, Roger Hilsman, or Robert Kennedy. The neglected factor is *the American people.*

I read the first, the secret letter from Khrushchev, on the evening of Friday October 26, as it came in on the wire from Moscow. It indicated to me, as I said previously, that Khrushchev was frightened and was throwing in the towel. There was one passage which to me was the key. Elie Abel cites rather fully the contents of this unpublished letter, some parts in direct quotes. So do Robert Kennedy and Roger Hilsman. None of them mention the passage which I recall as the key to why Khrushchev was frightened. Somewhere in the rambling letter Khrushchev mentions or implies that he knows the American people are *aroused*. It did not matter what he had thought of Kennedy; he had come to realize that Kennedy would have to act because the American people were aroused. We knew that the American people were intensely angry, that emotion was rising to a vehement pitch; we knew it from the press and the radio, from ourselves, from our friends, from Congressional statements. President Kennedy and Robert Kennedy certainly knew it. Robert Kennedy relates in his book that on the Wednesday morning, October 24, when the quarantine went into effect, he said to the President, "I just don't think there was any choice, and not only that, if you hadn't acted you would have been impeached." The President thought for a moment and said, "That's what I think—I would have been impeached." [12]

How does the autocratic leader of Russia, the Soviet Union, know that the American people are aroused? Perhaps from the Soviet Embassy in Washington, from Soviet Ambassador Dobrynin; it would certainly be his responsibility to report to the Kremlin on popular American attitudes during the crisis. Perhaps Fomin, the presumed chief of Soviet intelligence in the United States, reported to Khrushchev on the emotional surge. How does an autocratic and Communist leader who thinks in terms of "manipulating" the mind of the masses, how does he understand what it means in a democracy, when the *people* are *aroused*? It is puzzling, but Khrushchev had been to the United States and he was an extraordinary man. At any rate, Khrushchev, to my reading of this unpublished letter, was clearly aware that the American people were aroused and he understood what that meant.

There is some collateral published evidence on this point. In relating the contents of the October 26 letter, Elie Abel states the following: "But he [Khrushchev] asked the President to believe in himself, to agree that passions ought to be controlled on both sides." [13] However, the passions of the Russian people had not been aroused. During the period from October 22 to October 28, the Soviets had not failed to inform their people about the Cuba crisis; they could hardly ignore it in view of the seriousness of the crisis and the volume of broadcasting from other countries on the subject. In fact, the Soviet propaganda on Cuba during this period was quite voluminous. However, the emphasis was placed upon the United States-Cuban rather than the United States-Soviet aspects of the crisis, which tended to blunt the impact of the story as far as Soviet audiences were concerned.

Another piece of collateral published evidence appears in the third paragraph, the major operational paragraph in the Khrushchev letter of Sunday October 28, in which Khrushchev accepted President Kennedy's propositions set forth in his letter of the previous day, and stated that the Soviet government had ordered the offensive arms to be dismantled, crated, and returned to the Soviet Union. One of the reasons given in the preamble portion of this third paragraph justifying this order is as follows: "To reassure the American people who I am certain also want peace, as do the people of the Soviet Union." [14] You would only want to reassure the American people if you realized that the American people were aroused.

Although ten years have passed, it is still too early to appraise the outcome of the Cuba missile crisis in proper historic perspective. While the brief tank incident at Checkpoint Charlie the previous year may have been the first confrontation of U.S. and Soviet armed forces, the Cuba missile crisis was the first direct nuclear confrontation of the United States and the USSR—it was the first nuclear confrontation in history. Had the Soviet Union not backed down, nuclear war appeared imminent. At the time it was clear that in this test of will the United States had won a notable victory which made its impression on world public opinion. On the other hand, it would have been a mistake for us to overestimate the element of victory involved. The Soviets had ventured forward into an area of maximum U.S. national security interest. They had moved into an exposed position where military advantage was entirely on our side. If the United States was not ready to accept quietly the installation of Soviet missiles in Cuba, the Soviets had no alternative except to withdraw them, unless they were willing to go to all-out war, which they quite evidently were not. Moreover, by acting quickly, and obtaining a U.S. commitment not to invade Cuba, the Soviets secured the Castro regime from removal by U.S. military force. They may have hoped to achieve an improvement of Cuban relations with the United States and the Latin American countries. After the dust had settled, they doubtless expected to be able to return to the long-term use of Cuba as a Communist bridgehead in the Western Hemisphere.

President Kennedy made no victory claims himself, and he explicitly instructed all members of the executive branch not to make any statements to the press claiming any kind of victory. There was personal nobility in this, particularly in view of the rough handling which Khrushchev gave him in Vienna the year before. More important was the immediate vision to the future; President Kennedy wanted to utilize the outcome of the Cuba missile crisis to introduce a basic improvement of U.S.-Soviet relations. It is customary for Soviet policy to move toward a *détente,* after a forward rush has been stopped, and Khrushchev responded in statesmanlike fashion. As a consequence, significant agreements in the arms control field were reached. The first agreement was the Partial Nuclear Test Ban Treaty of July 1963 which the United States had been seeking for many years. In November 1963 the United States and the Soviet Union accepted a UN resolution that nuclear weapons must be excluded from outer space; pursuant to this resolution, in 1967 the Outer Space Treaty was adopted which prohibits installation of military bases on the moon or other celestial bodies, and the placing of mass destruction weapons in orbit around the earth or otherwise stationing them in outer space. Likewise, in 1963 the hot line was installed between the White House and the Kremlin as a direct result of the Cuba missile crisis, its aim being to avoid nuclear war by misunderstanding—both sides had experienced the acute delicacy of timing and the danger of communications delay during the missile crisis. Continuing steps in the arms control field have been taken up to the present: the Treaty on the Nonproliferation of Nuclear Weapons was signed July 1, 1968, and went into effect March 5, 1970; the Treaty Banning Emplacement of Nuclear Weapons on the Seabed was signed by sixty-two nations in Washington, February 11, 1971; and the strategic arms limitation talks between the U.S. and the USSR began in November 1969 and are continuing as of this writing (February 1972). Also, in this period of *détente* between the U.S. and USSR, some bilateral agreements have been achieved: a consular convention, a civil air agreement, and vastly expanded cultural exchange agreements. In most recent years there has been a tentative movement toward cooperative, if not joint, scientific and space exploration projects. It is remarkable that the *détente* has persisted to the present and borne some fruit, despite the Vietnam war. Were this U.S.-USSR *détente* to continue undisturbed and broadened in the next decades leading to a fundamental understanding between the two powers, the Cuba missile crisis will be seen as the all-important beginning.

Meanwhile, of course, the Soviets have utilized this period of *détente* to build up, not on a crash basis, but at a measured pace, their intercontinental ballistic missile force to near parity with the United States, or perhaps even above parity. If there is to be a confrontation again with the Americans, from their standpoint the Soviets will be better prepared and in a more equal position. However, the Soviets do not want nuclear confrontation any more than we do. The Soviet leadership has been aware for more than a decade of the folly of mutually destructive strategic nuclear warfare. This awareness was signalized at the Twentieth Party Congress in 1956 by the renunciation of the doctrine of the inevitability of war between capitalism and communism. This awareness, however, did not prevent them from blundering into Cuba.

One lesson that both nuclear powers learned in the Cuba missile crisis was to avoid situations which might possibly lead to a nuclear confrontation. This aim dictates, particularly, caution and restraint in the use of either powers' own armed forces. Our own performance in Vietnam, has hardly been exemplary on this score.

The Cuba missile crisis outcome did not eliminate the threat of nuclear war nor did it necessarily introduce a basic reconciliation. Nor has it meant the end of the cold war, the "protracted struggle" in Marxist-Leninist terms. What it did was make very clear the outer limit of the frame within which political and military action in international affairs dare take place. If policy is, as Bismarck said, "die Kunst des Möglichen," the "art of the possible," the Cuba missile crisis revealed the limit to the possible in today's world.

3
Myths, Slogans, and Vietnam
Specious Abstraction And Foreign Policy

One of the wisest men who has lived in this country during this century, Alfred North Whitehead, in his Lowell lectures in 1925 at Harvard, pointed out a fallacy which causes great confusion in philosophy. It is called the "Fallacy of Misplaced Concreteness," that is, the accidental error of mistaking the abstract for the concrete.[1] Professor Whitehead cited many examples, particularly referring to the characteristic scientific philosophy of the seventeenth century with its distinction between primary and secondary qualities. This conception of the universe he found "quite unbelievable" because it was framed in terms of high abstractions, and the paradox arose because we had "mistaken our abstraction for concrete realities."[2]

Of course, abstraction is essential to the thought process; "you cannot think without abstractions."[3] Whether in philosophy, science, or foreign policy, we think in abstract terms and in differing levels of abstraction. The disadvantage of exclusive attention to a group of abstractions, as Whitehead points out, is that you have abstracted from the remainder of things and, if the excluded things are important, the chosen modes of thought are not able to deal with them. Hence, it is most important "to be vigilant in critically revising your modes of abstraction."[4]

The fallacy of mistaking the abstract for the concrete is not limited to science and philosophy. Specious abstraction occurs in all fields of endeavor as a prominent source of error. The more complex the affairs, the more prevalent becomes specious abstraction; the more significant the issue, the more dangerous.

Formulation of American foreign policy is a thought process, and not nearly as primitive a one as some critics believe. Unfortunately, however, our traditional policies and some on-going policies have been replete with diverse forms of specious abstraction as well as other forms of miscalculation. The most flagrant example from which our nation is still suffering is U.S. policy in Vietnam. Whitehead wrote in 1925: "We all know those clear-cut trenchant intellects, immovably encased in a hard shell of abstractions" [5]—how better describe the inner circle of political and military advisers who formulated U.S. policy on Vietnam from early 1961 to March 1, 1968 (the day Clark Clifford replaced Robert McNamara as Secretary of Defense). Whitehead spoke of the "accidental" error of mistaking the abstract for the concrete which was doubtless true of seventeenth-century scientific philosophy—in foreign policy the error is more apt to be willful than accidental. In the case of our Vietnam policy, it was certainly willful, perhaps even obsessive.

If all thought is by way of abstractions, how shall we avoid the pitfalls of specious abstraction? If we acknowledge that in foreign policy decisions, thought must be directed toward the concrete, we must then ask what is *concrete* in this context so that the word will have some meaning. Let me suggest the following to delineate what is *concrete* in foreign policy:

> —to seek attainable national goals—if politics is the "art of the possible," then policy should not seek "the impossible," the unattainable;

—to serve necessary national purposes—national survival is doubtless the ultimate such purpose, but more than mere survival is involved, healthy social development, institutional strength, and individual happiness as well;

—to recognize and acknowledge the legitimate interests of other nations—this means that we must understand other nations, their nature, historic roots, their aspirations, etc.;

—to relate national aims and policies constantly to the rapidly changing world political configuration.

Doubtless there are other ways to delineate the concrete in foreign policy; the foregoing is meant to be suggestive, not exhaustive.

Myths and legends, which are either accidentally or deliberately created, are abstractions which often serve as ingredients in the formation of foreign policy. The *Dolchstoss,* or stab-in-the-back, legend which explained away the defeat of the "invincible" German army in World War I was a constant background feature in the Nazi mentality and in the formulation of a foreign policy which required invincible military prowess for its fruition. There is a danger that a comparable legend may gain currency in this country in the wake of our disengagement from Vietnam, namely, that the civilian-imposed restraints on military tactics in the air and in the field, for example, bombing targets in North Vietnam and restrictions on ground troop movements into border sanctuary areas, frustrated our armed forces and denied them the victory they would assuredly otherwise have achieved. This legend is not sustainable by the facts—though no one denies that we had the nuclear capability of "bombing North Vietnam back to the Stone Age," which would hardly have been a triumph of foreign policy in an undeclared limited war, not to mention the moral aspects nor the international repercussions.

One of the most pernicious legends which has hampered American foreign policy during the past twenty years is the legend that "we," "U.S. foreign policy," or "the State Department" lost China to the Communists. This legend, fostered by the very active "China lobby," constrained and intimidated the government in every effort to reformulate our policy toward Communist China. It created the force which drove out of the State Department at a critical time our foremost China experts, John Carter Vincent, O. Edmund Clubb, John Paton Davies. Were these men so wrong, who may have regarded the Maoists as Chinese reformers, Communist to be sure, but more nationalist than Soviet Communist? Perhaps they did not perfectly appraise the Marxist-Leninist aspect of Maoism, but they certainly understood the nationalism of China and the impossibility of its subordination to Kremlin communism. Whether they anticipated the early Sino-Soviet rift in their thought, I do not recall, but I am sure they would have recognized its meaning. They knew China, the great essentially nonexpansionist Middle Kingdom. If they had not been sacrificed to the insensate passion of a legendary figment, they might have ten years later been at high enough positions in the State Department to bring some deep understanding of China into the consideration in the early sixties of our policy toward Vietnam.

This unhappy legend has gradually faded, and more and more Americans now seem prepared to acknowledge that the outcome of such cataclysmic historic events as the Chinese civil war cannot be determined by foreigners. Thus we had come to an intellectual posture where we could entertain the idea of normal relations with Communist China, and in 1971, with the invention of "pingpong diplomacy," the Chinese arrived at a corresponding posture, more important for U.S.-Chinese relations even than answers to the seemingly insoluble Formosa problem.

More pernicious as abstractions perhaps than the legends and myths in foreign policy and even more prevalent, are the slogans. Slogans are abstract verbalizations of policy. They are designed for easy public understanding in a democracy; they aim to catch the public attention and imagination, to inflame passions and to fortify will. Sometimes the slogans refer to real and meaningful policies; sometimes they merely reflect wishful thinking, or are concocted for domestic purposes, while being patently spurious for foreign policy. Slogans, and particularly an interconnected set of slogans, have a life and vitality of their own; they are apt to become an intrinsic part of the mental-image world of the policy maker as well as of the informed public. The policy makers themselves come to *think* in terms of their own slogans, and, worse, become unable to think in other terms—it is in this sense that policy makers become captives of their own slogans.

Policy by slogan is not unique to American democracy, nor to Western democracy. Sloganeering may well be intrinsic to modern mass society, Communist as well as non-Communist, deriving in part from modern communications techniques and media which are designed to inform and hold together the popular masses in the social process. Certainly policy by slogans is perhaps as prevalent in the Communist world as in Western democracies. Indeed, the question arises as to what extent Communist ideology is being undermined in this process. Has the Communist ideology become a slogan, or rather a collection of slogans? To whom are the slogans still meaningful? Probably to the party leadership and other

95

self-chosen captives among the party faithful; probably very little to the broad masses.

Let us consider briefly some examples of slogans in recent American foreign policy. "Unconditional surrender" was enunciated by Franklin D. Roosevelt in Casablanca at a press conference on January 24, 1943. Grant's Civil War use of the term was in the background of its formulation, but it was not an impromptu casual usage. Roosevelt had World War I in mind in this as in so many other elements of his policy; he wanted the Germans to be obliged to admit military defeat so unequivocally that no new *Dolchstoss* legend could arise. He had discussed this formulation with Churchill and received British government approval of its enunciation. Nevertheless Churchill was never happy with this slogan; Stalin sought modification, believing it would stiffen German resistance; General Eisenhower sought clarification for the same reason. Roosevelt never wavered, and refused every request to qualify "unconditional surrender." He regarded it probably as a rallying cry to fortify the intense domestic exertions, and, more important, as a unifying goal for Allied exertions, a common denominator overriding the many disagreements and mutual suspicions.

Did the "unconditional surrender" demand lengthen the war against Germany or Japan? The answer with respect to Japan is uncertain. It can be argued that the shock of the atomic bomb brought the end of the war against Japan and that the end of the war would not have come so soon had it not been for Hiroshima and Nagasaki. On the other hand, the State Department Japanese experts Joseph Grew and Eugene Dooman had urged the President since early May 1945 to issue a statement clarifying "unconditional surrender" and indicating that the existing imperial dynasty might by retained.

In the early winter of 1944, I served on the Interdepartmental Committee working on the surrender terms
for Germany. After we concluded our work, a similar
committee was established for the surrender terms for
Japan. This latter committee sought a member who had
participated in the previous work on the German surrender terms and who might hence be able to explain the
background thinking involved in aspects of the German
document. It was my good fortune to be assigned to sit
with the Japan committee. My chief recollection of this
committee work is the violent dispute on the issue of the
retention of the Emperor. Was the Emperor to be held
responsible like Hitler and to be treated like Hitler? The
foremost Japan expert at the table was Eugene Dooman.
I recall the impressive cogency, passion, and brilliance
of his argumentation on the need for retaining the Emperor, both to accomplish the surrender and to facilitate
a democratic reconstruction of Japanese social and political life. In comparison, the talk by the emissaries of
MacLeish, Acheson, and Elmer Davis was the abstract
generalistic prattle of men unfamiliar with the specific
concrete realities.

The battle within the State Department on the issue of
the Emperor continued unabated until the Potsdam Declaration of July 26, 1945; influenced by Cordell Hull's
and James F. Byrnes's rigid insistence on unconditional
surrender, President Truman did not include even then
the clear statement on the Emperor issue desired by the
experts. In the end, of course, Japan's surrender was not
really unconditional, since the maintenance of the Emperor as head of state was a condition stipulated by the
Japanese and accepted by the Allies. Thus, there remains
a lingering doubt whether, if the course advocated by
Grew and Dooman had been followed, that is, a clear
statement in May 1945, of acceptance of the imperial

institution in the Japanese surrender, the peace-desiring elements around the throne might not have been successful before August in overcoming with the Emperor's help the militarist elements who were advocating war to the bitter end. Had this been achieved, the United States would not bear the guilt of having dropped atomic bombs without warning on a civilian population.

The answer with respect to Germany is likewise difficult. Goebbels and the German propaganda machine made persistent and insistent (almost gleeful) use of "unconditional surrender" to stiffen German popular and military resistance by painting the cataclysmic effects on the German people of submission to this demand. The German generals in postwar interviews have confirmed the view that German military resistance to the end was fortified by reaction to the "unconditional surrender" demand. General Eisenhower and SHAEF headquarters thought the same, and, from April 1944 on, sought without avail to have the demand clarified. Evidence is strong that the "unconditional surrender" slogan may have lengthened the war against Germany. If so, the value of its pronouncement is cast in grave doubt. The Allies did not need this slogan to inspire their effort, and whatever beneficial efforts it may have had on the Allied side, they would certainly be outweighed by the disadvantage resulting from the stiffened German resistance caused by the slogan. One comes to the conclusion that the slogan was not necessary and that, even if this were to be our policy to the end, it would have been better left unsaid.

John Foster Dulles was one of the master sloganeers of the postwar period. "Liberation," "agonizing reappraisal," "massive retaliation" were among the many catchwords he put forth. Dulles produced the "liberation" of Eastern Europe in a presidential campaign speech in 1952 at Buffalo, New York, a city with a large population of Eastern European extraction. It was the Republican answer to "containment" which was merely defensive, as the Republican platform had stated. We heard much of "liberation," or "roll-back," during those years in the State Department. No one working on Eastern European affairs took it seriously. It never was real. It never was a policy. In some senses, it was a cruel hoax. A slogan concocted for domestic political purposes during a presidential campaign, it was then reiterated in declaratory statements as if it were a policy, particularly in the early years of the Eisenhower administration. Perhaps it was just wishful thinking; "roll back the iron curtain," as if it might happen if one said it often enough. Its emptiness was revealed during the events in East Germany in June 1953 and in Hungary in 1956. "Agonizing reappraisal" was a phrase Dulles used in mid-December 1953 to warn the French government that it must ratify the European Defense Community or face a reconsideration by Washington of U.S. commitments to Europe, implying possible withdrawal. In August 1954 the French parliament voted against the EDC. As State Department officers at the time commented, "we agonized; but that's all. We didn't reappraise, certainly not in the sense indicated." As a matter of fact, together with the British, we quickly moved to the rearmament of Germany within NATO. "Massive retaliation" was a threat, a military doctrine, and slogan, all in one. It was a threat to retaliate against open Communist aggression anywhere by use of nuclear weapons. It was military doctrine because of the Eisenhower administration's determination to cut the military budget and to do this by relying on strategic nuclear weapons while reducing the conventional military forces. As a threat, it may have frightened Dulles's countrymen more than the enemy. Certainly we who were working on foreign affairs lived with the devout hope that it was mere rhetoric, as it turned out to be.

"Containment" became a slogan, but it was much

more. It was real policy. It became real policy in 1946 and 1947, and was enunciated, in part, by President Truman in March 1947 in his message to Congress on the Aid to Greece and Turkey Bill, saying that the United States would "support free peoples resisting direct or indirect aggression seeking to impose on them totalitarian (i.e., Communist) regimes." The brilliant article by George Kennan entitled "The Sources of Soviet Conduct" in the July 1947 issue of *Foreign Affairs* set forth in authoritative terms the full meaning of the containment policy. Kennan wrote that, "the main element of any United States policy toward the Soviet Union must be that of a long-term, patient but firm and vigilant containment of Russian expansive tendencies," [6] and that the Soviet pressure against the free institutions of the Western world . . . can be contained only by the adroit and vigilant application of counterforce at a series of constantly shifting geographical and political points, corresponding to the shifts and maneuvers of Soviet policy.[7]

Containment was never merely a negative defensive policy, although Dulles and others often criticized it as such. Kennan's original article suggests that it might be "possible for the United States to influence by its actions the internal developments, both within Russia and throughout the international Communist movement . . . to promote tendencies which must eventually find their outlet in either the break-up or the gradual mellowing of Soviet power." [8] The point was to "contain," but thereby and otherwise seek to promote *evolutionary* change in the USSR so that the Soviets would become easier to live with, and perhaps even "partners" in some senses on the world political scene. The containment policy may have led under Dulles to excessive commitments in unreal alliances. Also it was certainly misapplied in Vietnam. But the policy itself cannot be faulted for these aberrations. Intrinsically sound, it has governed U.S. policy toward the Soviet Union in a consistent and meaningful way. Doubtlessly we were too hopeful twenty years ago about the timing and speed of evolutionary change in the Soviet Union. Kennan himself in 1947 wrote of what it might mean if we were able to *contain* Soviet power over a period of ten to fifteen years. Yet there have been perceptible changes in the Soviet Union. There are also mutually recognized growing areas of common interest, for example, arms control, trade, international scientific cooperation, educational and cultural exchanges, air travel, and others. More important, there have been great changes in the world political scene. The advent of communism to China was not clearly foreseen in 1947; the intense current conflict between Communist China and the Soviet Union was not foreseen in the 1950s. With all our great and laudable "containment" efforts, it is ironical to recognize now, as we must, that Communist China *contains* the Soviet Union much more effectively than we, by setting limits to the expansion of its power in Asia and elsewhere, and by contesting its leadership of the world Communist movement. The brutality—born of fear—of Soviet occupation of Czechoslovakia in August 1968 and the strenuous Soviet efforts to codify the *status quo* in Europe by contractual agreements have been results of Chinese containment pressure.

One other aspect of Kennan's original concept should be mentioned. The possibility of the United States influencing this evolutionary change is a question of the degree to which—in Kennan's language of 1947—"the United States can create among the peoples of the world generally the impression of a country which knows what it wants, which is coping successfully with the problems of its internal life and with the responsibilities of a

World Power, and which has a spiritual vitality capable of holding its own among the major ideological currents of the time." [9] How pathetic Kennan's language of 1947 sounds today! Our failure to live up to this requirement is one of the most worrisome aspects of our current situation in international affairs. It is strange that by misapplication of the containment policy in Vietnam, we have created a major factor gravely undermining the internal strength and unity essential to its fulfillment.

Language has doubtless never been static. However, we have become more conscious of its changes, presumably because of the accelerated rate of change due to the modern mass information media. If the newspapers and television spread a word repetitively, it becomes readily a part of the current language; if they tend to omit words, these will tend toward obsolescence. By constant repetition in the mass media, words or phrases may also lose their appeal; new phrases are sought because people weary of the old ones. Even if the situation connoted by a phrase remains constant, or when not constant, if the meaning of a phrase is still significant, there develops a tendency to reject not only the word but the reality to which it refers.

The phrase "cold war" was also a slogan, but it expressed a reality of political warfare, of conflict between the U.S. and the USSR, between the non-Communist free world and the Communist world. Moreover, it expressed the novel condition of "neither peace nor war," which the United States experienced after World War II for the first time—we were wont to return to peace after war. Somehow recognition of the cold war helped this nation gird itself for the struggle. Now people are tired of the cold war, tired of the unending hot war in Vietnam, tired of the prospects of other so-called limited wars, and concerned about the possibility of a nuclear confrontation. People are tired, in fact, of the word *war*, not to mention the reality war. Hence "cold war" as a slogan has fallen into desuetude, but primarily as a result of an emotion derived from word weariness. At the time of the Soviet occupation of Czechoslovakia, we were told that we must take appropriate action—we did nothing—but we must not return to the cold war. Why not? Suppose the Russians return to the cold war, or suppose they have never really abandoned the conflict, the political and ideological struggle which they euphemistically call "peaceful coexistence"—a term so readily misunderstood in the West. This brings us to a grave question. Do we create conflict or promote or sustain conflict when we recognize it as enduring conflict? Do we make it *endure* by regarding it as enduring? No more, in my opinion, than we are able to do away with conflict by wishing it did not exist and failing thus to recognize it. The conflict will endure for a long time, and we shall know when it ceases.

r eading the history of our involvement in Vietnam in preparation for a lecture led me to the melancholy conclusion that the only man at the top echelon of the United States government who was sound on Vietnam in the past twenty-five years was Franklin D. Roosevelt, who wanted to prevent the French return to Indochina and to have Indochina at the end of World War II put under United Nations trusteeship. Roosevelt was not only motivated by his antipathy for the French and his contempt for their colonial accomplishment—in fact, he told Secretary Hull on January 24,

1944, "The French have had the country (Indochina) for 100 years, and the people are worse off than they were at the beginning"[10]—but he also had a prescience of the anticolonial wave to sweep the world in the wake of World War II. Indochina was inconsequential to U.S. national security interest then as FDR understood, and the advent of the Chinese Communists subsequently did not necessarily change this.

There are so many facets to the folly of U.S. massive military involvement in Vietnam: ignorance of the area, failures of political judgment and insight, diverse military miscalculations in strategy and tactics, basic misconception of the nature of the struggle. American political and military leaders seem to have been caught in a web of abstraction spun by themselves. The folly of Vietnam has been the most complete triumph of "specious abstraction" in the history of our foreign affairs. The web of abstraction is clearly and neatly set forth in Townsend Hoopes's *The Limits of Intervention*, together with incisive character portrayals of the principal figures in the inner circle of Vietnam policy determination during the Kennedy-Johnson administrations from early 1961 to March 1968. The extraordinary persistence of the inner circle in its effort to fulfill its idea would have been so laudable were the idea not so specious. It is a token of the power of specious abstractions and of the captivity in which they may hold men, that it took a new man, a fresh mind not committed to the web, Clark Clifford, to see through the speciousness with the aid of concerned and thoughtful second-level officials, and to break the web.

Let us set down some of the strands in this web. The thought of the American policy makers during the 1950s was dominated by the idea of an expansionist Communist monolith which needed to be "contained."

This monolith included the Soviet Union at its head, Communist China, the Eastern European satellites, and the small Communist-controlled Asiatic countries, North Korea and North Vietnam. By 1960–61 it was quite clear that deep conflict had arisen between the Chinese Communists and the Soviets and that the national aspirations of the Eastern Europeans were driving them to seek as much independence from Soviet imperial control as they could achieve. The Sino-Soviet conflict did not fully surface publicly until several years later, but the United States government in 1960–61 possessed information demonstrating that the Communist monolith no longer existed. Chinese nationalism had asserted itself definitively against Russian control. Tito had done the same in 1948; so there was even a previous example to facilitate understanding. Yet the cataclysmic break-up of the Communist monolith was never properly taken into consideration in the formulation of our Vietnam policy.

Perhaps a consciousness of the disruption of the Communist monolith did filter through in the form of an assertion of Chinese expansionism as the force to be contained and in the repeated efforts to enlist Soviet support to bring an end to the Vietnamese conflict. We hardly recognized that the new rivalry of the Soviets and the Chinese forced the Soviets to compete with the Chinese in support of the North Vietnamese regime in its just "national liberation struggle." All our attitudes toward Communist China, our attitudes toward the North Vietnamese were conditioned and determined by the Korean War—Dean Rusk as assistant secretary of state for the Far East was one of the men who met with President Truman on the fateful Sunday afternoon in June 1950 when the decision was made for the United States to intervene militarily against the North Korean military aggression. Over ten years had passed, and the circumstances in Vietnam were very different.

There were probably few areas in the world about which American knowledge was less in 1950 and the early 1960s than Indochina. Our area knowledge of Indochina was slight to nonexistent. The Harvard China expert, Professor J. K. Fairbank, was reported by the press in the spring of 1970 to have commented that there was not even now one professor in the United States devoting his time exclusively to Vietnamese studies. Perhaps this is disputable, maybe one or two could be found. Certainly there was no institute for Vietnamese area studies in an American university until the fall of 1969 when the belated Center for Vietnamese Studies was opened at Southern Illinois University with the help of a $1,000,000 AID grant—and being belated, has labored under manifold difficulties, the greatest, of course, faculty and student hostility.

We stumbled into the Vietnam war, in part, through ignorance and unfamiliarity with the area. How silly to regard the North Vietnamese Communists as the spearhead of Chinese Communist expansionism—the North Vietnamese having resisted Chinese rule for a thousand years (111 B.C. to A.D. 965) and then over the next thousand years maintained a many-times threatened national autonomy over against the Chinese empire. Ho Chi Minh and the Vietnamese would as likely have served Chinese expansionism as Tito and the Yugoslavs have served Soviet expansionism. In 1968 in Zurich, I gave a lunch for Douglas Pike, the USIA expert on the Vietcong, which leading Swiss experts on Southeast Asia attended. Pike had to leave early for the airport accompanied by several guests. Two Swiss experts who remained at the table belabored me, the local American official representative, saying, "What is the matter with you Americans? You supported Tito during the war and after the split with Moscow, why didn't you realize that Ho Chi Minh, who had worked for the O.S.S. during the war, was as much a national Communist as Tito, and that a Communist Vietnam under him would probably have been a bar rather than an aid to Chinese expansionism?"

Moreover, China, the Great Middle Kingdom, does not need to expand. Our top political leaders for two decades have transposed expansionism, which is the key to Russian and Soviet history, onto China where it has not historically applied—and important as Communist ideology may be, it does not *ipso facto* override traditional attitudes based on geography, size, population, and more than two thousand years of history. As Professor Fairbank has written, "the best way to stimulate Chinese expansion is for us to mount an over-fearful and over-active preparation against it. History suggests that China has her own continental realm, a big one; that Chinese power is still inveterately land-based and bureaucratic, not maritime and commercial; and that we are likely to see emerging from China roughly the amount of expansion that we provoke." [11]

The domino theory failed to recognize the likelihood in view of past history that a Vietnam united under the Communists would be more apt to serve as an impediment than an aid to Chinese expansionism. Certainly after the Khrushchev ouster in 1964, it became clear that a central Soviet interest in the North Vietnamese regime lay in Hanoi's capability to impede the spread of Chinese hegemony in Southeast Asia. While U.S. intelligence estimators recognized this fact, U.S. policy never took cognizance of it. The domino theory likewise failed to recognize the individuality of the Southeast Asia countries; granted they were small and weak in power, they were not blank dominoes—a wonderful image for a specious abstraction. The domino theory may possibly turn out to be a self-fulfilling prophecy; if so, only because of our doing. There is no doubt that we have made North Vietnam a formidable military power; we elevated a low-level guerrilla civil war into a modern war, and our military pressure has brought modern arms, communications, and methods to the North Vietnamese.

If, because of the domino theory, Chinese Communist "expansionism" had to be contained, why should we have drawn the line in South Vietnam? In 1969 a retired Foreign Service officer China hand said, "We never should have gone into South Vietnam in 1954. Diem, his seeming strength, sucked us in. We should have taken the line at Thailand." Thailand, an independent country, had never fallen under colonial domination.

We first slipped into our role in Vietnam supporting the French in 1949–50, and by 1954 we were giving major military economic and equipment aid to the French; in fact we were footing nearly 80 percent of the bill. When the French sought direct military intervention to avert their impending collapse at Dien Bien Phu, a split JCS, British opposition, Congressional resistance, and Eisenhower's residual caution saved us from becoming the handmaiden of moribund French colonialism.

Unfortunately, and how unwisely, we chose soon thereafter, quite contrary to American tradition, to replace the French in Vietnam, supporting a regime which had no legitimacy for the Vietnamese people, but only for a social class produced by colonialism. The inspiration for this new policy apparently came from John Foster Dulles. There are some very revealing passages in the transcripts of interviews with Dulles's colleagues contained in the Oral History Project in the John Foster Dulles Library in Princeton. After the Geneva Conference, General Goodpaster relates: "On studying this affair

(Geneva), Mr. Dulles thought it was perhaps not quite down the drain. Everyone else, I think, felt that it was— he felt that there might be something in this that would be worth trying to salvage, trying to sustain." [12] Before General J. Lawton Collins made his trip to Vietnam in 1954 to assess the situation, he recalls that Mr. Dulles said to him, "Frankly, Collins, I think our chances of saving the situation there are not more than one in 10." [13] Six months later, Dulles was so pleased at the progress of Collins's mission, he said to him that "we had increased our chances down there to something like 50 to 50 rather than one to ten" [14]—the first of a series of miscalculations of an optimistic nature that American political and military leaders have made persistently during the past fifteen years. However, there is a more important lesson here: does one gamble the national interest, the interests of the American people on a one to ten chance? Can it ever be sound policy to involve the United States in a gamble of such odds? Perhaps it might be considered, if vital United States national security interests were involved. But they were not.

A former American ambassador in Saigon during the late fifties didn't agree with the foregoing. He believed that it was worth the effort to give economic, technical, and military aid to the South Vietnamese regime. The mistake, in his opinion, was to introduce United States armed forces to fight in Vietnam. When was the decision made? By Lyndon Johnson with the massive intervention of American combat forces in the spring and summer of 1965? It seems to me that the fundamental decision was taken earlier by President Kennedy in October 1961 when Kennedy decided to alter the bounds of a conventional MAAG effort and to permit the introduction of American military advisers in the field. As a consequence of this decision there was a quantum jump from the 600–800 MAAG complement to 16,000 American advisers, pilots, and supporting military personnel in 1963 and to 25,000 by 1964. One often reads from Kennedy admirers that Kennedy would never have gone along with the massive intervention of American military forces, that he would have extricated the United States, recognizing the damage that was being done to the nation. Against this view, however, stands Kennedy's decision in 1961 to put United States military forces in the field, and also the fact that his advisers were the same men who advised President Johnson. It was a tragedy that Lyndon Johnson, out of the ambivalence of his position as president by assassination and out of loyalty to Kennedy, kept the same political and military advisers. Perhaps these men gave him the advice responsive to his own nature, but he deserved better advice. A strong man with unsurpassed skill in Congressional affairs, he had great understanding of domestic affairs, but unfortunately a limited knowledge of foreign affairs. Caught in a tight web of specious abstraction in foreign policy—a web spun primarily by others, he was not the man, unassisted, to break the web. No President in this century, except perhaps Woodrow Wilson, has been so much like the heroic figure of a Greek tragedy. I am sure that future American historians—despite his memoirs—will be kinder to LBJ than his contemporaries.

A Far East historian told me in autumn 1965, "We are looking at Vietnam as if it were a military problem. It is really a political problem. There is no military solution to the problem." In John McAllister's book, *Vietnam: The Origins of Revolution,* the political problem emerges with clarity, namely, the problem of establishing a government with popular support in the countryside, in the villages as well as in the towns. We did not help the South Vietnamese accomplish this purpose by the intervention of modern military prowess. How win the people of the countryside by destroying their villages, killing civilians, by helicopter gunships and B-52s, by defoliation and other military gimmicks and gadgets? I recall officer friends saying with pride in 1965–66 that we were fielding the best equipped, best supplied, finest U.S. army in our history. The finest put to a mistaken purpose—a modern army is not designed to fight a guerrilla war in a strange foreign country. The miscalculations of our military, the unfulfilled promises of the "end in sight" are too numerous to contemplate without sadness. But one cannot expect from the military leadership a political wisdom greater than that of the political leadership. The military were given an impossible task. With bravery, imagination, and superior fire power, they made a valiant attempt; in no significant battles were they defeated. Yet we have learned that it is possible to lose a war while winning all the battles.

In February 1965 McGeorge Bundy made a trip to Saigon, and on his return prepared a memorandum for the President recommending the bombing of North Vietnam. Rostow and others had previously advised such a course. Perhaps there were other memoranda before the President recommending this course, but we had the impression that the President's approval was accorded by "signing off" on Bundy's memo. The basic argument appeared soon thereafter in the press and has been often repeated. By bombing North Vietnam on a gradually increasing scale, we would slowly increase the level of pain until the other side feels it is too much to bear and desists. Had the former Harvard dean forgotten his Greek mythology? The answer to this specious abstract thinking lies in the story of the little old Greek peasant who was able to carry a full-grown eight-hundred pound bull on his back up the 250 steps to the temple entrance and back down. How was he able to accomplish this? The Greek peasant carried the bull on his back up and down the 250 steps on the day the bull was born and once every day thereafter.

In March 1965 a counsellor of the Japanese Embassy in Washington, talking about the new U.S. policy of bombing North Vietnam, politely said that he saw no alternative. However, he did not "believe that it would be effective—we did not understand Asiatic psychology." The bombing of North Vietnam, as should have been expected, strengthened the Communist regime there, united the people with the regime, raised popular morale in the north for the struggle, lead to increased Soviet and Chinese deliveries, and rather than reducing infiltration from the north, brought about an increase and the strengthening of the NVN and VC forces in the south.

Townsend Hoopes writes with great personal admiration and sympathy for Robert McNamara, but his tale makes eminently clear the unique role that Clark Clifford played in President Johnson's decision in March 1968 to deny Westmoreland's request for some 200,000 more American troops, to deescalate American involvement in Vietnam, to cease bombing the populated areas of the north, and to withdraw from the presidential election. It also makes clear that if the President had not chosen previously to shuffle McNamara off to the World Bank, that if McNamara had been still Secretary of Defense in March 1968, the President's momentous decisions reversing irrevocably our course in Vietnam would not have been made, and that instead we would have continued the "more of the same" policy. Hoopes reveals in *The Limits of Intervention* how this would have resulted from McNamara's "managerial" efficiency. General Wheeler made the trip to Saigon in February 1968 which brought back Westmoreland's request. If McNarama had not been in his final month of office, he would have gone to Saigon, and his judgment rather than Westmoreland's alone would have determined the request. As Hoopes explains, at every critical juncture McNamara had flown to Vietnam to bargain with Westmoreland on manpower and discretionary authority, having reached his own conclusions before departing Washington and having prepared a draft report to the President for his return. In each case he prevailed upon the military to scale down their requests. "It was a technique which exemplified Mc-Namara's mastery of . . . managed decision-making: by holding control within very narrow channels, developing an advance position and moving fast, he *finessed serious debate on basic issues* [my italics] and thus saved the President from the unpleasant task of arbitrating major disputes within his official family." [15] With this matchless managerial efficiency our military manpower in Vietnam increased twenty-five-fold—from 21,000 to 510,000—in three years, but to no avail. With McNamara firmly in the saddle, "managing the problem," there would have been no request for 206,000 men, rather an agreement to send perhaps 50,000 troop reinforcements, and there would have been no fundamental reappraisal of policy.

Need the lesson be stated? We Americans are masters in managerial methodologies—are not the Europeans correct who so often say that there is no technological gap between the United States and Western Europe, but rather a managerial gap? However effective managerial methodologies may be in implementing sound fixed policy, they are no substitute for policy consideration, and they are dangerous if their pursuit tends to suppress consideration of the real policy issues. Managerial methodologies are, after all, high-class abstractions; they become *specious* when they obfuscate policy or inhibit unremitting policy review.

One more word from Hoopes on McNamara—and

this for the behaviorally minded political scientists with their quantification lust, to ponder. Hoopes describes him in the summer and fall of 1967 as a man in deep doubt forced "to accept the realization that, in the major decisions of the war, rigorous logic and quantification analysis had conspiciously failed." [16]

There is a reciprocal relation between *hubris* and specious abstraction. A set of accepted specious abstractions engenders self-assurance, and with self-assurance comes pride, prideful sure knowledge, prideful correct policy. Pride in itself fosters blindness, as do specious abstractions, and the two together mutually support and augment the blindness so characteristic of willful mistaken policy. The pride was nurtured by a sense of overweening power, still echoing in the childish phrases, "we cannot be defeated," "we cannot be humiliated." The Washington inner circle believed that the United States was so strong that it could accomplish anything; hence the stubborn misuse of military power after all else failed, hence the proud thought that we were "nation-building." South Vietnam was a fragmented society, ethnically, religiously, economically, socially with the city-land split; its government administration was inefficient, corrupt, weak. Can one build on quicksand, on weakness? Besides, it was just the weaker part of a divided country. Dean Rusk used to say *ad nauseam*, "if only the neighbor in the north would cease his aggression." Of course, there was "aggression" from the north, but it was also a civil war in the south, and in the one country, Vietnam, including both north and south. Can South Vietnam ever stand on its own? Certainly the United States, a foreign power, cannot create, establish, or maintain at tolerable cost a state unless there is a real potentiality for state-building. A State Department Vietnam expert in summer 1969 characterized the existing government as "firm jello." It might survive when we withdraw, he said, but the other side is "better organized and more dedicated." We cannot supply the dedication the South Vietnamese need to survive.

The United States has already lost the war in Vietnam. It does not matter whether a non-Communist South Vietnamese government survives after American departure or whether the Communists take over. Either way we have lost.

No war is won if the cost exceeds the potential gain. The cost of the Vietnam war to the United States in men, resources, internal disunity, and domestic neglect has long since surpassed any possible potential gain. A Pyrrhic victory is not a victory, but a euphemism for a type of defeat—old King Pyrrhus recognized this when he said, "Another such victory, and we shall be undone."

I agree with Townsend Hoopes who wrote in August 1969, "the American people have just about written off the Vietnam war." [17] The American people are busy in mind with more important domestic concerns; they are ahead of the Washington leadership. The Nixon Administration still seems enmeshed in the contradiction of seeking a U.S. "victory" simultaneously with withdrawal. It has moved much too slowly in withdrawal, seemingly reluctant to give the South Vietnamese the opportunity they need to stand on their own feet. It does not appear yet to have committed itself to complete withdrawal of U.S. military forces. I doubt that the American people will be satisfied with less. In the end, the Administration —perhaps it will have to be a new one—will catch up with the people.

Are there not lessons to be learned? How shall we avoid the fallacy of misplaced concreteness in foreign policy? How shall we recognize the specious abstractions? Of course, we should look to the spinners of the web, the men who formulate the policy, and learn to recognize with mistrust those "trenchant abstract intellects" so aptly described earlier by Professor Whitehead. More, though, we must seek guides which may help us avoid similar errors in the future. Let me suggest the following:

1. There must be a continuing consideration of national goals and policies at the same time as efforts are being made to realize the goals and implement the policies. Analogous to Whitehead's precept "to be vigilant in critically revising your *modes* of abstraction," we must be constantly watchful as circumstances change in the temporal flux for those circumstances which might oblige reconsideration and alteration of national goals and foreign policies. The Sino-Soviet conflict has probably been our most conspicious failure in this regard. In his belief that Kennedy would have extricated us, Hoopes cites the Khanh coup in 1964 as a likely occasion for such a decision; [18] it would have been.

Beware of fixations in general policy and exclusive concentration on ways and means, such as McNamara's managerial methodology. Be prepared to rethink the basic general policy—not necessarily every day—but periodically, and certainly whenever significant new measures in implementation are being considered. This is precisely what Clark Clifford did in March 1968.

2. Policy which deals with foreign areas and foreign peoples must be based on knowledge and understanding of the area. What a truism! But how often have abstract generalities determined American foreign policy toward an area, with little specific reference to the concrete realities of the area. On most areas, expert area knowledge is usually available to the U.S. government; often it is not consulted, or if it is, expert advice is readily ignored, and more readily overridden by some abstract

generality. On Indochina, our area knowledge was practically nonexistent. We have suffered grievously for policy based on ignorance.

3. Foreign policy must be continually related to domestic policy and the domestic scene. When foreign policy assumes a constant domestic scene, when it fails to take properly into account the effects of foreign policy on the domestic situation, it is generally doomed to failure.

Did our top political leaders consider before March 1968 the domestic implications of our Vietnam policy—the strain on our resources of manpower and material, the financial burden, the attendant inflation, the stubborn imbalance of payments, the student demonstrations, the draft-card burnings, the desertions to Canada and Sweden, the growing lack of popular support? If so, then with the same unrelenting miscalculation and bad judgment that characterized the whole effort. At any rate, we know that President Johnson's historic decision to reverse the course of American involvement in Vietnam was motivated considerably by a belated recognition of the domestic consequences, the internal disunity, and the neglect of essential domestic concerns.

4. National interdependence is a characteristic of the current period. It is reflected in the numerous regional arrangements to which the United States is a party—some, like NATO, real and essential to our national interest, others much less real and quite insignificant. In the immediate post–World War II period, U.S. leadership inevitably took on hegemonic forms. It is no longer possible nor desirable with our old allies nor with the newer ones to exert hegemonic leadership. If we have allies, we must learn to listen to them, to heed their views. In Vietnam we went it essentially alone. At no time did we receive either government or popular support from our

NATO allies, although the British government did its loyal best. The Far Eastern allies cheered our efforts, mostly with lip service and token contributions, except for the South Koreans. They saw our sacrifices in their interest, but did not regard their interest as sufficiently involved to bring them to share in the sacrifice. It was Clark Clifford's cognizance of the views of the Far Eastern allies which brought the first glimmering in him that led later to his rescue deed. He relates how in the late summer of 1967, with General Maxwell Taylor, he visited our Pacific allies to seek an increase in their troop commitments in South Vietnam. The pleas fell on deaf ears and it became apparent to him that the other countries did not share our concern. He returned home troubled. In his words, "Was it possible that our assessment of the danger to the stability of Southeast Asia and the Western Pacific was exaggerated? Was it possible that those nations which were neighbors of Vietnam had a clearer perception of the tides of world events in 1967 than we? Was it possible that we were continuing to be guided by judgments that might once have had validity but were now obsolete?" [19] He was not in the inner circle, committed and captive; so he was able to heed the views of others, our allies.

5. Prestige is always a major factor of consideration for the policy makers of a great power. It is an abstract psychological imponderable, and readily is subject to the fallacy of misplaced concreteness. Prestige has a significance, but not in itself, only when related to reality. Intellectually, we have been saying for over fifteen years that there are "limits to power"; in practice we Americans have finally learned it in Vietnam. Just as there are limits to power, there are limits to prestige. Policies motivated by concern about maintaining prestige are apt to be questionable. Nor is prestige to be maintained by per-

sistence in mistaken policy. Prestige is related to the criterion of success, success in domestic accomplishments, in social well-being, and success in foreign ventures. Infallibility is an exclusive prerogative; it is not expected of men in domestic or in foreign affairs, either by our countrymen or others. The tendency of power concerned with prestige to clothe itself with infallibility is just again the Emperor on horseback without clothes before the public view.

Recognition of mistakes in human affairs, early or late, is more beneficial than damaging to prestige, individual or national.

4
The Continuing Revolution
Science, Technology and Foreign Affairs

We are living in the age of a scientific and technological revolution, and my discussion will concern aspects and implications of this revolution. It is a truism that we are living in a revolutionary age, but there are varying perceptions as to the real nature of the revolution. There is the "permanent revolution" of communism against capitalism, and more recent phenomena with a revolutionary aspect, such as New Left anarchism, or the revolutionary aims of new nations liberated from colonialism. These are real phenomena, but they seem to be surface phenomena compared to the revolution which we will be considering. The scientific and technological revolution is the central factor changing the nature of human existence, and altering not only social and national life, but also the previously established premises for international relations.

Our discussion will seek to focus on the current impact of scientific and technological developments on foreign affairs. It will not attempt to be exhaustive—that would hardly be feasible. It will aim to sketch a broad panorama, pointing out basic issues and outlining some of the novel problems confronting mankind. It will deal with the accelerated rate of change due to science and technology, the catalytic role of World War II, the significance of the atom bomb, the global character of foreign affairs, the mismatch between rates of technological and social change, the role of scientists on the international scene, the problems of environmental pollution and population growth, transnational activities and resources such as outer space, the oceans and the seabed, weather forecasting and modification. Finally, we shall consider briefly the pressures toward rational solutions imposed by these new problems and the general direction of their possible resolution.

For most of his existence (about 250,000 years) man was one among many species on the earth. During most of this time he was a hunter-gatherer, and if you include hominids, his ancestors in the family of man, he was probably a hunter-gatherer for at least five million years. One first great revolution took place thirteen or fourteen thousand years ago, when man began to cultivate food crops, domesticate animals, and erect permanent settlements. It was the revolution of agriculture, and it radically changed his environment. Hence, it is not new for man to change his environment.

Around 4500 B.C. written language was developed. By 2000 B.C., a code of laws emerged in Egypt; use of metals started, mathematics and astronomy began. By 500 B.C. we had the great age of Greek thought. About five hundred years ago, with Copernicus, Kepler, Galileo, da Vinci, and Gutenberg, came the beginning of modern science. In the words of Professor Donald Hornig, former science adviser to the President, "Modern science as a systematic interpretation of nature in terms of a general theoretical framework was born through astronomy, and da Vinci began the systematic development of imaginative technological applications of science."[1] About two hundred fifty years ago with the invention of the steam engine came the Industrial Revolution and the subsequent transformation of the developed societies. With its problems and evils the Industrial Revolution which took place from 1820 to 1860 in Britain and later elsewhere was a process "highly mysterious to contemporary thought." [2] Men just did not know how to handle this process and the problems that arose. We do not appear to be in the same circumstance with respect to the current phase of the scientific and technological revolution; we have been tardy in recognizing the problems: environmental pollution, population explosion, etc., but at least we are beginning to recognize and face them.

With his new-found ability to understand the environment through science and to control it through technology, man has taken over the planet, its space and its resources, and is preparing himself to explore the interplanetary realm, if not yet the universe. He appears no longer just as *one* among many species on the earth— "a species that can break out of the biosphere of our planet Earth is different from the species bound by its limitations." [3]

It is difficult to define the present stage of the scientific and technological revolution. It has been called the "postindustrial revolution." Rather than attempt a definition, let me cite the major components. Our present postindustrial scientific and technological revolution can be subdivided into a "set of revolutions," [4] each one with profound influence and manifold problems: the military revolution, nuclear weapons, and ballistic missiles; the revolution in transportation and communications; the medical revolution with the attendant population explosion; the revolution in the use of natural resources and chemical substitutes; the high efficiency of agriculture fostering urbanization; the computer revolution with automation and control by computers, and accumulation, retrieval, and dissemination of information by computers.

One of the dominant characteristics of the contemporary revolution is the increasingly accelerated rate of change derived from the growth and present luxuriance of science and technology. There are certain oft-repeated statistics used as background illustrations for this point: ninety percent of all the scientists who ever lived are alive today; three-fourths of all scientific publications have appeared in the past twenty-five years since World War II; in the more advanced and industrialized nations, the number of people employed in scientific and technical work has been doubling every ten years. It is startling to realize how many of the basic elements of our present civilization have been discovered or developed fully in this century: the communications net, radio, television, long-distance telephone network, communications satellites; large-scale use of aluminum and plastics; fungicides and pesticides; sulfa drugs, penicillin, and other antibiotics; nuclear power, the jet airplane, and rockets. It is estimated that over half of the products manufactured by American industry now did not exist twenty years ago.

Behind this rapid advance is a basic change in methodology, perhaps related to the sheer proliferation of science and technology. Scientific and technologic advances are still occasionally the intellectual work of scattered individuals, but now they are primarily the product of directed team effort, of research institutes, research companies, or the research division of large corporations. They are not so much based on experience, trial and error, as on knowledge systematically acquired through formal education and purposively applied to a recognized task. Knowledge is producing both the structural elements and the dynamism of our new world— which has been called the "research society" [5] by James R. Killiam of M.I.T., the President's first science adviser; and called the "knowledge society" [6] by Peter F. Drucker.

The accelerating rate of change is reflected in the growth of technological innovation and speed of wide application of such innovation. Consider how the interval between discovery and application in physical science has been shortened during the past two centuries, as exemplified by the following table: [7]

Photography	—	112 Years	—	1727–1839
Electric Motor	—	65 Years	—	1821–1886
Telephone	—	56 Years	—	1820–1876
Radio	—	35 Years	—	1867–1902
Radar	—	15 Years	—	1925–1940
Atomic Bomb	—	6 Years	—	1939–1945
Transistor	—	3 Years	—	1948–1951

An example of the same process in the chemical industry is the following: "Only ten years ago it used to take from 5 to 7 years for a chemical product to advance from the laboratory to the production stage; the process has now been shortened to from one to three years." [8]

It is clear from the structure and expanse of science and technology that the rate of growth of science, of technological innovation, and of industrial application is apt to continue. In fact, as we shall see later, it will have to continue in order to meet the problems being caused by the present technological developments.

Science and technology have always played a role in warfare. Innovators—whether the innovation was in military equipment or in tactical techniques—had a decided advantage. The epic victory of the Swiss mountaineer foot-soldier over the Austrian cavalry at Morgarten in 1319 is a classic example of both innovative features: boulders which were suddenly rolled down steep hills on the Austrian force strung out on a narrow road along the side of Aegeri Lake and divided by the undulating hills, panicked the horses, throwing heavily armored riders in the lake or on the ground and the marching lines into confusion, so that the Swiss could charge down the hills with sword and dagger to slaughter the cavalrymen immobilized on the ground by their heavy armor and to rout the others. The boulders were a simple form of military equipment, nonfabricated to be sure, but excellent in effect when used with tactical insight. A more conventional example is the technological advantage in small arms enjoyed by the Prussian armies which facilitated their military victories during the 1860s and 1870, leading to the unification of Germany. It is probable that during much of prehistory as well, technological innovation was crucial for the spread and survival of peoples, and that man's large brain size (which makes possible modern scientific thought) was in the evolutionary process a product of natural selection, partly due to conditions of group conflict.

There are two great examples in World War II of the role of science and technology in warfare, radar and the atomic bomb. Radar won the Battle of England in 1940. Churchill paid a memorable and well-deserved tribute to the RAF pilots who saved England from the Nazi bombing onslaught—"never have so many owed so much to so few." But the unsung hero was the British chemist, Sir Henry Tizard, "the most valuable scientific mind that in England has ever applied itself to war." [9] It was his foresight in 1934 that led to the development and deployment of radar installations in England by 1940, making possible the RAF victory. This remarkable story is told in C. P. Snow's book, *Science and Government*. The war against Japan could have been won without the atom bomb; however, the surrender was, in fact, effected in 1945 by its use.

While innovations play a role in warfare to the advantage of the innovator, war pressures likewise play a role in the development of technology. One does not have to embrace the Hegelian concept of the general beneficial effect of war on a society to recognize the catalytic effect of war on science and technology. For example, as Dr. Franklin P. Huddle states in his study, *The Evolution of International Technology:* "The American Civil War had a profound effect on technology. For the first time, . . . 'the technological resources of a whole nation were ultimately mobilized to overwhelm an opponent. There was mass production of weapons and ammunition, of uniforms and boots; canned food was supplied to armies transported for the first time by rail.' " [10] World War II played a particularly significant role in scientific and technologic development. It is hardly likely that radar, with its manifold uses, would ever have been developed with the same speed and thoroughness, had it not been for the pressure on British scientists to prepare the air defense of a small, densely populated island, an ideal target for Nazi bombers. Certainly the magnetron, which C. P. Snow terms "probably the most valuable single device in the Hitler war," [11] and upon which all advances in radar after 1940 have depended, would not have been invented at the time, were it not for the intensive, directed British effort to improve their radar capability for air defense.

The story of the atom bomb is better known. Apprised of the theoretical possibility of constructing a nuclear fission bomb based on scientific discoveries in 1939, and fearful that the Nazis might succeed first in developing such a weapon, the British and Americans pooled their resources in scientific talent, and by a massive effort in this country achieved the production of fission bombs in five years. Why didn't the Nazis succeed? Partly, they had radically diminished German scientific strength by their racial policies,[12] and, partly, the remaining German scientists may not really have tried because of a subtle inner rejection of Nazism. Confident of blitzkrieg success, Hitler was not interested in projects requiring extensive support for some years. With the Fuehrer uninterested, nobody else cared. As Max von Laue, a German Nobel Prize winner told a foreign friend at the time: "No one ever invents anything he doesn't really want to invent." [13]

The computer is another instance of a war-induced technological advance. Computers were first developed for the complex calculations of artillery trajectories—mathematicians had served with distinction with artillery batteries in World War I, but they were in short supply in 1941. [14]

More significant even than its generative effect on particular scientific and technological discoveries, World War II had a catalytic effect on the organization of scientists and engineers for purposes of research and technologic invention. For the first time, scientists and technologists were mobilized for war. To be sure, some scientists had provided technical support in England to the armed forces in World War I; in the United States, the National Research Council was established as an arm of the National Academy of Science, and the National Academy offered its services to the President in 1916. However, the mobilization was very partial, as indicated by Rutherford's bitter complaint when the young British atomic physicist Moseley was killed in action in the Dardanelles. [15] In World War II, scientists and technologists were mobilized in a systematic and organized way, as befits a total war, to resolve military problems by scientific analysis, basic theoretic advance, and technologic innovation. The revolutionary changes in warfare came from the scientific, engineering and industrial community as a whole, rather than from the specific disciplines seemingly related to the military problems. As Dr. Hornig points out, radar "was to a considerable extent developed by nuclear physicists because prewar electrical engineering neglected electromagnetic theory which was critical to the development of microwave devices." [16] Also, in the development of the atomic bomb, physicists, chemists, and engineers performed tasks for which they had never been trained. Trained as a physical chemist, Hornig's assignment was to design the firing unit, a task of electrical engineering. Teams of scientists produced the major new weapons and provided the operational research which resolved complex military problems by collective scientific analysis. The point is that science per se, research-mindedness, scientific problem-solving talent were utilized on a large scale in organized ways directed at specific tasks across the whole broad range of military activities.

As a result of the World War II experience, science and technology themselves became recognized in the United States as national resources, worthy of government financial support. This recognition did not come at once. Had it not been for the foresight of some of the military, the rapid post–World War II demobilization might also have broken the bond between science and the military forged by the war. It was principally the Office of Naval Research which, realizing the need for a broad scientific and technical base for military defense in the new technical age, first invested in basic research of abstract theoretical nature in the universities as well as in technologically advanced industries.[17] In 1950 the National Science Foundation was established with the express purpose of government support of science; then also the Atomic Energy Commission, the National Institutes of Health, and the National Aeronautics and Space Administration, as well as, to a lesser extent, the old-line

Departments of Agriculture, Commerce, and Interior engaged in support of academic research.

The close collaboration of government, science, and industry which was developed during World War II was thus continued after the war, first through the foresight of some military scientists, and then as a result of cold-war pressures. In two decades from 1945 to 1965, federal government expenditures on science and technology increased from $40 million per year to $15 billion per year. Most of this has been expended on technology in industry, but $1.3 billion in 1965 went to universities proper, not including research institutes attached to universities. In the fiscal year 1968, the federal government expenditure peaked at $17 billion and has remained above $16 billion since then. The close collaboration in the United States of government, industry, and the university is envied by many other countries since it has contributed so much to our rapid technological advance and economic growth. However, this collaboration is now under attack, from those concerned perhaps legitimately about the power of the military-industrial complex, and from those academic circles concerned less legitimately about government control of, or intervention in, academic life.

The first atom bomb was exploded in 1945; the first thermonuclear bomb was ex ploded in 1951. These two explosions represented the most novel and unique "advance" achieved by science and technology. Moreover, they signified an essential change in the basic conditions of human existence and world politics. Through science and technology man has created the capability of destroying himself. Perhaps he cannot yet blow this planet earth to bits; perhaps he cannot even yet destroy all men. However, he can probably destroy human civilization as we know it—this civilization which is the product of millions of years of human evolution.

The megaton hydrogen bomb delivered to densely populated areas in sufficient numbers could kill tens of millions of people and devastate urban civilization. Very large areas of the adjacent countryside would be contaminated with lethal effects by the fallout. The 1970 Yearbook of the Stockholm International Peace Research Institute estimates the world's nuclear stockpile as amounting to 50,000 megatons, which "would represent about 15 tons of TNT per person on the globe, or—and this is more meaningful—about 60 tons per person in the NATO and Warsaw Pact nations taken together." As the survey points out, "Such an 'overkill' is so fantastic that whether the true figure is twice or half as high seems to matter little." [18] Moreover, there is a theoretical probability that if a sufficiently large number of fission and fusion bombs are exploded, the concomitant release of radioactive particles will so increase the radioactivity in the radiation background of the atmosphere that all human life will be killed. At least all human life in the nothern hemisphere might be killed, assuming that the bomb explosions would take place in the northern hemisphere, in which lie the great powers of the opposing blocs. It has been estimated that the atmospheric nuclear tests held before the partial test-ban treaty of 1963 released some 100 megatons of fission energy resulting in an average exposure of one-tenth to one-twentieth of a radiation unit to each individual in the northern hemisphere. If the 50,000 megatons of the world nuclear stockpile were expended in a nuclear war, each person would be exposed to 25–50 radiation units. The lethal radiation dose is 400 units for man. If the SALT negotiations, which seek to limit strategic nuclear systems at current levels, fail, then a continuation of the nuclear arms race could produce a tenfold increase in megatonnage in the next decades. "If that happens," Bernard T. Feld of MIT states, "man will be setting the stage for the ultimate catastrophe." [19] At least for the northern hemisphere—perhaps the broad doldrum belt at the equator would so restrict the passage of radioactive matter into the southern hemisphere's atmosphere that it would be spared the fate of the northern one.

Ever since the American monopoly on nuclear weapons was broken by the Soviets, a dominant purpose of American foreign policy has been to avoid strategic nuclear warfare. Since it has been regarded as unthinkable that this American democracy—though it cast the atom bomb on Japan—would ever initiate general nuclear warfare, the rationale of the maintenance of a strong nuclear arsenal has been based on our capability to survive an enemy nuclear first-strike so as to be able to deliver a devastating nuclear counterattack. Knowledge of this capability, it has been assumed, would deter any potential enemy. The Soviets, the only power with a comparable nuclear capability, have manifestly accepted the same dominant purpose, to avoid a nuclear holocaust. At the Twentieth Party Congress in 1956, Khrushchev made the fundamental ideological shift from the doctrine of the "inevitability of war" between the Soviet Union and the capitalist states, which had been formulated by Lenin and reiterated by Stalin. Khrushchev said then that "war is not a fatalistic inevitability." During the Cuba missile crisis of 1962 it was quite clear that both great powers were animated by a common desire to avoid nuclear warfare. The Chinese have disputed the Soviet ideological shift on the "inevitability of war" at a time when they do not yet possess the capability for real nuclear warfare. However, the Chinese are cautious in their actions. If and when they become a major nuclear power, they will doubtless no longer be preaching the inevitability of war to the death between communism and capitalism.

For twenty-five years men have been conscious of the "quick death" of a nuclear holocaust as a possible consequence of our triumphant advance in science and technology. Now in the past few years, suddenly a rapidly growing awareness has emerged of the possibility of a "slow death" by manmade ecological maladjustment as a result of our advances in science and technology. We shall return to the ecological problem later.

Thus far we have been looking at modern technology from the negative side. There is a positive side. Modern technology which has created the possibility of world destruction is also laying the foundation for a world civilization and creating the possibility of a world community of man.

The atom bomb has been, in a sense, a symbol for the great technological changes which were eating away the presuppositions of the traditional century-and-a-half-old isolationist policy and promoting the transformation of American foreign policy after World War II to an acceptance of responsible participation in world affairs in peacetime. Isolationism meant avoidance of responsible participation, a sensible policy for a weak new country in the world of that time. The United States was the great nonaligned power of the nineteenth century, and we should have remembered that when tempted to pass judgment on the nonalignment policy of the new weak nations in the twentieth century. It is because advancing technology had changed the presuppositions of our traditional foreign policy that this transformation was *responsive* to the real nature of the revolutionary age. The geographic isolation of North America was lost by transportation means—the airplane, fast ocean vessels; by communication means—telegraph, radio, and telephone. Now we have supersonic ballistic missiles which can hit any target on the earth, and simultaneous TV all over the world by communications satellite. The visit of man to the moon has indicated how small the planet earth has become. The "detached and distant situation" which Washington spoke about so movingly in his Farewell Address no longer applies to the United States, nor to any other country.

As a result of technological developments, foreign affairs have become global in nature. In previous centuries the continents were relatively separate. What happened in China several hundred years ago had little or no relation to events in Europe. There are no far-off, remote places in the world of modern transportation and communication. The continents are no longer separate in their historical development. Previously, foreign policy considerations were limited primarily to Europe—to the balance of power among European states. Even in the eighteenth and nineteenth centuries, as European influence and power spread to overseas continents, foreign policy was still the affair of the European powers. Now the overseas possessions have become free. New nations have arisen as independent actors on the world political scene, and they are all participating in one way or another, in the UN and its agencies, if not in the big power conflict. Foreign affairs are now taking place on a global scene, and foreign policy has to be formulated with global considerations.

Some observers regard nationalism as the most potent force in the twentieth century. It broke down empires after World War I and spread triumphantly throughout the world after World War II with the European loss of colonial possessions. The Communist monolith was short-lived as a result of Chinese nationalism and the nationalist aspirations of the East European states. De Gaullist nationalism has been a counterpart in the West. There is a rampaging nationalism about in the world, and yet at the same time as a result of technological forces about which we have been talking, there is proceeding necessarily a real decline of nation-state sovereignty. It is possible that there is an inner dialectic operating here, or perhaps more likely, just the overlap of contradictory historic forces.

The decline in nation-state sovereignty is seen most clearly in the economic and financial interdependence which has been institutionalized among the non-Communist countries in the wake of World War II. Economic interdependence has come through progressively liberalized trade, achieved by multilateral agreement on reciprocal tariff concessions under GATT. Fifty-three nations with eighty percent of all world trade participated in the so-called Kennedy Round, three years of intensive tariff negotiations, ending in June 1967. Financial interdependence was achieved through the Bretton Woods Agreement of 1945, whereby the United States and forty-three other countries created the International Monetary Fund (IMF) and the International Bank of Reconstruction and Development (IBRD) or World Bank. The aim was to introduce monetary order into a world of independent and interdependent nations. The International Monetary Fund has in the past twenty-five years served well the new "world economy" which emerged after World War II as a result of technological advance. It is the electronic media which have been creating common economic desires and demands and has made the whole world, in Marshall McLuhan's words, a "global village" or in Peter Drucker's words, a "global shopping center." [20] Through the institutional powers of the IMF, a relative financial stability has been sustaining a phenomenal world economic development and world trade growth. As of this writing (February 1972) it is not yet clear despite the agreement on new exchange rates what changes in the previous rules will ultimately result from the United States decision of August 15, 1971, to suspend gold payments, but the past success of the IMF as well as a general awareness of financial interdependence militates for the effective continuation of the IMF under different arrangements and with altered operational rules.

A second institution serving the world economy has grown up since World War II, the "multinational" corporation. In Peter Drucker's words, "the multinational corporation . . . is largely the result of a deliberate planning effort which sees the economy of the entire free world as one and then tries to find places where economic resources produce the greatest result and bring the highest return. The rationale is increasingly not the inability to export over tariff barriers, but the need to plan, organize, and manage on a scale appropriate to the magnitude of technical and managerial resources required for modern technology, economical operations, low cost production, and mass distribution." [21] A multinational corporation produces and operates in many different countries; it can transfer capital, personnel, and resources across national frontiers; the research and development laboratories are scattered throughout the world and usually are staffed on a multinational basis. Also the main office is staffed on a multinational basis; for instance, thirty-two nationalities are represented in the IBM World Trade Corporation in New York which is headed by a Frenchman, Jacques Maisonrouge. As a token of the power of the multinational corporation, it should be noted that American multinational companies have been credited with making the European Common Market a reality by recognizing the big market opportunity it offered and acting quickly to move into this potential market.[22] Peter Drucker has termed the management meeting of the multinational corporations "the only truly supernational occasion in the world today. Here men of different nationalities, each a member of his own culture and proud of it, come together in a common purpose. The purpose is an economic one and therefore very easy to define, to measure, and to control." [23] Perhaps this is an overstatement, perhaps there are other "supernational occasions," but this is an important insight nonetheless.

The world economy is coming into being despite political fragmentation. However, the decline of nation-state sovereignty is taking place in the political as well as the economic realm. It may be seen in the trend toward federal organization, such as the European Common Market and the tentative efforts along federal lines in the Middle East and Africa. It is also evident in the search for collective security through alliances such as NATO and the Warsaw Pact and through the existing international organization, the United Nations. Whatever its shortcomings, the United Nations in its many organs, specialized agencies, and multifarious activities attests to the decline of national sovereignty. This decline has not, however, brought us close to a coherent world order, much less world government. In a recent article entitled "The Reluctant Death of Sovereignty," the British historian Arnold Toynbee poses the question: "Will allegiance to the fatal ideal of national sovereignty be transferred to the ideal of world government in time to save mankind from self-destruction?" [24]

We are coming now to the crucial question. Science and technology continue to better conditions of men and nations and at the same time create new dangers, not only in warfare but in peace as well. Rapid changes brought on by technology are causing strains and stresses on the institutional structure of society. They are causing such strains within individual nations, and many problems they have created are transnational and cannot be handled by one country. Science and technology have outgrown the institutional framework of nations acting independently. Moreover, they have also outgrown the institutional framework of existing international institutions, which in general lack the competence and authority to deal with the problems.

The crucial question has been stated by Dr. Simon Ramo as follows: "We are already sensing the possibility that the greatest problem of this century may be the gross mismatch between the rate of technological change and our ability to match such change with appropriate social advance. We doubt our capacity to organize, select, and manage so as to be able to utilize science and technology to the utmost on behalf of society." [25] This applies obviously in the national sphere, despite long-established institutional structures and deep popular attitudes which foster cooperation and accept social welfare as a national goal. But it applies even more poignantly in the international sphere, where the institutional structures are new, weak, and uncertain, lacking jurisdictional competence, and where crosscurrents of national interests and ideological aspirations hinder cooperation and obscure the community of man.

Who shall save us? The scientists? Shall the scientists become our statesmen? That would not be easy to accomplish, nor is it clear that the attributes of mind which distinguish leading scientists are the same as those which characterize leading statesmen. If politics is an art, "the art of the possible" as Bismarck said, then we cannot expect scientists to possess qua scientists special proficiency in this art. Hence if we were able to turn over the affairs of state to scientists, it is not likely that our problems would thereby be solved. Nonetheless, it is most important that scientists represent an international community. Science is intrinsically international in character. Scientists work at common problems from the same fundamental premises, using the same methods of experiment, and seeking to discover the basic laws of nature. There are no distinct national styles in science. The reason for this is that theory must be checked by experiment.

The internationality of science is maintained by an established worldwide communication pattern. The scientific journal is the heart of this pattern. The chemistry department library of a large American university receives each month some two hundred and fifty journals from all over the world. Then there are journals which print significant findings from all the journals published anywhere; for example, *Chemical Abstracts,* which is read by most American chemists, abstracts over five thousand chemical journals. Also many scientists carry on an extensive personal correspondence with fellow scientists in other countries. Large international meetings organized by the great international scientific unions or smaller symposia on specialized topics bring together personally scientists from all over the world. It is no surprise to note that the great all-encompassing ICSU, the International Council of Scientific Unions, had its origin in this century. The International Association of Academies was founded in 1900, to be succeeded in 1919 by the International Research Council, which in turn was succeeded in July 1931, by the International Council of

Scientific Unions. ICSU at present has fifty-seven national members, and fourteen scientific members; these scientific members are international scientific unions, such as the International Union of Astronomy, Mathematics, Pure and Applied Physics, etc. These organizations sometimes organize international collaborative efforts, one of the most important of which was the International Geophysical Year of 1957–58, which was initiated by the ICSU and included on its planning committee representatives of the International Scientific Unions interested in that program. Also the ICSU has cooperated with the World Meteorological Organization in the World Weather Program. Similarly, in the field of oceanography, a special committee on oceanographic research of ICSU is cooperating with the International Oceanographic Commission of UNESCO.

Scientific and technological exchanges across the Iron Curtain are of particular importance. The USSR is the only country in the world with which the United States conducts cultural, educational, scientific, and technical exchanges by means of comprehensive, formal intergovernmental agreement. Exchange programs with the other Communist Eastern European countries are conducted without intergovernmental agreements. The first agreement, sometimes called the Lacy-Zarubin Agreement after its signers, was concluded in Washington on January 27, 1958, and covered the years 1958 and 1959. Subsequent agreements for a two-year period have been negotiated alternatively in Moscow and Washington. The last agreement was signed at Washington on February 10, 1970, for the period 1970–71.[26] The agreement provided for exchanges in the fields of science, technology, agriculture, public health, and medical science, education, performing arts, publications, exhibits, motion pictures, radio and television, culture and the professions, and athletics. At the same time, as part of the exchanges agreement for 1970–71, agreements were negotiated between the National Academy of Sciences of the United States and the Academy of Sciences of the USSR, as well as between the American Council of Learned Societies and the Academy of Sciences of the USSR, providing for the continuance of contacts between American and Soviet scientists and scholars. Similarly, a memorandum on cooperation in the peaceful uses of atomic energy between the United States Atomic Energy Commission and the State Committee of the USSR for the Utilization of Atomic Energy was also negotiated as part of this exchanges agreement. However limited the actual exchanges and however restricted they may be in practice, their importance cannot be overemphasized in keeping alive a line of communication across an ideological chasm and in bearing witness to mutually recognized common interests. It is the international language of science and technology, as well as of the arts, which makes possible this communications line.

If scientists, engineers, and technologists are members of a large international community of people with a common basis for mutual understanding and a common method of analyzing and resolving problems, then surely scientists and technical people should be brought into the policy level of government decision-making nowadays. This has already taken place in the United States government and in some Western European countries. Both Kosygin and Brezhnev are former engineers and a surprisingly large number of other members in the Soviet Politburo have technological training and experience.[27] This shows the technocratic aspect of Soviet leadership, although political policy may not yet have been affected on most key issues. Nevertheless, we must recall that scientists have undoubtedly played a significant role in

143

arms control agreements. For instance, although it is not always recognized as such, the Antarctic Treaty of 1959 was really the first arms control agreement. It provided that the Antarctic was not to be used for military purposes, and that there were to be no nuclear explosions nor disposal of radioactive waste material there. This treaty also insures the freedom of scientific investigation in the Antarctic area, the exchange of scientific information and personnel, and also—and this is particularly significant—mutual inspection of facilities. I do not believe that it is generally known that this epoch-making Antarctic treaty was a direct result of the international scientific cooperation in the Antarctic program of the International Geophysical Year of 1957–58.[28] However, it is well known that the concern of American and Soviet scientists as well as the scientists of other countries about the possible dangers of increasing the radioactivity level in the upper atmosphere by continuing nuclear weapons tests in the atmosphere undoubtedly played a significant role in leading to the readiness of the major parties to seek an arms control agreement in this field. Also scientists actively participated in the negotiations which eventually led to the signing of the partial nuclear test ban treaty of July 1963.

On January 25, 1967, Professor Hornig, then science adviser to the President, gave a memorable talk to the Panel on Science and Technology of the House Committee on Science and Astronautics indicating how the international scientific community can contribute positively to international relations. Fittingly entitled "Science and Technology as a Vehicle for Promoting World Comity," the talk closed with, "I have one final plea too. Since this world scientific and technical community has so much in common, I think it would be wise to bring it further into the discussion of the large group of international problems which are not in themselves technical, but which have large technical components, where the analytical cast of mind and insight into the nature of technical change might be put to use. This has already occurred in some parts of the world, but usually not to the extent that it has within the United States, where scientific and technical people are now present at the policy level in every major part of the government. It seems to me we can make progress on the world scene if the particular flavor brought by the scientists and the engineers are incorporated intimately into our discussions of disarmament, world economic development, world food, population control—in short, to the total development of mankind so that he can gradually free himself from the restraints of nature and realize the goals of his dreams." [29]

environmental pollution, as is well known, is not merely a national problem. Let me cite an example: Norway lies in a somewhat remote situation, across the North Sea from England and separated by water from the main body of the European continent. On January 11, 1970, the *New York Times* published a long article on the Norwegian concern about air and water pollution coming from abroad. The concern related to the rising acidity in rain and snow attributed to wastes from Britain and West Germany. The problem had been dramatized a year previously by the "black snow," actually a grayish snow with black spots, which fell on eastern Norway and western Sweden. The blackness was caused by combustion pollutants with high content of sulfuric acid, which came from air over the

Ruhr in West Germany. Trapped by inversion, this air moved first east, then came back north over Sweden and Norway. Such air patterns as well as the prevailing southwesterly winds from England have contributed to increased acidity in Norwegian precipitation with adverse effects on Norwegian soil and water. High acidity could reduce the growth of trees by as much as five percent a year. Although there are no local pollution sources in southwest Norway, the rivers there have shown increasing acidity, presumably derived from the prevailing southwesterly winds from England. The Norwegians regard pollution from abroad as a greater problem than local pollution. Norwegian scientists say: "our fresh water fish and our forests will be destroyed if these developments continue uncontrolled." [30]

Norway and Sweden have raised the international issue at the Council of Europe, but as a Norwegian said, "The international question is so difficult because it requires so many separate political decisions and it takes so long to get around to doing anything." [31]

In response to a query in a conversation in January 1965, Professor Hornig, then the President's science adviser, said to me: "If river water pollution continues unabated at the present rate throughout the world, in fifty years the oceans will all be polluted." Shall we have "dead oceans"—no fish, no plant life—like the "dead sea," Lake Erie?

My first personal encounter with the problems of environmental pollution control came in January 1965, when participating in the pilot course given by the Foreign Service Institute on the subject of "Science, Technology, and Foreign Affairs." During the course the class was broken up into small committees, each of which was assigned a current problem. My committee was assigned the problem of environmental pollution control. While the details of the problem are not relevant here, the solution put in the form of a recommendation for United States policy seemed realistic to us.

"We recommend that the United States put forward a resolution in the United Nations General Assembly along the following lines:

"1. All member states shall be encouraged to study the problems of environmental pollution on a local and national basis, and to exchange information with one another on this subject;

"2. All member states with common environmental problems as riparian or adjoining states should be urged to consult with one another on environmental pollution measures and to coordinate their actions in their common interest;

"3. A new UN commission, under the United Nations Economic and Social Council, will be established to serve as a clearing house for the exchange of information on environmental pollution and to carry out research on all problems of environmental pollution, including particularly those of a broad international and planetary nature;

"4. The new UN commission shall seek to advise member nations with respect to their own local and national pollution control measures;

"5. The new UN commission shall study regional pollution problems, hear complaints of any country alleging pollution originating in another country, and advise the countries of a regional area on common pollution control measures;

"6. The new UN commission shall seek to encourage regional and international agreements for environmental pollution control, as required;

"7. The new UN commission shall report on its activities and make recommendations, to the Economic and Social Council, and through the Council to the United Nations General Assembly."

Imbued by a sense of the urgency of the problem and regarding the proposal as practicable, on February 8, 1965, we sent identical memoranda to the Foreign Service officer on the staff of the President's science adviser, to the director of the Office of International Scientific and Technological Affairs in the State Department, and to the director of the appropriate office in the State Department's International Organization Bureau, proposing that the United States take an initiative along the lines of the foregoing proposal in the United Nations. The memorandum argued as follows:

"The problem of environmental pollution control is receiving increased attention in the United States and elsewhere, and properly so. As pointed out in the body of our paper, the problem is now a serious one and is likely to become even more serious in the ensuing decades. At present the problem is being worked at on a piecemeal basis, both here and abroad. It would be desirable to draw international attention to this problem and to establish some international mechanism for intensified study of the problem and for coordination of research as well as pollution control measures. Drawing international attention to the problem may even have a salutary effect in promoting United States national efforts in this field."

What happened? Nothing. The United States government did nothing. I don't know why. Perhaps it was Vietnam which had already become such an obsession at the top levels in government that it effectively precluded positive initiative on other subjects. However our proposal was in a committee paper prepared as a training exercise in an FSI course; we had no jurisdictional competence on this issue; the proposal was sent out as a message addressed hopefully to someone who did have jurisdictional competence. It is very difficult to accomplish anything in government unless one is in the line of command or operation. Otherwise, one can sometimes accomplish things through one's friends, if they happen to be in the proper line of command. Some months later, we learned from the Foreign Service officer on the President's science adviser's staff in the White House that the paper had been referred to the specialist on environment in the White House science and technology staff.

Several years later, the Swedish government took the initiative in the United Nations General Assembly, and the United States representative on December 3, 1968, made a strong statement joining Sweden and other nations in the resolution adopted that day, calling for an international conference in 1972 on the problems of the human environment. In the April 1970 issue of *Foreign Affairs,* George Kennan proposed the establishment of an international environmental agency in an article entitled "To Prevent a World Wasteland: A Proposal." A report in the *New York Times,* May 24, 1971 on a conference at Rensselaerville, New York, of international scientific leaders dealing with the UN Conference on the Human Environment, to be held in Stockholm, June 1972, contained the following: "The hope was repeatedly expressed that the Stockholm conference would set the stage for decisive action. The most likely action now seems to be creation of a commission within the Economic and Social Council to provide an over-all coordination of such activities as global monitoring of the environment and analysis of problems arising from the exploitation of natural resources and rapid urbanization." This is so reminiscent of our 1965 proposal that it is difficult to beat down the emotion of sadness at the slow pace of response, while environmental pollution continues unabated. Moreover, as of this writing (February

1972) there is doubt that any such commission or other effective institutional arrangement will be established at the Stockholm Conference. The secretary general of the conference believes that new international machinery could only be established after the functions to be performed at international level had been clearly defined and the capacity of existing agencies to perform these functions assessed. The United States and perhaps other developed countries are leaning toward the idea of a small staff attached to the office of the UN Secretary General to coordinate UN environmental activites among the UN specialized agencies.

In the last two or three years there has been a plethora of words about the problems of environmental pollution control, but not much substantial progress. There are some functioning regional and bilateral agreements on environmental pollution matters, primarily on water pollution. The United States and Canada have a bilateral arrangement going back to 1909 with respect to the U.S.-Canadian boundary waters, under which the International Joint Commission was established, one of whose functions was to see that the waters would not be polluted by either side so as to injure the inhabitants or property of the other. In recent years efforts have been made to reactivate the work of the International Joint Commission on pollution matters. The U.S.-Mexican International Boundary and Water Commission performs the same functions in respect to the boundary between the United States and Mexico. The International Commission for Protection of the River Rhine against Pollution was formed in 1950 by Switzerland, France, Luxembourg, the Federal Republic of Germany, and the Netherlands. A joint testing of water quality was undertaken. In 1965 these countries signed a formal treaty, giving a firm legal base to pollution control measures, and they undertook to study the origin of the pollution and to recommend to the signatory governments appropriate antipollution measures. An International Water Preservation Commission for Lake Constance was established in 1959 by Germany, Austria, and Switzerland. By 1968, about forty European and ten extra-European bilateral agreements had been drawn up dealing especially with water pollution. However, in most cases, no specific water standards have been set. As Abel Wolman wrote in 1968, these agreements have failed "to come to grips with the hard-core questions as to who was to institute corrective measures and who was to pay for them. . . . real international controls have not come into being." [32]

Is it surprising? Think of the difficulties on the international scale, with several governments involved, even friendly ones. Compare this with the national problems, where federal, state, and local jurisdictions may be involved in the same problems. The Potomac, the Hudson, the Delaware, the Mississippi, the Missouri and all our other great rivers flow through many states, and often through giant metropolitan areas. We have come to recognize the problems of water pollution, but we have not solved the problems of conflicting jurisdiction and pollution control organization.

Environmental pollution is no respector of ideologies or competitive socioeconomic systems. Communist Eastern Europe is now plagued with pollution problems. In the industrial districts of southern Poland, Czechoslovakia, and western Hungary, air pollution levels have been comparable to that in New Jersey. Rumania, with its speedy prideful industrialization, is now beset with air and water pollution. The Council for Mutual Economic Assistance, including representatives from Bulgaria, Czechoslovakia, East Germany, Hungary, Poland, Rumania, and the USSR has approved common criteria and standards of purity for surface waters, as well as principles of water classification. Nevertheless, many of the tributaries and certain parts of the main Danube River already show signs of heavy pollution. For several years, the World Health Organization has been working on a project to prevent pollution in the Danube Basin, on the grounds that it may be easier to prevent pollution than to clean up pollution after it has occurred, as in the case of the Rhine, on account of the international difficulties involved. The Soviet Union is not immune. Water pollution has afflicted the Angara River, with its vast electric power and manufacturing complex, and the sturgeon fisheries on the Volga River and the shores of the Caspian Sea. In recent years the Russians have been restricting local consumption of caviar in order to obtain the hard currency from the export of their dwindling production of caviar—indeed they have begun to experiment with the production of artificial caviar! Consider Lake Baikal, in Siberia, the largest, oldest, and deepest body of fresh water on earth—its pure waters contain a thousand species of plants and animals known nowhere else. Some six years ago, despite protests from scientists in the USSR and abroad, pulp mills began to discharge their sulfurous effluents into the lake. Recently, as a result of the continuing scientific protests, a report has indicated that the Soviets may be taking steps to clean the effluents or to divert them into a stream not running into Lake Baikal. This is just one example of many showing that the conflict between scientists and environmentalists on one side and industrial managers on the other cuts across diverse socioeconomic systems.

As mentioned earlier, we have had since 1958 agreements with the Soviet Union on exchanges in the scientific, technical, educational, cultural, and other fields. It is very significant that the agreement signed February

10, 1970, for the two-year period 1970–71 introduced a new category, "Man and His Environment," which provides for exchanges in oceanography, urban transportation, air and water pollution, management systems, social security, and agricultural economics. This shows that the Soviets recognize that they have the same problems we have and they they want to get the benefit of any solutions we may have achieved. It does not necessarily mean that they are yet ready for joint collaboration and real cooperation in this field. Nevertheless, it is a hopeful sign.

In theory there is one certain way to avoid pollution. An example is the Aegerisee, the only unpolluted lake in Switzerland. My wife and I lived on the shores of the Aegerisee in 1938–39, and when we returned to Switzerland in 1966, we marvelled at how undisturbed the beautiful woodland-meadow contours of the Aegerisee valley had remained. Once in conversation with Silvan Nussbaumer, the head of the Oberaegeri community and president of the Executive Council of the Zug Canton, we learned why the Aegerisee was the only unpolluted lake in Switzerland. Nussbaumer was known as *der Amerikaner;* he had been born in South Dakota, and his mother and brothers live in the United States; he was visiting Nussbaumer relatives in the Aegerisee valley in the summer of 1939 when the war broke out and was unable to return home; after some months he was mobilized into the Swiss army. He told us that he had refused every request of industry to establish a plant on the shores of Lake Aegeri; he wanted to keep undisturbed the nature and scenery and to develop the valley as a rest and recreation area. This is not a feasible general solution; we need industry, of course, to maintain our technological society. Yet it is rather touching to think that it was the insight of *der Amerikaner* which prevented the pollution of the lake and preserved the lovely scenery of this valley.

There is a major concern with respect to environmental pollution which must be stated. Before we achieve the capability of intervening deliberately to control environmental pollution, inadvertent total changes in the world environment may take place with major effects. For example, the increase of carbon dioxide in the atmosphere may induce global temperature changes; in the past one hundred years, with the massive burning of fossil fuels, atmospheric carbon dioxide has increased by about ten percent. Given the rapidly increasing rate of fuel consumption, it will probably increase by another fifteen percent by the year 2000. Will the resulting "greenhouse" effect cause a permanent warming of the earth's climate, melting the polar ice caps and bringing perhaps a rise in the world's sea level which will flood the great coastal cities—Leningrad as well as New York? No one is sure. Secondly, the contamination of the upper atmosphere by jet aircraft and rocket exhaust may be of practical significance. Clouds thus formed may reflect the sun's infrared rays, possibly bringing about a cooling effect. No one really knows. Thirdly, the use of pesticides and fertilizers to meet mounting needs for food is a potential danger—large concentrations are being found in some plants and animals.

Dr. Jerome Frank of Johns Hopkins has expressed his deep fear and concern as follows: "Humans may be in the same plight as a frog placed in a pan of cold water which is very slowly heated. If the rise in temperature is gradual enough he will be boiled without ever knowing what happened to him." [33] Well, unfortunately, man is different—he will probably know.

What we need, what mankind needs, is an "ecological early warning system." We require also international institutions having scientific and managerial skills, competence, and authority – with capabilities for overseeing broad areas of activity and the power to establish standards and regulations. This presupposes constructive relations between nations and international institutions. And this presupposes changes in the attitudes of men and nations – working together for common advantage must become more important than gaining transient competitive advantage.

Nations must also learn to cooperate to control world population growth. The population explosion is a result of the medical revolution mentioned earlier as one of the elements in the scientific revolution. It is not a result of sharply increased birth rates, but rather comes from the worldwide spread of modern sanitation, epidemic control, health measures, and modern medical practice. These have produced a sharp decrease in infant mortality and an increase in life expectancy. The decreasing death rate rather than the increased birth rate has produced the population explosion.

It took around 250,000 years for the earth's population to reach its first billion inhabitants, about A.D. 1830. During the Magdalenian period fourteen thousand to twelve thousand years ago, the world contained perhaps ten million persons. It took a hundred years to A.D. 1930 to add the second billion, and thirty years (between 1930 and 1960) to add the third billion. The fourth billion will be added by 1975. Assuming present trends of high fertility and declining mortality, the fifth billion will be achieved in nine years, the sixth in eight years, the seventh in five years, so that by the year 2000 the world's population would stand at around 7.5 billion.

In 1965, two out of three of the world's 3.3 billion inhabitants lived in less developed countries, i.e., lived at subsistence levels. By 1980 with the world's population over four billion, three out of four will be living in less developed countries. By the year 2000 with around seven billion, nearly four out of five will live in the less developed areas of Asia, Africa, and Latin America, with one out of five in the developed world, that is, in Europe, the USSR, North America, Japan, Australia, and so forth.

Why did the current population explosion happen so suddenly? In Western Europe by 1800, at the beginning of modern sanitation and scientific medicine, annual birth rates were about 35/1000 and annual death rates (varying with famines or epidemics) were about 28–30/1000. The population growth rate was about 0.5 percent per year. Death rates went down slowly for the next century or more as public sanitation spread and medical science grew. Birth rates also went down slowly as the industrial revolution developed, more and more families moved from rural areas to the cities, increasing numbers of women took jobs, lengthening education became desirable or compulsory, and parents decided to have fewer children. By the early or mid-twentieth century, the demographic transition had been made; annual birth rates had dropped to 15–18/1000, annual death rates had dropped to 10–12/1000 and population growth rates were again 0.5 percent per year, or a little more. It is important that during this one hundred or more years of the demographic transition in Europe, as birth rates followed death rates downward, the population growth rates never exceeded 1.5 percent per year and in most countries, most of the time did not exceed one percent.

In the less developed countries, the situation has been materially different. Until about the 1940s, birth rates were at traditional levels of 40 to 50/1000 and, in many countries death rates were still at 38/1000 or more. Beginning in the 1950s (two decades earlier for some Latin American countries), public sanitation and the sudden widespread availability of fully developed modern medicine plus massive United Nations programs to stamp out malaria brought about rapid, substantial reductions in death rates, particularly among infants and children, in nearly all developing countries. Birth rates remained unaffected, staying at levels higher than European levels had ever been. Population growth rates rose rapidly to 2.5 percent, 3.0 percent, 3.5 percent, or even more. The drop in death rates is still continuing in many countries, particularly in Africa, and population growth rates there can be expected to move from present levels of about 2.3 percent to levels comparable to the 3.0 percent average of Latin America. For these less developed countries, one-half of the demographic transition —the drop in death rates toward modern levels—is rapidly being accomplished. The other half—a comparable drop in birth rates to modern levels—is still to be accomplished.

Will there be food enough to feed these coming billions, even at subsistence levels, or will there be widespread famine and mass loss of life? No one knows. Much has been written about the "green revolution," the new strains of wheat and rice which under controlled conditions in certain parts of the developing world have produced fabulous yields. Whether these yield increases can be sustained and improved over a wider area is uncertain.

How shall the less developed countries break out of poverty? The rate of population growth in the developing world renders difficult, if not impossible, attainment of rapid increases in per capita income. Two-thirds of the world population live in countries where per capita income is less than $300 per annum and often less than $100 per annum. With a GNP growing at an annual rate of five percent in a stationary population, it takes twelve years to double per capita income. If population is rising at 2.4 percent (the projected average rate for the less developed world), it will take twenty-seven years to achieve a doubling in per capita income. Doubling at this rate is not likely to represent a satisfactory fulfillment of economic expectations. Despite all the economic and technical aid from the developed countries to the less developed, the economic gap between them has been widening rather than lessening and primarily because of the population growth.

What is being done with respect to birth control? The burden of assistance has been borne by private organizations like the International Planned Parenthood Federation, the Ford and Rockefeller foundations, the Population Council, or by bilateral programs, for example, those of the Swedish and the United States governments. In 1968 commitments of major agencies to population programs amounted to nearly eighty million dollars—not very much in view of the enormity of the problem. A world population conference was held under UN auspices in 1964. The UN Population Trust Fund was established by the Secretary General in 1967. Contributions to the fund from Sweden, the United States, Denmark, the United Kingdom, and others, amounted to only two million dollars in 1968—very little, showing some belief in a multilateral approach and disbelief that the UN system can handle the problem efficiently.

It must be borne in mind that the technology for birth control is available: contraceptives such as the intrauterine loop, the pill, and the sterilization of either man or woman. Decisive are the social attitudes with respect to the use of birth control measures, and the major problem is to spread knowledge of the need for birth control, and then to spread the information on birth control measures to families concerned, as well as to provide the means and facilities for birth control.

The population problem is enormous, but some progress has been made. A relative population stabilization has already taken place in some advanced countries —Sweden, Hungary, Bulgaria, Austria, Ireland, East Germany. Japan has been notably successful in a birth control program initiated in 1952; a birth rate of 34 per 1000 shortly after World War II dropped to less than 17 in the mid-1960s—special factors played a role in this success, however; 99.8 percent of the Japanese people have a basic education and the Japanese government is strong and effective. Indeed, Japan had been so success- ful that a growing labor shortage in its rapidly expanding technological economy led the Japanese Government in the summer of 1969 to advocate that Japan's birth rate which had fallen below the average of other advanced nations should be increased back up to that average level. Korea started government-supported family planning late in 1961. The population growth rate had been brought down from 3 percent to 2.5 percent by 1968; it is ex- pected that the growth rate will be brought down under 2 percent before the end of 1973. If so, Korea will be the first poor country to bring down the birth rate so rapidly —it is still poor, despite its economic success; the annual income per person has risen from $80 in 1962 only to $120 in 1968. At the end of 1961, the birth rate in Tai- wan was 3.8 percent. As of July 1967, with one of every five fertile mothers between the ages of 20 and 44 using the loop, it is estimated that the birth rate was brought down to 2.85 percent. Whereas the average rate of popu- lation increase was 3.4 percent from 1950 to 1967, the rate of population increase had declined to 2.3 percent at the end of 1967. In ten years from 1956 to 1966, the birth rate in Puerto Rico fell nearly 20 percent as a result of work of a family planning association. When the Of- fice of Economic Opportunity provided funds in July

1966, under a government-sponsored community action program, the birth rate declined another 9 percent in one year.

The foregoing indicates what can be accomplished by family planning, but there have been significant failures in national birth control efforts, not to mention the many areas where no serious effort has been undertaken. Planned parenthood was introduced into the United Arab Republic in the early 1950s; in the early 1960s the government openly adopted a planned parenthood policy. Nevertheless the Egyptian population increased 50 percent, from 20 million to 30 million, from 1950 to 1968; while the birthrate went down from 4.3 percent in 1950 to 3.9 percent in 1967, the death rate decreased slightly faster so that the growth rate during this period has hovered around 2.5 percent. India is one of the major problems of population growth. With a present population under 550 million, at the current growth rate of 2.5 percent India will have a population of a billion in about twenty years. India's official family planning program which was commenced in 1951 has been notably unsuccessful. The Indian government aimed during 1960–1970 to reach 50 percent of the population with birth control information; it is estimated, however, that only 4 percent were actually reached, and of these, half stopped the use of contraception by the end of the decade. In contrast to Japan and Korea with their high literacy rate, India is greatly impeded in its birth control measures by the high stand of illiteracy, 60 percent to 70 percent—it has been remarked that the government of India spends less on education than the women of the United States on lipstick. Nevertheless, the 1971 Indian census found a population of 547 million instead of the expected 561 million; since the difference of 14 million does correspond with the 12 to 15 million figure of births prevented which was calculated from the operations of the family planning program, the Indian program may finally be *beginning* to have some impact. However, according to a Population Reference Bureau report of December 1970, "Even if Indian parents were to alter their family patterns so drastically that by 1985 they were producing only enough children to replace themselves, such is the momentum of population growth that the ultimate population of India would still exceed a billion. That is the inevitable consequence of having a population of which nearly 45 percent is under 15 years of age with many fertile years ahead."

The population growth problem is so intractable because social attitudes, motivation, and personal choice play a crucial role. The average Indian couple wants at least two surviving sons; since daughters are approximately as numerous as sons, the large family tradition will keep India's birth rate high unless there is a basic change in motivation. Although the Japanese government undoubtedly promoted the postwar population control effort, many Japanese demographers regard the success as largely the result of spontaneous personal choice in the sense that the highly literate Japanese people in the near-starvation conditions of a war-ravaged economy decided to limit the number of their children. The factor of motivation shows itself clearly in Eastern Europe. In 1967, five of the nine countries in the world with the lowest birth rate were Eastern European: in ascending order, Hungary, Rumania, Bulgaria, East Germany, Czechoslovakia. Anyone familiar with the sorry psychic life of these people become captive of an alien system will recognize the element of personal choice in these low birth rates. The issue of government regulation or coercion over against free choice as the means of accomplishing population control has been basic in current discussion. It is interesting to note that the 1971 National Academy of Science committee report, "Rapid Population Growth: Consequences and Policy Implications," pleads against coercion and expresses the view that economic development, economic and health security will lead to voluntary birth control where information and techniques are available.

Even if population and family planning programs are prosecuted with all possible vigor, the Rockefeller Panel Report on World Population concludes that in the year 2000, instead of a world population of 7 to 7.5 billion, we will have a world population of 6 or possible 5.5 billion. This might make a crucial difference, even if the problems of overpopulation remain. Overpopulation is a threat to both national and international stability, bringing about pressures of crowding, acute need for resources, and failure to meet expectations. Likewise, population growth adds to the environmental pollution problems which we previously discussed – the demands made by expanding populations in developed and developing countries alike are increasing the threat to our environment. While food production continues to increase with the growing world population, there is a limit – the air, water, and soil supplies are relatively constant; renewable, but, for the most part, not expandable. In time, with population growth and pollution, we may simply reach the limit of fresh air and water, and of soil. Were the world population to reach only 5 to 6 billion at the century's end, then population experts estimate "hopefully" that it might reach zero population growth with 10 billion, thirty to fifty years later. A 10 billion world population, it is adjudged, would stretch the world's resources to the utmost.

It is pertinent here to reflect on the views of the Soviet scientist, Andrei Sakharov, which were privately circulated in the USSR, and reprinted in the *New York Times*, July 22, 1968:

It is apparently futile to insist that the more backward countries restrict their birth rates. What is needed most of all is economic and technical assistance to these countries. This assistance must be of such scale and generosity that it is absolutely impossible before the estrangement in the world and the egotistical, narrowminded approach to relations between nations and races is eliminated. It is impossible as long as the United States and the Soviet Union, the world's two great superpowers, look upon each other as rivals and opponents.

does competitive exploration of outer space really make sense? President Kennedy made a specific offer to the Soviets to undertake with us a joint effort at moon exploration. Perhaps the offer was somewhat rhetorical, and we did not persist in the proposal. However, the Soviets showed no interest, doubtless because the technology of space exploration, at least the rocket booster part, is so closely related to military missilry. At any rate, the race to place a man on the moon in the sixties was, for us, a costly venture. In the light of other national needs, we might in hindsight question the priority of this goal and the forced pace at which it was pursued. If world power prestige was the primary purpose, it is ironical to note that our landings on the moon in 1968–70 which initially excited the imagination of the world's peoples and thereby elicited admiration for our technical prowess, nevertheless came at a low point of American national prestige as a great power, resulting from our disastrous military adventure in Vietnam as well as the manifest internal disunity and the disintegration phenomena within our society.

The challenge of space exploration is, of course,

much deeper than the histrionic and hysterical national competition for moon landings and space probes. Outer space, the planetary system, and indeed the universe offer a new frontier for human exploration. Man's knowledge embodied in science and man's inventiveness embodied in technology have made possible exploration in this new frontier. It is the nature of modern man to explore, wherever he can, and so space exploration is responsive to the deepest urgings of the human spirit. While science and technology have made space exploration possible, the space exploration effort itself has been a major stimulant to scientific and technological development. Moreover, this scientific and technological development has not merely served space exploration, but its products have industrial ramifications and thereby practical uses. This is the phenomenon of "spin-off."

Some overall benefits are claimed. The space program, it is said, brought a "think big, think new" attitude both to government and industry alike. Stimulated too by the Soviet Sputnik success, it led to a thoroughgoing review of the nation's educational system, at first concerned with the need to produce more scientists and engineers, but quickly moving into the general quality of education, teaching techniques, etc. The nation's technology base and its skills were enhanced generally by the space program. "The country had never built a piece of equipment as complex as the Apollo spacecraft with its two million different parts that all had to function properly. Nor had it attempted anything comparable to sending a Surveyor spacecraft two hundred twenty-five thousand miles to the moon, slowing it down to land gently on the lunar surface, then having it respond to commands to take photographs and perform other scientific chores and relay the data back to earth." [34] Likewise new managerial skills were perfected. "The Apollo lunar-landing program was the largest single research program ever attempted by the United States. It required the melding together of input from thousands of companies and hundreds of thousands of persons, where requirements and skills were forced to criss-cross technical disciplines in unprecedented volume." [35]

There are varying views, some positve and some skeptical, as to the value of the nonspace applications of space technology. It is still too early to draw up a balance sheet, to relate costs to social and economic benefits, to evaluate the distortions in national research and development expenditures and in the use of scientific and engineering personnel which may have been imposed by the space program. Moreover, some years ago, the director of NASA's Technology Utilization Program stated that the benfits from industrial applications never will be the justification for the high costs. As for the manifold detailed forms of spin-off, perhaps we can regard as an unbiased source a United Nations study prepared for a conference in 1968 which contains the following on practical applications of space science and technology:

It is not at all surprising that space exploration has produced so much in the way of new knowledge. Think of what is involved in a reasonably complicated manned space mission. To see that it is accomplished successfully, scientists and engineers have had to devise life-support systems capable of operating in a very hostile environment for periods ranging from a few minutes to perhaps a year or longer. They have had to design and develop switches, valves, and filters which function with hitherto unattainable reliability. They have made new bio-engineering instrumentation, microminiaturized electronic parts, new alloys, new adhesives and new lubricants.

They have had to find new and ingenious ways of bending, shaping and joining materials and structures of every conceivable kind. They have had to devise pumps that will handle almost unbelievable amounts of the most volatile fuels that exist. They have had to develop exotic materials that could be forged into a heat shield capable of withstanding the five thousand degree F. temperatures encountered during re-entry into the earth's atmosphere at speeds of 25,000 miles an hour. They have had to take the fuel cell from the laboratory curiosity stage to a device already under serious consideration for lighting homes and powering automobiles. They have had to advance the state-of-the-art enormously in measuring, sensing and testing, and they have had to raise the reliability of systems, sub-systems and components to levels never previously dreamed of. . . .

Obviously, many of the advances made in the course of space research are important to industry generally. Remote control systems offer a typical example. Developed only a few decades ago to handle radioactive materials, they were developed still further for use in the hostile environment of space. The same kind of system is now being used on submarines and in plants where toxic or explosive materials are handled, and the concepts are already being studied for use in artificial limbs.

Temperature controls, basic to progress in space technology, are now being used to set operational limits in petroleum refining processes. Space research during the last ten years has almost doubled the temperature capabilities of advanced alloys and refractories. Payload limitations aboard space vehicles have resulted in the development of microminiaturized electronic devices of better reliability and longer life expectancy than their much heavier and bulkier predecessors, and these are already being used by industry. Thus integrated circuits are now beginning to be used in making better and smaller industrial, office and even home electronic devices.

The metal fabrication field is particularly interesting. The weight limitations imposed by the efficiency of today's rocket engines made it imperative to find substitutes for the heavy metals in almost every part of a space vehicle. New techniques have been developed, in the course of space research, for joining aluminium, titanium, beryllium and the refractory metals, through the use of such new tools, developed in the same way, as electron guns, plasma guns and lasers. These techniques are just as applicable to making better hardware as they are to making rockets.

There have in addition been specific transfers of space technology to other industries. An electromagnetic hammer that is capable of smoothing and shaping metal without weakening it, for example, is now being used in the shipbuilding and automotive industry. A ceramic-bonded dry lubricant, developed for use on a rotating seal of a pump for liquid-rocket propellants at high temperatures under vacuum, is now being used to coat bearings.

Reports on aerospace research have helped improve methods of growing crystals for industrial use. Space metallurgists found that a hexagonal crystal structure provided a better bearing material than any other, and the new alloys discovered in this research appear to be useful in a number of industrial and commercial devices. . . . A small remote sensor designed to report extremes of temperature aboard space vehicles is now available commercially for use in laboratories and industrial plants as a probe for obtaining accurate temperature measurements at inaccessible points.

A six-legged walking vehicle proposed for unmanned exploration of the moon has been redesigned as a walking chair for crippled children. The vehicle can cross rough terrain and surmount obstacles that would stop an ordinary wheelchair. And an unusually tough coating developed for spacecraft is the basis for a new paint.[36]

The UN report points out how difficult it is to assign money values to the benefits which might accrue from the use of communications, meteorology, navigation, or earth-resources satellites. However, it refers to an estimate by the World Meteorology Organization that "further improvements in weather forecasts made possible by the use of meteorological satellites may, by 1975, allow direction of the time of planting and harvesting on a worldwide basis with such reliability that about $15 thousand million dollars might be saved annually on harvests which are now being lost." [37] Such an accomplishment, however, would require a stand of directed national effort and international cooperation far beyond what exists today.

Let us consider now the stand of international cooperation in space activity. It should be noted, first, that space programs were initiated in the context of an international cooperative effort. It was at a 1954 meeting of the International Geophysical Year International Committee in Rome, that scientists proposed that artificial satellites be introduced as a contribution to the IGY program, providing thus the original stimulus for both the United States and Soviet space programs. Nevertheless, the space programs have never been carried out on an international cooperative basis as potentially possible.

To the credit of the United States, it has maintained a large diverse program of international cooperation in space exploration with all countries desiring to cooperate. Up to October 1969, NASA had launched twelve foreign satellites in cooperative projects where the foreign countries design, construct, and pay for the satellites. We launched at our expense. The countries involved have been Canada and the Western European countries. Moreover, many individual experiments by foreign scientists have been flown on our own United States satellites. One of the first experiments on the surface of the moon was a Swiss device to investigate the solar wind and its composition. By October 1969, lunar surface materials had been given not only to American scientists, but to thirty-six foreign scientists as well, whose proposals for analysis had been accepted. Nearly half of NASA's scientific sounding rocket launches are conducted in cooperation with other countries; almost two dozen countries are involved, including India, Brazil, Pakistan, Argentina. Some forty countries and many hundred of scientists, have been involved in cooperative ground-based observations carried out abroad in support of orbiting satellite projects. The European Space Research Organization, ESRO, including ten European countries, has likewise been a significant asset in international scientific cooperation. An extensive and unprecedented information exchange arrangement exists between the European Space Research Organization and NASA. The international use of American weather satellites has become routine; some fifty countries have installed the simple equipment which permit them to receive data from our satellites daily and directly. Similarly, there are international programs related to our own geodetic satellite projects, with thirty-seven countries cooperaitng. There is also extensive cooperation in tracking stations, close relationships with the ESRO and French tracking nets, and then, too, cooperation in tracking stations with many countries in Africa, Asia, and South America, with the costs of operating the stations borne in some cases by the host countries.

Competition has been overriding in the relations between the United States and the USSR with respect to space exploration. There has been no substantial but rather token cooperation with the Soviet Union in the areas of weather satellite data, satellite communications experiments, mapping of the geomagnetic field. In October 1969, Arnold Frutkin, assistant NASA administrator for international affairs, said: "We have throughout the years made many overtures, but we have unfortunately very little to show for them." [38] As he relates, Soviet officials have spoken of total disarmament or withdrawal from Vietnam as prior conditions, but the Soviets have not developed significant international cooperation with other countries not involved in Vietnam. Only in 1969 did they begin flying experiments for other countries, and these only Communist Eastern European countries. Soviet policy in this field demonstrates clearly the dominance of ideology and of political conflict over possible international cooperation. However, a change of Soviet attitude is possible, and we have been continuing our efforts to elicit Soviet cooperation.

An historic breakthrough in U.S.-Soviet cooperation in space exploration may have been achieved in October 1970.[39] For the first time four Soviet specialists participated in the work of the Space Rescue Committee of the International Academy of Astronautics, meeting in Constance, West Germany. During this conference arrangements were made for a formal meeting of American and Soviet space experts to consider the questions of space rescue operations. On October 29, 1970, NASA disclosed that an agreement had been signed in Moscow calling for a series of meetings by three committees of technical experts from both countries to draw up designs for mutually compatible rendezvous and docking systems for spacecraft.[40] Both the Americans and the Soviets are thinking in terms of large space stations or space laboratories in earth orbit. Compatible rendezvous and docking systems are not likely to be available until the late 1970s. Since October 1970, meetings of the technical experts have been held alternately in Moscow and Houston; recent newspaper reports as of this writing (February 1972) indicate that the United States and the Soviet Union are close to an agreement which could lead to a joint manned space flight. Meanwhile, the United States and the Soviet Union exchanged samples of lunar soil at a formal ceremony in Moscow on June 10, 1971; also an announcement was made on December 30, 1971 of an agreement for an exchange of information on the biological effects of space flight, with meetings of experts to be held for this purpose at least once a year. Another more superficial, yet not insignificant, sign is the fact that while an American astronaut was not permitted to attend the funeral of Col. V. M. Komarov after the crash of Soyuz 1 in April 1967, the American astronaut Col. T. P. Stafford, as President Nixon's representative, attended the funeral in July 1971 of the three astronauts of Soyuz 11. Pregnant words were spoken on August 23, 1971 at the National Press Club in Washington by Col. D. R. Scott, commander of Apollo 15, who said that he knew six Russian astronauts, would be glad to fly with them anywhere, and hoped to get the chance. He continued, "In this manner we can tie the countries together. Science has a common language. And among pilots, flight has a common language" (*New York Times*, August 24, 1971).

It may be taken for granted that on the Soviet side also it is the scientists who are pressing for cooperation. An indication of this is contained in a Pravda article by Boris N. Petrov, a Soviet space scientist: "Space exploration is becoming increasingly complex. Under these conditions, thought should be given to the development of collaboration among scientists and specialists of different countries. We already have effective examples of collaboration in this field. Under a program of collaboration among nine Socialist countries, four research satellites of the inter-cosmos series and the geophysical rocket Vertical I have been launched, and collaboration is continuing with France and some other countries. An agreement has been reached between the U.S.S.R. and the United States for collaboration in some aspects of space research." [41]

Aside from a desire for a space rescue capability, there is another factor which will impel Soviet-American cooperation in space exploration—the cost factor. Space exploration is becoming too costly for any single country. The USSR as well as the United States has pressing domestic problems. Just as the cost factor of an unlimited arms race may drive the Americans and Soviets to some successful accomplishment in the SALT talks, similarly the cost factor may lead ultimately to more comprehensive collaboration in space exploration. There is a precedent of some cooperation in high energy physics, another costly effort requiring big and expensive atom-smashing machines. In 1970, five high-energy American physicists undertook cooperative experiments at the Institute of High Energy Physics at Serpukhov, near Moscow, while two Soviet scientists participated in the 1970 summer study program of the National Accelerator Laboratory in Batavia, Illinois.

In a sense, the ocean and the seabed are comparable to outer space in relation to the present stage of human development; they are both frontiers for exploration and exploitation, the ocean being perhaps man's last frontier on earth. This comparability is attested by the achievement of disarmament treaties prohibiting the use of nuclear weapons in outer space or on the seabed, the Outer Space Treaty which went into effect on October 10, 1967, and the Treaty Banning Emplacement of Nuclear Weapons on the Seabed which was signed on February 11, 1971. In this connection, it is interesting to note the common language used in the preambles of the two treaties: "Recognizing the common interest of all mankind in the progress of the exploration and use of outer space for peaceful purposes," and "Recognizing the common interest of mankind in the progress of the exploration and use of the seabed and the ocean floor for peaceful purposes."

Through millennia man has used the seas and the

oceans in order to travel from land to land and to obtain food. The oceans cover around seventy percent of the earth's surface; the overwhelming majority of states have sea or ocean shorelines, but despite their diverse claims most of the waters of the oceans are international. The ocean is probably the ancestral home of all life; it is one of the most powerful natural forces on earth, particularly through exerting great influence on the weather cycles. Despite long familiarity with the oceans, man's knowledge of the ocean and the seabed is still very limited. The first scientific deep-sea surveys of the oceans and the ocean floor were undertaken around one hundred years ago. Recent rapid technological progress, such as underwater photography and television, the echo-sounder, the scanning sonar, etc., have provided us with a knowledge of the ocean floor contour, indicated its geological structure, and revealed vast mineral resources on and under the ocean floor. As Arvid Pardo says, "Thus man has probably been able to acquire more knowledge about the deep seas and the ocean floor in the past fifteen years than in the preceding two thousand years." [42]

For thousands of years, mankind has been taking fish and other seafoods from the oceans. Occasionally one reads optimistic reports that utilization of the oceans could provide a solution to the food problems of the world's expanding population. Such optimism is not supported by the technical experts in the field. The great majority of marine plants are microscopic in size. As to the use of such plankton plants as food, it is said that "the outlook is poor and there is little hope that any use will be made of them for human food. Many are inedible, some poisonous and all immensely expensive to collect. Harvesting animal plankton is almost equally unlikely." [43] Since most marine plants are small and free-floating, they are not likely to serve as a primary food source; the large seaweeds are a very small percentage of the sea plant life, and their growth is restricted to shallow water which is unpolluted, a condition increasingly difficult to find. The situation with respect to sea fauna is already precarious. Whale and seal stocks are not likely to survive unless vigorous conservation measures are taken. The blue whale, especially, is in a critical situation; in 1930–31, eighty thousand blue whales were caught, in 1963–64, only 372. The International Whaling Commission was unable to impose sufficiently stringent regulations against the interests of the countries concerned. Overexploitation sharply reduced seal populations years ago, although the situation of the Pribilov fur seal has been restored through the agreement between the United States, Canada, the USSR, and Japan. However, under the most favorable circumstances the great sea mammals can only be an insignificant source of food for the growing world population. Fish are a more significant resource, but the situation with respect to fish is likewise becoming alarming. Fishing methods have become too "efficient," with the result that there is much wasteful overfishing, stimulated by a need to justify costs in the short term. Ocean salmon fishing in the Atlantic illustrates the problem, intensive fishing which brings in immature and inedible fish can threaten the survival of the species and destroy a potentially rich food source. Ocean fishing is expanding with great rapidity, even in several of the smaller developing countries. An expert has stated: "Ocean fishing power on a world-wide basis is growing at a much more rapid rate than the means of measuring its effect on the fish stock it is being applied against. . . . The nations devote their ocean research funds to the development of fisheries, but they are laggardly in providing research funds for the detailed biological and population dynamics research which alone can give guidance in the solution of the problems which expanding fishing effort creates." [44] Thus lack of knowledge is hindering the development of agreements which in themselves for other reasons would be extremely difficult to bring into force. Fishing agreements have been made among the major fishing powers, but they have been limited and partial, with uncertain success. One problem, of course, is that the high-seas fisheries are a common property resource; not being owned by any party, no one is responsible for their proper management. Hence each nation is readily moved to seek to obtain a maximum share for itself.

The aquaculture concept of enclosing large areas of the sea for the purpose of breeding and protection of marine animals is not regarded as feasible at this time. Experts believe that an effort to separate off parts of the sea would result in deficient oxygen levels; besides, the most valuable fish require large areas of open oceans and large amounts of food and oxygen. Aquatic farms, as at present, can be maintained at the edge of the sea, but this area nowadays tends to be more heavily polluted.

Food from the sea amounts at present to one percent of the food for the world's population. Even if the amount of food taken from the sea were to be quadrupled, it would only meet four percent of today's food needs. Hence food from the sea is not likely to solve the world's food problems.

As Rachel Carson pointed out over ten years ago, "the ocean is the earth's greatest storehouse of minerals." [45] Estimated offshore reserves of petroleum, natural gas, and sulphur are enormous. In 1965 natural gas reserves under the United States Continental Shelf were estimated at 150 trillion cubic feet. In 1966 world offshore petroleum reserves were estimated at 2.5 trillion barrels, not including the rich petroleum deposits under the Arctic Continental Shelf of the Soviet Union and the major oil fields off northern Alaska. Beyond the geophysical continental shelf, the sediments of the ocean are believed to contain enormous quantities of valuable minerals and other substances. Manganese nodules, a hard mineral resource, commonly found on the surface of the ocean floor at depths between 4,500 and 19,000 feet, are currently being given particular attention, inasmuch as technological planning for collection of these nodules on a commercial basis is proceeding rapidly. These nodules vary in chemical composition, but they are known to contain manganese, iron, copper, nickel, cobalt, and other minerals. Tonnage estimates for Pacific Ocean nodules range from 9 to 170 trillion tons. Although the nodules grow slowly, there are believed to be so many nodules that their growth is estimated to be outstripping the world's consumption of manganese and other substances.

Can the great mineral resources of the ocean be exploited without catastrophic pollution, without upsetting the ecologic balance in the oceans? We are all familiar with the problems of oil pollution as a result of oil spills, such as the Torrey Canyon disaster, as well as the accidents in offshore petroleum mining despite our highly developed petroleum technology, which have caused serious contamination off the California coast at Santa Barbara and in the Gulf of Mexico. There are, of course, similar threats of pollution from the exploitation of mineral resources. For instance, mining which has been taking place in the shallow waters around Indonesia has already had a considerable deleterious influence on the coral fauna and on fish populations chiefly because of the large amount of sediment turned up in this activity. The main method of nodule harvesting is expected to be from a moving submerged platform operating like a giant vacuum cleaner; these may seriously upset the seabed environment. Shall the technologically advanced countries rush into competitive national exploitation of the ocean floor minerals, with inadequate knowledge and unconcern of the ecological hazards?

There is an alternative. We are indebted to Arvid Pardo, permanent representative of Malta to the United Nations, for this alternative, long known as the "Maltese proposition" for the internationalization of the seabed, and it may well turn out that this will be an exemplary case of the influence one man of foresight from a small country may have on the affairs of mankind. At the United General Assembly in the fall of 1967, Ambassador Arvid Pardo proposed adoption of a resolution with the following concepts:

1) "The seabed and the ocean floor are a common heritage of mankind and should be used and exploited for peaceful purposes and for the exclusive benefits of mankind as a whole." [46] The needs of poor countries should be considered in the distribution of financial benefits deriving from the exploitation of the seabed for commercial purposes.

2) Present claims to sovereignty over the seabed should be frozen until further study.

3) The UN should establish a committee to study the problems of an international regime over the deep seas and ocean floor, to draft a treaty to safeguard the international character of the seabeds, and to provide for the establishment of an international agency to insure that national activities in the deep seas and on the ocean floor will conform to the provisions in the proposed treaty.

Many countries supported this resolution and eventually, on January 14, 1969, the United Nations General Assembly set up the Committee on the Peaceful Uses of the Seabed and the Ocean Floor beyond the limits of national jurisdiction, composed of forty-three states. In the same resolution the General Assembly welcomed the

United States' proposal for an international decade of ocean exploration, and called for intensified activities in the scientific field.

On May 23, 1970, President Nixon issued a statement, little noted by the press, enunciating United States policy for the seabed. This statement seems so important that I should like to quote the following portions:

"The nations of the world are now facing decisions of momentous importance to man's use of the oceans for decades ahead. At issue is whether the oceans will be used rationally and equitably and for the benefit of mankind or whether they will become an arena of unrestrained exploitation and conflicting jurisdictional claims in which even the most advantaged states will be losers.

"The issue arises now—and with urgency—because nations have grown increasingly conscious of the wealth to be exploited from the seabeds and throughout the waters above and because they are also becoming apprehensive about ecological hazards of unregulated use of the oceans and seabeds. The stark fact is that the law of the sea is inadequate to meet the needs of modern technology and the concerns of the international community. If it is not modernized multilaterally, unilateral action and international conflict are inevitable." [47]

The President's statement then endorsed the general concepts of Malta's proposal, unfortunately without referring specifically to it, and called upon the United Nations to adopt a treaty renouncing all national claims over the seabed resources beyond a depth of 200 meters, agreeing to regard these resources as the common heritage of mankind, and establishing an international regime for the exploitation of seabed resources beyond this limit.

Pursuant to the President's statement, on August 3, 1970, the United States representative on the United

Nations Seabeds Committee submitted to that committee a draft "United Nations Convention on the International Seabed Area." [48] Some of the provisions of the convention draft are as follows: The international seabed area, beginning at the 200 meter isobath is a common heritage of all mankind. No state may acquire rights in this area or in its resources, except as provided in the convention. The seabed is open to use by all states and is reserved exclusively for peaceful purposes. It guarantees that revenues will be devoted to international community purposes, particularly to the economic advancement of developing countries. It assures accomodation of the different uses of the marine environment—this is important since there may be a conflict between different uses, for example, extraction of oil or metals and harvesting of fish in the same area at the same time. A large number of regulatory provisions are included to protect the marine environment from pollution. Uniform rules are stipulated concerning exploration and exploitation of all international seabed resources. It provides for a coastal state trusteeship in the area beyond the 200 meter boundary embracing the continental margins, with the precise seaward limit still to be determined. The rights and responsibilities of the trustee state are set forth. A new international organization is to be established called the International Seabed Resource Authority, having comprehensive rule-making authority beyond the 200 meter boundary, functional responsibilities including inspection of all licensed activities in the same area, licensing responsibilities beyond the trusteeship area, adjudication of all disputes arising under the draft convention, with special procedures for approving the delimitation of all boundaries required by the draft convention. The principal organs and certain procedures of the International Seabed Resource Authority are likewise set forth.

This extensive draft convention was presented to

the committee just as a basis for discussion. The subject is extremely complicated. It will be years, if ever, before a final convention will be concluded. However, it is a positive approach to a very significant issue.

On December 17, 1970, the United Nations General Assembly adopted resolutions containing a declaration of principles governing the seabed, reserving the seabed exclusively for peaceful purposes and the use of its resources in the interests of mankind, and, convening in 1973, a Conference on the Law of the Sea.[49] This conference would deal with the foregoing United States' and other proposals for the establishment of an international regime for the seabed, and a broad range of related issues including those concerning the high seas, the continental shelf, the territorial sea, fishing and conservation of the living resources of the high seas, the preservation of the marine environment (including prevention of pollution), and scientific research. However, it will certainly not be clear and easy sailing. There is already a serious warning signal. The Soviet Union and its allies did not support these resolutions. Moreover, after a quietly held four-day conference in Riga during April 1971, the Soviet bloc established an International Coordinating Center of Marine Exploration in the Soviet Union.[50] This center will be open to members of the Council of Mutual Economic Assistance or COMECON, the economic alliance of the Soviet and Eastern European Communist countries. According to an interview with the head of the Soviet delegation, published in the Latvian newspaper – but not in the major Soviet national newspapers, which is itself enlightening [51] – joint expeditions of the COMECON members are being planned to the Atlantic and Indian oceans to select prospective sites for mineral exploitation. Exploration efforts would be directed toward finding oil and gas fields as well as deposits of gold, tin, nickel, and other metals which are limited in supply on the Soviet Union's land mass. Thus the Soviet bloc seems to be trying to move rapidly and unilaterally before an international authority on the exploitation of seabed resources can be established.

While the Soviet attitude may well impede and render more difficult establishment of an International Seabed Resource Authority, it is unlikely to be able to thwart the measure, particularly in view of the strong interest of the developing countries in obtaining economic assistance through a share in the revenues from exploitation of the seabed resources. The majority of the UN members are developing countries. The UN resolutions of December 17, 1970, cited previously were adopted by affirmative votes ranging from 104 to 111, with abstentions ranging from 6 to 16, and 7 negative votes being cast by the Soviet Union and its allies only against the convening of the Conference on the Law of the Sea in 1973. Even if the marriage of traditional Russian expansionism with the Communist universalist ideology has produced the most aggressive nationalism in the world today, the Soviets are not insensitive to the demands and attitudes of a majority of the world's nations nor to the imperatives of ecological considerations. The concerted Soviet COMECON effort may perhaps be designed to prepare the technological basis for a manifold participation of the European Communist countries in seabed resource exploitation under an international authority, if its establishment becomes unavoidable.

Senator Claiborne Pell, chairman of the Ocean Space Subcommittee of the Senate Committee on Foreign Relations, has been one of the foremost American proponents of internationalization of the seabed. In the fall of 1967 he introduced in the Senate the first proposals designed to encourage international cooperation to this end; he participated from 1967 to 1970 as an adviser to the United States delegation to the Seabed Committee.

In a statement made on November 26, 1970, in Committee I (Political and Security) of the UN General Assembly, Senator Pell expressed views so germane to our general topic that they are worth quoting at length:

"Like him [Ambassador Pardo], I had for some time been concerned that the advancing pace of technology, both military and industrial, would soon signal a new era of conflict on the ocean floor. . . . We do not want to see a 'flag nations' rush toward new colonial empires. Rather, we wish to see the ocean resources and usufruct available to all the world's peoples. . . .

"The moment is, however, a fleeting one. The technology is within our reach now. And now is the time that we must decide whether those who possess it will work out their own means of accommodation or whether we will plan ahead for the equitable sharing of benefits from what is truly the common heritage, and perhaps the most valuable heritage, of mankind. In truth, this is the world's new frontier — and its last frontier where we have a choice of developing it sensibly and peacefully for the benefit of mankind.

"Mr. Chairman, in stressing the importance of diplomacy keeping abreast of science and technology, I think this committee's overwhelming commendation of the draft seabed arms control treaty is well worth recalling. That commendation evidenced a strong conviction to prevent the extension of the nuclear arms race to a new vast area. The wisdom of that decision cannot be contested. We must strive for a similar diplomatic ability to insure the best use of advances in undersea technology, which is now making the theoretical wealth of the seabed an actuality. . . .

"The General Assembly can delay progress on international solutions. But it cannot delay technology; it cannot delay the problems; and it cannot delay the pressures for unilateral solutions to these problems and the conflicts that will inevitably result if unilateral actions are taken. In brief, in every year that passes, unilateral actions will reduce our options and prejudge our decisions until the opportunity will be lost to provide for the common benefit of all. A few technologically advanced states will be wealthier. . . .

"It is important to act with urgency to establish internationally agreed rules which will assure the harmonious use of the seas and the seabed—for commerce and transportation, for the production of food, and in the development of other resources—to insure that man's marine activities are regulated to prevent pollution.

We have seen about us the effects of greed, of indifference to the future, of disregard for the waste of resources, and the indignities to nature which may be irretrievable. Surely it is not necessary to repeat the mistakes of the past.

"The future compels greater unity as our global interests increasingly outweigh our individual differences. It is often hard in this forum to imagine a time of such unity; but imagine it we must, because there is no real alternative. This is one of the times when we have within our grasp the means of dealing with a problem which has no national history, and which knows no national boundaries, and to resolve it in the kind of global framework that we must construct for the future." [52]

The oceans, which earlier served as barriers, have for several millennia increasingly become bridges for the movement of man from continent to continent, and for the intermingling of human affairs. As mentioned earlier, the oceans are a major force in the creation of weather through their great influence on the weather cycles. But in this century man, through science, may also become a force in the creation of weather.

More than fifteen years ago the famous mathematician, John Von Neumann, said that man's ability to intervene deliberately in processes of weather and climate "will merge each nation's affairs with those of every other, more thoroughly than the threat of a nuclear war or any other war may already have done." [53] The nuclear physicist Edward Teller is known for his assiduous concern about United States national security interests. Hence it is of particular significance to note his comments on weather modification at hearings before a House committee in 1963. Teller said that if weather modification is feasible, violent disagreements will arise on the question of how weather should be influenced. This will necessarily create issues between the capitalists and the Communists. "The situation where the Russians can influence weather and we can't is one which I would rather see not arise." [54] He then points out that foresight may prevent insoluble situations from arising. "To try to agree on the atom now is not quite easy. To try to agree on the weather may be easier. The fullest exploration of meteorology requires, in any case, international cooperation. . . . If we establish collaboration now, then at the time we get to the threshhold of practical application, we will have a group of people talking to each other, we will have an organization with responsible lines of information and command, so that you can have more easily put before you the problems and the alternatives. We should start friendly collaboration on this shrinking globe before we are faced with an insoluble situation. In the end, I believe that it will be necessary to agree on all these things, including weather, with the Russians and again whatever we can do on a joint effort, I would welcome." [55]

There are three aspects to the weather problem: (1) knowledge of the basic principles of atmospheric processes; (2) forecasting of weather; and (3) modification of weather, perhaps leading eventually to control of major weather conditions. The knowledge of our atmospheric environment has grown slowly during the past 2500 years. The rational-minded Greeks raised the study of the atmosphere out of the context of mythology and began the scientific interpretation of systematic observations; Aristotle, around 350 B.C., summarized all then-existing knowledge in his *Meteorologica,* which remained the authoritative work for nearly two thousand years. The invention of the thermometer, the barometer, and the hygrometer during the sixteenth and seventeenth centuries brought a second major advance. Many great scientists dealt with atmospheric problems: Galileo, Pascal, Descartes, Newton, Franklin, LaGrange, LaPlace, et al. A third major advance took place in 1820 when Brandes prepared the first weather map; this led to the preparation of weather forecasts based on systematic observations of the successive states of the atmosphere. During the past twenty-five years, from weather observations data and from studies on the basic physics of atmospheric processes, a reasonably coherent picture has emerged of the basic scientific problems in meteorology. Mathematical simulation models of the atmosphere using computers have enabled rapid progress in the understanding of the physics of the atmosphere.

During this decade the science of weather prediction is expected to achieve the capability of accurate ten- to fourteen-day weather forecasts. As a result thousands of lives and billions of dollars in property may be saved which are annually lost in unexpected weather disasters, floods, blizzards, hurricanes, tornadoes, etc. The more accurate forecasts will be accomplished by the world weather program which was initiated in 1967 by the

World Meteorological Organization. The first step beyond local studies of the atmosphere was taken in 1853 at a meeting of maritime nations which initiated a program of weather observation over the ocean for safety purposes at sea. The International Meteorological Organization was founded in 1878 by the directors of the national weather services with the aim of systematic observation of weather. This cooperative effort developed well over the next seventy years, providing weather services for navigation and agriculture, and exchanging weather information along air routes and at airfields. After World War II the organization was reconstituted as the World Meteorological Organization (WMO), which in 1951 became a specialized agency of the United Nations. At present more than 130 countries are members collaborating in a worldwide exchange of meteorological information, with the methods of weather observation, coding, and transmission being determined by WMO regulations.

For weather predictions in excess of a few days, the earth's atmosphere must be treated as a single dynamic system. It must be borne in mind that specific air masses may travel around the globe several times in two weeks. The atmosphere is a global phenomenon, and weather changes in particular regions are determined by global circumstances. For a two-week weather forecast, data over the entire globe, from high in the atmosphere to the ocean's surface, are needed. Yet as late as 1970, it has been estimated that only twenty percent of the world is covered by adequate weather and marine observations. The World Weather Watch, initiated at the 1967 WMO meeting, aims to fill the gaps. It "includes the design, development, and implementation of an international system for the regular observation of the atmosphere over the entire globe and for the rapid and efficient communication, processing, and analysis of worldwide weather data." [56] It is expected that the full Watch will not come into being until the late '70s. Recent studies have indicated that an additional 270 stations for ground-level observations are required and that the observation program at around 1,400 established stations is incomplete. In the past, very few weather measurements have been taken in uninhabited areas and over the three quarters of the earth covered by oceans. To fill these gaps, more than a hundred ships will be equipped with surface and upper air instruments and about forty new land stations and seven new weather ships around the Antarctic are planned. Ground-level observations are to be supplemented with weather satellite information, special aircraft reconnaissance flights, meteorological rockets, constant altitude balloons, and data from automatic weather stations. The World Weather Watch is likewise establishing a worldwide telecommunications system for transmitting and collecting weather observations. To facilitate the collection and exchange of meteorological data, world meteorological centers are being established at Washington, Moscow, and Melbourne, Australia, and regional meteorological centers elsewhere, equipped with computers of sufficient speed and capacity to process the global meteorological data in the manner required.

Also in 1967 the World Meteorological Organization and the International Council of Scientific Unions met and agreed upon the Global Atmospheric Research Program (GARP), whose aim is "to develop an understanding of the global atmospheric circulation in sufficient depth to permit the mathematical/physical prediction of weather two or more weeks in advance, to provide the basis for physical explanation of world climate, and to make possible the scientific exploration of the possibilities and limitations of large-scale climate modification." [57] GARP is proceeding along vigorously, with three kinds of data-gathering experiments being planned: first, a series of studies of the planetary boundary (the atmospheric layer immediately above the surface up to a few thousand feet); secondly, an experiment planned for around 1973 in the tropics where our current knowledge is slight; thirdly, a global meteorological experiment extending for a year to provide research scientists with a complete set of global data—this experiment is planned for the mid-1970s.

Eugene Skolnikoff has pointed out that these two related programs, the WWW and the GARP, may create requirements for new or revised international machinery to operate the program as they develop. The implications of the knowledge required through these programs may also establish a requirement for controlling the application of this knowledge in accord with internationally agreed purposes. "At least, the development of the knowledge in an international environment creates the opportunity to prepare international means to monitor its application." [58]

Efforts at human weather modification are not new. Rainmaking has been an occult "science" probably for many millennia, and some primitive tribes today still believe in their witch doctors' abilities. For twenty years, early in this century, a Charles Hatfield of Kansas conducted a business of rainmaking primarily in the dry midwestern areas of North America. Hatfield was so lucky that on most occasions rain did occur; once at Medicine Hat, Canada, six days after he set up his equipment, the rainfall totaled over an inch and farmers began to ask Hatfield to turn it off. Since 1946 serious efforts at local weather modification have been made by cloud-seeding, either with dry ice or silver iodide. There is experimental evidence that rainfall can be increased locally by cloud-seeding from five to twenty percent. T. F. Malone anticipates that by 1980 "naturally occurring rainfall can be either augmented or diminished locally by proven techniques," and that by the end of that decade "the probability is high that rainfall several hundred miles downwind from the site of the operations can be increased or decreased at will." [59] It is easy to foresee the problems which may arise between nearby countries as a result of this capability, for example, claims that water has been deprived one nation by the action of another, or that excessive rainfall is a result of such action. Experiments in cloud-seeding with silver iodide in order to reduce hail damage have been undertaken with spectacular success reported from the Soviet Union and with mixed results from other countries, including the United States. An experimental effort ten years ago to suppress lightning by the introduction of silver iodide into the thunderclouds did not result in any significant reduction in the occurrence of the lightning. However, silver iodide was used successfully in August 1969, in reducing the maximum velocity of a hurricane by thirty-one and fifteen percent on alternate days. In view of the extensive damage that hurricanes cause, it might seem desirable to modify them if possible, but grave questions arise. Caribbean hurricanes are a major source of water for parts of the United States and the Caribbean region. If their courses were diverted or their power reduced, certain areas might be deprived of an important source of water. Tampering with hurricanes will not be useful until we understand the full consequences of any modification so that the interests of the countries and regions concerned can be properly taken into consideration.

There has been considerable speculative discussion among meteorologists of possible large-scale climate modification. For instance, it has been suggested that the

Arctic ice cover or the Greenland ice cap could be melted by spreading a layer of carbon black all over it; the purpose would be to make the climate of the northern hemisphere milder and to provide increased moisture for the vast Siberian and North American regions. However, the effect of melting the Arctic ice cover is disputed, varying from forecasts of an entirely beneficial effect with a more temperate climate and increased rainfall in Siberia, Northern Canada, Europe, and as far south as the Sahara, to predictions of a new ice age, and the flooding of major coastal cities as a result of the ocean level increase caused by the melting of the Greenland ice cap. To warm the northern hemisphere climate, Russian scientists have also proposed pumping water out of the Arctic Ocean at the Bering Strait, thus accelerating the flow of warmer Atlantic water into the Arctic basin, with the flow direction to be controlled by means of a dam across the Bering Strait.[60] There is, of course, still much uncertainty as to the likely effect of such an undertaking, but there is little doubt that such a project is becoming technologically feasible.

We are probably entering a period where our understanding of weather processes would make possible eventually rational decisions on large-scale weather modification. Thomas Malone has pointed out three recent scientific and technological developments of major importance in this direction: first, "understanding of the physical processes occurring in the atmosphere has now progressed to the point at which they can be expressed in the equations that constitute mathematical models . . . ; second, the advent of high-speed electronic computers has hastened the possibility of integrating the nonlinear, partial, differential equations governing atmospheric motions by numerical methods"; third, capabilities are expanding "of making the observations and measurements specifying the initial and final atmospheric conditions that must be reconciled by the computerized atmospheric models if they are to be meaningful." [61] These three advances make possible not only the development of quantitative techniques for weather forecasting, but also will permit an examination through simulation techniques of possible deliberate interventions in atmospheric processes, enabling an assessment of consequences and limitations.

Who shall guide and control the use of the capability of weather modification? Insofar as minor local modifications are concerned, which affect the weather only within the territory of one nation and with no adverse effect on weather conditions in the territory of any other nation, then presumably the state would control the use of weather modification technology over its own territory. The situation with respect to large-scale weather modifications is obviously different. In a lecture before the Fifth Congress of the World Meteorological Organization in 1967, E. K. Federov, chief of the USSR Hydrometeorological Service, stated: "It is not difficult to understand that the problem of transforming the climate on a world or regional scale is by its very nature, an international one, requiring the united efforts and the coordination of the activities of all countries. Ever more rapidly humanity is approaching the stage in its symbiosis with nature, when it can turn to practical account all the natural resources of the earth and when, as a result, it will become capable of thinking in terms of natural phenomena on a planetary scale. . . . It is hardly necessary to prove that, in these circumstances, all mankind should regard itself as a single whole in relation to the surrounding world. There is no other way." [62]

The voice and language of a Russian scientist on meteorological affairs is the same as that of an American scientist or a European scientist. In a talk in Zürich in 1967, the German physicist, C. F. von Weizsaecker, said that in ten years perhaps we will sufficiently comprehend the principal factors in the creation of major weather conditions so that in twenty years we should be able technically to produce the major weather conditions. He added, if we can do this, then we must have in thirty years a sufficiently strong world organization to prevent the misfortune which would otherwise be produced by this technical capability.[63]

When the capability for weather modification is eventually achieved, minor climatic modifications affecting weather conditions only over the territory of one nation will properly be under the control of the state concerned; however, even in such cases, there will have to be some accepted international means for consideration and adjudication of claims of adverse effects by other countries. Who will guide and control modification on a regional or international scale? In its 1971 report, "The Atmospheric Sciences and Man's Needs: Priorities for the Future," the National Research Council's Committee on Atmospheric Sciences recommended that the United States government introduce in the UN General Assembly a resolution "dedicating all weather-modification efforts to peaceful purposes and establishing, preferably within the framework of international nongovernmental scientific organizations, an advisory mechanism for consideration of weather-modification problems of potential international concern before they reach critical levels." [64] This is a laudable forward-looking proposal. Doubtless it is realistic in the given situation of intergovernmental relations. Is it not in essence, however, timid? To whom shall this advisory body offer its advice, to nations or to international bodies? The World Meteorological Organization assisted by the International

Council of Scientific Unions has demonstrated a high level of international cooperation in the exchange of weather information, in weather forecasting, and in research. When the time comes, will the countries of the world be ready to accord to the WMO and ICSU, or some new World Weather Control Agency, the jurisdictional competence and the authority to regulate and operate weather modification in the interest of all countries and all peoples? It is difficult now to imagine such a time, but is there any other way?

Can the problems created by science and technology be solved through science and technology? None of them can be solved by an attempted escapism, a return to a nontechnological world.

It may be necessary, however, to consider the control or suppression of some particularly potentially dangerous technology. Eugene Skolnikoff discusses this subject in the last chapter of his book entitled *Science, Technology, and American Foreign Policy*. He points out that the limited test ban treaty has the effect of retarding technological developments by slowing research and development in weapons. The non-proliferation treaty has a similar effect. Skolnikoff raises the need to consider the internationalization of science support as a means of improving the prospects for control of dangerous technology. International sponsorship will help reduce the fear of scientific technological surprise. We are unfortunately very far from an international understanding of this type. In this connection, we may recall the Soviet rejection in 1955 of President Eisenhower's proposals to insure against surprise attack. The Soviets probably never appreciated the deep sincerity and pathos of this American proposal, grounded as it was in the poignant memory of Pearl Harbor. The Soviets rejected the proposal out of hand as an effort to "spy" on them. There is no sign as yet that the Soviet secrecy attitude, which led to this unfortunate rejection, has changed. Nevertheless we have to consider and be prepared to put forward ideas such as international control of dangerous technology in the hope that their attitude may change.

Let us return to the question: Can the problems created by science and technology be solved through science and technology? Most of these problems can be, but not by science and technology alone. Usually economic factors, social attitudes, and public policies are also involved. Most problems of air and water pollution are soluble by science and technology. Are we ready to pay the cost of finding the solutions, and more important, of imposing these solutions on industries and individuals? Although public policy statements about environmental pollution are abundant, the actual expenditures and actions have been minuscule in comparison with other national policies. As mentioned earlier, the techniques controlling the population explosion are available, but changes in social attitudes and customs throughout the world are required before they will be used effectively.

In a speech in 1969 Lee DuBridge, then the President's science adviser, said that he was often asked: "if we can land on the moon, why can't we clean up our cities?" Developing the technology of landing on the moon was relatively easy, he said. The laws of nature have been well known for a long time; engineering skills to manufacture the spacecraft were available. The problems of our cities and the other social problems are not all that easy, he said. We have learned to discover and use laws of inanimate nature, but we do not understand the laws governing human nature.

Science and technology are the products of human reason. The revolutionary age in which we live is the result of the application of scientific and technological achievement, however unfortunate some of the results may appear to us. We should not be surprised, indeed we should expect, that grounded as it is in human reason, the scientific and technological revolution is imposing strong and manifold pressures toward rational solutions of foreign affairs problems in the interest of mankind. To be sure, these pressures may not in the end be strong enough, and there are obviously counterforces of great strength that may lead to disaster.

The form of these pressures may be recapitulated as follows: the scientific revolution has created a global situation uniting all mankind; it has likewise posed a threat to human survival, which cannot be mastered unless rationality prevails; the host of problems created by technological advance, environmental pollution, population, weather modification, resource exhaustion, exploitation of ocean resources, etc., require rational solutions both on the national and international levels. Despite all the signs of internal American disunity and disintegration, I have faith in the strength and quality of our institutional structures, their resilience and adaptability. Hence I am optimistic with respect to the American national capability to solve these new problems created by scientific and technological developments, insofar as these problems can be solved on the national level. However, it is manifest that they cannot really fully be solved on the national level; they require either international or perhaps supranational solutions. And I am much less optimistic about the international capability of resolving the many new problems of our revolutionary age.

There is one hope though that mankind may achieve collective security through recognizing the threat to human existence; if he achieves collective security, he will be able thereby to move toward a solution of the other problems. Let me discuss collective security through external threat in the light of Swiss experience.

On the Rütli meadow overlooking Lake Lucerne, the mountain communities of Uri, Schwytz, and Unterwalden met in August 1291 to swear an oath of mutual assistance, to protect each other against any enemy in the interest of security and peace. This act of collective security set down in a treaty founded the Swiss confederation. The original confederation expanded partly by conquest, but more importantly by the voluntary association of adjacent cities and communities. This growth brought together peoples of diverse ethnic extraction, language, and religious confession. The pact of 1291 was expressly intended to last, "God willing, forever." Animated by the need for collective security to maintain independence, the Swiss confederation has endured for seven hundred years, only once losing its independence for a brief period when overrun by Napoleon's armies at a time of internal division and weakness.

What has held Switzerland together for seven hundred years? There are important factors such as the mountain topography, lack of mineral resources, the wild mountaineer spirit coupled with military skill. The overriding factor, however, has been the unremitting external threat. The first enemy was Austria, then the Duchy of Milan, later the Dukes of Savoy and of Burgundy, and France. The European revolutions and wars of the nineteenth century as well as World Wars I and II were all experienced as external threats by the Swiss, evoking mobilization for armed defense. On September 1, 1939, by the shores of Aegerisee, with all the church bells in the valley pealing, we saw the peasants one after another come striding down the hills, in uniform with rifles over their shoulders—dark faces lit with that singular Swiss fury, going to meet the external threat.

Does mankind need an external threat for collective security? Just think if the "War of the Worlds" were really to transpire, if the men from Mars were to invade, how quickly all creatures of this earthly family of man would join together to ward off the attack. The differences between white and black, Communist and capitalist, Arab and Israeli would vanish at once in the experience of the community of man against the foreign invader. With his live imagination and prescience, H. G. Wells wrote in 1898 how "humanity gathered for the battle," and at the end of his book how this invasion from Mars "has done much to promote the conception of the commonweal of mankind."

Human existence is threatened today as never before. The fruit of the scientific and technological revolution which has been the driving force of our civilization is an all-pervasive threat to human survival. As mentioned earlier, the threat is well known in its twofold aspect; first, the continuing danger of a nuclear holocaust—the quick death; secondly, the danger of ecologic maladjustment—the slow death, if the problems of environmental pollution (air, water, thermal change), the population explosion, resource exhaustion are not resolved.

Has man created himself the threats to human existence which will bring about collective security and international cooperation as would the external threat of invaders from Mars? It is clear that if we do not adapt successfully to these threats, the human species will decline, if not disappear, as have other species which did not adapt to changing conditions. As conscious creatures, we recognize the threats, but it is more difficult to envisage the proper actions, and much more difficult to carry them out.

As well as posing the threat to human survival, the scientific and technological revolution has created the new global situation in foreign affairs and brought into being transnational problems in such spheres as ecology, population, weather control, outer space, use of ocean resources, etc. The scientific revolution has indeed undermined or altered the presuppositions on which national foreign policy has been based for centuries. For one who retired in 1969 from the Foreign Service after twenty-eight years service, it is a shock to realize now that the basic framework of a life's work, devotion to the national interest, is no longer adequate to meet the present foreign policy realities. In the current situation, national interest is an intrinsically superficial phenomenon: universal ideologies, such as revolutionary world communism, are even more superficial. Of course, we shall worry along, endeavoring to protect our national interest, as we seek a new direction in our foreign policy responsive to present realities.

The only chance for human survival lies in the development of international institutions strong and resilient enough to direct and control the impact of technological development in the interest of all mankind. The United Nations is a weak reed in this direction, with a charter based on anachronistic premises. Perhaps it can be developed, with a new or amended charter. Amendment of the charter, however, is procedurally very difficult, requiring as it does under Article 108 of the charter an affirmative vote by two-thirds of the entire membership, and specifically including the five permanent members of the Security Council. The Review and Revision Provision under Article 109 is similarly restrictive, requiring a two-thirds vote of all UN members and a vote of any nine members of the Security Council to call a general review conference, and charter changes at the conference must be approved by two-thirds of the UN members, and also by all the permanent members of the Security Council. At present the Soviets have indicated firm opposition to any changes in the charter, while the French and British have expressed "grave reservations." The United States has given some lip service to the idea, but has not endeavored to exert leadership in that direction.

The situation, however, is not entirely hopeless. Under the pressure of transnational world problems, the specialized agencies of the United Nations, such as the World Meteorological Organization, the World Health Organization, the Food and Agriculture Organization, and newly created international UN organs, such as the proposed International Seabed Resource Authority, and a possible Environment Pollution Agency, may achieve new competence and jurisdictional responsibility over significant aspects of supranational human problems. In this way, they may come to serve the interests of all mankind, and by a steady development through these diverse sources a new world order may emerge. The goal will not be achieved presumably on the basis of a constitutional blueprint, but perhaps as the end result of the development of manifold international and supranational institutions. At any rate, the goal is a federal organization with real powers and a workable structure of governance.

Notes / Index

NOTES

I. THE BERLIN WALL

1. *Neues Deutschland*, March 27, 1959.
2. Department of State Publication 6972, *Background of Heads of Government Conference—1960* (Washington, D.C.: Government Printing Office, April 1960), pp. 295 f.
3. Ibid., pp. 315 f.
4. Ibid., pp. 329 f.
5. Ibid., pp. 387 f.
6. Ibid., pp. 461 f.
7. Department of State Publication 7257, *Background: Berlin—1961* (Washington, D.C.: Government Printing Office, August 1961), pp. 30 f.
8. Jean Edward Smith, *The Defense of Berlin* (Baltimore: Johns Hopkins Press, 1963), p. 260.
9. Ibid., pp. 269 f.
10. Ibid., p. 273.
11. Ibid., pp. 273 f.
12. Ibid., p. 274.
13. Ibid., pp. 282 f.
14. Geoffrey McDermott, *Berlin: Success of a Mission?* (London: Andre Deutsch, 1963), p. 32. Mr. McDermott also states on page 32: "The Americans would have liked to put on a show of force; but we and the French questioned whether this would improve matters, with large Soviet forces at the ready all around Berlin."

When Arthur Schlesinger was in Berlin, February 1962, accompanying Robert Kennedy, he asked Brandt whether, looking back, he thought the Allies should have done something to halt the Wall or to tear it down. Brandt replied: "If I were to say now that something could or should have been

done, it would be inconsistent with what I felt and said at
the time. I do believe that the Allies should have been much
quicker in their condemnation of the action. But that would
not have stopped the building of the Wall. On August 13 no
one proposed that we stop the Wall. We all supposed that
such action would run the risk of war." Arthur M. Schlesinger, Jr., *A Thousand Days* (Boston: Houghton Mifflin,
1965), p. 402.

15. Ibid., p. 52.
16. Early in March, Odintsov and his wife had come to our
    home in West Berlin for an *a quâtre* luncheon. The day be-
    fore the luncheon Odintsov called me to inquire whether he
    should not bring along his interpreter. I told him that there
    was no need; we could talk German together. Odintsov had
    a reputation among the American military as a man sin-
    cerely concerned that minor issues or clashes might some-
    how get out of hand and lead to real hostilities. For this
    reason I wanted to meet him on a social basis in order to try
    to develop a personal contact so that in any critical situa-
    tion he would not hesitate to use the official political adviser
    channel. His lady interpreter was the attractive wife of a
    young Soviet air force officer; she was reported through her
    family to have good contacts at high levels in Moscow; we
    assumed that she may also have been working for the KGB.
    At any rate it did not suit my purpose to have her attend
    the luncheon. Three weeks later Odintsov was transferred
    from Berlin to central Asia. His departure seemed precipi-
    tate; he did not make the usual official parting calls on his
    political adviser counterparts. Naturally we wondered at the
    time if his willingness to attend an a quatre luncheon had
    caused his sudden transfer. Odintsov was generally regarded
    as a real Soviet army officer. When after lunch we entered
    our library living room, a large room with built-in book-
    shelves and many books, he said, "A Soviet artillery officer
    doesn't need so many books." No skill at playacting is apt to
    produce such an impromptu remark.
17. It became clear, not on the first day of our meeting at
    Friedrichstrasse, but rather in the ensuing months, that
    Alexeiev was a Soviet intelligence officer. During the several
    occasions that General Watson and I met with Colonel
    Solovyev and Lieutenant Colonel Alexeiev, it was very notice-
    able how different Alexeiev's conduct was from that of
    Odintsov. At a commandant's meeting it was not customary
    for the political advisers to speak out freely unless requested
    by the commandant to make a comment. A political adviser

might make a suggestion to his commandant discreetly, either by whispering or passing a written note, if he deemed it necessary. Odintsov had been somewhat stiffly at attention in the presence of his superior officer. Alexeiev was quite different in manner, relaxed, freely interjecting comments, inclined to smiles and verbal humor. It was evident that he did not regard Colonel Solovyev as his commanding officer; indeed he acted as if he were the higher ranking officer. The tip-off as to Alexeiev's identity came, however, on that February 1962 day on the Gliennicke Bridge, when the Soviet master spy Abel was exchanged for the American U-2 pilot Powers. Accompanying Powers from the Soviet zone side to the middle of the bridge where the exchange took place were Shishkin, the "cultural attaché" of the Soviet Embassy in East Berlin with whom the American attorney James Donovan had negotiated, and Alexeiev dressed in civilian clothes. There was no reason for Lieutenant Colonel Alexeiev, political adviser to the Soviet commandant in East Berlin, to be participating in the exchange of spies on the Gliennicke Bridge.

18. Pryor's release was arranged in connection with the Powers-Abel exchange and took place just before the exchange on the Gliennicke Bridge. James Donovan, the New York lawyer who negotiated the exchange with Shishkin, of the Soviet Embassy in East Berlin, sought unsuccessfully to obtain also the simultaneous release of Maakinen, an American student at the Free University Berlin, who had been detained in the Soviet Union and imprisoned for espionage. When Shishkin protested that Donovan was seeking to obtain a 3 for 1 exchange, Donovan retorted, "3 mechanics for 1 engineer."

19. Department of State Publication 8007, *American Foreign Policy: Current Documents, 1962* (Washington, D.C.: Government Printing Office, 1966), pp. 714–15, text of statement issued by Soviet News Agency Tass announcing decision of the Soviet Defense Ministry.

20. During the Soviet blockade 1948–49, London was at one time a place of negotiations among the Western Allies. The American Ambassador Lewis Douglas was seeking instructions around 8:00 A.M. London time by telecon with the State Department. It was 3:00 A.M. in Washington. Under Secretary Robert Lovett with senior advisers was on the Washington side. The telecon apparatus broke down; while waiting for its repair, the advisers engaged in lengthy argumentation on the pros and cons of policy alternatives. Tired and exasperated, Under Secretary Lovett suddenly banged both fists on the

table, sprang to his feet, and said, "Boys, boys, stop it. Never mind the cheese; get me out of the trap."

2. THE CUBA MISSILE CRISIS

1. According to Arthur Schlesinger, Frost was not quoting an actual Khrushchev remark, but interpreting an anecdote Khrushchev had related from Gorki's memoirs where Tolstoy described himself as "too weak and too infirm to do it but still having the desire"; Khrushchev meant to say thereby that the United States is old, the Soviet Union young. The ideological content is just as clear in this interpretation. See Arthur M. Schlesinger, Jr., *A Thousand Days* (Boston: Houghton Mifflin, 1965), p. 821.
2. Roger Hilsman, *To Move a Nation* (New York: Doubleday, 1967), p. 189.
3. Andres Suarez, *Cuba: Castroism and Communism, 1959–1966* (Cambridge, Mass.: M.I.T. Press 1967), p. 93.
4. Ibid., p. 94.
5. Ibid., p. 115.
6. *New York Times Book Review,* January 24, 1971, p. 28.
7. Robert F. Kennedy, *Thirteen Days: A Memoir of the Cuban Missile Crisis* (New York: W. W. Norton, 1969), pp. 163–71.
8. Hilsman, *To Move a Nation,* p. 219.
9. Ibid., p. 220.
10. Ibid., p. 156.
11. Kennedy, *Thirteen Days,* pp. 202–3.
12. Ibid., p. 67.
13. Elie Abel, *The Missile Crisis* (Philadelphia: J. B. Lippincott, 1966), p. 181.
14. Ibid., p. 204.

3. MYTHS, SLOGANS, AND VIETNAM

1. Alfred North Whitehead, *Science and the Modern World* (New York: Macmillan, 1928), pp. 74 f.
2. Ibid., pp. 80 f.
3. Ibid., p. 85.
4. Ibid., p. 86.
5. Ibid., p. 85.

6. Reprinted in George F. Kennan, *American Diplomacy 1900–1950* (Chicago: University of Chicago Press, 1951), p. 119.
7. Ibid., p. 120.
8. Ibid., pp. 126–27.
9. Ibid., pp. 126 f.
10. Claude A. Buss, *The Far East* (New York: Macmillan, 1955), p. 714.
11. John K. Fairbank, "China's Foreign Policy in Historical Perspective," *Foreign Affairs* 47 (April 1969), 463.
12. Richard D. Challener and John M. Fenton, "Recent Past Comes Alive in Dulles 'Oral History,'" *Princeton Alumni Weekly* (March 14, 1967), p. 41.
13. Ibid., p. 42.
14. Ibid.
15. Townsend Hoopes, *The Limits of Intervention* (New York: David McKay, 1969), p. 163.
16. Ibid., p. 85.
17. Ibid., p. 231.
18. Ibid., p. 240.
19. Clark M. Clifford, "A Vietnam Reappraisal: The Personal History of One Man's View and How it Evolved," *Foreign Affairs* 47 (July 1969), 607.

4. THE CONTINUING REVOLUTION

1. Address by Donald F. Hornig, at the time Special Assistant to the President for Science and Techonolgy, at the dedication of the New Science Center, Wheaton College, Mass., October 19, 1968.
2. Barbara Ward, *Five Ideas that Change the World* (New York: W. W. Norton, 1959), p. 119.
3. Elizabeth Mann Borgese, "The Future of International Organizations: Last Days of the Superpowers," *The Center Magazine* 3 (July–August 1970), 7.
4. Roger Revelle, "Science and Social Change," in *Government, Science, and Public Policy*, a compilation of papers prepared for the 7th meeting, Panel on Science and Technology, House Committee on Science and Astronautics, 89th Congress, 2nd sess. (Washington, D.C.: Government Printing Office, 1966), p. 31.
5. Cited in Hornig's address, Wheaton College.
6. Peter F. Drucker, *The Age of Discontinuity: Guidelines to Our Changing Society* (New York: Harper and Row, 1968), pp. 38, 261–380.

7. Eli Ginsberg, *Technology and Social Change* (New York: Columbia University Press, 1964), p. 60; cited by Victor Basiuk, *Technology and World Power* (New York: Foreign Policy Association Headline Series No. 200, April 1970), p. 23.
8. Basiuk, p. 17.
9. C. P. Snow, *Science and Government* (New York: New American Library, 1962), p. 88.
10. Franklin P. Huddle, "The Evolution of International Technology," prepared for the Subcommittee on National Security Policy and Scientific Developments of the House Committee on Foreign Affairs by the Science Policy Research and Foreign Affairs Divisions, Legislative Reference Service, Library of Congress (Washington, D.C.: Government Printing Office, 1970), p. 12.
11. Snow, *Science and Government*, p. 44.
12. "Fully one-fourth of the German Nobel Prize winners were among those exiled. The number of science students in the German universities dropped by two-thirds between 1932 and 1937. Many of the scientific exiles migrated to the United States, thus greatly strengthening the nation's scientific resources for research and training. Among them were Leo Szilard, Eugene Wigner, Edward Teller, Enrico Fermi, James Franck, and Emilio Segre, to mention but a few." Everett Mendelsohn, "Science in America: The Twentieth Century," *Paths of American Thought*, ed. Arthur M. Schlesinger, Jr. and Morton White (Boston: Houghton Mifflin, 1963), pp. 437 f.
13. Robert Jungk, *Brighter than a Thousand Suns: The Story of the Men Who Made the Bomb* (New York: Grove Press, 1958), p. 94. Cited by Donald S. Detwiler, "Hitler's Fatal Mistake," *Air University Review* 21 (May–June, 1970), 89.
14. "During World War II, the rumor was deliberately circulated that the large analog computer under construction at the Massachusetts Institute of Technology by Dr. Vannevar Bush and his associates had proven impossible to complete. Actually, the machine's motors and wheels were busy spinning out artillery firing tables. As in Babbage's time, much of the impetus for modern computer development was military in origin. . . .

   "During World War II, at the Moore School of Engineering of the University of Pennsylvania, Drs. J. Presper Eckert and John W. Mauchly recognized the usefulness of the fact that a vacuum tube could be turned on and off in about a millionth of a second—thousands of times faster than the sluggish relay. By 1946, backed by the Army but too late for war use, Eckert and Mauchly had the ENIAC (Electronic Numerical Integrator and Calculator) ready. It was the first of the electronic digital computers and the most complex electronic machine in the world at that time.

"During World War II, Dr. John von Neumann, who later served as a member of the Atomic Energy Commission, was a consultant both to the Army's Aberdeen Proving Ground, for whom Eckert and Mauchly were developing their electronic computer, and the AEC's Los Alamos Scientific Laboratory, which was attempting to compute the characteristics and effects of atomic bombs. In the latter capacity, von Neumann became impressed with the need for rapid, extensive, and repetitive computations, and, in his Army work, he learned about the ENIAC. The two together stimulated him to develop the idea of the internally stored program, where the step-by-step directions for computation, called *instructions,* are stored within the computer, and computations progress without need for external guidance. The idea of *instructions,* as distinct from *data,* to be stored in the computer memory was von Neumann's landmark idea. It became a reality when a computer using internally stored instructions was built at the Institute for Advanced Study at Princeton, New Jersey, in 1952." William R. Corliss, *Computers* (Oak Ridge, Tenn.: U.S. Atomic Energy Commission, Division of Technical Information Extension, July 1967), pp. 7 f.

15. In his obituary of Moseley, published in *Nature* in 1915, Rutherford wrote: "It is a national tragedy that our military organization at the start was so inelastic as to be unable, with a few exceptions, to utilize the offers of services of our scientific men except as combatants in the firing line. Our regret for the untimely end of Moseley is all the more poignant that we cannot but recognize that his services would have been far more useful to his country in one of the numerous fields of scientific inquiry rendered necessary by the war than by exposure to the chances of a Turkish bullet." Sir Solly Zuckerman, *Scientists and War* (New York: Harper and Row, 1967), p. 13.

16. Donald F. Hornig, "The Changing Face of American Science," Robert A. Welch Foundation Research Bulletin No. 18, March 1966, p. 9.

17. Ibid., p. 17.

18. *New York Times,* November 30, 1970.

19. *New York Times,* December 9, 1970.

20. Drucker, *The Age of Discontinuity,* p. 80.

21. Ibid., p. 93.

22. Ibid., p. 95. As Drucker points out, this is a major theme of the 1967 European best-seller *Le Défi American*, by Jean-Jacques Servan-Schreiber; English translation, *The American Challenge* (New York: Atheneum, 1968), see particularly chapters 1 and 2.

23. Ibid., p. 97.

24. In a collection of major articles from *The Center Magazine*, *The Establishment and All That* (Santa Barbara, Calif.: Center for the Study of Democratic Institutions, c. 1970), p. 75.

25. This quotation was taken from an unpublished State Department paper. A similar statement by Dr. Ramo, Vice Chairman of the Board, TRW Inc. appears in a U.S. Chamber of Commerce pamphlet, *The Business of Progress*, May 1968, p. 27, as follows: ". . . we sense that the developing problem of this century is the gross mismatch between the rates of technological change and appropriate social advance. We question our capability to organize so as to make the best use of science and technology. We are not even able to prevent misuse of these tools."

26. *Department of State Bulletin* 62 (March 2, 1970), 260 f.

27. According to the official biographies published by *Pravda* after the conclusion of the 24th Party Congress in April 1971, the following members of the new enlarged fifteen-man Politburo have either technological education or experience:

Brezhnev studied at the Metallurgical Institute in his native city Dneprodzerzhinsk, then worked as an engineer at the iron and steel plant there.

Podgorny graduated from the Kiev Institute of Technology, worked as an engineer.

Kosygin graduated from the Textile Institute in Leningrad, was Director of the Leningrad Spinning and Weaving Mill.

Kirilenko graduated from the Aviation Institute in Rybinsk, worked as an engineer-designer.

Mazurov graduated from a secondary school specializing in motor transport, worked in a district road department.

Polyanskiy studied at the Kharkov Agricultural Institute.

Shelest trained as an engineer of metallurgy, worked in metallurgical factories.

Voronov studied at the Tomsk Industrial Institute.

Grishin trained at a geodesical technical school and a locomotive maintenance school, worked as a railroad engineer.

Kunayev graduated from the Moscow Institute of Non-

ferrous Metals and Gold, was a director of mines in Kazakhstan engaged in research, President of the Kazakhstan Academy of Sciences, member of the National Academy in the
Department of Sciences of the Universe and the Earth.
Shcherbitskiy graduated from a chemical engineering
college, worked in a coke-chemical plant in Dneprodzerzhinsk.
Kulakov trained as an agronomist.
Thus twelve of the fifteen Politburo members have a
background in technology. Of the remaining three, Suslov
graduated from the Moscow Economics Institute and taught
at Moscow University and the Industrial Academy in Moscow; Pelshe is a graduate of the Moscow Institute of Party
Theorists; and Shelepin studied at the Moscow Institute of
History, Philosophy, and Literature.

28. Laurence M. Gould, "Antarctic—Continent of International
    Science," *Science* 150 (December 31, 1965), 1725 f.
29. Panel on Science and Technology Eighth Meeting, Proceed-
    ings before the House Committee on Science and Astro-
    nautics, 90th Congress, 1st sess., January 24, 25, and 26,
    1967 (Washington, D.C.: Government Printing Office, 1967),
    pp. 82 f.
30. *New York Times,* January 11, 1970.
31. Ibid.
32. Abel Wolman, "Pollution as an International Issue," *Foreign
    Affairs* 47 (October 1968) 169.
33. Cited in Thomas C. Southerland, Jr., "The Battle over Amer-
    ica's Environment," *Princeton Alumni Weekly* (December 9,
    1969), p. 24.
34. Lincoln Bloomfield, ed., *Outer Space: Prospects for Man and
    Society* (New York: Praeger, 1968), p. 107.
35. Ibid.
36. *Space Science and Technology: Benefits to Developing Coun-
    tries* (New York: United Nations Publication, 1968, Sales
    No.: E.68. I. 11), pp. 27 f.
37. Ibid., p. 2.
38. Arnold Frutkin, "Status of International Cooperation in
    Space," Address at the IAA Orbiting International Laboratory
    and Space Sciences Conference, Cloudcroft, New Mexico,
    October 1, 1969.
39. *New York Times,* October 9, 1970.
40. *New York Times,* October 30, 1970.
41. *New York Times,* May 9, 1971.
42. Arvid Pardo, "Who Will Control the Seabed?" *Foreign Af-
    fairs* 47 (October 1968), 123 f.
43. M. M. Sibthorp, *Oceanic Pollution: A Survey and Some Sug-*

gestions for Control (London: David Davies Memorial Institute of International Studies, 1969), p. 4.
44. Ibid., p. 6.
45. Rachel L. Carson, *The Sea Around Us* (New York: Oxford University Press, 1961), p. 182.
46. Pardo, "Who Will Control the Seabed?" p. 135.
47. *Department of State Bulletin* 62 (June 15, 1970), 737.
48. *Department of State Bulletin* 63 (August 24, 1970), 209 f.
49. *Department of State Bulletin* 64 (February 1, 1971), 155 f.
50. *New York Times*, April 24, 1971.
51. Provincial newspapers in Communist countries are not kept under as rigorous guidance or censorship control as the major capital-city papers. Hence they often carry revealing items which do not appear in the national papers.
52. *Department of State Bulletin* 64 (February 1, 1971), 150 f.
53. John von Neumann, "Can We Survive Technology?" *Fortune* 51 (June 1955), 151.
54. *Hearings before the Subcommittee on Science, Research, and Development of the House Committee on Science and Astronautics*, 88th Cong., 1st sess., October 15, 16, 18, 22, 24, 29; November 5, 19, and 20, 1963 (Washington, D.C.: U.S. Government Printing Office, 1964), p. 119.
55. Ibid.
56. Richard Hallgren, "The World Weather Program," in *Global Weather Prediction: The Coming Revolution*, ed. Bruce Lusignan and John Kiely (New York: Holt, Rinehart and Winston, 1970), p. 22.
57. Thomas Malone, "An Overview," in *Global Weather Prediction*, p. 9.
58. Eugene B. Skolnikoff, "Functional Implications of Technology for International Relations," paper presented at 138th Meeting, American Association for the Advancement of Science, Chicago, December 28, 1970, p. 7.
59. Ibid., p. 5, cited from T. F. Malone, "Current Developments in the Atmospheric Sciences and Some of their Implications for Foreign Policy," papers presented at a Joint Meeting of the Policy Planning Council, Department of State, and a Special Panel of the Committee on Science and Public Policy, National Academy of Sciences, June 16–17, 1968, Washington, D.C., pp. 82–97.
60. P. M. Borisov, "Can We Control the Arctic Climate," *Bulletin of the Atomic Scientists* 25, No. 3 (March 1969), 43–48.
61. Malone, "An Overview," in *Global Weather Prediction*, p. 13.
62. E. K. Federov, "Weather Modifications," *World Meteorological Organization Bulletin* 16, No. 3 (July 1967), 130.

63. Professor C. F. von Weizsaecker, "Gedanken zur Zukunft der technischen Welt," Address at the Delegiertenversammlung des Schweizerischen Handels-und Industrie-Vereins, Zurich, September 16, 1967, pp. 8 f.

64. Committee on Atmospheric Sciences, National Research Council, *The Atmospheric Sciences and Man's Needs: Priorities for the Future* (Washington, D.C.: National Academy of Sciences, 1971), p. 79.

INDEX

Abel, Elie: on Cuba missile crisis, 75–76; mentioned, 79, 83, 84

Acheson, Dean, 36, 73, 79, 97

Adenauer, Konrad, 17, 19

"Agonizing reappraisal," 98, 99

Alexeiev, Lt. Col.: at Friedrichstrasse tank confrontation, 45–48 passim; mentioned, 52, 53, 204–5n

Allied Control Council, 10–11, 12

Amrehn, Deputy Mayor, 27

Antarctic Treaty, 144

Atom bomb: development of, 129–30; significance of, 132–33; as symbol of technological change, 135

Bay of Pigs, 18, 29, 60, 61, 62, 70

Berlin: division of, 10–12

Berlin blockade, 6–7, 24–25

Berlin crisis of 1958–62: beginnings of, 3–6; effect on refugees, 23; end of, 55–56; mentioned, 8

Berlin Wall: described, 19; Allied intelligence on, 19–20; decision to build, 21, 61; advantages to Communists, 24; as symbol of Communist failure, 24, 55; countermeasures against, 26–30, 31, 32–33, 35–38, 39; public attitude during crisis, 30–31; as factor in ending Berlin crisis, 1958–62, 55; mentioned, 40, 62

Brandt, Willy, 27, 32–35 passim, 203–4n

Bretton Woods Agreement (1945): results of, 137

Bundy, McGeorge, 111

Canada: agreement with U.S. on boundary waters, 150; in space program, 168

Castro, Fidel, 66–68, 70, 73, 81

China, 56, 69, 94, 101, 105, 107, 135

Churchill, Winston, 62, 96, 128

Clay, Gen. Lucius: and Berlin blockade, 6, 7, 24, 25; views on Berlin Wall, 25; and Friedrichstrasse tank confrontation, 42, 43, 44, 50; mentioned, 31, 34, 35, 40, 51

Clifford, Clark, 92, 104, 112, 116, 118

Clubb, O. Edmund, 94